ISBN 978-1-333-02278-5
PIBN 10453375

1 MONTH OF
FREE
READING

at
www.ForgottenBooks.com

By purchasing this book you are eligible for one month membership to ForgottenBooks.com, giving you unlimited access to our entire collection of over 700,000 titles via our web site and mobile apps.

To claim your free month visit:

www.forgottenbooks.com/free453375

English
Français
Deutsche
Italiano
Español
Português

www.forgottenbooks.com

Mythology Photography **Fiction**
Fishing Christianity **Art** Cooking
Essays Buddhism Freemasonry
Medicine **Biology** Music **Ancient
Egypt** Evolution Carpentry Physics
Dance Geology **Mathematics** Fitness
Shakespeare **Folklore** Yoga Marketing
Confidence Immortality Biographies
Poetry **Psychology** Witchcraft
Electronics Chemistry History **Law**
Accounting **Philosophy** Anthropology
Alchemy Drama Quantum Mechanics
Atheism Sexual Health **Ancient History**
Entrepreneurship Languages Sport
Paleontology Needlework Islam
Metaphysics Investment Archaeology
Parenting Statistics Criminology
Motivational

RECENT HISTORICAL BOOKS.

HENRY VIII. By A. F. Pollard, M.A., Litt.D., Professor of English History in the University of London. Crown 8vo, 4s. 6d. net.

NAPOLEON I. A Biography. By August Fournier, Professor of History in the University of Vienna. Translated by A. E. Adams. With 2 Photogravure Portraits and 7 Maps. 2 vols. 8vo, 21s. net.

A HISTORY OF WALES FROM THE EARLIEST TIMES TO THE EDWARDIAN CONQUEST. By John Edward Lloyd, M.A. With Map. 2 vols. 8vo, 21s. net.

HISTORY AND HISTORIANS IN THE NINETEENTH CENTURY. By G. P. Gooch, M.A. (Cantab.). 8vo, 10s. 6d. net.

THE FATE OF EMPIRES: being an Inquiry into the Stability of Civilization. By Arthur John Hubbard, M.D. (Dunelm). 8vo, 6s. 6d. net.

THE RISE OF SOUTH AFRICA: a History of the Origin of South African Colonisation and of its Development towards the East from the Earliest Times to 1857. By George Edward Cory, M.A., King's College, Cambridge, Professor in the Rhodes University College, Grahamstown, South Africa. In 4 Vols. 8vo.
Vol. I. FROM THE EARLIEST TIMES TO THE YEAR 1820. 15s.
    With Map, Plans, and Illustrations.
Vol. II. 1820-1834. 18s.

THE FIRST TWELVE CENTURIES OF BRITISH STORY: a sketch of the social and political conditions of the British Islands from the year 56 B.C. to 1154 A.D. With 20 Sketch Maps and 3 Photographic Reproductions of Medieval Maps. By J. W. Jeudwine, LL.B. (Camb.), of Lincoln's Inn, Barrister-at-Law. 8vo. 12s. 6d. net.

GARIBALDI'S DEFENCE OF THE ROMAN REPUBLIC. By George Macaulay Trevelyan. With 7 Maps and 35 Illustrations. 8vo, 6s. 6d. net.

GARIBALDI AND THE THOUSAND. By George Macaulay Trevelyan. With 5 Maps and numerous Illustrations. 8vo, 7s. 6d. net.

GARIBALDI AND THE MAKING OF ITALY. By George Macaulay Trevelyan. With 4 Maps and numerous Illustrations. 8vo, 7s. 6d. net.

THE FIRST DECADE OF THE AUSTRALIAN COMMON- WEALTH: a Chronicle of Contemporary Politics, 1901-1910. By Henry Gyles Turner. 8vo, 9s.

THE MAKING OF THE AUSTRALIAN COMMONWEALTH (1889-1900). A stage in the growth of the Empire. By B. R. Wise. 8vo, 7s. 6d. net.

A HISTORY OF ENGLAND FROM THE DEFEAT OF THE ARMADA TO THE DEATH OF ELIZABETH. With an Account of English Institutions during the Later Sixteenth and Seventeenth Centuries. By Edward P. Cheyney, A.M., LL.D., Professor of European History in the University of Pennsylvania. In 2 Vols. 8vo. Vol. I.

LONGMANS, GREEN AND CO., 39 Paternoster Row, London.
New York, Bombay and Calcutta.

THE POLITICAL HISTORY OF ENGLAND.

Edited by the Rev. W. HUNT, D.Litt., and

REGINALD LANE POOLE, M.A., LL.D.

8vo. 12 vols. 7s. 6d. net per volume.

VOL. I. FROM THE EARLIEST TIMES TO THE NORMAN
CONQUEST (to 1066). By THOMAS HODGKIN, D.C.L., Litt.D., Fellow of the British
Academy. With 2 Maps.

VOL. II. FROM THE NORMAN CONQUEST TO THE
DEATH OF JOHN (1066 to 1216). By GEORGE BURTON ADAMS. With 2 Maps.

VOL. III. FROM THE ACCESSION OF HENRY III. TO
THE DEATH OF EDWARD III. (1216 to 1377). By T. F. TOUT, M.A. With 3
Maps.

VOL. IV. FROM THE ACCESSION OF RICHARD II. TO
THE DEATH OF RICHARD III. (1377 to 1485). By C. OMAN M.A., LL.D. With
3 Maps.

VOL. V. FROM THE ACCESSION OF HENRY VII. TO
THE DEATH OF HENRY VIII. (1485 to 1547). By H. A. L. FISHER, M.A.
With 2 Maps.

VOL. VI. FROM THE ACCESSION OF EDWARD VI. TO
THE DEATH OF ELIZABETH (1547 to 1603). By A. F. POLLARD, M.A. With
2 Maps.

VOL. VII. FROM THE ACCESSION OF JAMES I. TO THE
RESTORATION (1603 to 1660). By F. C. MONTAGUE, M.A. With 3 Maps.

VOL. VIII. FROM THE RESTORATION TO THE DEATH
OF WILLIAM III. (1660 to 1702). By RICHARD LODGE, M.A., LL.D. With 2 Maps.

VOL. IX. FROM THE ACCESSION OF ANNE TO THE
DEATH OF GEORGE II. (1702 to 1760). By I. S. LEADAM, M.A. With 8 Maps.

VOL. X. FROM THE ACCESSION OF GEORGE III. TO
THE CLOSE OF PITT'S FIRST ADMINISTRATION (1760 to 1801). By the
Rev. WILLIAM HUNT, M.A., D.Litt. With 3 Maps.

VOL. XI. FROM ADDINGTON'S ADMINISTRATION TO
THE CLOSE OF WILLIAM IV.'s REIGN (1801 to 1837). By the Hon. GEORGE
C. BRODRICK, D.C.L., and J. K. FOTHERINGHAM, M.A. With 3 Maps.

VOL. XII. THE REIGN OF QUEEN VICTORIA (1837 to
1901). By SIDNEY LOW, M.A., and LLOYD C. SANDERS, B.A. With 3 Maps.

LONGMANS, GREEN AND CO., 39 Paternoster Row, London.

THE REIGN OF HENRY VII

THE REIGN OF HENRY VII FROM CONTEMPORARY SOURCES.

Selected and Arranged with an Introduction.

By A. F. POLLARD, M.A., Hon. Litt.D.

Three Volumes. Crown 8vo.

Vol. I. Narrative Extracts.
Vol. II. Constitutional, Social, and Economic History.
Vol. III. Diplomacy, Ecclesiastical Affairs, and Ireland.

LONGMANS, GREEN AND CO.,
LONDON, NEW YORK, BOMBAY AND CALCUTTA.

THE REIGN OF

H E N R Y   V I I

FROM

CONTEMPORARY SOURCES

[UNIVERSITY OF LONDON HISTORICAL SERIES, No. I.]

SELECTED AND ARRANGED IN THREE VOLUMES WITH AN
INTRODUCTION BY

A. F. POLLARD, M.A., Hon.Litt.D.

FELLOW OF ALL SOULS COLLEGE, OXFORD; PROFESSOR OF ENGLISH
HISTORY IN THE UNIVERSITY OF LONDON

VOLUME I

NARRATIVE EXTRACTS

LONGMANS, GREEN AND CO.

39 PATERNOSTER ROW, LONDON

NEW YORK, BOMBAY AND CALCUTTA

1913

INTRODUCTION.

§ 1. Sources for the History of Henry VII's Reign.

These three volumes spring from a humble cause and pretend to a modest ambition. Their production is due to the difficulty experienced in finding original sources accessible to the rapidly increasing number of historical students in the University of London, for the purpose of studying their selected subjects. The materials for history have, when published at all, been published in a disjointed, partial, and haphazard fashion by governments, academies, societies, and individual scholars without co-operation, consultation, or system; and the reign of Henry VIII is the only reign in English history for which an attempt has been made to collect and publish the extant original documents. For other periods the published sources are fragmentary, expensive, and often out of print; and students and teachers alike are often restricted to inferior materials, simply because to those alone have they access. Generally this defect has led to the preference of secondary sources, such as chronicles, memoirs, and histories, to records, state papers, and correspondence; and, in particular, for the reign of Henry VII even competent students of history have been content to rely on Bacon, whose portrait of the first Tudor, painted more than a century after his death, has recently been described as the only English historical composition worthy of the lineal and literal attention paid to Tacitus and Thucydides. These volumes will serve at least one good purpose by providing general students of history with materials for the reign of Henry VII somewhat more original and contemporary than Bacon's literary sketch. It is hoped, moreover, that the experiment, if successful, may be extended to other periods and to other countries until the whole field of history is covered with a groundwork of materials available and appropriate for students in university Schools of History.

But the scope of these volumes is circumscribed by their purpose, which is primarily to meet the needs of undergraduate students, and not to satisfy the requirements of original research. The main object has been simply to illustrate from contemporary sources the various aspects of Henry's government and the conditions, political, constitutional, social, economic, and ecclesiastical, of the England over which he ruled. Circumstances have forbidden prolonged search for unpublished documents, and there has been no attempt at a scientific edition. The life-work of several trained archivists could not be done in the few leisure hours that have fallen to me in the last fifteen months ; and so transcripts from foreign archives, Calendars of State Papers, and even those most defective of printed sources, the Law Reports, have necessarily been accepted for what they are worth without the collation of MSS. with one another or with the printed text or epitome. My task has been for the most part one of selection and arrangement, although some hitherto unprinted documents have been included, and attention is drawn to others in the notes. Nor have these texts been reprinted without examination. Some misprints in earlier editions have been corrected, some identifications supplied, and occasionally I have been compelled to differ from previous editors with regard to the dates they conjecturally assigned to their documents. Thus, in Campbell's "Materials" (i. 172) there is assigned to 1486 a letter which purports to be from Henry VII to the Duke of Exeter; but there was no Duke of Exeter in Henry VII's reign, the king is Henry VI, and the letter belongs to the earlier part of his reign. Again the same editor (*ibid.* ii. 244) assigns to 1487 a document which clearly belongs to 1488, and even Dr. Gairdner reverses the order of Nos. 31 and 32 of the present volume. The chronology of chroniclers needs continual verification, and editors of State Papers have not always borne in mind the Gregorian reform of the calendar.

The task of selection, moreover, has not been quite so simple as might be supposed. The paucity of original materials for the history of the period has become almost a commonplace; but any attempt to select from among them soon brings the conviction that this paucity has been exaggerated, and it would have been easier to expand these documents into thirty volumes than it has been to confine them within three. It is true that we have practically nothing in Henry VII's own hand, and very little in the writing of men like Morton, Foxe, Daubeny, Poynings, and Bray. But it is doubtful whether these eminent statesmen often wielded the pen. We are told by Bacon that the king himself kept a notebook in which he jotted down caustic comments on his friends and advisers, but that a pet monkey, not without instigation, tore this priceless record to pieces. Bacon terms this report "a merry tale," and it was hardly in keeping with Henry's secretive character to commit such matters to paper. Writing was the business of clerical experts, and a painful labour for laymen ; and even the matrimonial correspondence of princes was conducted in the hand of their secretaries. The Renaissance had not taught Henry VII and his councillors the *cacoethes scribendi*, and the rarity of their script does not demonstrate an unwonted destruction of sources. No doubt, a mere fraction of what was written by statesmen survives ; but that is true of every age before the eighteenth century, and if the attempt were made to deal with the materials for Henry VII's reign as those for his son's have been treated by Brewer and Gairdner, it would result in at least a dozen equally portly volumes. Henry VII's treaties alone, as printed by Rymer, would more than fill these three volumes ; Campbell's " Materials," selected from two or three years of the reign, run to two, Gairdner's " Letters and Papers " to two more, and his " Memorials " fill a fifth. The statutes are almost as bulky as the treaties, and extant reports of legal cases are not less lengthy. There are hundreds of private letters, while the financial records of the reign call loudly for editing and elucidation. Foreign correspondence, although only the contents of the Spanish and North Italian archives have been calendared, occupy the best part of three volumes, and there is much material yet to be found for the commercial history of Henry's reign in the archives of the cities of the Netherlands and North Germany.

Nevertheless the collection and publication of all these sources would leave valuable records unexplored. The history of England was still in Henry's reign to a large extent local, and until the local archives of England have been examined and their contents collated, a good deal of light will be lost. In the archives of Colchester there is a private journal of Henry's first parliament, the only document of its kind known before the reign of Elizabeth ; from those of York we derive the best illustrations of Yorkist sympathies after Richard III's defeat. Hardly less important are those of Exeter and Bristol in the south-west, Norwich in the east, and Leicester and Nottingham in the midlands. Nearly half the entries in Campbell's "Materials" relate to Henry as Duke of Lancaster and not as King of England ; and the records of the provincial governments, the Councils of the North, and of Wales, and the West were kept, and to some extent have been retained at the cities in which they sat. The centralization which eventually brought to London nearly all the records of government was not yet accomplished.

In selecting from materials, the printed portions of which are extensive enough by themselves, the method or methods adopted must appear more or less arbitrary, and the result be incomplete. All that has been possible has been to illustrate, and not to provide a comprehensive basis of evidence for, the history of Henry's reign. In view of the abundance of documents, and of the value of the historical training which their study provides, it has been determined to exclude all extracts from histories, even from one so nearly contemporary as Polydore Vergil's, and from the contemporary fragments by

Bernard André. History is distinguished from its materials by the author's desire to tell a story, which is rarely free from an element of falsification ; and legends may grow without design. An original manuscript by Bernard André described how Henry after the battle of Bosworth entered the city of London *lætanter ;* a copyist transcribed the adverb *latenter,* and in Bacon's speculative mind *latenter* became "himself not being on horseback, or in any open chair, or throne, but in a close chariot, as one that having been sometimes an enemy to the whole state, and a proscrib'd person, chose rather to keep state, and strike reverence into the people than to fawn upon them " This almost ranks with the pages of moral reflections on the sloth of Alfred the Great's sailors, into which Simeon of Durham was betrayed by misreading *cum dom' iret* as *cum dormiret.*[1] Even when the historian's reflections are based on facts, it is well for the student occasionally to have the opportunity of differentiating between the food for thought and the finished product.

The elimination of the historian still left difficulties enough with regard to the documents. A few of the more important treaties have been printed *in extenso,* because serious historical students should know what public instruments are like, with all their prolixity and minuteness ; and without the labour of reading and translating one or two treaties, it is impossible to realize the extent to which international relations are matters of detail. We are always striving to amass the pounds without the trouble of collecting the pence. Similarly, a few cases from the Courts of Star

---

[1] Plummer's " Alfred the Great," p. 64.

Chamber and of Requests have been printed at length, because concrete examples of the procedure of those famous institutions convey a more vivid impression than pages of description. But we have had to be content with samples, and to epitomize most of the treaties required to illustrate Henry's foreign and commercial policy. Even when a despatch has been printed in full in Gairdner's " Letters and Papers " or elsewhere, conditions of space have often necessitated the preference of epitomes contained in the Spanish and other Calendars. The briefer communications which passed between private individuals have on the other hand been printed, sometimes with omissions, but without condensation.

These letters, written in English, involve difficulties of spelling which do not occur in the stereotyped Latin of official correspondence. English spelling was uniform in Henry's reign only in the bizarre appearance it presents to modern readers ; and editors have differed about the respective advantages of modernizing the spelling and of literal reproduction. Halliwell in his " Letters of the Kings " and Miss Wood in her " Letters of Princesses " modernized their text ; Dr. Gairdner printed the " Paston Letters " as they were written, and the same plan was adopted by the editors of the " Plumpton Correspondence " and the " Cely Papers " for the Camden Society. Sir Henry Ellis in his eleven volumes of " Original Letters " was not quite consistent, and of one document at least he printed the first half in modern, and the second half in sixteenth-century English.[1] It is hoped that these volumes contain no

[1] " Original Letters," 2nd ser. ii. 215-6.

vagary quite so erratic ; but it was obviously impossible to re-edit the above collections and reduce their spelling to uniformity. The letters are accordingly reprinted in the spelling of the editions from which they are taken. The same plan has been followed in reprinting statutes. Most of them have been taken from the " Statutes of the Realm " with its modern spelling ; but a few of the earlier Acts of Henry VII's parliaments have been reprinted from Caxton's original edition of 1489. The student who troubles to compare Caxton's text with the " Statutes of the Realm " should remember that it was not in Caxton's time considered necessary to publish statutes with literal fidelity to the statute-roll, any more than the proclamation of a statute necessarily embodied all its provisos and machinery. The published version was for popular use, the text of the statute-roll for the judges of the High Court of Parliament. Some liberties have been taken in the matters of punctuation and the use of capitals ; the original statutes were, of course, innocent of the former, and English scribes in Henry's reign were undecided between the modern English and German ideas about capital letters.

The arrangement of these documents presented almost as many difficulties as their selection. The easiest and least useful plan would have been to make the whole series chronological ; but history can only be understood through the collection and correlation of phenomena, and it seemed expedient to arrange these documents under certain heads. The first volume attempts by means of narrative extracts to give a general view of the chronological history of the reign ; and it is hoped that something has been gained by a liberal interpretation of the epithet " narrative ". A speech in Parliament, the preamble to an Act, a despatch, a private letter, a political poem, even an inscription on a tomb,[1] may supply chronological information that will be sought in vain in chronicles and histories ; and the varied sources, from which these narrative extracts have been drawn, provide light from many quarters, and thus create a better perspective than illumination, however brilliant, from a single point of view. But this very comprehensiveness renders impossible hard and fast distinctions ; and documents, which have been used to illustrate the narrative, might equally well have been employed to exemplify diplomacy. Foreign relations, again, cannot be sharply distinguished from commercial intercourse, nor social from economic history. Nevertheless it has appeared advisable and feasible to arrange the documents in the second volume under Constitutional History and Social and Economic History, and those in the third under Foreign Affairs, Ecclesiastical History, and Ireland.

On all these aspects of Henry's reign these volumes will provide the student with the materials for forming a judgment ; but they will not supply that judgment ready made, nor relieve him from the task of drawing his own conclusions. History can never be an exact science, because it deals with realities and not with abstractions, with human affairs and not with hypotheses. Men have been content to accept with unanimity Euclid's fiction that a line is length without breadth, because, except for the sake of lucidity, it does not matter how a fiction is stated. But they have never agreed

[1] Vol. i. No. 56.

about the facts or theories of human progress, and the judgments of men and events by their contemporaries were just as capricious and contradictory four centuries ago as they are to-day. One tells us that Henry VII spent all his leisure poring over his accounts, another that he only cared for amusements ; against assertions that he spent nothing we have to set the sums he lavished on jewels and entertainments, and against Morton's fork and Empson's fines the release of all prisoners in London for debts of less than 40s. His haggling with Ferdinand of Aragon over the distressful Catherine's dower conflicts with the charm of his correspondence with his mother ; and his harshness to Warwick and Suffolk, with his fidelity to his ministers, only one of whom encountered the fate so common to Tudor statesmen. The simple facts of history prove on examination to be as fictitious and as fallacious as the elements of geometry or of chemistry. They are little more than convenient hypotheses, suited to juvenile students.

The test of the student's historical competence lies in his capacity to weigh and interpret conflicting evidence, but he does well to accept assistance ; and, in spite of adverse criticism, Bacon's "Henry VII" remains an indispensable guide to the understanding of Henry's reign. Bacon is incomparably the greatest man who has ever tried to elucidate Henry's mind and policy ; and his sources of information were not so inadequate as seriously to impair the value of his judgment. He was a careful student of Henry's legislation, and some of the constitutional maxims embedded in Bacon's general works were derived from his study of Henry's practice.

Moreover, the opinion of a Lord Chancellor, and of one of the greatest of them, on questions of legislation and judicature, is generally worth having; and none but the sorriest pedant would permit the defects in Bacon's historical knowledge and the laxity of his imagination to blind him to the historical value of Bacon's political insight and experience. Of modern writers on Henry VII fewer than half a dozen need be considered. Dr. Gairdner has in his prefaces to the three volumes he contributed to the Rolls Series, and in his more popular lives of "Richard III" (with an Appendix on Perkin Warbeck) and "Henry VII," done more than anyone else to reveal the sources for the history of the reign. Dr. Wilhelm Busch has in his "England under the Tudors" (Vol. i.; Eng. trans. by A. M. Todd) reduced practically all the materials available at the date of writing (1895) to a succinct though not very lucid narrative, which may be supplemented by Mr. Fisher's illuminating volume in the "Political History of England" Two of the best of Stubbs' "Seventeen Lectures on Mediaeval and Modern History," are devoted to Henry's reign; and reference should be made to Mr. Leadam's learned prefaces to his "Select Cases" from the Courts of Star Chamber and of Requests, published by the Selden Society, and to Mr. Kingsford's admirable edition of the well-known Brit. Mus. Cotton MS. Vitellius A. xvi. and other chronicles, which formed the basis of the later works by Fabyan, Hall, Holinshed, and Stow. The following paragraphs do not profess even to sketch the history of Henry's reign, but merely to make some general remarks for consideration in the light of these documents.

b

§ 2. POLITICAL AFFAIRS.

Distant as Henry Tudor was from the direct line of succession to the English crown, and dubious as his retention of it long appeared to be, the throne afforded him the only prospect of tolerable security. The Wars of the Roses removed his competitors with murderous rapidity, and Richard III accelerated Henry's progress to perilous eminence by disposing of less dangerous rivals. The assassination of the princes in the Tower, far from smoothing Richard's thorny path, rendered the world too small to hold both him and the Earl of Richmond ; and the Wars of the Roses culminated in a duel. Neither competitor could be safe, so long as the other lived ; the question for both was one of the crown or of death by battle, murder, or attainder. The Tudor orphan was proscribed and hunted as far as the arm of Richard III's diplomacy could reach ; and Richard's retention of the throne would sooner or later have involved the Earl of Richmond in the fate which he inflicted upon the Earls of Warwick and Suffolk. The battle of Bosworth settled the issue in Henry's favour, but it was mainly a personal matter. Stanley held the balance, and Stanley was not partial to any political principle. There was no popular revolt against Richard's rule, and the lamentation of the city of York over the death of its "merciful" king [1] cannot have been feigned. A generation of butchery had hardened men's hearts ; they might well be indifferent to the fate of princes, and in any case they were not certain that the murder, if murder there was, was Richard's work. He may have been the monster of iniquity depicted by Tudor writers, but there is little

[1] Vol. i. No. 9.

evidence to show that England was deeply impressed by the fact. He had ruled well enough ; in the south he had given men peace, in the north he was remembered for the reconquest of Berwick from the " auld enemy ".

If Henry was to keep the throne, he must create his own credentials. There was nothing divine about his descent ; and though something was made of the " verum Dei judicium "[1] at the battle of Bosworth, the God of Battles was a fickle and dangerous deity to invoke. Hymen might be more steadfast, and Henry's marriage with Elizabeth of York was as essential to his position as was William III's with Mary II to his.

The marriage blunted the edge of Yorkist jealousy, and gave the party at least an excuse for feeling that it was represented on the throne. But we misapprehend the nature of Henry's problem, if we think of a party as being the greatest of his difficulties. The problem was not a party, but a frame of mind. If there had ever been, before the Tudors came to throne, a law-abiding English people, that characteristic had certainly disappeared in the fifteenth century. In 1411 a judge waylaid a peer with 500 hired bravos, and then pleaded in Parliament that he did not know his conduct was illegal.[2] Respect for law and order did not improve as the century grew older, and these documents amply illustrate the comprehensive determination of men in all classes to have their will, with or without the law. The law, indeed, was regarded mainly as a means of oppression, and its chaotic condition rendered it the facile instrument of chicanery and force. Machiavelli ascribed

----

[1] Vol. i. No. 15.   [2] " Rot. Parl.," iii. 649.

the political evils of the time to weakness of will, but he had in mind the impotence of the State. There was will enough and to spare in the individual, but it was anarchic and insubordinate ; and the great political need of the time was the subjection of the over-mighty subject, the restraint of individual greed and irresponsible power, by the will of the community in the interests of law and order.

In this respect the terms Yorkist and Lancastrian were distinctions without a difference ; and it is as irrelevant to discuss, as it is impossible to determine, whether Henry VII pursued a Yorkist or a Lancastrian policy. It has been said—in Wellington's phrase— that he " dished the Whigs," and it is true that there is little novelty or originality in his legislation or methods of government. That is because the issue was essentially one between order and disorder ; and the government, whether Yorkist or Tudor, was necessarily on the side of order. In the south-east, which was growing commercial and peaceful, feeling was generally with the government ; in the north and in Cornwall, where feudalism still prevailed, sentiment was as much against the government as it was in Ireland thirty years ago. Juries would not convict on a prosecution by the Crown, even where the Crown was not prevented by feudal liberties from prosecution ; lordship was more than the law and the prophets ; [1] and the King's peace was a reign of riot. The fact that prerogative Councils were set up for the North, the Marches of Wales, and the West, but not for the Midlands or South-East

[1] "Paston Letters," vol. i. p. 156. "Get you lordship . *quia ibi pendet tota lex et prophetæ*".

indicates the difference in social conditions between the different parts of England.

But these divergences were not Yorkist and Lancastrian. Henry VII's proclamation against the northern rebels in 1489 [1] charging them with a desire to " rob, despoil, and destroy all the south parts of this his realm, and to subdue and bring to captivity all the people of the same," echoes the Yorkist appeal of 1461 against " the misruled and outrageous people of the north parts of this land coming hitherward, purposing the utter destruction as well of this country as of you and other our true subjects and also the subversion of the commonweal of all this land ".[2] There was substance in this divergence, and it remained a cause of distraction in English politics for centuries after Henry's reign ; but the identification of either north or south with either Yorkist or Lancastrian was an accident depending upon the personal affiliations of the monarch who happened to be on the throne. There was neither party nor principle in the plots against Henry VII ; they represented merely personal discontents, abetted by foreign rivals, and fed by endemic disorders. They grew dangerous chiefly when they coincided with the resistance which uneducated people are always liable to offer to taxation required for national purposes. The rioters who slew the Earl of Northumberland in 1489, "renied their taxes to pay " ; [3] the Cornishmen rose because they refused to be taxed for the defence of the

---

[1] Vol. i. No. 53.

[2] Nicolas, " Proceedings of the Privy Council," vi. 309-10.

[3] Vol. i. p. 75. Skelton's reference to that " dolorous Tuesday " (p. 76) enables us to date Northumberland's death 28 April.

Scottish borders; and taxes or rumours of taxes were the occasion of most revolts in the Tudor period. They illustrate on the one hand the progress of national government and of its financial requirements, and on the other, the adherence of the more backward parts of the realm to mediaeval and local liberties, and their consequent indifference to national growth. Had this indifference been general, it must have been fatal to Henry and to the New Monarchy, of which he was the principal architect. But the Midlands, the South, and the East, while never enthusiastic supporters of Henry VII, gave no countenance whatsoever to conspiracies against him. Lovell's rebellion was merely a local and personal manifestation. The force which sent Lambert Simnel up like a rocket was provided from Burgundian and Irish sources; and Perkin Warbeck could only forage in Celtic fringes and foreign purlieus. When his followers landed at Deal, the men of Kent gave short shrift to their pleas and pretences.[1] Progressive England had no liking for Henry's taxation; but it realized the worth of his rule, and felt even less dissatisfaction with his government than it had with Richard III's.

The most conclusive testimony to the success of Henry's administration consists perhaps in the feebleness of the indictment which Perkin Warbeck brought when he made his second invasion from Scotland.[2] The obscurity of his Tudor descent is cast in Henry's teeth; his " caitiff and villain " councillors; the proscription of Warbeck's adherents; Warwick's imprisonment and disinheritance; "the great and execrable offences

[1] Vol. i. Nos. 79-82.	[2] *Ibid.* No. 108.

daily committed and done by our foresaid great enemy
and his adherents in breaking the liberties and franchises of our Mother Holy Church, to the high displeasure of Almighty God "; the " daily pilling of the
people by dismes, taskes, tallages, benevolences, and
other unlawful impositions and grievous exactions ";
and so forth. The liberties of the church had been
slightly curbed with the assent of Pope and prelates [1];
the preference of " caitiff and villain " councillors, which
was a stock complaint against Tudor monarchs, might
touch a sympathetic chord in noble breasts ; and the
references to Warwick's misfortunes and to Henry's
financial exactions would reach a wider audience. But
this was not a programme on which to effect a revolution in favour of an adventurer, who came in the train
of a foreign enemy, pledged to abandon Berwick and
to pay 100,000 marks to James IV ; [2] and Henry refused
to enter London in triumph over the capture of such
a contemptible foe.[3]

It had always been Henry's cue to assume contempt
for Warbeck's cause and person ; [4] but Perkin had given
him six years of serious anxiety, and some authorities,
though not the best, have been unconvinced of the truth
of the official account of the pretender's origin.[5] The
comparative success of Simnel's imposture, which is
not seriously doubted, destroys the theory that there
must necessarily have been a substratum of truth in
Perkin's pretensions. Nevertheless, Henry's poet laureate, Bernard André, gives colour to the suspicion that

[1] See vol. iii. pt. 2. [2] Vol. i. p. 138.
[3] *Ibid*. No. 125. [4] Vol. iii. No. 6.
[5] See, for instance, " Annals of England," Oxford, 1876, pp.
279-81.

Perkin was not merely the son of a boatman of Tournay, by recording the story that he was godson to Edward IV; and Bacon embellished the tale.[1] Another, still more curious, was revealed by the publication in 1913 of the first volume of the Calendar of Milanese State Papers. In February, 1495, Maximilian, King of the Romans, told the Milanese envoy at his court that Sir Robert Clifford had communicated to Henry VII the fact that Perkin was not the son of Edward IV, as he claimed to be, but the son of Edward IV's sister, Margaret of Burgundy, and of the Bishop of Cambray.[2] It is a story similar to those told about Queen Elizabeth, in which no serious historian places any credence. But Maximilian's object in repeating this scandal about his wife's step-mother is difficult to understand, more especially as he was still himself an active supporter of Perkin's pretensions. In 1498 the bishop was in England on an embassy from the Netherlands, and specially desired to see Perkin, as, Puebla tells us, "he had formerly transacted business with him". Henry thereupon summoned Perkin from the Tower and questioned him in Puebla's and apparently in the Bishop's presence. If there was any truth in the story, this confrontation must have afforded Henry some grim amusement, which would not be lessened by Perkin's answer, as reported by Puebla, to the effect that Margaret of Burgundy knew as well as he did that he was not the son of Edward IV [3] The story would not be inconsistent with Perkin's upbringing by foster parents in humble circumstances in Tournay; it would explain some of

[1] Busch, "England under the Tudors," i. 336.
[2] Henry of Bergen (1450?-1502); vol. i. No. 77. [3] Ibid. No. 134.

the mystery about his career; and yet it would not be one which Henry could publish, for princes observed even then the *convenances* in their relations with one another. The year of Perkin's capture, which was the central year of Henry's reign, was also its *annus mirabilis*. The Scottish invasion had been repulsed ; Warbeck's attempts on Ireland had been frustrated by Waterford's loyalty; the second rebellion of the turbulent commons of Cornwall had ended in smoke ; and Cabot had discovered Newfoundland.[1]　Foreign princes began to respect Henry's accomplished facts, and their envoys in England impressed upon them the strength of his position.　" I repeat," the Milanese envoy informs his master, Ludovic Sforza,[2] " that this present state is most stable, even for the king's descendants, since there is no one who aspires to the Crown ; with concord at home they have no occasion to fear " : and again, " from this time forward he is perfectly secure against Fortune " [3]　" Henry is rich," wrote two Spanish envoys from London in July, 1498, " has established good order in England, and keeps the people in such subjection as has never been the case before." [4]　" His Majesty can stand," reiterates Soncino, " like one at the top of a tower looking on at what is passing in the plain." [5]　" England," averred Puebla early in 1500, " has never been so tranquil and obedient as at present." [6]　More material rewards were reaped than this chorus of appreciation.　Ferdinand and Isabella finally made up their minds that Arthur would be a suitable match for their daughter Catherine, and con-

---

[1] Vol. ii. Nos. 161-2.　　　　[2] Vol. i. No. 118.
[3] I, 121.　　[4] I, 132.　　[5] I, 137.　　[6] I, 145.

tributed to the prospects of the pair by smoothing the way, through Ayala's agency, for peace between England and Scotland.[1] Louis XII of France hastened to surrender John Taylor who had planned Warbeck's first Irish adventure,[2] and further strengthened Henry's position by reviving the Orleanist claims to Naples and thus involving France in a perennial contest with Spain for Italian supremacy.

The union between Prince Arthur and Catherine was cut short by the prince's death in April, 1502 ;[3] and the marriage between Catherine and her brother-in-law Henry, which Louis XII's attack upon Ferdinand led him and Isabella instantly and urgently to press forward,[4] was delayed until after Henry VII's death. The fact that the Spanish alliance had become less necessary for England than the English alliance was for Spain had probably more to do with the delay than the scruples of conscience about the marriage, which are said to have troubled Henry VII and awoke with such painful results in the breast of Henry VIII twenty-five years later. Henry's declining years were devoted to cultivating Habsburg friendship in the Netherlands, and his relations with Ferdinand were far from friendly. Catherine was therefore placed in a painful position ; a betrothal was contracted between her and Henry, but her youthful *fiancé* was induced to protest in solemn form that the promise was made against his will and invalid. Ferdinand had paid but half of the dower promised on Catherine's marriage with Arthur ; the remainder was not forthcoming,[5]

---

[1] I, 122, 133.   [2] I, 57, 141.   [3] I, 157.   [4] I, 160-1.
[5] " Spanish Calendar," i. 435, 513, 529.

and Catherine wrote to her father that the reason for her treatment was his inability to fulfil his engagements. Henry VII declined responsibility for Catherine's maintenance pending a settlement of this question, though Catherine's complaints of her poverty must be taken with some reserve, and the "liberality" for which she is praised seems to have been extravagant. In March, 1509, there were still 30,000 crowns left of the first half of her dower which had been smuggled out of England to be beyond Henry's reach ;[1] and Catherine's complaints of her father's ambassadors[2] are even louder than her lamentations over her lot.

The truth is that her relatives were not at all a happy family ; a Spaniard complained that her sister Juaña "had an obdurate heart and no piety," and Catherine herself was not altogther discreet in public or private affairs. Her father and her brother-in-law, the Archduke Philip, were at loggerheads over the government of Castile ; and Catherine appears to have sided with Philip,[3] whom Ferdinand accused of being the cause of her misery.[4] These quarrels were reflected in the ranks of Catherine's household servants, with which Henry declined to interfere ; and it is impossible to determine the balance of truth in the mutual recriminations between her and her father's ambassadors. One of these went so far as to intimate that Henry's coldness to Catherine was justified by the conduct of the father confessor to whom she was too deeply attached.[5]

These bickerings hardly relieve the dulness of the last

[1] I, 213.   [2] I, 193, 198, 212, 215.
[3] " Spanish Calendar," i. 231.
[4] *Ibid.* i. 400.   [5] I, 211, 213, 214.

seven years of Henry's reign. The absence of domestic
incident might suggest that England was enjoying the
proverbial happiness of a people without a history. Only
one Parliament met between 1497 and the end of the
reign [1]; after Warbeck's execution there was no war
and no insurrection; and the workings of treason were
doubtful and obscure. The fate of the Earl of Warwick
or complicity in the schemes to release him terrified
the Earl of Suffolk into double flight from England,[2]
and in February, 1502, Sir William Courtenay, who had
married Edward IV's younger daughter, Catherine, Sir
James Tyrrell, and others were sent to the Tower for
favouring Suffolk's party.[3] Another of the Queen's
kinsmen, the young Marquis of Dorset, followed.
Tyrrell, Sir John Wyndham, and others were brought
to the scaffold three months later.[4] Dorset and
Courtenay were transferred in October, 1507, from the
Tower to Calais, where, says the chronicler, " they were
kept prisoners in the castle as long as King Henry the
Seventh lived, and should have been put to death if he
had lived longer "; [5] ever since the Duke of Gloucester's
murder at Richard II's command, the transference of
prisoners to Calais had been ominous of their fate. If
Dorset and Courtenay gained, Suffolk himself was the
loser by Henry's death. His capture had been one of
the main objects of Henry's diplomacy for four years,
and he fell a victim into his hands through the storm
which cast the King of Castile on English shores in
January, 1506. But Henry had made a promise which
his son did not respect; and Suffolk was brought to

[1] I.e. in 1504; see Vol. i. No. 168.   [2] I, Nos. 142, 153.
[3] I, 156.   [4] I, 158.   [5] I, 201.

the block in 1513, as a preliminary precaution to Henry VIII's invasion of France.

Suspicion became almost a disease in Henry's mind. The strength of his position, which enabled him to bring such offenders with impunity to the Tower and the block, should have been an argument for lenity. But Henry had developed some of the foibles of Louis XI. "He is growing very devout," wrote Ayala in March, 1499 ; [1] and he hunted out relics with almost as much zest as he did traitors. Morton's death in 1500 is said to have removed a wholesome influence, which saved the King from unpopular courses, though Morton survived the worst blot on Henry's reign, the judicial murder of Warwick, and himself incurred " the great disdain and great hatred of the Commons of this land ".[2] The death of Sir Reginald Bray in 1503 cannot have influenced Henry's conduct ; the loss of his Queen earlier in that year might more reasonably be thought to have had more effect, but no councillor exercised an appreciable control over Henry's policy. Fox is the most familiar figure during the closing years of his reign, but it is to Oxford that Spanish and Flemish diplomatists are represented as ascribing the greatest influence. Subsequent writers laid the responsibility on the shoulders of Empson and Dudley, who are hardly mentioned in diplomatic correspondence ; and it would, indeed, be strange that the reputed victim of Henry's most famous fine should thus be linked with his most infamous financial agents. But this representation is in part at any rate due to editorial error. The Provost of Cassel does, indeed, clearly refer to Oxford as " un

des grands, et, comme l'on nous dit, le principal person-
nage de ce royaume " ;[1] but that does not imply political influence, and when Puebla is made to say that
" the Lord Great Chamberlain, who is of his blood, is
more in his confidence than any other person,"[2] there
is a manifest confusion between Oxford, who was Lord
Great Chamberlain, and Sir Charles Somerset, Lord
Herbert, who was illegitimate son of Henry VII's cousin
the third duke of Somerset, and was appointed Chamberlain of the Household in 1505. However that may be,
Empson and Dudley, who had both been Speakers of
the House of Commons, traded upon their sovereign's
taste for finance, and developed a skill in extortion[3]
which darkened the close of Henry's reign and helped
his successor to make the scaffold a popular institution.

§ 3. CONSTITUTIONAL ASPECTS OF THE REIGN.

While the political history of Henry's reign has
attracted some learned and competent critics, it cannot be said that its constitutional aspects have received adequate attention ; and the opening chapters of
Hallam, after nearly a century, still remain the favourite
recourse for students and teachers. It has been well
said, in criticism of Hallam's treatment of the seventeenth century, that he thought there was a definite
constitution and that the Stuarts broke it.[4] The
criticism applies with greater force to the earlier period.
A constitutional historian is apt to regard the constitu-

---

[1] I, 208.   [2] I, 199.
[3] See Vol. i. Nos. 209-10 ; Vol. ii. Nos. 23-30.
[4] Gooch, " History and Historians in the Nineteenth Century,"
p. 293.

tion as complete when his book is finished; and the
circumstance that the greatest of English constitutional
historians stopped in the Middle Ages has led his
readers to antedate the completion of the English constitution. It is not easy to define at the present day;
it was still more difficult in 1485; and no satisfactory
attempt has been made to determine what was and
what was not constitutional during the Tudor period.

In the first place there had as yet been no definition
of the prerogative of a national king. It is true that
we read in the Middle Ages of a *prærogativa regis* and
its limitations; but these referred to the king as a feudal
landlord. They deal with the obligations of suit and
service attached to the land, with the relations between
landlord and tenant. Except in so far as the subject
was a tenant of the Crown he had few dealings with it.
The tenants of Henry VII himself were in a very different
position from his other subjects. Those on the lands of
the Duchy of Lancaster were free from tolls throughout
the realm and exempt from all other jurisdiction; on
the other hand, if they were bakers and competed with
the ducal baking-houses, their ovens were destroyed.[1]
The relation of the King to all Englishmen, irrespective
of tenure, was a different and a very indeterminate
matter, which could only develop with the elimination
of feudal ideas from the sphere of government, and with
the gradual destruction of those mediaeval "liberties"
which cut so much of the country out of the national
system and subjected it to private jurisdiction. In 1348
the Commons had petitioned the Crown against these

---

[1] Campbell's "Materials," i. 604-5; ii. pp. xvii. 50, 531; it was
the same with their stalls and shops.

liberties as tending to the destruction of the common law and to the oppression of the people; and nearly two centuries later Parliament transferred these liberties to the Crown.[1] That Parliament should have authority to destroy a single privilege was itself an anti-feudal idea connected with the growth of national sovereignty and of statute law.

The varieties of law, and their relations to one another, were much in the minds of statesmen in Henry VII's reign, and the Chancellor generally touched on the subject in his opening speech to Parliament.[2] Most of these varieties, like Divine law, the law of Nature, and the law of Nations, were regarded as direct or indirect emanations from God, with which no human authority could interfere, except by way of interpretation. But side by side with these, and ever encroaching upon them, was the positive law, created and imposed by man. This might be the canon law of the Church, the civil law of the Empire, or the municipal statutes of some more local body, a Parliament, a City Council, or a Guild. Richard II had first of English kings learnt the lesson of Pierre Dubois, and claimed for the national monarch the legislative monopoly possessed by Roman Emperors: and this conception, modified by feudal ideas and customary law, became the basis of the

[1] "Rot. Parl.," ii. 166; 27 Henry VIII, c. xxiv. This statute was the completion of a gradual process; the Crown had long tended to monopolize liberties through attainder and forfeiture. Henry VII himself is perhaps Duke of Lancaster rather than King of England, grand seigneur rather than sovereign. It was a case of Aaron's rod swallowing all the rest; the greatest feudal magnate gained the Crown.

[2] Cf. Vol. i. Nos. 45, 83, 105, 168.

modern royal prerogative. It was still in 1485 in a crude, amorphous condition without definite limitations, because men only trouble to limit powers which may conceivably be exercised. No one has thought to limit a despot's power over rain or sunshine, and the law of the air has only just come within the sphere of practical politics. Similarly, no mediaeval monarch had been prohibited from keeping a standing army in time of peace, because it had not entered men's minds that a mediaeval king should ever possess the financial resources adequate to its maintenance. His actual power was small, and the need for defining his pre-rogative only grew with the New Monarchy and with the concentration in the hands of the Crown of those fragments of sovereign power, called liberties, which had been so lavishly distributed among over-mighty subjects.

The power of making positive law could only de-velop in royal hands. For one thing, legislation grew out of jurisdiction, and began as the judgments of a court.[1] Parliament was the King's High Court ; even to-day an Act of Parliament is strictly speaking an Act of the King in Parliament, and in 1485 it was so in a very real sense. The circumstance that Parliament was the chief court in the land led to the theory that the chief matters could only be decided there ; but while legislation was to be enacted *in* Parlia-ment, it could only be enacted *by* the Crown. Certain formulae about the advice and consent of Lords and Commons had come into use ; but they had not yet been stereotyped, and were by no means essential to the

[1] McIlwain, " The High Court of Parliament," 1911.

validity of statutes made in Parliament. Many of
Henry's VII's Acts, indeed, begin "Prayen the Commons"; but many others " The King, remembering,"
without the least indication of advice or consent by
anyone else. An Act of Attainder was even passed
without the consent of the Commons ; the judges, it is
true, decided that it was not therefore valid,[1] but their
decision did not apply to other kinds of legislation, and
in 1504 Henry was empowered by Parliament itself to
repeal Acts of Attainder on his sole authority.[2] The
" Rolls of Parliament" teem with " provisions " made
by the King in person in Parliament ; and the difficulties
in which this casual method of legislation involved the
clerks are illustrated by the following entry : " Item,
quædam Provisio facta est per Dominum Regem in
Parliamento prædicto pro David Philip, armigero ; sed
cui Actui debeat affilari, ignoratur ; tenor tamen Pro-
visionis illius sequitur, et est talis . . ."[3] " Howbeit,"
writes one of Sir Robert Plumpton's correspondents of
the Act of Attainder passed in Henry's first Parliament,
"there were many gentlemen against it ; but it would
not be, for it was the King's pleasure."[4]

Dr. Gairdner has pointed out that the royal veto was
never used in Henry's reign,[5] and has naturally suggested that this circumstance indicates a fairly comprehensive control over legislation before it reached the
throne. But the methods by which this control was
exerted have never been explained ; and before we can
understand any explanation we must clear our minds of
the familiar notions of Parliament. In Henry's reign we

[1] Vol. ii. No. 14. [2] Ibid. No. 13. [3] Ibid. No. 12.
[4] Vol. i. p. 32. [5] " Henry VII," p. 212.

have as yet no " Lords' " or " Commons' Journals ". We have merely the " Rolls of Parliament," and the Rolls are the records of a court, kept by royal clerks. Parliament, as such, has no officials of its own ; Chancery is the office of Parliament, and supplies all the machinery that Parliament possesses, its presiding officer the Lord Chancellor, its writs of summons, its legal advisers, its clerks, and its forms of procedure by bill and petition. There is nothing called the House of Lords, either as a building or as a body of men. There are, indeed, Lords of Parliament; but there are also Lords of the Council, just as to-day there are Lords of the Treasury, Lords of the Admiralty, and others whose Lordship is purely official ; and it is not till 1544 that we get the earliest reference to a "House " of Lords.[1] In Henry VII's reign the " Lords "—including judges, masters in chancery, law officers of the crown, and royal secretaries— sat "in Camera Magni Consilii vocata le Parlement Chambre " ; [2] they sat in a council chamber, were all the King's councillors, and were regarded as such, not as " Peers," a word unknown to the parliamentary records of the reign.

Near the " Parliament Chamber " was the " Parliament House " " The same day," write the burgesses for Colchester, whose diary for the Parliament of 1485-6 has been preserved in the Colchester archives, " it pleased the King and all his lords for to send for Master Speaker and all the House into the Parliament chamber." [3]

[1] Parry, " Parliaments and Councils of England," p. xlii.
[2] " Rot. Parl.," vi. 232 a.
[3] W. G. Benham, " The Red Paper Book of Colchester," pp. 60-4 ; cf. Campbell's " Materials," i. 82, 333.

c *

The "Domus Communis" in which the Commons
deliberated was in the fourteenth and fifteenth centuries the Chapter House of Westminster Abbey; and
they are supposed to have continued meeting there
until 1547, when they were transferred to St. Stephen's
Chapel. In any case their discussions were no part of
the proceedings *in* Parliament, and consequently there
is no reference to them in the "Rolls". The Commons
only appear *in* Parliament[1] on rare occasions, to hear
the chancellor's opening speech and prorogation, to present the Speaker, or to announce by his mouth the result of their deliberations; they only appear at the bar,
and generally on their knees, and the Speaker alone
of the Commons may speak in the Parliament chamber.
His regular petition for freedom of speech is for himself
alone, and refers only to what he says in the Parliament
chamber as the prolocutor of the Commons; his principal
claim is that he may withdraw or correct any resolution
which he may have misreported; and it has nothing to do
with the domestic debates in the "Domus Communis,"
which is outside "the Parliament chamber," and of
which the clerk of Parliament takes no cognisance. It
does not, however, follow that the Commons have complete liberty of action even in their own House. So far
as petitions were concerned there was little or no restraint; and most of these appeals to grace were presented by the Commons on behalf of—*ex parte*—some
corporation or individual. But a bill, *formam cujusdam
Actus in se continens*,[2] was a different matter; it not only
contained a petition, but dictated the form of answer;
and to the end of the Tudor period procedure by bill was

[1] E.g. Vol. i. p. 25.   [2] See Vol. ii. No. 12.

thought to trench on the royal prerogative. Elizabeth, whose action was generally based upon precedent, directed the Speaker to refuse leave to introduce bills of a certain character;[1] and it is probable that in Henry VII's reign, before bills could be introduced into the House of Commons, leave had to be given through the Speaker by the King or the Lords in the Parliament chamber.

There is not the least doubt that the constitutional questions involved in Henry's legislation were discussed and settled by the judges before the bills were introduced into Parliament; and some of the most interesting of the following documents[2] illustrate this practice. It is unfortunate that the text is so badly edited; and the attempts of the non-legal mind to elucidate its meaning can be little better than guesswork. The printed editions of these "Reports" give us no information as to their *mise-en-scène*. The judges are seen discussing general constitutional questions, and we are forcibly reminded of Bacon's approval of frequent consultation by the Crown with those "lions under the throne". But the method by which these questions were brought before them, the court in which they sat, and the precise effect of their judgments are left obscure. One is tempted to see in these sessions a relic of the High Court of Parliament before it contained representative elements, and when there might be a "plenum parliamentum" without specially summoned magnates or elected knights of the shire and burgesses.[3] At any rate, an important

[1] D'Ewes, "Journals," p. 213; Prothero, "Select Documents," 2nd ed. p. 120.

[2] E.g. Vol. ii. Nos. 6, 7; Vol. iii. Pt. 3.

[3] Maitland, "Memoranda de Parliamento," Rolls Ser., pp. xxxv ff.

part of the work of the Lords of the Great Council in the Parliament chamber was the examination of bills before or as soon as they were introduced into the "Parliament House"; and in 1536 Lord Darcy complained that, whereas the Lords had previously been accustomed to obtain copies of bills introduced into the Commons that they might take legal opinion as to whether they were constitutional, recently they had experienced great difficulty in so doing "partly through default of those of the Chancery in the use of their office amongst the Lords"[1]

The credit for the legislation enacted under these conditions, upon which Bacon has passed an encomium, must therefore be divided between Henry VII and his judges. Its characteristic was "the revival of moribund legality and the construction of an efficient machinery for its enforcement"; Henry's statutes "were for the most part not novel in kind, but an endeavour to enforce existing laws".[2] It was remarked by a contemporary that he would like to govern after the French fashion,[3] and Dr. Busch has ascribed to this predilection the statute of 1495 dispensing with a jury of indictment, and legalizing action upon common informations in cases of livery, etc. The coincidence of this Act with the careers of Empson and Dudley as "common informers" has perhaps given it undue notoriety; for a similar Act had been passed in 1468, and petitions against its non-execution had been presented in the parliaments of 1472

---

[1] " Letters and Papers of Henry VIII," Vol. xii. pt. i. No. 901 [39, 40].

[2] Leadam, " Star Chamber Cases," Vol. i. pp. lxiv, xcv.

[3] Vol. ii. Nos. 2, 45.

and 1482. Similar precedents may be found for most of Henry's Acts; the remedies were well-nigh as ancient as the disease, of which complaints had been heard for nearly two centuries. The Statute of Fines, which legal historians persist in representing as Henry VII's invention, merely repeats an earlier Act;[1] and the nearest approaches to novelty in Henry's legislation may be found in the principle of Poynings' Laws, in the restriction of benefit of clergy and right of sanctuary, in the subjection of municipal law-making to the supervision of Chancery, and in the protection given to the subjects of a *de facto* king against prosecution for treason.[2] The novelty lay in execution; there had been lack of power, if not also lack of will, to enforce the law. Henry VII supplied both these qualities in a fuller measure than any of his predecessors, though complete cure was not to be effected for long years after his death. Sometimes, no doubt, Henry's zeal for execution carried him too far. The monstrous fine inflicted on his host, the Earl of Oxford, was hardly the act of a gentleman; but neither was the Earl's in parading illegal retainers before his royal guest, and it was Henry's duty to be a king before he was a gentleman. He, too, like James I, caused comment by hanging thieves, perhaps without a trial.[3] But he did not alter the judges' tenure of office from *quamdiu se bene gesserint* to *durante bene placito*.[4]

Even his famous Star Chamber Act of 1487 comes

---

[1] Busch, p. 295 *n.*
[2] Vol. ii. No. 9 ; Vol. iii. Pt. 3.
[3] "Venetian Calendar," i. 782.
[4] Campbell's "Materials," i. 592.

under this rule. As early as 1355 a select body of councillors sat for judicial business in a room called the Star Chamber. New forms of writ, infringing the common law, such as *sub poena* and *certis de causis* had been invented by John de Waltham, who became Master of the Rolls in 1381. By statute 31 Henry VI, c. 2, the issue of writs of privy seal had been legalized summoning before the King or his Council offenders in cases of " great riots, extortions, and oppressions " Parliament resisted this extension of the Council's jurisdiction, and in 1390 the Council admitted that cases concerning the common law should be sent before the judges. But in 1423 it reserved cases of too great might on one side and unmight on the other ; in 1426 it added to the reservation " other reasonable cause " ; and these received parliamentary sanction in 1429. A further Act of 1453 was so similar to that of 1487 that it might well have been regarded as the foundation of the Court of Star Chamber. Henry VII's statute improved upon the Act of 1453 (a) by extending the number of offences with which the Court was thenceforth by consent of Parliament competent to deal ; (b) by giving statutory sanction to the issue of writs of Great and Privy Seal ; and (c) by extending to all cases covered by the statutory jurisdiction the ancient practice of examining defendants upon oath.

The Court was little more than the Privy Council in another form ; and it exercised an almost indistinguishable jurisdiction. But it sat in public, while the Council sat in private, and judges always attended the Star Chamber, while they seldom attended the Privy Council. There were other differences in *personnel ;* councillors who were not privy councillors sat in the Star Chamber, and it was claimed in Elizabeth's reign that a peer, as an hereditary councillor of the Crown, had a right to sit in the Star Chamber. The claim was not allowed, but the composition of the Court was always doubtful. The statute of 1487 enabled the famous seven to exercise certain kinds of jurisdiction, but in 1493 it was laid down that the only judges of the Court were the Chancellor, Treasurer, and Lord Privy Seal.[1] This decision, however, was soon ignored; in 1529 the Lord President was added, and later, in the sixteenth century, the Court seems to have been the Privy Council, *plus* the judges, holding a public sitting for certain judicial purposes in the Star Chamber. The jurisdiction of the Court was also gradually extended beyond the limits of 1487 to cases of forgery, perjury, contempt of proclamations, frauds, duels, and other offences.

This list of crimes and misdemeanours, which the Common Law courts were unable to check, illustrates the need for some such institution as the Star Chamber ;[2] but its main justification lay in the breakdown of the jury system. Documents printed in these volumes and elsewhere show that trial by jury might in effect be a contest in perjury, and that the conscience of jurors was seldom proof against the pressure of bribery or force that might be brought to bear upon them by their powerful neighbours. It should, no doubt, be remembered that the judicial functions now discharged by juries were something new, and that jurors probably still

[1] Vol. ii. No. 35.

[2] Cf. Fortescue, ed. Plummer, p. 22, who describes the Star Chamber as a "national blessing".

regarded themselves as little more than witnesses, expected to do their best for their friends and not to judge impartially between the parties to the suit. The function and the merit of the Star Chamber was to put a greater fear before their eyes than that of local magnates; but even in this business of dealing with weak or dishonest juries, the Star Chamber was not in Henry's reign engaged on a novel task. Sixty years earlier the Court of Star Chamber, advised by the judges, was sitting upon a corrupt body of jurors.[1] Well might successive Chancellors open Parliament with exhortations to justice, and dwell with eloquence upon the Augustinian question, "sublata justitia, quid aliud sunt regna quam magna latrocinia?"[2]

While Morton and Warham talked of justice, their hearers murmured of taxation. Queen Elizabeth once admitted to a foreign diplomatist that there was plenty of money in England but that it was difficult of extraction;[3] and the circumstance that every revolt against the first two Tudors was occasioned by taxation shows that their difficulty was no less. Yet the sums were in inverse proportion to the hubbub raised by taxation. The yield of tenths, fifteenths, and subsidies sank as the wealth of the country rose; instead of real tenths being levied, the total sum had become stereotyped in the fourteenth century, though deductions were constantly made for towns and cities that professed to be decayed. Then, too, the tenths and fifteenths were collected by nominees of the local members of Parliament. "This

[1] Nicolas, "Proc. Privy Council," iii. 213.
[2] Vol. i. Nos. 45, 167.
[3] "Political History of England, vi. 188.

year," writes a London chronicler of 1489, " was granted unto the king toward the defence of Brittany, whereupon he had expended great sums of goods, the tenth penny of men's lands and goods moveable ; but it was so favourably set by the commissioners that it amounted to nothing so much in money as men deemed it would have done." [1] Whenever the sheep came to be shorn there was much cry and little wool.

There were two obvious causes for this discrepancy. Direct taxation was spasmodic ; it was not a regular annual charge, to which men grow accustomed and for which they make allowance. Only seven Parliaments met in the twenty-four years of Henry's reign ; none of them sat four months ; and some provided no supply. Taxes were not voted oftener than about once in six years ; it is true that payment was usually spread over two, but even so, the normal taxpayer had only to open his purse about once in three years. He was none the more grateful for that ; the income tax would to-day create far more friction if it were only collected once in three years, and if no one knew beforehand when it might be levied. It was the irregularity of direct taxation in the Tudor period that caused the hardship and provoked the discontent. There was little complaint about customs, except among merchants, because the ordinary taxpayer was not sufficiently educated to trace any connexion between the prices he paid and the duties levied by the King. The second cause of the outcry against taxation was simply the feebleness of national sentiment. The strength and soundness of a State depends upon the readiness of its members to vote

[1] Vol. i. No. 55.

and pay taxes for national purposes; but the Cornishmen's patriotism was so local that they thought it monstrous to be compelled to contribute to the expense of defending the Scottish borders, and even to the London chronicler an assessment is "favourable" when the taxpayer escapes, and the Government is left without financial resources to discharge its national duties.

It may be, however, that the most substantial cause for discontent consisted in the assessment. It is clear that local commissioners treated their localities with the greatest tenderness, but we have little information about the apportionment among individuals of the local assessment; a shire or town might be lightly assessed, but individuals might be heavily taxed, and what we know of local justice would not lead us to expect much fairness in the distribution of the burden. The extent to which the "commons" participated in the revolts against taxation, while the well-to-do townsfolk held aloof, suggests that meagre returns to the Exchequer might be compatible with grievous exactions from the poorer classes. If this were so, there was justice, if there was also illegality, in the forced loans and benevolences Henry raised. The benevolence is said to have been invented by Edward IV, but the forced loan at any rate was an earlier expedient, and the Privy Council records for 1435 contain a long list of person, cities, and towns from which sums were to be required.[1] Their collection from cities and towns might merely reproduce what injustice there was in the assessment of tenths and fifteenths; and while Henry VII made the city of London pay heavily for a renewal of its charter, he levied his benevolences

[1] Nicolas, "Proc. Privy Council," iv. 316-29.

as a rule from individuals. An Act of Richard III
had declared them illegal, but Parliament condoned and
enforced their payment when levied by Henry VII;[1]
and if Archbishop Morton devised the famous fork that
bears his name, it is satisfactory to find that he did not
himself escape the dilemma, but had on one occasion to
pay what would now be some £15,000.[2] It is probable
that in effect benevolences represented a rough and
partial equalization of financial burdens. Clerical ex-
emptions from tenths and fifteenths were a scandal;[3]
lay assessments were a farce. At the end of the Tudor
period Sir Walter Ralegh declared in Parliament that the
£3 or £4 at which men were rated in the subsidy-books
might stand for their real income or for less than its hun-
dredth part, while Cecil averred that in one shire no
man's lands were assessed at more than £80 a year, and
no one's income in London at more than £200. Subsidies, he asserted, were " imposed for the most part upon
the meaner sort of her majesty's subjects "[4] In Henry
VIII's reign Secretary Paget expressed his preference
for a benevolence over parliamentary taxation, because, among other reasons, a benevolence "did not
grieve the common people ".[5] Those who paid benevolences were the chief beneficiaries of Tudor government, and they contributed least to the regular
forms of taxation. Tudor autocracy, in this as in
other respects, attempted by extra-legal means to redress a balance unfairly tilted by middle-class predomin-
ance in the House of Commons.

[1] Vol. ii. No. 29.   [2] Ibid. No. 27.   [3] Vol. iii. Pt. 2.
[4] " Political Hist. of England," vi. 463, 472-3.
[5] "Letters and Papers of Henry VIII," 1544, Pt. ii. No. 689.

This political influence of a narrow class was as marked in local as it was in national politics. No doubt it was ultimately based on the greater capacity and sense of responsibility possessed by the well-to-do; and the turbulence of the commons was as much the reason as the excuse for the restriction of the municipal franchise at Leicester, Northampton, and Exeter.[1] But the local magnates of the towns were at least as locally minded as their humbler fellow-townsmen. At York civic patriotism manifested itself in a mutual bond to ignore all outside jurisdiction.[2] London prohibited its merchants from frequenting other fairs and markets in order to compel resort to its own; and the conflict of the municipal laws of guilds and other corporations with one another and with the royal prerogative provoked an important step towards the centralization of sovereignty in 1504, when an Act of Parliament subjected local legislative powers to the control of the central government. It was also a step towards the modern "concession" theory, according to which corporations exercise authority solely through explicit or implicit delegation from the State, and not in virtue of any original or imprescriptible right. Bacon was expressing the civilian's prejudice against all associations save the State, when he described the guilds as "fraternities in evil "[3]

§ 4. SOCIAL AND ECONOMIC HISTORY.

The time has long since passed when politics and the Constitution were considered exhaustive of the content of English history; and no apology is needed for the

[1] Vol ii. Nos. 98-100.   [2] *Ibid.* No. 94.
[3] Vol. ii. No. 104; Leadam, "Star Chamber," Vol. i. p. cli.

illustrations of English manners and customs included in the second volume. They are naturally derived for the most part from Venetian comments, and no one was better fitted than a Venetian diplomatist, with his cosmopolitan outlook and experience, to appreciate the salient points in English national character. Insularity is what we expect ; it was hardly more marked than the peninsularity of Spain, and we are told that the vulgar of both countries imagined that there was no other.[1] A greater freedom of manners than obtained after the rise of Puritanism was also natural ; but the Venetian's comments on the draconian severities of English parents must be discounted by Dudley's complaints of maternal doting, while the statement that apparently the English never fell in love should be interpreted as meaning that they did not express their passion with Italian exuberance.[2] The more sordid features he notes in middle-class family life were the excrescences of that development of commercialism which characterized Henry's reign.

The domestic effects of that movement were not so marked as they became in the next generation ; but we have Acts of Parliament to restrain enclosures, the increase of pasture, the decay of husbandry, the growth of usury and of vagabondage.[3] Internal trade was becoming national rather than local, and such legislation as is devoted to this subject represents somewhat crude experiments to substitute national for local regulation. Matters such as the fixing of wages and hours of labour, and standards for commerce and manufacture, which had been determined by guilds and municipal corpora-

---

[1] Vol. ii. No. 112. [2] Ibid. Nos. 110, 111. [3] Ibid. Nos. 117-22.

tions, were now brought within the expanding scope of Parliamentary interference. Effective steps were at length taken to secure a national uniformity of weights and measures, licence was occasionally granted by Henry VII for the introduction of foreign clothworkers, and the currency was improved, notably by the first coinage of English sovereigns.[1]

But, as Dudley pointed out,[2] the encouragement of domestic trade and manufactures would be robbed of much of its effect without a proper vent in foreign markets ; and Henry's energies were largely devoted to promoting England's oversea commerce. There was hardly a State in Western Europe with which he did not conclude one or more commercial treaties. The problem was of some difficulty, for Englishmen were the last to concede to foreign merchants in England the privileges they claimed for themselves abroad ; and the question was complicated by rivalries among English merchants themselves. The individual was too weak and poor to face the risks of foreign enterprise with any prospect of success ; and foreign trade, so far as it was in English hands at all, was almost monopolized by one or two great corporations. Of these the most powerful comprised the merchants of the English Staple at Calais, and it has been said that they almost formed a fourth estate of the realm.[3] The " staple " included not only wool, but all " staple " products ; it was governed by the *lex mercatoria,* a form of " liberty," and its privileges

---

[1] Vol. i. No. 58 ; Vol. ii. Nos. 121-2, 129, 131 ; Campbell's " Materials," ii. 134.

[2] Vol. ii. No. 133.

[3] See " Cely Papers " (Camden Soc.), Pref. p. x.

overrode all local and municipal franchises. Its chief domestic rivals were the Merchant Adventurers, whose mart was established at Antwerp ; they were not less exclusive in their ambitions, and the process of freeing trade for the individual by destroying the liberties of privileged corporations made little, if any, progress in Henry's reign.[1] He was more successful in placing English and foreign traders on a footing of equality. In this respect English merchants had been at a considerable disadvantage, and their jealousy of the foreigner had no little justification. Owing to superior organization and enterprise, foreign merchants, such as the Venetians, but especially the merchants of the Hanse, had established themselves in a privileged position in London, Southampton, and elsewhere. The complaint that partial exemption from taxation gave them an unfair advantage over their English rivals was met by making aliens and denizens pay double taxes ; but the King retained and commonly exercised the power of granting wholesale dispensations, and the Hanse merchants paid at a lower rate than other foreigners.[2] This was a small grievance compared with the practical monopoly of the Baltic trade which Henry sought to break down by commercial treaties with Denmark and with Riga.[3] He also encouraged trade between England and the Mediterranean ports ; an English consulate was established at Pisa ;[4] Venetian merchants were tempted to make Southampton rather than the Netherlands the

---

[1] See W. R. Scott, " Joint Stock Companies," 3 vols., 1910-12.

[2] Vol. ii. Nos. 136-41 ; cf. Campbell's " Materials," i. 115, 373-7, ii. 245-7.

[3] II, 152, 154.   [4] *Ibid.* No. 143 ; cf. Campbell, ii. 288.

d

emporium of their trade; and Henry's importation of alum—indispensable to the soap manufacture—from other than Papal sources, involved him in the risk of excommunication.[1]

But it was with the Netherlands that England's commercial relations were most important. Their development would assist Henry's schemes for breaking down the monopoly of the Hanse; and apart from that, the Netherlands were England's best market. Political divergences, however, interrupted commercial friendship. Exasperated by Margaret and Maximilian's patronage of Perkin Warbeck, Henry in 1493 transferred the Merchant Adventurers' mart from Antwerp to Calais, and expelled the Flemish merchants from England. Six months later the Flemish government retaliated by prohibiting the import of English goods.[2] The Hanse merchants naturally profited by this quarrel, and the English apprentices somewhat illogically vented their resentment at their loss of trade in an attack upon the Steelyard, the house of the Hanse in London.[3] Mutual suffering from the interruption led in 1496 to the conclusion of the treaty subsequently known as the *Intercursus Magnus*, which is here printed in full.[4] Further advantages were secured for the English by the *Intercursus Malus* ten years later;[5] but Philip's death prevented its ratification, and Henry had to moderate some of the terms he had extracted from Philip's shipwreck in England. The treaty, thus modified, remained the basis of England's commercial relations with the

----

[1] "Venetian Calendar," i. pp. 160-1, No. 815; "Letters and Papers," ii. 168.

[2] Vol. ii. Nos. 136, 148.   [3] I, No. 69.   [4] II, 149.   [5] II, 155.

Netherlands throughout the following century, and the model for its negotiations with other states.

Shipping was, however, the greatest of England's interests, if not the greatest of its industries ; and Henry VII was the first English king to realize the importance of conducting English oversea trade in English bottoms manned by English seamen. Two Acts of Parliament, passed in 1485 and 1489,[1] were, although primarily concerned only with the wine and woad trade from Gascony and Guienne, the basis of legislation which culminated in the famous Navigation Laws of Oliver Cromwell and Charles II, enacted in 1650 and 1661 and repealed in 1849. There was English trade, if not English shipping, in the Mediterranean, or an English consul would not have been established at Pisa, nor a proposal made to set up an English staple there.[2] The North Sea fisheries on the Dogger Bank were beginning to assume the importance which ultimately precipitated Grotius' *Mare Liberum* and Selden's *Mare Clausum* and other Anglo-Dutch conflicts of the seventeenth century. The voyage to Iceland was an annual enterprise, regulated not only by royal injunctions, but also by Act of Parliament ; and the men of Bristol in particular, extending their Irish adventures, began to stretch out across the Atlantic.

Their leader came from Venice, but found his crews and capital in Bristol and in London. There can be little doubt that Henry VII would have encouraged Columbus but for the accident which intercepted the seaman's proposals ; and to the assistance he rendered to Messer Zoane Caboto witness is borne by the records

[1] II, 134-5. [2] "Venetian Calendar," i. pp. 185-6.
d *

of his privy purse expenses as well as by his commission authorizing Cabot to sail under his flag and plant it in new-found lands.[1] There was no hard and fast line between the crusaders and the early explorers, and the various " rewards " paid by Henry to priests who went on these voyages of discovery proves the existence of a religious motive ; but there was also the germ of that lust for dominion which became so marked a feature of Elizabeth's England.[2] No doubt the desire for trade gave zest to the search for dominion ; but greed alone would never have carried men in 80-ton vessels across the stormy Atlantic to uncharted shores. The accounts which the Milanese envoy gives of his conversations with Cabot,[3] and other documents here printed testify to his successful explorations, which were somewhat obscured by his son Sebastian's unfilial impiety in assuming the glory of his father's achievements. The continuous existence of an English colony in Newfoundland from 1497 to the present day is, however, a fable in which every Newfoundlander and no one else believes ; but Cabot's triumphant return was greeted with national enthusiasm. He himself went on, and, contrary to the general opinion, returned from, a second expedition in the following year ;[4] and his example was frequently followed by known and unknown mariners, until a voyage to " the new found isle " became a sort of forlorn hope for the restoration of the fortunes of the penniless scions of noble houses.[5] These were the rough drafts of a future expansion of England, which depended

[1] II, 160-171.   [2] " Political Hist. of England," vi. 306.
[3] II, 162.   [4] II, 169.
[5] " Letters and Papers of Henry VIII," iv. No. 3731.

for its success upon internal consolidation, the development of industry and commerce, the maintenance of peace at home, and the avoidance of war abroad.

§ 5. FOREIGN POLICY.

The concluding words of the preceding section sum up the objects of Henry's foreign policy. No English statesman achieved so much at so small a cost. It is a well-worn theme of historical disquisition to compare and contrast the foreign policy of Henry VII with that of Wolsey and that of Queen Elizabeth. So far as Wolsey is concerned it is a question of contrast. There was a fundamental divergence between Henry's patient craft and Wolsey's pyrotechnics; and the contrast in methods sprang from an equally fundamental divergence in personal character and in public aims. Henry disdained the pomp and circumstance of diplomatic power; no one set greater store by them than Wolsey. The king had the quiet hauteur of an aristocrat, born in England, but trained in exile; standing, to use Soncino's phrase, like one on a tower, he surveyed the arena with almost Olympic calm. The cardinal, sprung from the people, was ever climbing the heights of personal glory; and his brow was seldom free from the dust and sweat of the conflict. It might have cleared beneath the triple crown; and the merging of his ambition in the greater glory of the Catholic church might have given him something of the serenity which Henry obtained on the throne through the identification of his with his country's greatness. As it was, Wolsey's diplomacy was tainted by private un-English ends. England for him was a stepping-stone to Rome; and to achieve the papal tiara he must dazzle the eyes of the western world and play a great part on the stage of Europe. He sought to be the arbiter of Christendom that he might win the votes of its cardinals. The giddy eminence, that rose before the vision of the butcher's son from Ipswich, was beyond the reach of the English king. Henry's ambitions were centred in England. To the suffrage of Europe he was indifferent, and he held aloof from its abortive councils. Italy was, he said, too distant for English concern ; [1] he joined the Holy League as a matter of form ; with the Congress of Cambrai he had nothing to do ; and he had no reason to angle for votes in a papal conclave. His early acquaintance with foreign lands fitted him all the more to pursue an insular policy, and the sole aim of his dealings with other countries was to promote the welfare of his own. He struck out the path, and his grand-daughter trod in his footsteps.

Like her, he was parsimonious of the public purse, and hated war because war meant taxation, taxation meant discontent, and discontent involved friction, waste, and weakness. An overflowing exchequer, and not the empty bubble reputation, was the object of his desire. Such wars as he waged he turned to financial profit, and his brief campaign against France produced an income of 50,000 crowns a year from the French treasury for the rest of his reign. A little more glory might have cost him ten times as much. But he was no believer in peace at any price ; on the contrary, he always obtained a very high price for his peace. His subjects paid him to levy war, and his enemies

[1] Vol. i. No. 132.

bribed him to refrain. Yet the complete success of his policy did not render its inception an easy matter of course. It has been said that the Yorkists were soldiers while the Tudors were statesmen.[1] The comparison would be more pointed, if Lancastrians were substituted for Yorkists; for after all, Edward IV had set at Pecquigny an example upon which Henry VII improved at Étaples, and it was Henry V who gave the most striking proof of the harm which a brilliant soldier can do without the restraint of a statesman's mind. No doubt, if Henry VII had been as brilliant a soldier as Henry V, he might have attempted once more a fool's quest for the crown of France; none the less it needed a statesman to resist the temptation, for no expedient is more attractive than military adventure to the occupant of an unstable throne; and the lure was presented to Henry in a well-nigh irresistible guise when the Duchess of Brittany appealed to England for help against its absorption by France.

This was the touchstone of Henry's foreign policy, and the challenge of his statesmanship. Should he or should he not commit England to the task of preventing the union of Brittany with France, and thus renew the Hundred Years' War? It was clear that the step would mean permanent enmity between the two realms; and yet English interests might seem to demand that the risk should be taken. The triumph of France would greatly increase her strength, would bring her down to the English Channel along the whole of its length, and complete her position as England's rival on the sea. England's success on the other hand

---

[1] Gairdner, "Letters and Papers of Henry VII," Vol. i. p. xxvi.

would practically give her command of both sides of the
entrance to the Channel and prevent the consolidation
of her traditional enemy. Ferdinand of Aragon was
ever urging Henry to renew England's claims to Normandy and Guienne, and success in Brittany would add
to the feasibility of that project. Yorkist and Lancastrian would sink their mutual hostility in warfare
against the national foe; and both Ferdinand and
Maximilian promised assistance.

The pressure of sentiment and of apparent utility was
too strong to permit the occasion to pass without some
show of response on Henry's part; and after two years
of desultory operations in aid of Brittany, he crossed
the Channel in person in October, 1492. But a month
later he concluded the peace of Étaples,[1] and there is as
little doubt about the correctness of his conclusion as
there is of his intention so to conclude all along. The
assurances of Ferdinand were not worth the paper on
which they were written; the treaty of Medina del
Campo between England and Spain had, indeed, been
signed in 1489, purporting perpetual friendship and a
marriage between Arthur and Catherine; but the real
object, avowed from the first by Ferdinand, had been to
use England for the purpose of recovering Rousillon
and Cerdagne for Spain, and the treaty of Étaples barely
forestalled the peace concluded in January, 1493, between France and Spain, by which those two provinces
were ceded to Ferdinand and the treaty of Medina del
Campo was rendered void.[2]

Even less reliance was to be placed on the meteoric

[1] Vol. i. Nos. 64-5; Vol. iii. Nos. 3, 7.
[2] "Spanish Calendar," i. 21-2, 29, 34, 54-6, 62-3, 78, 90.

Maximilian whose orbit observed no regular course, and whose control over the chaotic government of the Netherlands could not prevent his wife's step-mother, the Duchess Margaret, from supporting every pretender to Henry's throne. Henry, as a *parvenu* king, had as yet no genuine friends among princes; they would wait and see before they plighted their friendship to him, and they would gladly make their profit out of war between England and France. For the war would be long and costly, unless England was early defeated. It was not in Henry's power to guarantee the Breton frontier against the armies of France, and the effort to defend it would have ruined his work in England. He might, it is true, have supported a national Breton resistance; but of this there was little sign. Henry knew from his youth the inside of the Breton court, and the Breton people were not prepared for a life-and-death struggle against a union with France. Peace had its perquisites no less than war, and Henry returned from Étaples, if not with honour, at least with substantial profits. Charles VIII abandoned the cause of Perkin, admitted Henry's title to the English throne, and paid him a handsome annuity to refrain from claiming the French.

The peace thus concluded was prolonged by the rash ambition of France. Italy tempted Charles VIII as France had tempted Henry V; and he, too, fell a victim to the seduction of a divided and almost defenceless neighbour. Frenchmen found the plains of Lombardy more enticing than the waves of the Atlantic; and, turning their backs upon the new world, plunged into the cockpit of the old. Ferdinand, whose conquest of

Granada from the Moors in 1492 [1] did for Spain what
the simultaneous acquisition of Brittany did for France,
likewise turned to enforce his claims upon Naples ; and
two generations of strife between the two great Catholic
powers made straight the path of the Tudors and the
Protestant Reformation. It was the English and not
the Spanish king who was now the *tertius gaudens*,
and Henry VII played the part with consummate for-
bearance. A less prudent sovereign would have inter-
vened by force of arms, but nothing would induce
Henry to break with France. This peace was the key-
stone of his foreign policy. It was far more significant
than his alliance with Spain ; for France was the nearer
neighbour and the older rival. There were no ancient
scores to be settled with Spain, and no traditional claims
to the Spanish throne. The Yorkists had been wise
enough to avoid the folly of Edward III and Henry V,
and Henry VII was not too proud to borrow prudence
from the dynasty he dethroned.

Spanish benevolence had been useful to Henry in
the early, unstable days of his rule ; but the value of
Ferdinand's friendship grew less with the lapse of
time. After the peace of Étaples, Spain was valued
mainly as a counterpoise to Maximilian, whose champion-
ship of Yorkist pretenders has been ascribed, in default
of more statesmanlike motives, to chivalry ; like the
partisans of the Tichborne Claimant, he did not like to
see a poor man kept out of his rights. The treaty of
marriage between Arthur and Catherine of Aragon
was concluded in 1497 at the height of the Warbeck
crisis ; and other Spanish diplomatists denounced

[1] Vol. i. No. 64.

Puebla's failure to make Henry to pay for his difficulties in the terms of the marriage treaty.[1]   Their
complaints show sufficient cause for Henry's conduct in
completing the match.   But the case was altered when,
after Arthur's death in 1502, Ferdinand and Isabella
became suitors for Catherine's marriage with Arthur's
brother.   In 1497 Henry was threatened in various
quarters, while only the life of her elder sister Juaña
stood between Catherine and the succession to the
thrones of Aragon and Castile.   In 1502 Henry was
secure, while Juaña's rapidly increasing progeny by the
Archduke Philip rendered Catherine's prospects of the
succession remote.   It is just possible, too, that the
success of Cabot and the voyages of his successors were
suggesting the possibility of Anglo-Spanish rivalry in
the New World ; and it is certain that Henry was now
more anxious for friendship with the Netherlands than
with Spain.

In 1496, the year of the *Intercursus Magnus*, Puebla
had written that Henry " esteemed Flanders more than
any other power " ;[2] and the adolescence of the Archduke Philip afforded a more promising basis than the
hostility of that inveterate Yorkist, the Duchess Margaret,
or the vagaries of his father the Emperor Maximilian, for
Anglo-Flemish friendship.   To obtain a firm grasp of
Philip's mind now became the main object of Henry's
foreign policy.   He had personal no less than national objects to serve ; through Philip he hoped to
lay hands on the fugitive Earl of Suffolk as well as
to foster English trade and frustrate the designs of
Ferdinand.   The death of Queen Isabella in 1504 had

[1] Vol. i. No. 132.   [2] " Spanish Calendar," i. p. 103.

shaken Ferdinand's hold on Spain; he had no title to Castile, which he could only administer in the name of his daughter Juaña. But Juaña's power had gone to her husband, and Philip was henceforth styled King of Castile. To fortify himself against his children, Ferdinand made terms with France at the Treaty of Blois in October, 1505; [1] Isabella's death had discounted the victories of Gonsalvo di Cordova, and the Italian prey was divided with Louis XII. Ferdinand also married a French wife, Germaine de Foix; and this Franco-Spanish *entente*, which Henry sought to neutralize by negotiations for a marriage between his son and a French princess,[2] threw him more than ever on to the side of Philip and the Netherlands. Similar considerations mollified Maximilian's antagonism to the Tudor king, though his sentiments towards Henry never grew warmer than that form of gratitude which consists in the anticipation of financial favours to come. Maximilian was always needy, and he confessed that his principal object was to extract money from Henry VII; [3] he was always embarking on hopeless quests.

Henry thus was involved in a series of somewhat sordid family squabbles and marriage negotiations. Ferdinand and Maximilian intrigued against one another for the control of their common grandchildren's fortunes; and even Catherine was used in the conflict. Philip and Juaña themselves were not on the best of terms; Philip detested his wife's Spanish household, and Juaña her husband's Flemish councillors. The Spaniards tried to prey upon Flanders, and the Flemings

---

[1] "Spanish Calendar," i. 450
[2] I, 177, 205.   [3] *Ibid.* i. 587.

hoped to prey upon Spain. But Philip could hardly reach Spain without Henry's assistance ; and Henry lent him large sums for equipment, and successfully mediated with Louis XII for the peace of Flanders during the archduke's absence.[1] The extent to which Philip was already indebted to Henry before he embarked in January, 1506, renders it difficult to estimate the extent to which Henry took advantage of Philip's storm-driven visit to English shores. He departed from Henry's presence bound by the *Intercursus Malus* and by a treaty for Henry's marriage with Margaret of Savoy, the regent of the Netherlands ; and before he set sail from Falmouth, the gates of the Tower closed behind Suffolk.[2]

Philip's death in the following autumn gave Fortune's wheel a turn in Ferdinand's favour. Juaña lost her reason, and her eldest son Charles was a child of six in the Netherlands, clearly incapable of disturbing Ferdinand's occupation of Castile. That realm was almost a no-man's-land, and it seems as though Henry in his old age began to build " castles in Spain ". He suggested his marriage with Juaña,[3] condoning her mental affliction for the chance of ruling Castile. But it is difficult to debit so cautious a king with so wild an adventure. He could not hope to establish his rule in the heart of Spain ; he continued to press for his marriage with Margaret of Savoy ;[4] and the real object of his schemes appears to have been the marriage of Charles with his daughter Mary and the safeguarding of Charles's pros-

[1] Vol. i. No. 175 ; iii. Nos. 19-21.
[2] Vol. i. No. 189 ; Vol. iii. Pt. 1.
[3] Vol. i. No. 202 ; Vol. iii. Pt. 1.
[4] Vol. i. No. 194 ; Vol. iii. Pt. 1.

pects. These seemed doubtful enough. Ferdinand was said to be his grandson's principal enemy;[1] he was enraged at the conclusion in 1507 of the treaty of marriage between Charles and Mary Tudor;[2] and the birth of a son to him and Germaine de Foix, for which the Aragonese longed with a truly provincial patriotism,[3] would have deprived Charles of the succession to Aragon, Naples, and Navarre, and have broken up that Spanish union which is reckoned as Ferdinand's greatest achievement. Germaine's child died at its birth a few days after the close of Henry's reign;[4] and Ferdinand's historical reputation as the founder of modern Spain was rescued from shipwreck. Henry's own fame as the architect of union between England and Scotland rests on equally mortal foundations; he cannot have looked forward to the death without issue of two of his sons and of all his surviving son's children, which led to the union of the crowns in the great-grandson of the marriage between James IV, and his daughter Margaret.

§ 6. ECCLESIASTICAL AFFAIRS.

Henry's reign was the eve of the Reformation, and it is natural to scan its records for signs of change. If no signs are forthcoming, one historian will interpret their absence as proof that the breach with Rome was the unheralded act of royal caprice; and another will talk of the darkness before the dawn, the hush before the storm. If there are signs, the one will try to ignore, and the other to magnify, their significance.

[1] Vol. i. No. 207. [2] Vol. iii. Pt. 1.
[3] Ibid. Stile's report. [4] Gomara, "Annals," p. 26.

Fortunately, perhaps, the reign does not lend itself to
partisan declamation. Its greyness is too obstinate to
be pronounced either black or white, night or day;
and the signs that are found in the various aspects of
the relation between church and state do not all point
in the same direction. The religious upheaval of the
sixteenth century was due in England to four principal
causes of disturbance. One lay in the relations between
England and the Papacy; another in the authority
over the laity wielded by the church; a third in the
exemption of churchmen from temporal jurisdiction;
and a fourth in rejection of Catholic dogma. None
of these four was inseparable from the other three,
although the second and third are commonly classed
together as the liberties of the church, and all four did,
in fact, co-operate in producing the Reformation.

The first of these in itself involves three distinct
relationships, that of the Crown with the Papacy, that
of the Crown with the English church, and that of the
English church with the Papacy. In none of them
is there any evidence of serious friction during Henry's
reign. It may be argued that the king was too much
master of the situation to tolerate conflicts, and that this
fact in itself proves the case for that sort of sovereignty
which Henry VIII established *de jure* as well as *de
facto* over the church. No Pope ventured to dispute
Henry VII's nominations for English preferments; and
they were made with strict regard to the interests of the
Crown. Morton, Deane, Warham, Foxe, Ruthal, Sherborne, Urswick, and others received their bishoprics
and deaneries as rewards and endowments for civil
and not for spiritual services; and popes agreed that

churchmen, if not the church, should serve the state.
The pope, indeed, only made one English cardinal
when Henry suggested five;[1] but he placed his papal
censures and dispensations freely at Henry's disposal.[2]
There were occasional disputes over more material and
costly papal commodities, such as alum;[3] but they were
kept within decent limits, and the pope even agreed to
such limitations of clerical privilege as Henry imposed
in his Parliament. From so accommodating a catholic
jurisdiction, Henry appeared to derive as much profit
as he could ever hope to do from an insular royal
supremacy.

On the other hand, it may be contended that the
harmony was due to Henry's orthodoxy and respect for
the papal see. He personally converted a heretic at the
stake; and, further, he burnt the heretic.[4] His judges
declared that Parliament had no power over the spiritual
sphere, and that no statute could, for instance, make a
king an ecclesiastical person;[5] and the grossest abuses
among the clergy were left for Morton and Convocation
to reform. If promotions to sees were made at Henry's
suggestion, they were also invariably made by papal
provision.[6] He was content if ecclesiastical revenues
went to his ministers, without keeping sees vacant to
profit his privy purse. Henry, indeed, characteristically
regarded his relations with church and Papacy as a
sound business connexion. Collections at court for papal

---

[1] "Venetian Calendar," i. 173-4.
[2] Vol. i. p. 160; Vol. iii. Pt. 2.
[3] *Ibid.*; "Venetian Calendar," i. 160-1.
[4] Vol. iii. Pt. 2.
[5] McIlwain, "High Court of Parliament," pp. 277-9.
[6] See Le Neve's "Fasti," ed. Hardy.

objects produced disappointing returns, and Henry's response to the Pope's appeal for a crusade against the Turks was marked by a bland assurance of impotence upon which a twentieth-century Concert of Europe could not have improved.[1] But there was no adequate force or motive to induce him to forgo the benedictions and benefits of papal benevolence. He himself augmented and adorned the material fabrics of the church by his buildings at Windsor and Westminster Abbey; he befriended the Friars Observants, and encouraged his mother's ecclesiastical foundations at Oxford and Cambridge ; and thrice he received from the Pope the sword and cap of maintenance.[2]

When King and Pontiff agreed so well, there was little chance of protest from English clergy ; and no sign of official remonstrance has been discovered in Henry's reign against royal or papal sovereignty. No chapter resisted a royal nomination or a papal provision. The statutes of *provisors* and *præmunire* had not been passed to protect English clergy, but to preserve royal and baronial rights of advowson and jurisdiction. Henry kept proctors at Rome to promote his suits in the papal curia ;[3] and if the King was pleased to waive his statutory powers, the English church had no constitutional or other means of enforcing their execution. The alleged independence of the English church left no traces in Henry's reign. Morton had to seek exceptional powers from Rome before he could attempt to reform St. Albans. Great abbeys had independence enough,

---

[1] " Venetian Calendar," i. 181.

[2] Cf. Vol. i., p. 251, vol. ii. No. 115, 20 Jan., 1497.

[3] Campbell's " Materials," i. 176, 323 ; ii. 297, 369, 396.

but theirs was a peculiar and not a national liberty; they were independent of English bishops but not of Roman popes. The Pope taxed the English clergy without their consent, and for protection against his demands they relied on royal mediation. The Pope (or a General Council) could alone legislate in spiritual matters for the whole of the English church; and the provincial powers enjoyed by the Convocations of Canterbury and York were sparingly used. Some instructive complaints were brought to their notice, but the remedies of Convocation for clerical evils were apparently limited to matters of clerical dress.[1]

The serious grievances, to which allusion is made in these documents, did not arise from that clerical jurisdiction over laymen about which so much is heard in the next generation. There are indeed municipal quarrels with bishops and abbots, as at Coventry, York, and Stratford-on-Avon;[2] but these arose from the fact that the bishop or abbot was a great lord with a liberal franchise, and not from his ecclesiastical character. The evils that called for public action in Henry VII's reign grew out of immunities of the clergy. A fierce Protestant declared in Elizabeth's reign that the principal liberty of the church had been a liberty to sin;[3] but he hardly exaggerated the words of the Italian observer of Henry's reign who had no Protestant bias to warp his judgment.[4] The two grossest of these aids to evildoers were the benefit of clergy and the right of sanctuary. To judge by the evidence of Henry VII's reign, the efforts of Henry H to bring criminous clerks to justice had been vain;

---

[1] III, Pt. 2.   [2] Vol. ii. No. 102; Vol. iii. Pt. 2.
[3] "Political History of England," vi. 362.   [4] III, Pt. 2.

and the remedies adopted by Henry VII's Parliament seem lame and halting enough. Any one who could read had been entitled to benefit of clergy for every crime he committed; henceforth it needed episcopal or other unexceptional testimony to the criminal's genuine clerical character to save him more than once from retribution. If this were not forthcoming the criminal was, for his second murder or theft, to be punished like a layman. Identification was secured by branding first offenders on the ball of the left thumb with an M for murder—the "brand of Cain"—and a T for theft or other crimes. Real clergy were, after conviction, claimed by the church and subjected to penance or even imprisonment.[1] It was an ingenious division of authority to leave the judgment of criminous clerks to the lay courts, and reserve execution to the church, which was prohibited by the law of God from shedding blood. But Parliament, having once tasted the forbidden fruit of clerical liberty showed a desire for more; and in 1491 the benefit of clergy was similarly restricted to persons in holy orders in the case of deserters from the army and of servants who murdered their masters. Fraud on the part of debtors in sanctuary had been restrained by Act of Parliament in 1487, but the limitation of the right of sanctuary itself was left to papal bulls obtained by Henry VII, which restricted its protection to first offenders.[2] The meagreness of these measures of reform may be ascribed either to Henry's desire to keep on good terms with the church, or to the fact that the spiritual peers were a majority in the Parliament chamber. Perhaps with the fear of Henry IV's mis-

[1] Vol. iii. Pt. 2. ; Busch, pp. 271-3.   [2] III, Pt. 2.

e *

fortunes after Archbishop Scrope's execution, before his eyes, he always pardoned his clerical traitors, numerous though they were.[1] But the judges sometimes tried by judicial interpretation to go further in the way of limiting clerical liberties than they were authorized by the statute-book.

The worst of these abuses were, no doubt, committed by criminals who were not churchmen in any real sense of the word ; and the fault of the church lay in its tenacity of its liberties and in its tenderness to every scoundrel who had any pretence to clerical privilege. Notorious crimes like the murder by a monk of the prior of Sheen, and scandals such as the siege of the prior of Christchurch by his bishop and a band of retainers,[2] must have been rare. So, too, must such gross immorality in high places as that with which the abbot of St. Albans was charged by Cardinal Morton. But if prelates could do such things, they would be more or less rife in humbler clerical spheres. No English bishop to-day is ever suspected of crime or immorality, but clerical criminals do appear now and then in the police courts ; and for every immoral abbot in Henry's reign it is safe to assume a good many immoral monks, especially when the assumption tallies with such evidence as we possess. To put the matter as moderately as possible, 'it is clear that clerical virtue was becoming an insufficient foundation for the imposing superstructure of clerical liberties ; and a beginning was made in Henry's reign of the attack on clerical privileges in the matters of taxation and jurisdiction.

---

[1] Cf. Vol. i. p. 100n, 122.
[2] Vol. i. No. 165 ; Vol. iii. Pt. 2.

The Catholic faith was another question. The connexion between Lollardy and the Reformation is one of
the unsolved problems of history ; but of the existence
of serious heresy in England in Henry's reign the details collected here can leave no doubt ; and there is a
strong presumption in favour of ecclesiastical continuity
in this respect. The doctrines of Reginald Pecock were
heterogeneous rather than heterodox ; and the facts
that he sternly condemned Lollardy but was himself
condemned by the Catholic Church, while they suggest a
certain affinity with the modern Anglican position, make
it difficult to attach its precise significance to the statement of the Venetian envoy in England in 1476 that
English churchmen and graduates studied little else
than Pecock's works, in spite of Edward IV's zeal for
their extirpation.[1] It seems at least to indicate an
heretical predisposition in clerical circles, and early in
Henry's reign charges of heretical preaching were brought
in Convocation. Clerical heretics were, however, submissive to authority in the last resort, and it was only
laymen or women who carried their stubbornness to
the stake. They were of course humble folk, mainly
connected with London and the Chilterns ; but the life-
history, were it ascertainable, of Joan Bourchier, who
was burnt in 1496 at the age of eighty, would probably
throw some light on the persistence of Lollard opinions.
Heresy was, however, in the air in other realms than
England ; a Spanish ambassador warned Henry VII
against infection through fugitives from the Spanish
Inquisition,[2] and Soncino speaks of the appearance of a
"new sect" in England without any great astonish-

[1] "Venetian Calendar," i. pp. 134-5.   [2] "Spanish Cal." i. 205.

ment.[1] With regard to the new faith as with regard to
the new world and old Ireland, the reign of Henry VII
was a time of small beginnings.

§ 7. IRELAND.

Although Ireland gave Henry VII abundance of
trouble, the Irish problem had not assumed the exasperat-
ing form it took after the Tudor and Stuart plantations.
In spite of the statute of Kilkenny, the line between
Anglo-Irish and " wild " Irish and their respective habits
was disappearing; and one of Poynings' Acts which prohibited the Celtic war-cry, "cromaboo," also prohibited
"butleraboo," which was clearly of mixed descent.[2]
The problem was not one of racial hatred, but one of
law and order. The crimson stains of Irish history have
been ascribed to the instigation of Saxon statesmen or
the imagination of Saxon historians ; but in the " Annals
of Loch Cé," [3] we have a native record of battle, murder,
and sudden death so remote from Saxon infection that
throughout our period there is no reference to Poynings'
Laws, to Henry VII himself, or even to those counterfeit
Irish royalties, Lambert Simnel and Perkin Warbeck.
These "Annals " relate to Ulster, then one of the wildest
Irish districts ; but in Munster, Connaught, and Leinster,
where men of Norman and English descent had sup-
planted native chieftains, the same features of tribal warfare were reproduced in the form of family feuds. In
the Pale and in the ports there was a greater semblance
of order ; but, except in Waterford, the greater order did

---

[1] "Milanese Cal." i. p. 380.   [2] III, Pt. 3.

[3] Rolls Series, Vol. ii. pp. 183-213 ; it has not appeared necessary to reproduce here these Ulster faction fights of four centuries ago.

not involve greater loyalty to the Tudor. Richard of York is said to have left behind him a grateful remembrance in Ireland; but the affection of Irish lords for Yorkist pretenders was assuredly not due to Richard's repute as a vigorous ruler. They had greater opportunities than English barons for realizing their common ideal of baronial independence; and Lambert and Perkin were to them simple stalking horses for its prosecution.

Vice-roys themselves had been infected by Irish patriotism; and Poynings' appointment and laws were designed less as a check upon Irish parliaments than upon more dangerous Irish deputies, who used Irish parliaments to foster their own ambitions. His statutes, which enforced the view of Irish dependence expressed by Henry's judges in 1485, were a comprehensive programme of reform;[1] but their execution was a task beyond Henry's resources, and Henry fell back on Kildare. The story of his selection represents well enough its motives.[2] Henry enlisted on the side of order the strongest personal factor in Ireland, and left Kildare with the responsibility and the expense of its government; on somewhat similar terms the Percies governed the Scottish Borders. It was not a heroic policy; but Henry could not afford a better. Even after the defeat of Spain and the plantation of Munster, the conquest of Ireland cost Elizabeth nearly five years' revenue. An effective English conquest and administration of Ireland might have involved Henry VII in some of the perils that attended the Lancastrian effort to conquer France. Ireland had to wait until England was stronger, and until the invasion of Ireland by English adventurers

[1] Vol. iii. Pt. 3.   [2] *Ibid.*

and foreign foes provided the English Government with the means and the motives for conquest commensurate with its risks.

The careful adjustment of his ambitions to his resources is the first of a statesman's duties ; and it is Henry VII's singular merit that he accomplished the objects he set before him, and refrained from pursuing quests which could only lead to disaster. A patient and grim diplomatist, he lacked the flamboyant spirit of Henry VIII and Elizabeth, and he never appealed to the mob, which never applauded ; for wisdom is not a popular quality. But no one knew his business better, or did his work more completely. His prescription for England's disorders was a sedative toned with iron and administered with unflinching resolution. He confined to the bounds of law and order a liberty that had run riot over the land ; and he gave the English State a framework of strength and unity that withstood the disruptive force of ecclesiastical revolution.

THE REIGN OF HENRY VII.

1485.

1.

[Extract from an oration said to have been delivered before Henry
VII at Cambridge about 1494, by John Blyth, Bishop of Salis-
bury; it is, however, doubtful whether Henry visited Cambridge in that year; and some of the orator's autobiographical
statements are inconsistent with the facts of Blyth's career
("Letters and Papers," i. 422-3).]

" Mater deinde viro orbata te peperit orphanum,[1] a 1457.
cujus uberibus mox abstractus, illorum custodiæ traditus
fueras qui bellis assiduis implicabantur. Castellum in
quo tenebaris obsessum in manus inimicorum tuorum
venit; qui tamen, Deo ita providente, te (ut præclarum
sanguine deceret) educaverunt egregie. Inde quæsitus
ad necem, patriam deserens, ubi ad cognatum tuum
regem Francorum ire destinaveras, in Minoris Britanniæ ducem utilius incidisti, quamquam ab eo rursum
tanquam captivus detinebare. Sed, pace cum eo facta,
quum in patriam redire statuisti, tanto ventorum im-
petu classis tua jactabatur ut vi compulsus retro retulisti
pedem, Deo rem ita disponente, ne forte in manus
inimicorum tuorum venisses qui tunc insidias parar-
ant tibi. Post hæc Britanni te venalem offerebant

---

[1] Henry VII was born on 28 January, 1457, at Pembroke
Castle; his father, Edmund Tudor, had died on 3 November, 1456,
and his mother, Margaret Beaufort, who was born in 1443, was not
yet fourteen years old.

1485. capitalibus inimicis tuis, nihil magis quam tuum· san-
guinem sitientibus.   Quid multis?   Convenit inter eos
de pecunia ; sed tu interea, Deo mirabiliter subveniente,
cum tuis omnibus effugisti salvus in Galliam.   Unde
quum denuo temptares venire in patriam, dirigente tunc
tuum iter et prosperante Deo, parva manu ingressus hoc
tuum regnum, regem qui tunc fuit cum universo ipsius
exercitu fudisti quamprimum."

2.

[Commines' "Mémoires," ed. Petitot, ii. 314-15.]

Le comte de Richemont m'a autrefois conté, peu
avant qu'il partist de ce royaume, que depuis l'age de
cinq ans il avoit esté gardé et caché comme fugitif en
prison.

Ce comte avoit esté quinze ans ou environ prisonnier
en Bretagne du duc Francois dernier mort, esquelles
mains il vint par tempeste de mer, cuidant fuir en
France, et le comte de Bennebroc,[1] son oncle, avec luy.
J'estois pour lors devers ledit duc quand ils furent pris.
Ledit duc les traita doucement pour prisonniers et au
trespas du roy Edoüard, ledit duc François luy bailla
largement gens et navires, et avecques l'intelligence
dudit duc de Boucquinguan,[2] qui pour icelle occasion
mourut, l'envoya pour descendre en Angleterre : il eut
une grande tourmente et vent contraire, et retourna à
Dieppe, et de la par terre en Bretagne.   Quand il fut
retourné en Bretagne, il douta d'ennuyer le duc par sa
despence ; car il avoit quelques cinq cens Anglois, et si
craignoit que ledit duc ne s'accordast avecques le roy
Richard, à son dommage ; et aussi on le pratiquoit de
deça : parquoy s'en vint avec sa bande, sans dire adieu
audit duc.   Peu de temps apres on luy paya trois ou

[1] Jasper Tudor, Earl of Pembroke.
[2] Henry Stafford, second Duke of Buckingham.

quatre mille hommes pour le passage seulement ; et fut 1485.
baillée par le Roy qui est de present, à ceux qui estoient
avecques luy, une bonne somme d'argent et quelques
pièces d'artillerie.[1] Il fut conduit, avec le navire de
Normandie, pour descendre en Galles, dont il estoit.

3.

[Richard III's proclamation against Henry Tudor, "Paston
Letters," iii. 883.]

R.R.

Ricardus etc. salutem. Precipimus tibi etc. For- 23 June.
asmoche as the Kyng our sovereign Lord hath certeyn
knowledge that Piers, Bisshop of Exeter, Jasper Tydder,
son of Owen Tydder, callyng hymself Erle of Pembroke,
John, late Erle of Oxon, and Sir Edward Wodevyle,
with other dyvers his rebelles and traytours, disabled and
atteynted by the auctorite of the High Court of Parlement, of whom many be knowen for open murdrers,
advoutrers, and extorcioners, contrary to the pleasure
of God, and ayenst all trouth, honour, and nature,
have forsakyn there naturall contrey, takyng them first
to be under th' obeisaunce of the Duke of Bretayn, and
to hym promysed certeyn thyngs whiche by him and his
counsell were thought thynggs to gretly unnaturall and
abominable for them to graunt, observe, kepe, and perfourme, and therfore the same utterly refused.

The seid traytours, seyng the seid Duke and his
counsell wolde not aide nor socour theym ner folowe
there wayes, privily departed oute of his contrey in to
Fraunce, and there takyng theym to be under the
obeisaunce of the Kynggs auncient enemy, Charlys,
callyng hymself Kyng of Fraunce, and to abuse and
blynde the comons of this seid Realme, the seid rebelles

[1] See below, p. 83.
1 *

and traitours have chosyn to be there capteyn one
Henry Tydder, son of Edmond Tydder, son of Owen
Tydder, whiche of his ambicioness and insaciable
covetise encrocheth and usurpid upon hym the name
and title of royall astate of this Realme of Englond,
where unto he hath no maner interest, right, title, or
colour, as every man wele knoweth ; for he is discended
of bastard blood bothe of ffather side and of mother
side, for the seid Owen the graunfader was bastard
borne, and his moder was doughter unto John, Duke of
Somerset, son unto John, Erle of Somerset, sone unto
Dame Kateryne Suynford, and of her in double avoutry
gotyn, wherby it evidently apperith that no title[1] can
nor may [be] in hym, which fully entendeth to entre
this Reame, purposyng a conquest.   And if he shulde
atcheve his fals entent and purpose, every man is lif,
livelod, and goddes shulde be in his hands, liberte, and
disposicion, wherby sholde ensue the disheretyng and
distruccion of all the noble and worshipfull blode of this
Reame for ever, and to the resistence and withstondyng
wherof every true and naturall Englishman born must
ley to his hands for his owen suerte and wele.

And to th'entent that the seid Henry Tydder myght
the rather atcheve his fals intent and purpose by the
aide, supporte, and assistence of the Kynggs seid auncient
enemy of Fraunce, [he] hath covenanted and bargayned
with hym and all the counsell of Fraunce to geve up and
relese inperpetuite all the right, title, and cleyme that
the Kyng[es] of Englond have, had, and ought to have,
to the Crowne and Reame of Fraunce, to gether with
the Duchies of Normandy, Anjoy, and Maygne, Gascoyn
and Guyne, castell[es] and townys of Caleys, Guysnes,
Hammes, with the marches apperteynyng to the same,

[1] For documents relating to Henry's descent and title to the
throne, see below, Vol. ii., Nos. 4-8.

and discevir and exclude the armes of Fraunce oute of
the armes of Englond for ever.

And in more prove and shewing of his seid purpose
of conquest, the seid Henry Tidder hath goven as well
to dyvers of the seid Kynggs enemys as to his seid rebelles and traitours, archebisshoprikes, bisshoprikes, and
other dignitees spirituels, and also the ducheez, erle-
domez, baronyes, and other possessions and inheritaunces
of knyghts, squyres, gentilmen, and other the Kynggs
true subjetts withynne the Reame, and entendith also
to chaunge and subverte the lawes of the same, and
to enduce and establisse newe lawes and ordenaunces
amongez the Kynggs seid subjetts. And over this, and
beside the alienacions of all the premyssez into the possession of the Kynggs seid auncient enemys to the
grettest anyntisshment, shame, and rebuke that ever
myght falle to this seid land, the seid Henry Tydder
and others, the Kynggs rebelles and traitours aforeseid,
have extended [intended] at there comyng, if they may
be of power, to do the most cruell murdres, slaughterys,
and roberys, and disherisons that ever were seen in eny
Cristen reame.

For the wich, and other inestymable daungers to be
escheuved, and to th'entent that the Kynggs seid rebelles,
traitours, and enemys may be utterly put from there
seid malicious and fals purpose, and sone discomforted,
if they enforce to land, the Kyng our soveraign Lord
willith, chargeth and comaundith all and everyche of
the naturall and true subgetts of this his Reame to call
the premyssez to there mynds, and like gode and true
Englishmen to endover themselfs with all there powers
for the defence of them, there wifs, chylderyn, and
godes, and heriditaments ayenst the seid malicious
purposes and conspiracions which the seid auncient
enemes have made with the Kynggs seid rebelles and

traitours for the fynall distruccion of this lande as is
aforesaid. And our said soveraign Lord, as a wele willed,
diligent, and coragious Prynce, wel put his moost roiall
persone to all labour and payne necessary in this behalve for the resistence and subduyng of his seid
enemys, rebells, and traitours to the moost comforte,
wele and suerte of all his true and feithfull liege men
and subgetts.

And over this, our seid soveraign Lord willith and
comaundith all his seid subgetts to be redy in there
most defensible arraye to do his Highnes servyce of
werre, when thy, be opyn proclamacion or otherwise,
shall be comaunded so to do, for the resistence of the
Kynggs seid rebelles, traitours, and enemys. Et hoc
sub periculo etc.—T. me ipso apud Westmonasterium
xxiij die Junij, anno regni nostri secundo.[1]

4.

[Henry's alleged manifesto to his army on the eve of the battle of
Bosworth, inaccurately reprinted in Halliwell's "Letters of
the Kings of England," i. 164, from Hall's "Chronicle". It
reads much more like Hall's composition than Henry's.]

22 August. If ever God gave victory to men fighting in a just
quarrel, or if He ever aided such as made war for the
wealth and tuition of their own natural and nutritive
country, or if He ever succoured them which adventured
their lives for the relief of innocents, suppressing of
malefactors and apparent offenders—no doubt, my
fellows and friends, but He of his bountiful goodness
will this day send us triumphant victory and a lucky
journey over our proud enemy and arrogant adversary.
For, if you remember and consider the very cause of our
just quarrel, you shall apparently perceive the same to

[1] Richard III's reign began on 26 June, 1483, so the third year
of his reign did not commence until three days after the date of
this proclamation.

be true, godly, and virtuous. In the which I doubt not _{August,} but God will rather aid us: yea, (and fight for us) than ^{1485.} see us vanquished and profligated, by such as neither fear Him nor His laws, nor yet regard justice or honesty. Our cause is so just, that no enterprise can be of more virtue both by the laws Divine and Civil ; for, what can be a more honest, goodly, or godly quarrel, than to fight against a captain being an homicide and murderer of his own blood and progeny?—an extreme destroyer of his nobility, and to his and our country and the poor subjects of the same, a deadly mall, a fiery brand, and a burden intolerable? Besides him, consider who be of his band and company,—such as by murder and un-truth committed against their own kin and lineage,— yea against their Prince and Sovereign Lord, have disherited me and you, and wrongfully detain and usurp our lawful patrimony and lineal inheritance. For he that calleth himself king, keepeth from me the crown and regiment of this noble realm and country, contrary to all justice and equity: Likewise, his mates and friends occupy your lands, cut down your woods, and destroy your manors, letting your wives and children range abroad for their living : which persons, for their penance and punishment, I doubt not but God, of His goodness, will either deliver into our hands as a great gain and booty, or cause them, being grieved and com-puncted with the prick of their corrupt consciences, cowardly to fly and not abide the battle. Besides this, I assure you that there be yonder in that great battle men brought thither for fear and not for love, soldiers by force compelled and not with good-will assembled,—persons, which desire rather the destruction than the salvation of their master and captain ; and finally, a multitude, whereof the most part will be our friends and the least part our enemies. For truly I doubt which is the greater, the malice of the soldiers towards their captain, or the fear of him conceived by his people. For surely this rule is infallible that, as ill men daily covet to destroy the good, so God appointeth the good to confound the ill; and of all worldly goods the greatest is, to suppress tyrants and relieve innocence, whereof the one is ever as much hated as the other is loved. If this be true, (as clerks preach) who will spare yonder tyrant, Richard, Duke of Gloucester, untruly calling himself king, considering that he hath violated and broken both the law of God and man? What virtue is in him which was the confusion of his brother and the murtherer of his nephews?[1] What mercy is in him which sleieth his trusty friends as well as his extreme enemies? Who can have confidence in him which putteth diffidence in all men? If you have not read, I have heard of clerks say, that Tarquin the proud for the vice of the body lost the kingdom of Rome, and the name of Tarquin was banished the city for ever. Yet was not his fault so detestable, as the fact of cruel Nero, which slew his own mother. Behold yonder Richard, which is both Tarquin and Nero! Yea, a tyrant more than Nero, for he hath not only murthered his nephew, being his king and sovereign lord, bastarded his noble brethren, and defamed his virtuous and womanly mother, but also compassed all the means and ways that he could invent how to stuprate his own niece under the pretence of a cloaked matrimony: which lady I have sworn and promised to take to my mate and wife, as you all know and believe.

If this cause be not just, and this quarrel godly, let God, the Giver of Victory, judge and determine. We

[1] For a discussion of the evidence upon which this charge is based, see Sir Clements Markham in "English Historical Review," vi. 250, 806, and Dr. James Gairdner, ib. vi. 444, 813.

have (thanks be given to Christ!) escaped the secret treasons in Brittany, and avoided the subtle snares of our fraudulent enemies there, passed the troublous seas in good and quiet safeguard, and without resistance have penetrated the ample region and large country of Wales, and are now come to the place which we so much desired. For long we have sought the furious boar, and now we have found him. Wherefore, let us not fear to enter into the toil, where we may surely slay him; for God knoweth that we have lived in the vales of misery, tossing our ships in dangerous storms. Let us not now dread to set up our sails in fair weather, having with us both it and good fortune. If we had come to conquer Wales, and had achieved it, our praise had been great and our gain more; but, if we win this battle, the whole rich realm of England, with the lords and rulers of the same shall be ours, the profit shall be ours, and the honour shall be ours.

Therefore, labour for your gain, and sweat for your right. While we were in Brittany, we had small livings and little plenty of wealth or welfare. Now is the time come to get abundance of riches and copie of profit, which is the reward of your service and merit of your pain. And this remember with yourselves, that before us be our enemies, and on either side of us be such, as I neither surely trust nor greatly believe. Backward we cannot flee; so that here we stand, like sheep in a fold, circumsepted and compassed between our enemies and doubtful friends. Therefore, let all fear be set aside, and like sworn brethren, let us join in one; for this day shall be the end of our travail and the gain of our labour, either by honourable death or famous victory; and, as I trust the battle shall not be so sour as the profit shall be sweet. Remember the victory is not gotten with the multitude of men, but with the courages of hearts and valiantness of minds. The smaller that our number is, the more glory is to us, if we vanquish. If we be overcome, yet no laud is to be attributed to the victors, considering that ten men fought against one ; and, if we die, so glorious a death in so good a quarrel, neither fretting time nor cancarding oblivion shall be able to obfuscate or raze out of the book of fame either our names or our godly attempt.

And this one thing I assure you, that in so just and good a cause and so notable a quarrel, you shall find me this day rather a dead carrion on the cold ground, than a free prisoner on a carpet in a lady's chamber. Let us, therefore, fight like invincible giants, and set on our enemies, like untimorous tigers, and banish all fear, like ramping lions. And now advance forward, true men against traitors, pitiful persons against murtherers, true inheritors against usurpers, the scourges of God against tyrants. Display my banner with a good courage ; march forth like strong and robustious champions, and begin the battle like hardy conquerors. The battle is at hand, and the victory approacheth, and, if we shamefully recule or cowardly flee, we and all our sequel be destroyed and dishonoured for ever.

This is the day of gain, and this is the time of loss ; get this day victory, and be conquerors ; and lose this day's battle, and be villains ; and, therefore, in the name of God and Saint George, let every man courageously advance forth his standard.

5.

[" Chronicle of Calais," Camd. Soc. p. i.]

22 August. Kynge Henry the Seventh enterid the realme of England, and landyd at Mylfordhaven with his army out of Britayné, in the monethe of August, in the yere of our Lord 1485. On seint Bartilmew's even he went

to the filde at Bosworthe hethe, and there was kynge August, Richarde slayne and the duke of Norfolke slayne, and 1485. the earl of Surrey the duke of Norfolkes sone taken prisoner, and the earl of Northumberland taken prisoner, the lord Sowche taken prisoner, and there was slayne Ratclife, Catesby, and gentle Brakenbery, and the erle of Shrowsbery was taken prisoner, and the lorde Lovell escaped and fled; and there was slayne of kynge Henry's party ser William Brandon, who bare kynge Henry's standard that day.

6.

[Kingsford's " Chronicles of London," p. 193.]

Also this yer the xxij day of August was the ffeeld of 22 August. Bosworth, where kyng Richard was slayne, and the Duke of Northfolk vpon his party, and therle of Surrey, son vnto the said Duke, was taken vpon the said ffeeld, and many other men slayn, as Brakynbury and other, by the power of kyng Henry the vij[th]. And after the ffeeld doon, the said Kyng Richard was caried vpon an hors behynd a man all naked to Leyciter, fast by the ffeeld; and there buryed w[t] in the ffreres.[1] And the xxvij day of August was the said kyng Henry brought in to the Cite, w[t] the Mayr, Aldermen, and the ffeli-shippys clothed in violet; and so to the palays at powles, and there loged.[2]

7.

[Circular letter of Henry VII after the battle of Bosworth, Halli-well, " Letters of the Kings of England," i. 169. The date of this circular can hardly be later than the morrow of Bosworth, because Henry was still under the impression that Surrey and Lovell had been slain.]

[1] The church of the Grey Friars, Leicester.

[2] Bacon's story of Henry's entrance to London in a closed carriage is a fiction evolved out of the misreading of André's *laetanter* as *latenter*. According to Harleian MS. 541 f. 217 *b*, Henry did not reach London until 3 September.

Henry by the grace of God, king of England and of
France, Prince of Wales, and Lord of Ireland, strictly
chargeth and commandeth, upon pain of death, that no
manner of man rob or spoil no manner of commons
coming from the field ; but suffer them to pass home to
their countries and dwelling-places, with their horse
and harness. And, moreover, that no manner of man
take upon him to go to no gentleman's place, neither in
the country, nor within cities nor boroughs, nor pick no
quarrels for old or for new matters ; but keep the king's
peace, upon pain of hanging etc.

And, moreover, if there be any man offered to be
robbed and spoiled of his goods, let him come to Master
Richard Borrow, the king's serjeant here, and he shall
have a warrant for his body and his goods, unto the
time the king's pleasure be known.

And, moreover, the king ascertaineth you, that Richard,
Duke of Gloucester, lately called King Richard, was
lately slain at a place called Sandeford, within the shire
of Leicester, and there was laid openly, that every man
might see and look upon him. And also there was
slain upon the same field, John, late Duke of Norfolk,
John, late Earl of Lincoln, Thomas, late Earl of Surrey,
Franceys, Viscount Lovel, Sir Walter Deveres, Lord
Ferrars, Richard Ratcliffe, knight, Robert Brackenbury,
knight, with many other knights, squires, and gentlemen : on whose souls God have mercy !

8.

[The " Rose of England " from " Bishop Percy's MSS.," ed. Hales
and Furnivall, iii. 189-94.]

Throughout a garden greene & gay,
a seemlye sight itt was to see
how flowers did flourish fresh and gay,
& birds doe sing melodiouslye.

in the midst of a garden there sprange a tree
which tree was of a mickle price,
& there vppon sprang the rose soe redd,
the goodlyest that euer sprange on rise.

August,
1485.

this rose was ffaire, ffresh to behold,
springing with many a royall lance ;
a crowned King, with a crowne of gold
ouer England, Ireland, and of ffrance.

then came in a beast men call a bore,[1]
& he rooted this garden vpp and downe,
by the seede of the rose he sett noe store,
but afterwards itt wore the crowne.

hee tooke the branches of this rose away,
and all in sunder did them teare ;
& he buryed them vnder a clodd of clay,
swore they shold neuer bloome nor beare.

then came in an Egle [2] gleaming gay,
of all ffaire birds well worth the best ;
he took the branche of the rose away,
& bore itt to Latham to his nest.

but now is this rose out of England exiled,
this certaine truth I will not faine ;
but if itt please you to sitt a while,
Ile tell you how the rose came in againe.

att Milford hauen he entered in ;
to claime his right, was his delight ;
he brought the blew bore [3] in with him,
to encounter with the bore soe white.

[1] Richard III.

[2] Thomas Stanley, afterwards first Earl of Derby, whose crest was
an eagle and child, and whose chief seat was at Latham.

[3] The crest of the Earl of Oxford, who commanded the vanguard
of Henry's army, was " a boar statant azure ".

August,
1485.
then a messenger the rose did send
to the Egles nest, & bidd him hye ;
"to my ffather[1] the old Egle I doe [me] comend,
his aide and helpe I craue speedylye."

saies, "I desire my father att my cominge
of men and mony att my need,
& alsoe my mother of her deer blessing,
then better then I hope to speede."

& when the messenger came before thold Egle,
he kneeled him downe vpon his knee,
saith, "well greeteth you my Lord the rose,
he hath sent you greetings here by me.

"safe ffrom the seas Christ hath him sent,
now he is entered England within."
"let vs thanke god," the old Egle did say,
"he shall be the fflower of all his kine!

"wend away, messenger, with might and maine ;
itts hard to know who a man may trust ;—
I hope the rose shall fflourish againe,
& haue all things att his owne lust."

then Sir Rice ap Thomas[2] drawes Wales with him :
a worthy sight itt was to see,
how the Welchmen rose wholy with him,
& shogged him to Shewsburye.

Att that time was baylye in Shewsburye
one Master Mitton in the towne.
the gates were strong, & he mad them ffast,
& the portcullis he lett downe.

[1] Thomas, Lord Stanley, had married Henry's mother, Margaret
Beaufort.
[2] See "Dict. Nat. Biog.," xlviii. 91.

& throug a garrett of the walls,
ouer Severne these words said hee,
" att these gates no man enter shall."
but he kepte him out a night & a day.

this words Mitton did Erle Richmond tell ;
I am sure the Chronicles of this will not lye ;
but when letters came from Sir William Stanley of the
    hold castle,
then the gates were opened presentlye.

then entered this towne the noble Lord
the Erle Richmond, the rose soe redd,
the Erle of Oxford with a sword
wold haue smitt of the bailiffes head.

" but hold your hand," saies Erle Richmond,
" ffor his loue that dyed vpon a tree !
ffor if wee begin to head so soone,
in England wee shall beare no degree."

" what offence haue I made the," sayd Erle Richmonde,
" that thou kept me out of my towne ? "
" I know no King," sayd Mitton then,
" but Richard now that weares the crowne."

" why, what wilt thou say," said Erle Richmonde,
" when I have put King Richard downe ? "
" why, then Ile be as true to you, my Lord,
after the time that I am sworne."

" were itt not great pitty," sayd Erle Richmond,
" that such a man as this shold dye ? "
such loyall service by him done,
the cronickles of this will not lye.

" thou shalt not be harmed in any case."
he pardoned him presentlye.
they stayd not past a night & a day,
but towards Newport did they hye.

but [at] Attherston these Lords did meete ;
a worthy sight itt was to see,
how Erle Richmond tooke his hatt in his hand,
& said, " Cheshire & Lancashire, welcome to me."

but now is a bird of the Egle taken ;
ffrom the white bore he cannot fflee.
therfore the old Egle makes great moane,
& prayes to god most certainly :

" O stedfast god, verament," he did say—
" 3 persons in one god in Trinytye !
saue my sonne, the young Egle, this day
ffrom all ffalse craft and trecherye ! "

then the blew bore the vanward had :
he was both warry and wise of witt ;
the right hand of them he tooke,
the sunn & wind of them to gett.

then the Egle ffollowed fast vpon his pray ;
with sore dints he did them smyte.
the Talbott he bitt wonderous sore,
soe well the vnicorne did him quite.

& then came in the harts head ;
a worthy sight itt was to see,
they jacketts that were of white & redd,
how they laid about them lustilye.

but now is the ffierce ffeeld foughten & ended,
& the white bore there lyeth slaine ;
& the young Egle is preserved,
& come to his nest againe.

but now this garden fflourishes ffreshly & gay,
with ffragrant fflowers comely of hew ;
& gardners itt doth maintaine ;
I hope they will proue iust & true.

our King, he is the rose soe redd,
that now does fflourish ffresh and gay.
Confound his ffoes, Lord, wee beseeche,
& loue his grace both night & day!

ffinis.

9.

[The council of York on the death of Richard III, Davis's "York Records," p. 218.]

Wer assembled in the Counsaill Chamber. Where
and when it was shewed by diverse personnes, and
especially by John Sponer,[1] send unto the feld of Rede-
more[2] to bring tidings frome the same to the Citie, that
King Richard, late mercifully reigning upon us, was,
through grete treason of the Duc of Northfolk[3] and
many other that turned ayenst hyme, with many other
lords and nobills of this North parties, was pitiously
slane and murdered, to the grete hevynesse of this Citie,
the names of whome folowethe hereafter. Wherfor it
was determyned for so moch as it was said that Therle
of Northumberland was commen to Wressill, that a
lettre should be consaved unto the said Erle, beseking
hyme to yeve unto them his best advise how to dispose
them at this wofull season both to his honor and

---

[1] He was "serjeant to the mace," and had been sent to Richard's
host on 16 August, ib. p. 214.

[2] The name by which the battle of Bosworth was known in York.

[3] An unsubstantiated rumour. On Saturday, 14 May, 1491, one
John Payntor was examined by the York council for saying "that
therle of Northumberland was a traytor and bytrayed Kyng Richard
with myche other unfittyng langage consernyng the said Erle".
Payntor's reply was to charge his accuser with sayinge "that Kyng
Richard was an ypocryte, a crochebake, and beried in a dike like a
dogge : wherunto the said John Payntor answered and said that he
lied, for the Kyngs good grace hath heried hym like a noble gentilman " (ib. pp. 220-1).

August,
485. worship, and well and prouffitt of this Citie, the tenor
wherfor foloweth hereafter ·—

"Right prepotent and right noble our moost honor-
able especiall and singler good lord, in our moost humble
wise we recommend us unto your good lordship, loving
almightie God of your home cummyng at this woofull
season, beseching your good lordship to be towards us
and this Citie as ye have be heretofore right good and
tendre lord, and soo to advertise us at this tyme as may
be to the honor of your lordship, the well and prouffit
of us, and sauffgard of this said Citie, wherunto we shall
applie us both with bodie and goods, and ever to owe
unto your lordship our faithfull hearts and true service;
ffurther we besech your lordship to yeve full faith and
credence unto our servaunt John Nicholson, the berer
hereof, in such things as he shall shewe unto your
lordship of our behalve, and the blessed trinitie etc.
Yours etc. Maire, Aldermen, Shereffe, xxiiij^{vi} of the
Counsaill of the Citie of York, with thole comunaltie of
the same."

10.

[Sir Thomas Lovell to his brother-in-law, Campbell's "Materials,"
i. 549.]

15 Septem-
ber. Brother Persone,—I mariveyll ye should be in any
dowte ffor the matter ye wrytte to me ffor, ffor I shewyd
you the kynges myud in sertein that Rydone and a
doctour Bothe showld go into Spayne, and so they shalle;
and Rydone must have the xl *li.* ye browte. And ye
may shewe also to my lord treshorer that he must
purvey ffor xxii *li* xiij*s* and iiij*d*, that is to sey, x *li.* ffor a
servaunt of the counte off Symy, and x *li.* ffor a gentill-
man off the kynges off Denmark and iiij marks ffor a
ffryer servaunt to the marchall off Bretayn.

11.

[Henry VII to Lord Stanley, Campbell's "Materials," i. 579.]

Henry etc.   To our right enterly beloved fader Lancaster,
Thomas Stanley, knight, Lord Stanley, and our wel- 15 October.
beloved brethern George Stanley, knight, Lord Strange,
Edward Stanley, knight, shriff of our countie palatyne and countie of Lancaster, and to every of theym,
gretyng. For as moche as we pleyne undrestondyng
that divers the subgettes of our cosyne Jame, kyng of
Scottes, in great nomber and multitude, ben in full
purpose to invade and enter this our reame, entendyng
to leaye seege to our town and castel of Berwik, and
the townshipes and mansions of our liege peaple in our
marches there to brenne, wast, and distroye, and the
same our liege peaple there dwellyng to take, slee, and
emprisone and devoure, and othre noyaunce to do,
asmoche as they cann and maye, trustyng to have aide
and favour at their comyng of divers riottuose and
evel disposed personnes in thoes parties, which of their
inward and froward malice and unnatural disposicion
entend the distruccioun of us and of our liege peaple,
by provokyng discensioun, discorde, and debate, as by
makyng of assembles and commocions of our peaple
steryng theym to the same dispocioun, whom and whos
malice we entend brifly to resiste and recountre, by the
grace of Almyghty God and help of our true and lovyng
subgettes. We, willyng the defense of this our reame
and marchis of the same, and of all our liege people,
trustyng in your great trouthes,; discrecions, and circumspect wisdomes, have assigned you and every of
you, joyntly and severally, to take mustres of all meenn
within our seid countie, aswel within libertates as without, beyng myghty and able to labour ; and everyman
after hys state, degre, condicioun, and facultie hymself

2 *

to array and arme defensibly for the warre, and they so arraied and armed, straitly chargyng theym to holde and kepe the same contynually with theym, so that they alwey and every tyme be redy armed and arraied, and to attende uppoun our seid entirely belovied fader Thomas, Lord Stanley, our welbeloved brethern George, Lord Strange, and Edward Stanley, knight, shirref of our seid countie or uppon any of them, when and as oft as it shalbe nedeful for the defence of our seid reame and marchis of the same, or for the subduyng of the said riotuos and evelle disposed personnes uppon short warnyng to theym gevyn by the seid Thomas, George, & Edward or any of theym. Wherefore we wol and straitely charge yow our seid commissioners and every of you, that, incontinent upponn the sight of this our commaundement, ye repaire, array, and arme your self and every of you, and over that cause al and every of our seid menn and subgettes to repaire array and arme theymself, and so arraied and armed to do, come, and be called bifore you at certeyn dayes and places by you to be lymytted, and our seid liege menn and subgettes not arrayed ne armed ye commaund and compelle onn our behalf to be arraied and armed in fourme aboveseid. And over this we yeve straitly in commaundement, by theis presentz, to al and singulre shireffes, maires, bailiffs, constables, and al othre our officers, ministres, liegmen, and subgettes whatsoever they be, aswel within franches as without, within our seid countie, that unto you they be attendant, assistent, behoyng, and obedient diligently in al the premissez. In witnes wherof we have doone to be made thes our lettres patentes undre the seale of our countie palatyne of Lancaster.

12.

1485.

[Henry VII to Henry Vernon, "Rutland MSS." (Hist. MSS. Comm.), p. 8.]

Trusty and welbeloved we grete you wele. And foras- London, 17 October. moche as it is commen unto oure knowlege that certeyne oure rebelles and traitours beyng of litill honour or sub- staunce confedered with oure auncient enemyes the Scottes ayenst their naturall dutees and allegeaunces, made insurrections and assemblees of oure pour subgettes in the north parties of this our realme, taking Robyn of Riddesdale, Jack St[raw], Thomolyn at Lath and Maister Mendall for their Capteyns, entendyng if they be of power, the fynall subversion and gode publique of this oure realme. We therfor woll and desire you that with all the power defensibly arrayed that ye can make, ye doo dispose you to come onto us in all haste possible to yeve your attendaunce and assistence unto us for the repressing of the malicious entent of our saide rebelles and traitours, not failyng herof in eny wise upon the feith and legiaunce that ye owe and bere unto us.

13.

[John de la Pole, Duke of Suffolk, to John Paston, sheriff of Suf- folk and Norfolk, "Paston Letters," iii. 887.]

Right welbeloved, we grete you well. And for as- Long Strat- ton, muche as the King our sovereigne Lord hath late ad- 20 October. dressed his letters of comission undre his seale unto us, reciting by the same that his highnesse undrestondith certayn his rebells associate to his old enmys of Scotlond, entending not only to trowble his peax, the nobles and subjects of this Reame to destroy, their goods and pos- sessions to spoill, and reward at thair liberties, but also the lawes of this lond and holy Chirche to subvert.

Our said moost drad soverayn Lord, as a Cristen Prince, . . . his said enmys and rebels to resist, hath

assigned and comaunded us to do all maner . . . and
others defensible able to labour, as well archers as
hobbyllers, to come before us and charge them . . .
armed and arayed, every man aftre his degre and power,
to attend uppon his person, and uppon us, to do him
service in defence as well of the Chirche as of the said
nobles and subjects of this Realm, against his said enmys
and rebels.

We therfore wull, and in our said sovereigne Lords
name straitly charge and comaunde you, that in all
possible hast ye do this to be proclaimed :—And that
all maner men able to do the King service, as well
knights, esquiers, and gentlemen, as townships and
hundreds, as well within franchesse and libertes as
without, within the counties of Suffolk and Norffolk,
and that they be charged to be redy at all tymes uppon
an howre warnyng, and ordered according to the last
comission afore this, to attend uppon his Grace and
uppon us to do him service, whatsoever they shalbe
comaunded, not failing herof, as ye wull answer at your
perile.   Geven at Long Stratton, the xx day of October.

And forthermore, that ye yeve credence unto our
servaunt this bringer, as this same day we receyved
the Kings commission at iiij. aftre none.

14.

[Opening of Henry VII's first Parliament, " Rot. Parl.," vi. 267.]

Memorandum, quod die Lune, die septimo mensis
Novembris, anno primo regni Regis Henrici Septimi,
videlicet, primo die Parliamenti, ipso Illustrissimo
Rege nostro in Camera communiter dicta Crucis, infra
Palacium suum Westmonasterium, regali solio sedente ;
Reverendus Pater Dominus Johannes Alkok, Wigor-
nensis Episcopus, Cancellarius Magnus Angliæ, causas
summonicionis Parliamenti admodum notabiliter pro-

nunciavit & declaravit; assumens hoc thema, " Intende
prospere, procede & regna". In quibus verbis intencionem
ostendit, quem suum [sic] haberent electi confluentes ad
hoc Parliamentum, quoniam precipue & principaliter,
non propter privatum & singulare comodum, set propter
eis & regno publicum & commune bonum. Et quomodo
unanimiter quantaque cum benevolencia & hilaritate
singuli eorum id promoverent & procurarent ostendit, ac
utilitatem regis & regni, una cum non mediocri pros-
peritate eorundem, necessario sequi ex eisdem; hec
notaus " Ibi intende prospere "; inducens hic historiam
quondam sedate discordie Rome relacione & consilio
cujusdam sapientis Agrippe nomine, de eventu discordie semell facte inter stomacum & omnia cetera
membra humani corporis; prout tradit ad longum
Titus Livius etc. Notavit insuper & declaravit fidelitatem quam subditi deberent continue & perseveranter
suis regibus; e conversaque vice, quam fidelitatem
reges ac principes debeant suis subditis, eos defeu-
dendo pro viribus, & providere ut equaliter, debite, &
rite justitia ministretur omnibus; & hec ostendit sub
hoc verbo in dicto themate; inducens etiam hic ex-
emplum apum; ubi ad plenum declaravit quinque bonas
proprietates apum; quarum quatuor primas applicavit
ad subditos, & quintam singulis bonis regibus & principibus applicari persuasit : ibi notaus quomodo princeps
apum sit sine aculeo pungitivo; insumans, quod per
locum, a forciori qui rationalis & rationalium princeps
est, jurisdiccionem suam cum clementia, benignitate
& pietate regere debet. Confirmans hoc ex interpretacione nominis, quia reges a recte agendo dicti sunt, ut
Sanctus declarat Isidorus Octavo Ethiologiarum, in quo
sic de regum proprietatibus perpulcre scribit regie
virtutes due sunt precipue, scilicet, pietas & justitia.
Ubi etiam ostendit, quod in regibus plus laudatur

pietas quam justitia. Et istud ibi confirmavit scitis sacrarum Scripturarum testimoniis : hoc inferens ex dicto Sancti Ambrosii in suo Examõn quod sicut finis tam principis, quam subditorum omnium bonorum apum, est operari, & educere ceram & mel, ceram ad cultum & obsequium divinum, atque ipsum mel in humanum proficuum & utilitatem ; Ita omne humanum Consilium atque Parliamentum versari debet solum circa ea que ad Dei & Ecclesie laudem, & Communitatis utilitatem conferre valeant. Scientes quoniam consilia, que in alterius horum detrimentum fuerit, scilicet, Ecclesie Christi, aut Communitatis, quamquam gentium & principum potentissimorum fuerint, Dominus dissipat, & consilium Domini manet in eternum. Et idem Reverendus Pater & Dominus ostendit ordinem postremo hujus incliti regni variis bonis & preclaris legibus ac institutionibus decorari, quibus bone execucioni mandatis, conclusit super hoc verbo finali thematis "Ibi regna" regem ac regnum sic prospere duratura, ut deletis tribus seculis de quibus commemorat Ovidius primo Metamorphoseos, argenteo scilicet æneo atque ferreo, id est avaritie, invidie & sedicionibus aliisque rapinis omnino deditis, aureum potiremus seculum ; quod seculum aureum ut facilius consequeremur, misit nobis propitius Deus alterum Josue regem strenuum & invictissimum propugnatorem nostrum, qui nos eruit a summa miseria, conabiturque totis viribus iniquos aut correctos reddere, aut evellere & extirpare ; Et hoc alitum suum regnum, bonis, probis & sapientissimis viris sic instaurare, refulcire & reillustrare, ut jubilantes de eo dicere debeamus omnes quod de Salomone legimus Israliticum populum applaudendo dixisse, "Vivat Rex, vivat Rex." Et cum Propheta sic orare continue, Domine salvum fac regem nostrum . ab omni adversitate mentis & corporis, ut nobis-

cum letos & prosperos plurimos durat anuos, & felicem
post se prolem regnaturum relinquat, quando perhenniter
& eterna felicitate remunerandum a nobis cum evocabit
Altissimus pro tantis suis bene meritis, quorum meri-
torum & premii nos esse participes concedat Deus, qui
sine fine vivit & regnat.   Amen.

15.

[Election of Thomas Lovell as Speaker, "Rot. Parl.," vi. 268.]

Item, die Mercurii, tertio die Parliamenti, præfati
Communes coram Domino Rege in pleno Parliamento
comparentes, presentaverunt Domino Regi Thomam
Lovell Prelocutorem suum, de quo idem Dominus Rex
se bene contentavit. ˊQui quidem Thomas, post excusa-
tionem suam coram Domino Rege factam, pro eo quod
ipsa sua excusatio ex parte dicti Domini Regis admitti
non potuit, eidem Domino Regi humillime supplicavit,
quatenus omnia & singula per ipsum in Parliamento
predicto nomine dicte Communitatis proferenda & de-
clarenda, sub tali posset protestacione proferre. & de-
clarare, quod si ipse aliqua sibi per prefatos socios suos
injuncta, aliter quam ipsi concordata fuerint, aut in
addendo vel omittendo declaraverit ea sic declarata per
predictos socios suos corrigere & emendare ; ˏ & quod
protestacio sua hujusmodi in Rotulo Parliamenti predicti inactitaretur. Cui per prefatum Dominum Can-
cellarium de mandato Domini Regis extitit responsum,
quod idem Thomas tali protestacione frueretur &
gauderet, quali alii Prelocutores, tempore nobilium
progenitorum ipsius Domini Regis Regum Angliæ, in
hujusmodi Parliamentis uti & gaudere consueverunt.
Subsequenterque, idem Dominus Rex prefatis Cõmini-
bus ore suo proprio eloquens, ostendendo suum adventum
ad Jus & Coronam Angliæ fore tam per justum titulum
hereditancie, quam per verum Dei judicium in tribuendo

26THE REIGN OF HENRY VII

November, sibi victoriam de inimico suo in campo, declaravit quod
1485.
omnes subditi sui cujuscumque status, gradus seu
condicionis fuerint, haberent & tenerent, sibi & heredibus suis, omnia terras, tenementa, redditus & here-
ditamenta sua, eisdemque gauderent, exceptis talibus
personis quales suam Majestatem Regiam offenderunt,
qui juxta eorum demerita in presentis Parliamenti Curia
aliter essent plectendi.

16.

[Parliamentary proceedings, " Rot. Parl.," vi. 287.]

19 Novem-   Memorandum, quod pro reformacione quorundam
ber.
enormium & inauditorum scelerum in regno Angliæ
usitatorum,necnon correccione perpetrancium eorundem,
quidam Articulus jurandus & promittendus in Parliamento predicto avisatus extitit, cujus quidem Articuli
tenor sequitur in hec verba.

Yee shall swere, that yee from henceforth shall not
reteine, aid ne comforte, any persoune oopenlie cursed,
Murderer, Felon, or outlawed Man of Felony, by you
knowen so to be, or any such persoune lett to be attacked
or taken therefore by the Order of Law, nor reteine anie
Man by Indenture or Othe, nor give Livere, Signe or
Token, contrarie to the Law, nor any Maintainance,
Imbracerie, Riotts or unlawfull Assemblie make, cause
to be made, or assent therto, nor lett nor cause to be
letted the execucion of any of the Kinges Writts or
Precepts, directed to such lawfull Ministres and Officers
as ought to have execucione of the same, nor lett any
Man to Baile or Mainprise, knowing and deeming him
to be Felon, upon your Honour and Worship. So God
you helpe and his Saints.[1]

    [1] A commission to administer this oath is printed in Rymer,
" Foedera," xii. 280, dated 4 January, 1486.

Super quo quamplures notabiles milites & armigeri, tam de Hospitio dicti Domini Regis, quam de Domo Communitatum ad præsens Parliamentum venire summoniti, decimo nono die Novembris, coram Domino Rege, Dominis Spiritualibus & Temporalibus, tunc presentibus, in Cameram Parliamenti vocati, articulo predicto primitus coram eis 'publice recitato, articulum illum singillatim observare & custodire super Sancta Dei Evangelia juraverunt & promisserunt.

Subsequenterque, eodem die, post recessum dictorum militum & armigerorum a Camera Parliamenti, Venerabilis Pater Johannes Wygornensis Episcopus, Cancellarius Angliæ, Dominis Spiritualibus & Temporalibus tunc presentibus ostendebat, qualiter supradicti milites, armigeri, & alii generosi, sacramenta sua, prout inter illos Dominos omnes appunctuabatur, prestiterunt; illos interrogans, si ipsi id idem facere vellent : qui respondentes, quasi una voce dixerunt, "parati sumus illud idem perficere"; facto intervallo, articulus supradictus, in presencia dicti Domini Regis, & ejus mandato, denuo extitit recitatus. Et eo audito, omnes prefati Domini tunc presentes, articulum illum in omnibus custodire, observare & performare, quilibet Dominus Spiritualis manum suam dexteram super pectus suum, & quilibet Dominus Temporalis manum suam dexteram super Sancta Dei Evangelia ponentes, sponte juraverunt & promisserunt.

Nomina Dominorum Spiritualium sacramentum predictum prestancium.

Archiepiscopus Ebor'.

Episcopi, videlicet.

London'   Exonien'
Bangoren'   Elien'
Cicestren'   Roffen'

Hereforden'   Wygorn'
Landaven'   Norwicen' &
Lincoln'   Meneven'
    Abbates videlicet.
    Westm'
    Glouc'
    Sancti Augustine Cantuar'
    Glaston'
    de Ramsey
    Cirencestre
    de Wynchecombe
    de Sancto Albano   &
    de Bello   Prior de Coventre.
Nomina Dominorum Temporalium sacramentum pre-
        dictum prestancium.
    Duces videlicet.
Bedford &
Suff'
    Comites, videlicet.
Lincoln'   Nottingham
Arundell'   Ryvers
Derbie   Devon &
Salop   Wiltes
    Viscount de Beaumont.
    Barones videlicet.
Grey   Grey de Wilton
Dudley   Beauchamp &
Bergeveny   Hastinges.
Fitzwalter

17.

[J. de Giglis, papal collector in England to the Pope, Campbell's
"Materials," i. 198.]

London, 6
December.
Beatissime pater, post humillimam commendationem
et pedum oscula beatissimorum. Post ultimas quas ad

sanctissimum patrem scripsi litteras, quo ad statum rerum istarum nichil aut parum est innovatum.   Agitur enim publicus regni conventus, quem dicunt Parliamentum, pro regni informatione, in quo aliqua sunt acta et in primis generalis abolitio omnium adversus regem commissorum.   Comes Northumbriæ qui captus et incarceratus fuerat est liberatus, sub cautione tamen omnium prælatorum et dominorum temporalium ac etiam plebeiorum.   Comes Sudræ adhuc detinetur.   Sed audio quod est hic liberabitur; filia major natu regis Edwardi declarata est ducissa Eboracensis.   Asseritur constanter quod rex eam sit ducturus in uxorem, quod omnes arbitrantur futurum regno saluberrimum.   Rex ipse prudentissimus habetur ac etiam clementissimus ; omnia videntur ad pacem disposita, modo animi hominum sint constantes.   Nichil enim magis est quod semper huic regno nocuit quam ambitio et cupiditas insatiabilis, quæ omnis infidelitatis atque inconstantiæ est mater, a qua si Deus nos liberaverit res regni hujus quietæ erunt. Cæterum, pater beatissime, humiliter supplico ut me commendatum S.V. suscipere dignetur atque ea concedere quæ ante me omnes collectores qui hic fuerunt sunt consecuti, facultates videlicet aliquas parvas et non multas, sine quibus et auctoritas languescit et res cameræ non potest utiliter geri; prosunt enim ad gratiam potentiorum michi conciliandam, sine qua nichil est quod bene in hoc officio agere possum.   Dominus autem, S.V. eminentiæ suæ diu incolumem præservet.

P.S.—Antequam has clauderem intellexi dominos Batenses et Sarisbruenses esse liberatos, amissis omnibus bonis, quod etsi antea intellexissem non scripsi quia pro certo non habebam ; ambo omnibus sunt exosi et non immerito.   Sunt hic nuntii regis Francorum, ducum Austriæ et Britanniæ, creditur quod cum illis pax futura sit.

18.

[Parliamentary proceedings, "Rot. Parl.," vi. 278.]

Memorandum quod decimo die Decembris, anno presenti, Communitates Regni Angliæ in pleno Parliamento coram Domino Rege comparentes, per Thomam Lovell prelocutorem suum, Regie Celcitudini humillime supplicabant, eandem Celcitudinem affectuose requirentes, considerato quod auctoritate dicti Parliamenti stabilitum est & inactitatum, quod hereditates regnorum Angliæ & Franciæ, cum preemenencia & potestate regali, sint, restent, remaneant & permaneant in persona ejusdem Domini Regis, & heredibus de corpore suo legitime exeuntibus, eadem Regalis Sublimitas vellet sibi illam preclaram Dominam Elizabeth, Regis Edwardi quarti filiam, in uxorem & conthoralem assumere; unde per Dei gratiam sobolum propagacio de stirpe regum a multis speratur, in totius regni consolacionem. Consequenterque, Domini Spirituales & Temporales in eodem Parliamento existentes, a sedibus suis surgentes, & ante Regem in regali solio residentem stantes, capitibus suis inclinantes, eandem requestam fecerunt voce dimissa: quibus quidem respondebat ore proprio, Se juxta eorum desideria & requestus procedere fuisse contentum. Subsequenterque, Venerabilis pater Johannes Wigornienis Episcopus, de mandato dicti Domini Regis, Dominis Spiritualibus & Temporalibus & Communitatibus tunc ibidem presentibus declaravit, quod idem Dominus Rex, certis de causis ipsum moventibus, presens Parliamentum suum prorogare disposuit, ipsos Dominos & Communitates exhortans ex parte ejusdem Domini Regis, & presertim justicia[s] pacis, ut unusquisque eorum, cum ad propria venirent, pacem Ecclesie Dei & Regni procurare, ac homicidia, latrocinia, murdra, roberia, raptus mulierum &

extortiones punire, necnon valentes mendicantes & December, vagabundos sub colore mendicii per proprias discur- 1485. rentes & discordias mendaciaque seminantes, secundum statuta inde edita castigare atrociter, & vinculis mancipare toto conatu curarent, ut Dominus noster Rex ipsis ad Parliamentum predictum revenientibus de eorum bonis gestibus iterum in executione permissorum causam redendi gratias speciales habere valeret. Post quam quidem exhortationem sic notabiliter factam idem Cancellarius, ex parte Domini Regis & ejus mandato declaravit, qualiter negotia Parliamenti predicti pro statu & defencione regni Angliæ, in eodem Parliamento communicata & ministrata, ante festum Natalis Domini tunc quasi in proximo existens, propter ipsorum negotiorum arduitatem, discuti non poterant nec finaliter terminari: quamobrem prefatus Dominus noster Rex presens Parliamentum suum usque in vicesimum tertium diem Januarii tunc proximum futurum duxit prorogandum, & illud sic realiter prorogavit ; omnibus & singulis quorum interfuit in hac parte firmiter injungendum quod ad dictum vicesimum tertium diem Januarii, excusacione quacumque cessante personaliter convenirent, ad communicandum tractandum & consenciendum super hiis que pro pleniori & saniori discussione, provisione, & determinacione negotiorum predictorum, favente Domino, contigerint ordinari.

19.

[T. Betanson to Sir Robert Plumpton, "Plumpton Correspondence," p. 48.]

Sir, if it please your mastership, on the satterday London, 13 after our Lady day, the Parlament was prolonged unto December. the xxvii [1] day of January, and then it begineth againe.

[1] Parliament was really prorogued until 23 January ("Rot. Parl.," vi. 278, 329). The "Lady day" of this letter refers to the conception

December, Sir, my lord Schanchler publyshed in the Parlament
1485. house the same day, that the Kings gud grace shall
weede my lady Elizabeth (and so she is taken as quene) ;
and that at the marage ther shalbe great justyng.
Also, Sir, ther be divers lords and gentlemen attended
[attainted] by the Parlament, which be these ; and first,
Richard late Duke of Glouceter, John Duke of Norfolk,
Thomas Erle of Surrey, Francis Lord Lovell, Walter
Lord Ferres, John Lord Such [Zouch]; knyghts, Sir
James Heryngton, Sir Robert Heryngton, Sir Richard
Charleton, Sir Richard Ritliff, Sir William Barkley, Sir
Robart Brakenbery, Sir Thomas Pilkynton, Sir Robart
Mydleton ; esqueres, Walter Hopton, William Catisby,
Roger Wake, William Sapcolt, Homfray Stafford,
Wylliam Clarke, Galfryd Seyngermen, Walter Watkyn,
herold of hermes, Richard Revell of Darbyshire, Thomas
Pulter of Surrey, Johne Walste, John Kendall secretory,
John Buke, John Ralte, William Brampton : the are
attended for certayne. Howbeit, ther was many gentlemen agaynst it, but it wold not be, for yt was the Kings
pleasure. Sir, here is much spech that we shall have
aschip agayne, and no man can say of whom ; but they
dem of Northernmen and Walchmen. And much spech
is in the Kyngs house and of his householdmen. Sir,
other tydings is none here as yett. Ther is much run-
yng amongst the lords, but no man wott what it is ;
it is sayd yt is not well amongst them. Sir, I send your
mastership a letter by Roger, Mr. Mydeton's man. Sir,
if ther be any newer things, your mastership shall have
word, if I can gett it caryed from London. In die
Lucie Virgin.

of the Virgin Mary, 8 December, and Parliament was prorogued on
10 December.

1486.

20.

[Campbell's "Materials," i. 282.]

Special pardon for Robert Throkmarton, late sheriff 8 Febru-
of Warwickshire and Leicestershire, for all fines and ^{ary.}
arrears of accompts touching his office, grounded upon
the following petition:—"Mekely besechethe youre
hyghenesse your trewe and feithfulle liege man and
servant Robert Throkmarton, squyer, late by your seid
hyghenesse incontynent after your most noble and
victorious acte of conquest in repressyng your gret
ennemyes, Richard, late duke of Gloucestre, and othir,
made and deputed sheriff of your countees of Warrewyk
and Leycestre, and whiche sheriffwyk your seid liege
occupied but by the space of one monethe or fulle litille
more, and in whiche tyme of occupacioun was within
this your realme suche, rebellioun and troble, and your
lawes not stablysshed, that youre seid liege neither myght
ne coude execut his seid office of sheriffwyk to eny profite
of your seid hyghenesse, and for which occupacioun your
seid liege is chargeable to accompte to your hyghenesse
afore the barons of your Exchequiere as though he had
occupied the same office peasibly by the space of an
hole halfe yere, where he therein never resceyved eny
peny, whiche accompt if he shuld soo make and
fynysshe wolle be to his utter undoyng. Please your
seid hyghnesse, the premysses considered at the reverence
of God, to graunt to your seid liege your gracious lettres
of pardon, in due and effectuell forme to be made under
youre brode sealle, accordyng to the tenure herafter
ensuyng, and he woll ever pray God for the conservacioun
of your most roialle astate."

1486.   21.

[Betanson to Sir Robert Plumpton, "Plumpton Correspondence,"
                              p. 49.]

London,   Sir, if it please your mastership, I have made a letter
15 Febru-
ary.   unto you afore Christenmas of such tydings as I know ;
but I was deceyved, for I went [*weened*] your mastership
had had it to within this ij dayes : and so ye shall have
one other with it both. Sir, if yt please you, these bene
the tydings that I know. The Kyng hat resumyde by
the Parlamentt into his hands all maner patayns, ȝeftys,
offyzs, that he dyd ȝiffe from the ij day of August unto
the iij day of January, and ther be many of his houshold
in yt plesyde with yt. Also he hath resumyde all maner
gyfts, patayns, offezs, that was geven from the xxiij
(*lege* xxxiii) yere of King Herre the vjth, by King
Edward the iiijth, or by King Edward his son the vth,
or by King Richard the iijth, into his hands. Also it is
in actte in the Parlament, that all maner huntyng in
parkes, chases, forest belonging to the Kyng, is made
felony. Also, Sir, the Kyng proposyth northward
hastyly after the Parlament, and it is sayd he purposses
to doe execution quickly ther on such as have offended
agaynst him. Sir, other tydings I know none as yet.
Sir, I besech you recomend me unto both my gud Ladis,
and I send them a pauper of the Rosery of our Lady of
Coleyn, and I have regestered your name with both my
Ladis names, as the pauper expresses, and ye be acopled
as brether and sisters. Also, Sir, these lords and
gentlemen that was attaynted, they gytt no grace, as
yt is sayd. No more, but I besech your mastership to
be gud master unto my father, and I shalbe your bed-
man, with Gods grace, who keepe you evermore in
great joy and felycyte. From London, *in crastino* St.
Valentin. Also, Sir, the King will come with great

company: as it is sayd, with x hundred men in harnesse, February, and with him mo then v or six schore lords and knights. 1486.
Also the Duke of Bedford goes into Wales to se that country. Also it is in actt, that all maner of profycyes is mayd felony. Sir, oder tydings I know none as yet, that be certayne.

22.

[Papal dispensation for the marriage of Henry VII and Elizabeth of York, Campbell's "Materials," i. 392.]

Innocentius episcopus, servus servorum Dei, ad per- 27 March, petuam rei memoriam. Romanus Pontifex, in quo Rome. potestatis plenitudo consistit, inter curas multiplices, quibus rerum negotiorumque varietatibus continue premitur, ad ea ex debito pastoralis officii sibi commissi solicite intendere debet, per quæ inter catholicos principes eorumque vasallos et subditos pacis et quietis coadjuvante Domino conservetur amœnitas, et quæ hiis contraria sunt ac scandala producunt per suæ vigilantiæ studium radicitus extirpentur, prout, personarum, locorum et temporum qualitate pensata, id in Domino conspicit salubriter expedire. Nuper siquidem pro parte carissimi in Christo filii nostri Henrici Septimi Angliæ regis illustris et dilectæ in Christo filiæ nobilis mulieris Elizabethæ claræ memoriæ Edwardi Quarti dicti regni olim regis primogenitæ, nobis exposito quod ipsi, ad submovendum contentiones quæ de regno ipso fuerant inter eorum prædecessores de Lancastria, de qua Henricus ipse rex, et Eboracensis, inclitis domibus et familiis dicti regni, de qua Elizabet, præfati originem trahebant, quarum occasione in regno ipso gravia scandala retroactis temporibus exorta fuerant, desiderabant invicem matrimonium contrahere ; sed quia quarto et quarto consanguinitatis et forsan affinitatis gradibus invicem conjuncti erant, eorum disiderium
3 *

hujusmodi in ea parte adimplere non poterant dispensatione apostolica desuper non obtenta. Nos, tunc cupientes perpetuæ tranquillitati paci et quieti dicti regni quemadmodum decet pium et communem patrem et pastorem omnium Christianorum, providere, ac discordiis, quæ in eo regno diu inter descendentes ex domibus prædictis, cum maximo ipsius regni detrimento, viguerant, finem imponere, illudque futuris dissentionibus occurendo pacatum et quietum perpetuis temporibus reddere, ac christiani sanguinis effusionem evitare, cum eisdem Henrico rege et Elizabetha ut, hujusmodi consanguinitatis et forsan affinitatis impedimentis non obstantibus, matrimonium inter se contrahere, et in eo postquam contractum foret remanere libere et licite possent, per alias litteras nostras gratiose dispensavimus, suscipiendam ex hujusmodi matrimonio prolem legitimam nuntiando. Cum autem, sicut accepimus, Henricus rex præfatus, quanquam non modo jure belli ac notorio et indubitato proximo successionis titulo, verum etiam omnium prælatorum, procerum, magnatum, nobilium, totiusque ejusdem regni Angliæ plebis electione et voto necnon decreto statuto et ordinatione ipsius Angliæ regni Trium Statuum in ipsorum conventu, Parliamento nuncupato, propter hoc publice et generaliter celebrato, jus ipsius regni Angliæ ad ipsum Henricum Septimum Angliæ regem suosque hæredes suo ex corpore procreandos indubitanter de jure pertineret eidemque delatum foret; ad omnes tamen discordias et dissentiones, quæ olim inter illustres Lancastriæ et Eboracensem domos prædictas viguerant, tollendas atque imperpetuum abolendas, ac pro firma et perpetua pace in eodem regno observanda, ad præcipuam et specialem ipsorum Trium Statuum dicti regni requisitionem, assenserit eandem Elizabetham principissam, immortalis famæ regis Edwardi præfati primogenitam et veram hæredem, du-

cere habereque in uxorem, dummodo primitus a nobis
oportuna dispensatio super impedimentis prædictis
obtineretur; nos qui una cum venerabilibus fratribus
nostris Sanctæ Romanæ ecclesiæ cardinalibus omnia
et singula supradicta paterna caritate considerantes,
non solum super matrimonio hujusmodi inter Henricum
regem et Elizabetham principissam præfatos ut præfertur contrahendo, ex causis supradictis per dictas
nostras literas dispensavimus, sed etiam prolem suscipiendam ex eo ad succedendum eisdem regi et Elizabethæ legitimam nuntiavimus, prout in ipsius dispensationis litteris plenius continetur, motu proprio, non ad
Henrici regis aut Elizabethæ prædictorum aut alterius
pro nobis super hoc oblatæ petitionis instantiam, sed
de nostra mera liberalitate et ex certa nostra scientia
hujusmodi dispensationem necnon matrimonium illins
vigore prædictæ contrahendum, seu cujusvis alterius
dispensationis desuper a sede apostolica vel illius pœni-
tentiaria aut legatis sive nunciis, ad id facultatem ab
eadem sede habentibus, forsan obtentæ, pro tempore
contractum, quarum quidem litterarum nostrarum et
aliarum prædictarum dispensationum tenores præsenti-
bus, acsi de verbo ad verbum insererentur, habere
volumus pro expressis, legitimamque liberorum successionem, ac etiam declarationem pronuntiationem et
decretum Parliamenti tam super titulo ipsius Henrici
regis quam super successione liberorum ac hæredum
suorum, necnon omnia alia et singula præmissa auctoritate apostolica præsentium tenore confirmamus et
approbamus, ac robur perpetuæ et inviolabilis vere
firmitatis obtinere eadem auctoritate pronuntiamus,
decernimus atque declaramus; supplemusque omnes et
singulos defectus tam juris quam facti, si qui forsan
intervenerint in eisdem aut aliquo præmissorum. Mone-
musque et requirimus, motu, scientia, et auctoritate

prædictis, omnes et singulos dicti regni incolas, et
ejusdem Henrici regis subditos, cujuscumque gradus,
status, seu conditionis existant, etiam si ducali vel
majori dignitate præfulgeant, eisque et cuilibet eorum
districte præcipiendo inhibemus ne ipsi aut aliquis
eorum novos tumultus, occasione juris succedendi hujusmodi vel quocumque quovis quæsito colore, aut quacumque alia causa, in eodem regno per se vel alium
seu alios movere seu moveri facere, dispensationi,
declarationi, et decreto hujusmodi, aut paci tranquil-
litative ipsius Angliæ regni contraveniendo quovis modo
præsumant sub excommunicationis et majoris anathematis pœna; quam omnes et singuli hujusmodi tumultus novos excitantes vel excitari facientes atque
pacem et regni præfati tranquillitatem posthac nequiter
perturbantes aut prædictis contravenientes exnunc
prout extunc et extunc prout exnunc (cujuscunque,
ut præfertur dignitatis, status, gradus, seu conditionis
existant, etiam si ducali aut majori præfulgeant dignitate) eo ipso incurrant, eosque incurrere et illius vinculo
innodatos et involutos ipso facto esse eisdem motu
scientia et auctoritate volumus, statuimus, decernimus
atque declaramus; a quo quidem excommunicationis et
anathematis vinculo ab alio quam Sede Apostolica præ-
fata, aut cui ipsa sedes id specialiter et specifice commiserit, præterquam in mortis articulo constituti,
nequeant absolutionis beneficium obtinere. Et si (quod
Deus avertat) contingat ipsam Elizabetham, prole ex
dicto Henrico rege non suscepta, vel suscepta non tamen
tunc superstite, decedere ante ipsum regem, eo casu
prolem ex ipso rege Henrico et alia quacunque ejus
legitima uxore ab eo superducenda, in omni jure hære-
ditario regni hujusmodi juxta antedictum ipsius Parliamenti decretum et hujusmodi nostrum, illius appro-
bationem, et confirmationem super hujusmodi decreto et

aliis prædictis, ut præmittitur, factam, succedere debere
similibus motu, scientia et auctoritate etiam decernimus
et declaramus, et ne, in hujusmodi eventum, quispiam
prolis præfatæ successionem hujusmodi, quovis quæsito
colore, impedire, aut (ad) impediendum novos tumultus
in eodem regno per se vel alios excitare vel excitari
facere vel procurare præsumat, sub præfatis censuris et
pœnis, quas omnes et singuli novos tumultus, ut præfertur, ex quacumque causa in contrarium excitantes
aut excitari facientes, eo ipso incurrant, et a quibus ab
alio quam Sede prædicta, et cui Sedes ipsa id specialiter
commiserit, absolvi nequeant, præterquam in mortis
articulo constituti, pari motu scientia et auctoritate
prohibemus. Et quoscunque, tam principes exteros
quam dicti regni incolas, præstantes opem et succur-
sum eidem Henrico regi, ejusve descendentibus in eodem
regno successoribus Angliæ regibus, contra eorum rebelles aut aliqua contra præmissa quovis pacto moli-
entes eisdem motu scientia et auctoritate benedicimus,
et illis, quos sic faciendo in tam justa causa decedere
continget, plenarium omnium suorum peccatorum in-
dulgentiam et remissionem elargimur ; et nichilominus
universis et singulis episcopis, monasteriorum abbatibus,
metropolitanis et aliarum cathedralium et collegiatarum
decanis, archidiaconis, canonicis, parrochialiumque et
aliarum ecclesiarum rectoribus sive vicariis perpetuis,
prioratuum et domorum cujusvis etiam mendicantium
ordinum prioribus et guardianis, et quibuscunque aliis
ecclesiasticis personis exemptis et non exemptis, similibus motu scientia et auctoritate sub interdicti ingressus
ecclesiæ in episcopos et superiores, ac excommunicationis
latæ sententiæ pœna in inferiores ab eis, eo ipso per eos
si non paruerint incurrenda ; mandamus quatenus ipsi
et quilibet eorum, cum pro parte præfati Henrici regis
hæredum et successorum snorum hujusmodi quorum-

cumque fuerint desuper requisiti ; contravenientes hujusmodi et novos tumultus excitantes in ecclesiis suis et
aliis locis publicis, inter missarum et aliorum divinorum
officiorum solemnia, necnon aliis temporibus congruis,
totiens quotiens requisiti fuerint, excommunicatos et
anathematizatos esse et hujusmodi sententias et censuras incurrisse publice nuntient, faciantque ab aliis
nunciari, et ab omnibus arctuis evitari, ac, legitimis
super hiis habendis servatis processibus, censuras et
poenas hujusmodi iteratis vicibus aggravent, contra-
dictores quoslibet et rebelles per censuram ecclesiasticam
et alia juris remedia, appellatione postposita, compes-
cendo, invocato ad hoc si opus fuerit auxilio brachii
secularis ; non obstantibus constitutionibus et ordina-
tionibus apostolicis concessis quoque per nos et Sedem
praefatam privilegiis et litteris apostolicis, quibus illa
etiam si de eis eorumque totis tenoribus, seu quaevis alia
expressio habenda esset, et in eis caveretur expresse quod
illis non intelligeretur unquam derogatum, nisi dum et
quotiens sub certis inibi expressis modo et forma con-
tingeret derogari praesentibus, pro expressis et insertis
habentes quoad praemissa specialiter et expresse dero-
gamus contrariis quibuscunque, seu si eisdem episcopis, abbatibus, decanis, archidiaconis, rectoribus,
vicariis perpetuis, prioribus, guardianis et aliis ecclesiasticis personis ac ducibus et aliis praedictis vel quibusvis
communiter vel divisim a dicta sit Sede indultum quod
interdici, suspendi vel excommunicari non possint per
litteras apostolicas, non facientes plenam et expressam
ac de verbo ad verbum de indulto hujusmodi mentionem,
et qualibet alia dictae Sedis indulgentia generali vel
speciali cujuscunque tenoris existat, per quam praesentibus non expressam vel totaliter non insertam effectus
earum impediri valeat quomodolibet vel differri, et de
qua cujusque toto tenore habenda sit in nostris litteris

mentio specialis. Nulli ergo omnino hominum liceat ^{March} hanc paginam nostræ confirmationis, approbationis, pro- ^{1486.} nuntiationis, constitutionis, declarationis, supletionis, monitionis, requisitionis, inhibitionis, voluntatis, statuti, decreti, prohibitionis, benedictionis, concessionis, mandati, et derogationis infringere etc.

23.

[Margaret, Countess of Oxford, to John Paston, " Paston Letters," iii. 890.]

Right trusti and welbiloved, I recomaund me unto Lavenham, you. And for as moche as I am credebly enfourmed that ^{19 May.} Fraunceis, late Lorde Lovell, is now of late resorted into the Yle of Ely, to the entente by alle lykelyhod, to finde the waies and meanes to gete him shipping and passage in your costes, or ellis to resorte ageyn to seintuary, if he can or maie ;

I therfor hertily desire praie you, and neverthelesse, in the Kinges name, streitly chargie you that ye in all goodly haste endevore your self that suche wetche or other meanes be used and hadde in the poorts, and creks, and othre places wher ye thinke necessary by your discrecion, to the letting of his seid purpose ; and that ye also use all the waies ye can or maie by your wisdom, to the taking of the same late Lorde Lovell. And what pleasur ye maie do to the Kings Grace in this matier, I am sure, is not to you unknowen. And God kepe you.

24.

[Henry VII to John Paston, sheriff of Norfolk and Suffolk, Campbell's " Materials," i. 451.]

Rex vicecomiti Norfolciæ et Suffolciæ, salutem. ^{West-} Præcipimus tibi firmiter injungentes quod statim post ^{minster,} ^{10 June.} receptionem præsentium in singulis locis infra ballivam tuam, tam infra libertates quam extra, ubi magis expediens videris ex parte nostra publicas proclamationes

fieri facias in hæc verba. For as muche as the king
our soveraigne lord, Henry the VIIth, by the grace of
God, king of Englond and of Fraunce, and lord of Irlond,
hathe credible informacioun that there is like to be open
werre had, moved, and stered, as well by water as by
lond, betwene hys cousyn Charles of Fraunce on the
oon partie, and his cousyne the king of Romannys oone
the other partie. Where uppone great navys of bothe
parties bythe in rigging redye to be sette unto the see,
wherthurghe hurte and prejudice, by the riottouse demeanyng of the said navyes, myghte sodenly growe unto
this his realme and to the subgettes of the same if no
remedie wer in that behalf foresene, ordyned, and pro-
vyded, which Gode defend. Our said soveraigne lord,
not willing any such hurte or prejudice to ensue unto
this his said realme, ne unto any of his said subgettes,
willeth, chargeth, and straitly commaundith alle and
everyche of his said subgettis that they and every of
them kepe watche and warde uppone the costes of the
see where nede shuld require, and that all bekyns and
other tokyns uppone the same costes be made redie to
be sette on fyre, and to warne all his said subgettis to be
redie and to comme and defend this his said realme and
his said subgettis, if nede be, according to their duteis,
in maner and fourme as in old tyme in like case bathe
ben used and accustumed. Et hoc sub periculo incumbenti nullatenus omittas.

25.

[Henry VII to the Earl of Northumberland, "Rotuli Scotiæ,"
ii. 471.]

Henrico comiti Northumbriæ datur potestas ad omnes personas de rumoribus in partibus borialibus novæ
insurrectionis incitandæ causa culpabiles arestandum.

Rex carissimo consanguineo suo Henrico comiti
Northumbriæ salutem. Quia credibiliter informamur

quod multa obloquia rumores & imaginationes in partibus June, 1486.
borialibus hujus regni nostri Angliæ nove insurrectionis
incitande & provocande causa per quosdam malivolos
maligno spiritu seductos, timorem Altissimi & sue
ligeantie debitum naturale retrahentes in abusione fideli-
um & diligentium subditorum nostrorum ibidem sedu-
ciose practicantur, seminantur, & alloquentur. Nos in-
convenientia multimoda, que per hujusmodi detractiones
consequi poterunt, amovere cupientes ut tenemur, de
fidelitate & circumspectione vestris plenius confidentes
assignavimus vos & vobis potestatem & auctoritatem
damus & committimus ad scrutandum & inquirendum
viis & modis quibus melius sciveritis aut poteritis de
omnibus & omnimodis hujusmodi malivolis obloquiis
rumoribus & imaginationibus hujusmodi utentibus & de
omnibus aliis in partibus predictis tam infra libertates
quam extra qui aliquid contra ligeantie sue debitum
in populo nostro commotionem & pacis nostre perturba-
tionem ac juris & legis nostri lesionem ibidem aliquo
modo facere committere aut attemptare presumant et
ad omnes illos quos in hac parte tam infra libertates
quam extra reos & culpabiles inveneritis de tempore in
tempus arestandum & capiendum & eos & eorum quem-
libet statim cum capti & arestati fuerint ad presentiam
nostram de tempore in tempus transmittendum trans-
mittive faciendum ut pro eorum punitione juxta eorum
demerita ordinare possimus quod punitio illa aliis cedat
in terrorem taliter imposterum perpetrandum. Et ideo
etc. Damus autem etc. In cujus etc.

26.

[Proclamations against rebels, Campbell's " Materials," i. 512.
    Similar letters were addressed to the sheriffs of Yorkshire and
    Cumberland, cf. *ibid.* i. 304-5].

Rex vicecomiti Northumbriæ, salutem. Præci- West-
pimus tibi firmiter injungentes quod statim post re- minster, 20 July.

ceptionem præsentium in singulis locis infra ballivam tuam, tam infra libertates quam extra, ubi magis expediens videris ex parte nostra publicas proclamationes fieri facias in hæc verba. Where Thomas Broughton, knyght, John Hodylston, knyght, William a Thorneburghe, William Ambrose, and other of their coadherentes, for their grete rebellyons and grevos offensez lately by theyme doone and commytted ayenst the most royalle persone of oure soveraigne lord Henry the VIIth, by the grace of God, kyng of Englond and of Fraunce, and lord of Irland, kepe theyme in hedylle and secret places, and over that have dysobeyed dyvers and many his lettres and pryve seales, to his gret displeasure and disobeisaunz, and to the gret trouble and vexacioun of his true liegemen and subjectes; oure soveraigne lord, willyng the good rule, tranquyllite, and restfulnesse of this his realme and of his subjectes of the same, straitly chargythe and commaundythe the seid Thomas, John, William and William, and their said coadherentez, that they and everyche of them, except Geffrey Frank, Edward Frank,[1] John Ward, Thomas Oter, and Richard Middylton, otherwise called Dyk Middylton, personelly appere before his highenesse, whersoever he be, withyn xl dayes next after this proclamacioun. And yf the seid Thomas Broughton, John Hodylston, Willyam, and Willyam, and theyre seid coadherentes, or any of theyme, except before except, absent themself, and of their obstinacye wille not appere and come to oure seid soveraigne lord as his true and obeyssaunt subjectes, that they and every of theyme so absentyng theymeself be had, taken, and reputed as his grete rebellez, ennemyes and traitours, and so forfeyt their lyvys, landez, and goodes, at the pleasure of the same oure

---

[1] An "Edmond Frank" and others were executed in the fifth year of Henry VII ("Greyfriars' Chron.," p. 25).

soveraigne lord. Et hoc sub periculo incumbenti July, 1486.
nullatenus omittas.

27.

[Submission of the rebels in Yorkshire, Campbell's " Materials,"
i. 535, cf. *ibid.* 541-2].

Rex omnibus ad quos etc., salutem. Sciatis quod nos 6 August.
de fidelitate, industria et circumspectione provida dilecti
et fidelis nostri Willielmi Tyler, militis, ac dilectorum
nobis Johannis Clerk, et Thomæ Lynom, seu eorum
duorum, quamplurimum confidentes, dedimus et com-
misimus ac tenore præsentium damus et committimus
eisdem Willielmo, Johanni et Thomæ plenam potestatem
et auctoritatem ad recipiendum et admittendum ad
obedientiam et ligeantiam nostras omnes et singulos
illos rebelles nostros, qui infra comitatum Eborum, et
præcipue infra dominia nostra de Midelham et Richmond,
nunc existunt, gratiæ et ligeantiæ nostræ se submittere
volentes, quos juxta discretiones suas expediens et
necesse viderint receptandos, ac eis, juxta discretiones
suas, promittendum, et sub sigillis præfatorum
Willielmi, Johannis, et Thomæ concedendum gratiam
et pardonationem nostras tam de vita, terris, bonis et
catallis suis, quam de quibuscumque proditionibus,
rebelionibus, feloniis, insurrectionibus, trangressionibus,
et aliis malefactis et offensis nobis, seu contra nos, per
eos seu eorum aliquem qualitercumque factis sive per-
petratis, necnon ad habendum et perquirendum de
gratia nostra litteras nostras patentes de hujusmodi
pardonatione, sub magno sigillo nostro, eis et eorum
cuilibet de præmissis conficiendas, ei pro eis prosequi
voluerint.

1487.

28.

[Campbell's "Materials," ii. 118.]

8 February.

Writ to Richard Eggecombe, knt, for the arrest of Henry Bodrugan, knt, and John Bemont and others, who have withdrawn themselves into private places in those counties, and stir up sedition and rebellion.

29.

[Henry VII to the Treasurer of the Exchequer, Campbell's "Materials," ii. 148.]

Coventry, 1 May.

Henry by the grace of God, etc. To the treasourer and chamberlains of our Eschequier that nowe be and that for the tyme hereafter shalbe, greting. Wher as of late by thadvyse of the lords and other nobles of our counsaill for diuers consideracions vs and theym moeuyng have seased into our hands all honors, castelles, manoirs, lordships, knights fees, aduousons, and alle othr lands and tenements, with their apportenaunces and all maner fefermes and annuitees by vs late assigned vuto Queene Elizabeth, late wyf to the full noble prince of famous memorye Edward the Fourth, and all and every of the saide honoures castells, manoirs, lordships, knights fees, aduousons, and all other lands, tenements with their appertenaunces, fefermes, and annuities haue assigned vnto our derrest wif the quene. Wherfor we woll and charge you that all suche sommes of money as is comen to your handes of any the p'misses, that ye anon vpon the sight of thies our letters make paiement vnto our said wif, or to suche persone or persounes as she hath and shall appointe and assigne to receyue the same. And from hensfourth yerely in likewise we woll and charge you that alle the issues, proffits, and reuenues that hreafter shall growe of the premisses and euery of them ye paie and deliuer to our said wif and to her receyuors. And also wher we of late haue graunted to our said wif c li. of annuitie yerely to be levied of all the manoirs, lands and tenements sumtyme of William Trussell, knight, nowe in our hands by reason of the nonage of the son and heir of the saide William, to haue to our said wif during the nonage of the saide heir, and as long as the saide manoirs and othr premisses shall abide and remaign in our handes. Wherfor we woll and charge you in likewise that of thissues and proaffits therof comen and that hereafter shall come to your bandes, ye deliuer c li yerely during the saide tyme to our said wif, or to such persone or personnes as she shall appointe to receyue the same. And thies our letters of pryue seall etc.

May, 1487.

30.

[Henry VII to the Earl of Ormonde, chamberlain to the Queen, Halliwell's "Letters of the Kings of England," i. 171.]

Right trusty and right well-beloved cousin, we greet you well, and have tidings that our rebels landed the fifth day of this month in our land of Ireland. Wherefore and forasmuch as we have sent for our dearest wife and for our dearest mother to come unto us, and that we would have your advice and counsel also in such matters as we have to do for the subduing of our said rebels, we pray you that, giving your due attendance upon our said dearest wife and lady mother, ye come with them unto us, not failing hereof as ye purpose to do us pleasure.

Kenilworth, 13 May.

31.

[The Earl of Oxford (?) to Sir Edmund Bedingfield, "Paston Letters," iii. 895.]

Where as I understonde by your late wrytyng un to me, that ye have ryght well endevyrd you to th' execusion of

May.

the Kynges comission and comawndment, in preparyng
your selffe with the jentylmen and other of the contre,
to be redy to do the Kyng servyce, whyche I have
shewid un to the Kynges Hyghnes, so that hys Grace
ys ryght well content and ryght thankfully acceptyth
the same, understondynge the ryght good myndys and
dysposyschon off you and off other jentylmen there
towardes hys Grace. How be yt, hys Hyghnes wull
not as zytte put you to ony further labur or charge, for
somoche as hys rebellys and enemyes be in to Irlande;
neverthelesse hys Grace wull that the contre be redy at
all tymis to do hys Hyghnes servyce up on resonabull
warnyng; for so moche as the Kynges Grace intendythe
to make provysyon to send an armi in to Irlonde in
haaste, nat knowyng as zytte whether that ye, and
other aboute you shall be desyird to bere ony charge
there to or no. And where as yt ys mervellyd that ye
had not the Kynges comysshon, under hys gret seall,
I send yt to you with thys my wrytyng, wyllynge you
nat to procede further to eny exechuson theroff tyll
swyche tyme as ye have other wise in comawndment,
alwey thankyng hertyly the jentylmen, and all other
for ther good wyllys towardes me.

32.

[Sir Edmund Bedingfield to John Paston, "Paston Letters," iii.
894.]

Right wurshypfull cosyn, I recomaund me un to you
as hertly as I can, letyng you wytte I was with my
Lorde Stuarde[1] as on Munday laste paste, by the desyir
of them that I myght not sey ney to. I herde all that
was seyd there, but they gaate non avawntage, wurde,
nor promyse off me; but they thought in asmoche as
they ware the beste in the shere, that every man owghte

[1] Robert, first lord Willoughby de Broke.

to wayte and go with them. Wherto yt was answerd that oure master [the Earl of Oxford], nexte the Kynge, havynge hys commysshon, muste nedys have the jentyl-men and the contre to a wayte upon hym by the vertu of the same; but yt was thought I owght not to obeye no copy of the commysshon, withoute I had the same under wexe, where in hathe ben gret argument, whyche I understoode by reporte a fortnyte paste, and that causyd me to sende unto my lorde to have the very commysshon, whyche he sente me, and a letter [No. 31], where off I sende you the copy here in closyd.

As for you, ye be sore takyn in sum place, seying that ye intende swyche thynges as ys lyke to folow gret mys-cheffe. I seyd I undyrstood non swyche, nor thynges lyke it; and yt ys thoughte ye intende nat to go forthe thys jorneye, nor no jentylman in that quarter but Robert Brandon that hath promysyd to go with them, as they seye.

I understonde Sir Wylliam Bolen and Sir Harry Heydon ware at Thetforde in to Kente ward, but they returnyd in to Norffolk ageyne; I thynke they wull not goo thys jorney, yff the Kynge nede : Ser Harry was at Attylborow on Saterday. I wene he had a vyce there to turne a zen; wher for cosyn, yt ys good to understonde the sertente what jentylmen intende to goo, and be as-suryd to go together, that I may have wurde; my cosyn Hoptun hathe promysyd that he wull be oon. As fore Wysman, he seythe he wull be off the same, but I can have no holde.

Furthermore, cosyn, yt ys seyd that after my lordys departyng to the Kynge ye ware mette at Barkwey, whyche ys construid that ye had ben with the Lady Lovell, but wrathe seyd never well ; and in asmoche as we understonde my lordys plesur, yt ys well doon we dele wysly therafter. And, nexte to the Kynge, I answerd

pleynly I was bownde to do him service, and to fullfylle
hys comaundment to the uttermest off my powere, by
the grace off God, Who ever preserve you to Hys plesur.

33.

[A letter of the Earl of Lincoln, styling Simnel Edward VI,
"York House Books," Vol. vi., f. 97.]

The same day was read a letter from the Earl of
Lincoln lately landed at Furness in the name of that
king calling himself king Edward VI.

By the king.

To our trusty and welbeloved the Maiour, his Brethren
and Commonaltie of our citie of York.

Trusty & wel beloved, We grete you well. And for
as much as we beene comen within this our Realme
not oonely by goddes grace to atteyne our Right of the
same but also for the Relief and Well of our said Realme
you and all other our true subgietts which hath been
greatly Iniured and oppressed in defaute of nowne ministration of good Rules & Justice desire therfor and
in our Right hearty wise pray you that in this behalve
ye woll show unto us your good aides and favours. And
where We and such power as we have broght with us
by meane of travayle of the se and upon the land beene
gretely weryed and laboured it woll like you that we
may have Relief and ease of logeing and vitailles within
our citie there and soo to depart and truly pay for that
that We shall take. And in your soo doing ye shall doo
thing unto us of Right acceptable pleasure And for the
same find us your good and soverain lord at all tymes
hereafter And of your dispositions herin to acertain us
by this bringer. Yevene undre our signett at Masham
the viii day of June.

34.   1487.

[" Chronicle of Calais," p. 1.]

Battayle at Stooke, anno 1487—Ther was slayne the 16 June.
erle of Lyncoln, syr Martyn Swarte, a Fleminge that
came into England with the forsayde erle out of
Flaunders from the dutches of Burgoyne kyng Edward
the fourth's systar, for she was the earles aunt, and she
would have made hym kynge of England, but the erle
was slayne and many other that bare armes that day,
and the lorde Lovell was nevar sene aftar.

35.

[Kingsford's " Chronicles of London," p. 194.]

Also this yere was Stoke feeld, wher by the kynges 16 June.
powre was slayne therle of Lyncolne, Maxten Swart, a
Ducheman, and moche of the people that came w^t theym.
And yet was that tyme false Englisshemen that were
bitwene the ffeeld and the kynges trewe people that
were comyng to hymward, which vntru persons said
that the kyng was fled and the feeld lost; wherby the
kyng was put from moche of his ayde, but yet god was
his helper and sent him the victory.

36.

[Simnel's rebellion, " Rot. Parl.," vi. 397.]

Forasmoch as, the xix^th day of the moneth of Marche 19 March.
last past, John late Erle of Lincolne, nothyng consider- 16 June.
yng the greate and sovereygn kyndnes that oure Sovereygne Leige Lorde that nowe ys, at dyvers sundry
tymes, contynuelly shewed to the said late Erle, but
the contrarye to kynd and naturall remembraunce, his
faith, trouth and allegeaunce, conspired and ymagyned
the most doloruse and lamentable murder, deth and
destruction of the roiall persone of oure said Sover-
4 *

eygne and Leige Lorde, and also distruction of all this
realme, and to perform his said malicious purpose,
traiterously departed to the parties beyond the see,
and ther accompanyed hymselfe with many other false
traitours, and enemyes to our said Sovereygne Leige
Lorde, by longe tyme contynuyng his malyce, prepared
a grete navye for the coostes of Brabon, and arryved
in the portes of Irland, where he with Sir Henry
Bodrugan, and John Beaumound, squier, ymagyned
and conspired the destruction and deposition of oure
said Sovereygne Liege Lorde ; and for the execution of
the same ther, the xxiiiith day of May last passed, at the
Cite of Develyn, contrarie to his hommage and faith,
trouth and allegiaunce, trayterously renownced, revoked
and disclaymed his owne said most naturall Sovereygne
Leige Lorde the Kyng, and caused oone Lambert
Symnell, a child of x yere of age, sonne to Thomas
Symnell, late of Oxforde joynoure, to be proclaimed,
erecte and reputed as Kyng of this realme, and to hym
did feith and homage, to the grete dishonour and despite
of all this realme ; and frome thens, contynuyng in his
malicious and trayterous purpose, arived with a greate
navie in Furnes in Lancashire, the iiiith day of June
last past accompanyed with a greate multytude of
straungers, with force and armes, that ys to saye,
swerdys, speris, marespikes, bowes, gonnes, harneys,
brigandynes, hawberkes, and many other wepyns and
harneys defensible ; and frome thens, the same day, he
with Sir Thomas Broughton, knyght, Thomas Haryngton, Robert Percy of Knaresburgh in the countie of
Yorke, Richard Harleston, John a Broughton, brother
unto the said Sir Thomas Broughton, knyght, Thomas
Batell, James Haryngton, Edward Frank, Richard
Middelton, squiers ; Robert Hilton, Clement Skelton,
Alexander Apilby, Richard Banke, Edmund Juse,

Thomas Blandrehasset, gentilmen; John Mallary of _{June,}
Lichbarowe in the countie of Northampton, Robert ^{1487.}
Mallary of Fallesley in the same countie, Gyles Mallary
of Grevysnorton in the same countie, William Mallary
of Stowe in the same countie, Robert Mannyng late of
Dunstaple, Willyam Kay of Halyfax gentilman; Roger
Hartlyngton, Richard Hoiggessone, John Avyntry, Row-
land Robynson, yomen; with many other ill disposed
persones and traytours, defensible and in like warrely
maner arrayed, to the nomber of viii M persones,
ymagynyng, compassyng and conspiryng the deth and
deposition, and utter destruction of oure said Soveraygne
Leige Lorde the Kyng, and the subversion of all this
realme, for the execucion and perfourmyng of the said
myschevous and traiterous purpose, contynuelly in hos-
tyle maner passed fro thens from place to place, to they
come to Stoke in the countie of Notyngham; where,
the xvi day of June last past, with baners displayed, 16 June.
levied warre ayenst the persone of his Sovereygne and
naturall Leige Lorde, and gave to hym myghty and
stronge batell, trayterously and contrarie to all trouth,
knyghthode, honour, allegeaunce, feith and affyaunce,
intendyng utterly to have slayne, murdred and cruelly
destroyed oure foresaid Leige Lorde and most Cristen
Prynce, to the uttermost and grettest adventure of the
noble and roiall persone of oure seid Leige Lorde, distruction, dishonour and subversion of all this realme.
For the which malicious, compassed, greate and heynous
offence, not alloonly commytted ayen oure said Sovereygne Lorde, but also ayenst the unyversall and comen
wele of this realme, ys requisite sore and grevous
punycion; and also for an example hereafter, that non
other be bold in like wise to offend: . . . [attainder
enacted].

54 THE REIGN OF HENRY VII

1487.

37.

[The Earl of Northumberland to Sir Robert Plumpton, "Plumpton Correspondence," p. 54.]

Richmond, 23 June.

Cousin Sir Robart, I commend me unto you: and wher it is so that diverse gentlemen and other commoners, being within your office at this tyme, hath rebelled against the king, as well in ther being at this last felde, as in releving of them that were against the Kings highnes, I therfore on the kings behalfe strictly charg you, and on myne hartely pray you, for your owne discharg and myne, that ye incontinently after the sight hereof, take all such persones as be within your office, which this tyme hath offended agaynst the king, and in especiall John Pullen and Richard Knaresborough : and that ye keepe them in the castell of Knarsbrough, in suer keepeing, to the tyme be ye know the kings pleasure in that behalfe. And that this be not failed, as ye love me ; and to give credence unto this bearer, and God keep you. Written at Richmound, the xxiii day of Juyn. Se that ye faile not, as ye love me, within the time, and as ever ye thinke to have me your good lord, and as ever I may trust you.

38.

[Henry VII's second parliament. Morton's address, "Rot. Parl.," vi. 385.]

9 November.

Memorandum, quod die Veneris, nono die Novembris, anno regni Regis Henrici Septimi post Conquestum tertio ; videlicet primo die Parliamenti, Reverendissimus pater Johannes Archiepiscopus Cantuarensis, Cancellarius Angliæ, in presentia prefati Domini Regis, sede regia in Camera communiter dicta Crucis infra Palacium suum Westmonasterium sedentis, ac quam plurimum Dominorum Spiritualium & Temporalium, nec non Communitatis Regni Angliæ, ad dictum Parliamentum

de mandatis Regiis convocatorum, ex ipsius Domini November,
Regis mandato, causas convocacionis ejusdem Parlia- 1487.
menti egregie pronunciavit & declaravit, assumens pro
themate hanc seriem verborum, "Declina a malo &
fac bonum, inquire pacem & persequere eam." Super
quo Reipublice curam concernentia quatuor perornate
declaravit : Primum equidem, divertendum esse a malo
quatriplici de causa ; prima, quia omne peccatum turpe ;
secunda, quia omne peccatum injustum ; tertia, quia
omne peccatum inutile ; quarta, quia omne peccatum
est causa pene. Hanc tripartitam causam immo et
cetera que in sermone subsequuntur, particulatim &
distincte, Ciceronis & philosophorum gentilium persuasionibus Veteris & Novi Testamentorum auctoritatibus doctorumque per Ecclesiam approbatorum decretis,
summa maturitate gravitateque profunda congestis, quam
dilucide explicavit ; ut nec proximo aut principi,
patrie aut regno vecordia, secordia, ignavia, violacione
juramenti, pseudo scissitantibus prophetis, aut quavis
alia arte proditoria malum . . . esse, singulis palam
auditoribus reliquit manifeste declaratum. In secundo
principali, persuadebat bonum esse faciendum, nam in
divertendo a malo, culpam . . . & hoc bonum est ; sed
in faciendo bonum, palmam pietatis adquirimus, & id
melius est. Hoc in loco, eos qui non propulsant reipublice injuriam nec defendunt si possint, tam esse in
vicio asseruit, quam si parentes, amicos aut patriam
deserant, imo & proditores sunt veritatis. Tertio
membro principali, inquirere pacem cuique opus per-
oravit, cum pax super omnia prodest ; hujus tamen
pacis due partes reperiuntur principales : una est pax
mala & culpabilis, & ista est triplex ; una sophistica,
que consistit vel in diviciis, vel in deliciis, vel in
fastigiis ; alia pax mala dicitur sophistica & ficta ; tertia
diabolica, que pessima dicitur : & . . . partes sunt

November, 1487. pacis male & culpabilis. Alia est pax bona & laudabilis,
que multiplex est: quedam interna, que est hominis
ad seipsum; alia fraterna, hominis ad hominem; ista
duplex est, nam quedam est domestica, scilicet patri-
familias in domo sibi commissa; secunda, politica,
que reipublice causa geritur, ad quam tria necessaria
requiruntur; primum, Regis & populi ad Deum rever-
entia cum timore; secundum, Regis providentia cum
amore; tertium, subjectorum ad Principem obedientia
cum honore. Hec declaravit planius persuasionibus,
auctoritatibus & Sanctorum decretis, & hoc pro tertio
membro principali. Ultimo membro, persuadebat nos
prosequi pacem, quia cum triplex nos hostis perturbat,
viriliter nos agere oportet, ut confortetur cor nostrum,
quod in celesti propria reperietur, ubi pax & plenitudo
pacis permanet in evum. Amen.

1488.

39.

[Campbell's "Materials," ii. 244.]

Greenwich, 15 Febru-
ary.   Grant to Thomas Lovell, the King's counsellor, and
a knight for the king's body of the lordships and manors
of Bodrugan, *alias* Bodrygan, Tregryan, *alias* Tregrehan,
Tremordret, Trevelen, Pentrasawe, Trethek, Trelowthas,
Treworrak, Cosawys, Trevagh, Resogowe, Dorsett,
Tucoys, Penrynborough, Pencoys, Huntingdon and
Castell Trehillock, Crukevallaunce [or Trukevallance]
Trevisethek, and Trernborough, co Cornwall, and all
lands etc., in those places forfeited by Henry Bodrugan,
knt, the traitor, under an Act of parliament holden 9
November 3 Hen. VII.

40.   1488.

[The expedition to Brittany, Campbell's "Materials," ii. 249, 251.
  There are various similar commissions, including one (*ibid.* ii.
  403) to impress soldiers and provide victuals.]

Commission to John Turbervile, knt, John Moton 19 Febru-
and Roger Hopton, to take the musters etc. of Charles ^{ary.}
Somerset, knt, and of the men in his company, about
to proceed to sea in three Spanish ships in resistance of
the king's enemies.

Commission to Charles Somerset, knt, to be captain
and admiral of the fleet in its present voyage (nothing
in these presents to be taken to the prejudice of John
earl of Oxford, who holds the said office for life).

41.

[Verses presented to King Henry the Seventh at the feast of St.
  George celebrated at Windsor in the third year of his reign,
  Skelton, "Works," ed. Dyce, ii. 387.]

O moste famous noble king ! thy fame doth spring and 23 April.
    spreade,
Henry the Seventh, our soverain, in eiche regeon ;
All England hath cause thy grace to love and dread,
Seing embassadores secke fore protectyon,
For ayd, helpe, and succore, which lyeth in thie elec-
    tyone.
England, now rejoyce, for joyous mayest thou bee,
To see thy kyng so floreshe in dignetye.

This realme a seasone stoode in greate jupardie,
When that noble prince deceased, King Edward,
Which in his dayes gate honore full nobly ;
After his decesse nighe hand all was marr'd ;
Eich regione this land dispised, mischefe when they
    hard :
Wherefore rejoyse, for joyous mayst thou be,
To see thy kynge so floresh in high dignetye.

April,
1488.
Fraunce, Spayne, Scoteland, and Britanny, Flanders
  also,
Three of them present keepinge thy noble feaste
'Of St. George in Windsor, ambassadors comyng more,
Iche of them in honore, both the more and the lesse,
Seeking thie grace to have thie noble begeste
Wherefore now rejoise, and joyous maiste thou be,
To see thy kynge so florishing in dignetye.

O knightly ordere, clothed in robes with gartere!
The queen's grace and thy mother clothed in the same;
The nobles of thie realme riche in araye, aftere,
Lords, knights, and ladyes, unto thy great fame
Now shall all embassadors know thie noble name,
By thy feaste royal; nowe joyeous mayst thou be;
To see thie king so florishinge in dignetye.

Here this day St. George, patron of this place,
Honored with the gartere cheefe of chevalrye;
Chaplenes synging processyon, keeping the same,
With archbushopes and bushopes beseene nobly;
Much people presente to see the King Henrye:
Wherefore now, St. George, all we pray to thee
To keepe our soveraine in his dignetye.

42.

[William Paston to Sir John Paston, "Paston Letters," iii. 904.]

Hening-
ham,
13 May.
Aftyr all dewe recomendacion, pleasyt yow to undyrstonde that my lorde hathe ben with the Kynge in
Wyndesour at Seynt Georgys Feste, and ther at the
same feste were bothe the inbacetours of Breten and of
Flaundyrs, as well fro the Kynge of Romayne as fro the
yonge Duke [Philip]. But I can not schew yow the
certeyn whedyr we schall have with them warre or
pease; but I undyrstonde for certeyn that all suche
capeteyns as wente to the see in Lente, that is to sey,

A NAVAL ENCOUNTER 59

Sir Charlys Somersett, Sir Richard Hawte, and Sir May, 1488.
Wylliam Vampage, makythe them redy to goo to the
see ageyn as schortely as they can, to what intente I
can not sey.

Also, where as it was seyde that my Lord Woddevyle
and other schulde have gone over in to Breten, to have
eyded the Duke of Breten, I can not tell of non suche
eyd. Butt upon that seynge ther came many men to
Sowthehamton, where it was seyd that he schulde have
takyn schyppyng, to have waytyd upon hym over; and
soo whan he was countyrmaundyd, thos that resortyd
thedyr, to have gone over with hym taryde there styll
in hope that they schuld have ben lycensyd to have gone
over; and whan they sey [saw] no lykeleod that they
schuld have lycens, there was ijC. of them that gete them
in to a Breten schyppe, the whyche was late come over
with salte, and bad the mayster sett them a lond in
Breten. And they had nott seylyd not paste vj. leges
butt they aspied a Frencheman, and the Frencheman
mad over to them; and they ferde as thow they wolde
not have medylde with them, and all the Englysche
men went undyr the hetchys, soo that they schewyd
no more but those that came to Sowthehamton with
the schype, to cawse the Frenchemen to be the more
gladder to medyll with them; and soo the Frencheman
burdyd them, and then they that were undyr the hetches
came up, and soo toke the Frencheman, and caryed the
men, schyppe, and all in to Breaten.

Also, ther was ther an inbacetour fro the Kynge of
Schottes, who is now put in grete trobyll be hys son
and other of the lordes of hys londe.

Syr, as I came homewerde be London, I speke there
with Emonde Dormand, and he seyd that he had wretyn
onto yow, but he had none aunswere; wherfor he prayd
me that if I knew ony man comynge towerdes Nor-

whyche, and I wold wrythe on to yow that he ferythe,
if ye see none other dyreccion, that he schall be comittyd
to the Flete.

Also he schewyd me that Herry Wyott wholde fynde
the mene to have yow condemnyd, and recover the obligacion of xl. *li* ageyns yow, and soo he seythe he whote
nott how to doo, for he is halfe dysmayd; he ferythe
lesse that he schall never come home. But he intendythe to plede the obligacion fulfylyd at Norwyche, for
he seythe ther is non other remedy to save yow fro the
condemnacion, tyl that he herythe otherwyse from yow,
whyche he thynketh longe aftyr.

43.

[Giovanni de Giglis, papal collector in England, to Innocent VIII,
" Venetian Calendar," i. 172-3.]

London,
5 October.
Announces receipt of a brief dated 3rd June, desiring
him to apply to the Archbishop of Canterbury, for
redress against some Franciscan Friars, who last Lent,
under pretence of certain indulgences, collected pecuni-
ary alms in England. Had the brief been delivered in
due time, its injunctions would have been most punctually obeyed; but now, as the Friars have long since
betaken themselves with the money to Paris, whence
they came, it cannot be recovered here, though otherwise all parties would have endeavoured, as fitting, to
obey the papal order; and the collector expresses his
belief that the money might be easily recovered from
the convent in Paris, which it was said to have reached.
The death of the Duke of Brittany is reported, and that
well nigh the whole province is already in the hands of
the French, or about to pass into their possession.
Flanders is in the situation known to your Holiness.
At Calais, an English city in France across the Channel,
a French plot has been discovered, about which a great

stir was made at first, but now it does not seem so perilous an affair. The King has reinforced the garrison with 1,500 soldiers, artillery and stores. There are ambassadors here from the Commons of Flanders, and some are also expected from the King of the Romans.[1] Anticipates the renewal of commerce which had been interrupted for many years ; but is apprehensive of war with France. Negociations are on foot for an alliance between the King of England and the King of Castile, and for the marriage of their children ; though this is not yet public. Henry VII expects to hold a parliament shortly, in which all matters will be discussed, and the collector will then transmit more certain intelligence. The Archbishop of Canterbury (John Morton) is prime minister, well adequate to everything, excellently deserving of the Apostolic see and of his Holiness, and worthy of honour. Cannot either omit mentioning the very good will borne towards the Pope by the King's Procurator at the Roman Court, the Bishop of Limerick (John Dunmow), which entitles him to commendation etc.

44.

[Ferdinand and Isabella to their ambassador in England, De Puebla, " Cal. of Spanish State Papers," i. 29.]

After the conclusion of the alliances, the King of England shall bind himself to make war upon the King of France every time and whenever Spain is at war with France, and whenever he is requested to do so ; also he shall not be at liberty to make peace or alliance with France, or any truce, without our express consent, *except* the King of France do *really* give back to the King of England the Duchies of Guienne and Normandy. In that case the said King of England is at liberty to

[1] See below, Vol. ii., Nos. 145-7.

conclude peace and alliance with the King of France.
In the same way we bind ourselves to make war on the
said King of France every time and whenever the said
King of England is at war with France, and we are
requested by him to do so, and will make no peace or
alliance with the King of France, or assent to any truce,
without his (King of England) consent, *except* the said
King of France give back to us our counties of Roussillon and Cerdaña, in which case we shall be at liberty to
conclude peace and alliance with France. These conditions are the same for both parties.[1]

1489.

45.

[Opening of Henry VII's third parliament, " Rot. Parl.," vi. 409.]

13 Janu-
ary.
Memorandum quod die Martis terciodecimo Januarii,
anno regni Regis Henrici Septimi post Conquestum
quarto; videlicet primo die Parliamenti, Reverendissimus Pater Johannes Archiepiscopus Cantuariensis,
Cancellarius Anglie etc. . . . causas convocacionis
ejusdem Parliamenti egregie & notabiliter pronunciavit
& declaravit; assumens pro themate verborum seriem
subsequentem. " Oculi Domini super justos, & aures
ejus ad preces eorum." Super quo Davitico textu
commendatam justiciam ejusque justitie tres species,
communitativam, distributivam, & eam que virtus
specialis est, equalitatem constituens in communita-
cionibus & distribucionibus, palam ac dilucide explanavit;
justitie legalis naturam, imperio, regno, provincie, &
civitati quam maxime perutilem exposuit: Primo
inquam quid sit ipsa; secundo, que ipsius principia;
tertio, quomodo ejus fieri debeat execucio; & quarto,

---

[1] See below, Vol. iii.

qualis finis & effectus justitie, & quomodo necessaria
populi multitudini : triplex asseruit justicie principium;
emanativum, ex quo ejus origo derivatur, puta a Deo,
que Lex eterna merito appellatur, a qua Lex naturalis
ceteris creaturis impressa inextinguibilis dicitur, malo
semper in homine remurmurans, a qua omnia nature
precepta derivata consistant : principium justitie im-
perativum fit Imperator, Princeps & Communitas,
auctoritate quorum subditi ad justiciam legalem ob-
servandam inducuntur, cujus finis est pax temporis ;
media huic fini convenientia sunt legum & statutorum
moderata disciplina, et officiorum moderata distributio,
bonorum premiacio, transgressorum punicio, & cetera
hujusmodi : Principium justitie susceptivum est hominum congregacio, quam ad justitie precepta suscipienda
necesse est esse capacem & aptam : Preterea hec ipsa
congregacio subdita & fidelis suo Principi ipsum ut
tueantur & defendant necesse est, non ut principatum
teneant, quia principatus populi deficit a principatu
& regimine optimatum, & iste quam maxime imperfectus
est in ordine ad regni principatum, in quo unus principatus secundum virtutem, quia & alii imperfecti & de-
fectum includunt, iste optimus est in omnes principandi
modos, assimilati uni Divino, a quo totus mundus ab uno
Creatore gubernatus est. In principatu res publica
viget, justitiaque floret, nam personas non respicit,
munera contempnit, veritatem ubique servat. Hic
justus fortis est, potens & constans in exequendo, justus
hic patiens, nil absque maturitate precipitante puniens,
tranquillus in discutiendo causasque diffiniendo, rigidus
pecc[at]oribus, servans equitatem in decernendo, maturus
& diligens in discuciendo, & ea que ad judicii rectitu-
dinem requiruntur observando, non timore, cupiditate,
premio, odio vel amore, quovis pacto turbatus ; in omni
sua justa accione appetitus rationi obedit, animadverti-

tur enim, quanta illa res sit quam efficere velit, ne major vel minor cura & opera suscipiat, quam causa postulat, & debite & caute moderatur que suam dignitatem attinent : modus enim est pulcherrima virtus, & injusticia pessimum vicium ; remota prefecto justicia, que sunt regna nisi latrocinia ? Siccine ergo extollens justicie naturam & qualitatem membratim, tamen summa cum gravitate, habundantissimis Canonum auctoritat[ibus] & Scripturarum, sua quam protulimus reverendissima dominacio cunctis coram luculentissime explanavit.

46.

[Margery Paston to Sir John Paston, " Paston Letters," iii. 907.]

As towards the brekyng up of the Parlement, many lykelywoodes ther be, that it schuld contynew no wyle, and these be they. My Lord the Archebyschop of Yorke departyd as zysterday, and my Lord of Northethomyrlond schall goo as on Fryday ; and also all schuch folkys as schall goo in to Breten schall be at Portysmouth on Satyrday cum forthnyth, and the Munday after on see bord, at wech seassun the Kyng intentyd to be ther to take the mustyrs.

And as for thos jantylmen that toke schyppyng to a gon over in to Breten up on a fortnyth a goo, that is to sey, Syr Richard Egecum, the cowntroller, Sir Robert Clyfford, Sir John Trobylvyll,[1] and John Motton, sarjent porter, be a ryvyd ageyn up on the cost of Yngland, save all only Syr Richard Egecum, wech londyd in Breten, and ther was in a towne callyd Morleys, wech a non up on hys comyng was besegyd with the Frenchmen, and so skapyd hardly with hys lyff, the wech towne the Frenchemen have gotyn, and also the towne callyd Breest ; how be it the castell holdyth, as we here say.

[1] Turbervile.

And ther be apoyntyd serteyn captens at thys seasun, February, wech be Lord Bruke, Sir John Cheney, Sir John of [1489,] Arundell, Sir John Becham, Sir John Gray, myn broder Awdley, myn unkyll Syr Gylberd Debnam, and Thomas Stafford, and many odyr knytys and esquyrys.

47.

[Ducal secretary to Gian Galeazzo Sforza, Duke of Milan, "Milanese Calendar," i. 248.]

The King of England on the 10th of February took Milan, St. Omer; 3,500 English entered the gates at the third 15 March. hour of the night shouting "Burgundy and England." The French sent a large force against them but it availed them little. The courier who brought the letters from Antwerp was present, also a Venetian merchant. These say that the people of England, that is to say, nobles, clergy and commons, have granted an aid of 300,000*l.* sterling or more than a million ducats for three years to the king, above his ordinary revenue. They did this so that he might make war on France.

48.

[William Paston to Sir John Paston, "Paston Letters," iii. 908.]

As for my Lord Treserer, he was not with the Kynge Sheen, of all the counsell tyme, the whyche was endyd on the 7 March. iij[de] day of Marche. And theder came my Lorde of Northethombyrland the fyrste day of Marche, and departyd the even afore the makyng of thys letter, and hath endentyd with the Kynge for the kepynge owt of the Schottys and warrynge on them, and schall have large money, I can not telle the some for certeyn.

Also ther is an rover takyn at Brystowe, on [*one*] Cowper, as I wene, and he is lyke to be hanged, and he

confessythe more of hys felawis. Also Edward Heestowe
of Dovere is apechyd of treson of many straunge poynts ;
and hys accuser and he were bothe afore the Kynge, and
then they were takyn apert. And he hymselfe confessyd
it that hys accusere accusyd hym of, and many other
thyngs more than he was accusyd of. And he had many
lords and gentylmen to aunswere for hys trowthe and his
demenynge afore tyme, for, as I hard sey, bothe the
Kynge in a maner, nor non of the tother lords nor
gentylmen belevyd not hys accuser, tyl that he confessyd
it hym selfe; and so he is in the Towre and lyke to be
dede.

As for the Kynges comynge into the contre. On
Monday come fortenyght he well lye at the Abbey of
Stratteforde and so to Chelmnsford, than to Syr Thomas
Mongehombrey, than to Hevenyngham, than to Col-
chestyr, than to Ipswyche, than to Bery, than to Dame
Anne Wyngfelds, and so to Norwych ; and there woll he
be on Palme Sunday Evyn, and so tary there all Ester,
and than to Walsyngham. Wherefore ye had nede to
warne Wylliam Gogyne and hys felaws to purvey them
of wyne i now, for every man berythe me on hande that
the towne schalbe dronkyn drye as Yorke was when the
Kynge was there.

Syr, Mayster Sampson recomaunde hym on to yow,
and he hathe sende yow a rynge be Edmonde Dorman,
and besydys that he requeryd me to wryte on to yow
that it were best for yow to purvey yow of some gentyl-
meny thynges ageyns the Kyngs comyng, for suere he
well brynge yow gests i now, and therefore purvey yow
theraftyr. Also he sendythe yow worde that it is my
lords mende [the Earl of Oxford's] that my syster with
all other godely folkys ther abowt scholde acompeny
with Dame Elsebethe Calthrop because there is noo
grete lady ther abowte ageyns the Kyngs comyng, for

my lorde hathe made grete boste of the fayre and goode March
gentylwomen of the contre, and so the Kynge seyd he 1489.
wolde see them sure.

Syr, my lorde hathe sente on to the most parte of the
gentyl men of Essex to wayte upon hym at Chelmnys-
ford, where as he entendythe to mete with the Kynge,
and that they be well apoyntyd, that the Lankeschere
men may see that ther be gentylmen of as grete sobe-
staunce that thei be able to bye alle Lankeschere. Men
thynke that ye amonge yow wol doo the same. Your
contre is gretely bostyd of, and also the inabytors of the
same. I beseche you to remembr my hors that ye pro-
misyd me. God kepe yow.

49.

[Henry VII to the Earl of Oxford, " Paston Letters," iii. 913.]

Right trusty and entierly beloved cousin, we grete you Hertford,
well. Inasmuch as it hath liked God to sende us good 22 April.
tidinges oute of Bretayn, such as we dought not but
that ye be desirous to undrestonde, we wryte unto
you of them as thay be comen to our knowlage, and as
foloueth.

The Lord Malpertuis, now late with us in ambassade
from our dere cousine, the Duchesse of Bretayne,
shippid at our porte of Dortmouth and arrived at Saynt
Powle de Lyon, in Bretayn, on Palme Sonday, at
iiij. after noone, from whens he wrote us the disposicion
and the state of the countre there, and of the landyng,
and the demeanyng of oure armee. We received his
wrytyng on Monday last, at evynsong tyme; and be
cause he was of Bretayn borne, and favorable to that
partie, we ne gave such trust to his tidinges, as was
thought to us surete to wryte to you theruppon.

This daye, aftre High Masse, comyth unto us from
5 *

oute of Bretayne forsaid, and with a new ambassade
from our said cousine, Fawcon, oon of our pursivantes,
that ratifieth the newes of the seid Lord Malpertuis,
which ben these.

After the garysson of Frenshmen in the towne of
Gyngham had certeinte of the landyng of our armee,
thei drewe downe the fabours of Gyngham, and made
thayme mete to defende a siege; but assone as they
ondirstode that our said armee jornayned towardes
theim, thei left the same Gyngham, where our said
armee arrived the Thursday next before Palme Sonday,
and was received with procession, logged and received,
refreshed in the town iiij dayes. And goyng towardes
the said Duchesse, thei must passe to the castell and
borugh of Monconter. In that castell was also a
garnisson of Frenshemen, which incontinently, upon
worde that our said armee drwe towardes theym, the
Frenshmen did cast downe gret parte of the walles, and
fled from thens; in that castell and borugh our seid
armee kept thair Estre. The castell of Chawson, ad-
joyning nere to the towne of Saynt Bryak, was also
garnisond with Frenshmen; that castell they set on
fire, and soo fled in the townes of Henebone and Vannes,
[? which] were garnisond with Frenshmen, which breke
downe the walles of the townes, and putte them selff to
fligth. Th'inhabitantes a bought Brest have layd siege
therunto and goten the Base Courte of the Frenshmen,
or the departyng of our said pursivaunt. The garnson of
the towne of Concarnewe, which is oon of the grettest
strengthes of all Bretayn, was besieged in like wyse, and
drevyn to that necessite that thei with in offerid, ar his
said departyng, to avoyde the towne with staffe in
hande; how that is takyn, or what is more done sithens,
he cannot telle.

Oure said cousine, the Duchesse, is in her citee of

Raynes; and our right trusti knyght and counsellour, April, 1489. Sir Richard Eggecombe, there also, havyng cheeff rule abowte her; and the Marchall of Bretayn arredieth hym to joyne with them in alle haste with a gode band of men. Mony noble men of that countree repair to our said armee to take their partie.

These premisses in substaunce we have be wrytyng, aswell from the cheff capytaynes of our said armee, as from our comptrollour forsaid. And that our said armee, blessed be God, hath among theyme selfe kepte such love and accorde, that no maner of fray or debate hath bene bitwene theym sithens the tyme of thair departing out this our Reame.

50.

[The Earl of Northumberland to Sir Robert Plumpton, " Plumpton Corresp.," p. 61.]

Right hartely beloved Cosin, I comaund me unto Semar, 24 April. you, and for right weighty consideration me moving concerning the pleasure of the Kings highnes, on the behalve of his grace, charg you, and on my desire pray you, that ye with such a company, and as many as ye may bring with your ease, such as ye trust, having bowes and arrowes, and pryvy harnest, com with my nepvew, Sir William Gascougne, so that ye be with me upon munday next comeing at nyght, in the towne of Thirske; not failing herof, as my speciall trust is in you, and as ye love me.

51.

[The Earl of Oxford to Sir John Paston, " Paston Letters," 914.]

Right worshipfull and right welbeloved, I comaunde 30 April. me to you. And for asmoche as it is certeinly unto Hertford. the Kynges Grace shewed that my Lord of Northumber-

land havyng the auctorite to se the Kynges money
levied in the North parties, had knowleche that certeyne
persones of combnes [companies?] wer assembled at
Topclif, and at a nother lordship of his nygh to the same,
saying that they wolde pay no money ; my seid Lord of
Northumberland heryng therof, and that they wer but
naked men, addressed hym self towardes theym withoute
eny harneys in pesible maner, trustyng to have appeased
theym. Howe be it, as hit is seid, that he is distressed
and that they have taken hym or slayne hym ; whiche
the Kyng entendeth to punysshe. I therfore desire
and hertely pray you in all godely haste to be with me
at Hedyngham, there for to knowe more clierly the
Kynges plesir in this behalve. . . .

Also I send to you a comyssion of licence to shepp
corne, which I pray you to do to be proclaymed in all
haste.

52.

[Proclamation of the northern rebels, "Paston Letters," iii. 916.]

To be knowyn to all the northe partes of England, to
every lorde, knyght, esquyer, gentylman, and yeman
that they schalbe redy in ther defensable aray, in the
est parte, on Tuysday next comyng, on Aldyrton More,
and in the west parte on Gateley More, the same day,
upon peyne of losyng of ther goodes and bodyes, for to
geynstonde suche persons as is abowtward for to dystroy
oure suffereyn Lorde the Kynge and the Comowns of
Engelond, for suche unlawfull poyntes as Seynt Thomas
of Cauntyrbery dyed for ; and thys to be fulfyllyd and
kept by every ylke comenere upon peyn of dethe.

And thys is in the name of Mayster Hobbe Hyrste,
Robyn Godfelaws brodyr he is, as I trow.

[Henry VII's proclamation against the northern rebels, Campbell's ' "Materials," ii. 447.]

Writ to the sheriff of Kent, directing him to publish 10 May. in his county and the liberties thereof the following proclamation :—For asmoche   as   the   kynge oure soueraigne lord for the defence of this his realme of England, and for repressing, punysshement and subduyng of his greate rebelles and traitours of the north parties of Yorkshire, which of late in their rebellious and riottous assemble seduciously and traiterously ayenst al humanyte cruelly murdred and distroid his most dere cosyn the erle of Northumberland, a pere of this realme, and of the kyngis most noble blode, and do yet con- tynue their seid riottous assembly, dayly callinge and assemblyng to theym robbers, theves and alle ill disposed persons, and in mayntenaunce of ther tresoun and murdre intende not only the distruccion of the kynges most noble person and of alle the nobles and lordis of this realme, but also the subuersioun of the poletique wele of the same, and to robbe, dispoyle and distroye alle the southe parties of this his realme, and to subdue and brynge to captiuite alle the people of the same,[1] intendeth therfore in his most royalle persoun, atte his greate costes and charges, with his lordis and nobles accompanyed with a greate arme to go toward the seid parts, and put hym selfe in deuour to recounter and subdue theym by Goddis grace of ther seid malicious purpos and intent ; and our seid souereyng lord the king of his blissid mynd and disposicioun willing thes parties nowe in his absence to be suerly kept and de- fendid as welle from the invasions and assaultes of his aduersaries and enmyes outewardes as from alle other rebellious insurreccious and vnlawfulle assembles of

[1] See Introduction.

riottours robbers and vagabundis, straitly commaundeth
and chargeth alle his true liegemen and subiectis that
they and euery of theym be atte alle tymes arredied in
their best and defensible arraye to be attendaunte vuto
the justices of the peas, the shirrive and to other hauyng
ther the kynges auctoryte, and them ayde, assiste and
obeye in alle thingis as apperteignyth fro tyme to tyme;
and that alle gentilmenne reciauntes within the seid
shire, not appoynted to go with the kynge in this viage,
kepe hospitalite and be resident att ther places to see
the gode rule of the contre; and also that all shirriffes,
maiers, bailliffes, constables of townes and villages, and
alle other officers assigned for the conseruacioun of the
kynges pease putt theym selff in deuour to represse, subdue, and make to seace alle maner of insurreciouns riottes
routtes, vnlawfulle assembles, and alle othre mysdoers,
vagabundis, fynders and makers of new rumours and
tydynges, to attach, arrest and ymprisone, and after
ther dimeritis to correcte, and alle other thingis to doo
that shalbe for the conseruacioun of the peas and gode
rule and gouernaunce and defense of the seid shire; and
that they nor none of theym faile this to doo vppone
payne of forfaiture of alle that they may forfaite and
their bodies at the kynges wille.

54.

[Skelton's lament vpon the "Doulourus dethe [28 April] and muche
    lamentable chaunce of the most honourable Erle of North-
    umberlande," "Works," ed. Dyce, i. 6-14.]

I wayle, I wepe, I sobbe, I sigh ful sore
The dedely fate, the dolefulle desteny
Of hym that is gone, alas, without restore,
Of the bloud royall descending nobelly;
Whose lordshyp doutles was slayne lamentably
Thorow treson, again him compassed and wrought,
Trew to his prince in word, in dede, and thought.

Of heuenly poems, O Clyo, calde by name
In the colege of Musis goddes hystoriall,
Adres thé to me, whiche am both halt and lame
In elect vteraunce to make memoryall!
To thé for souccour, to thé for helpe I call,
Mine homely rudnes and dryghnes to expell
With the freshe waters of Elyconys well.

May,
1489.

Of noble actes aunciently enrolde
Of famous pryncis and lordes of astate,
By thy report ar wont to be extold,
Regestringe trewly euery formare date ;
Of thy bountie after the vsuall rate
Kyndell in me suche plenty of thy noblès,
These sorowfulle dites that I may shew expres.

In sesons past, who hathe herd or sene
Of formar writyng by any presidente
That vilane bastarddis in their furious tene,
Fulfylled with malice of froward entente,
Confetered togeder of commonn concente
Falsly to slee theyr moste singuler good lord?
It may be regestrede of shamefull recorde.

So noble a man, so valiaunt lord and knyght,
Fulfilled with honor, as all the world doth ken ;
At his commaundement which had both day and nyght
Knyghtes and squyers, at euery season when
He calde vpon them, as meniall houshold men ;
Were not these commons vncurteis karlis of kind
To slé their owne lord? God was not in their myud.

And were not they to blame, I say, also,
That were aboute him, his owne seruants of trust,
To suffre him slayn of his mortall fo?
Fled away from hym, let hym ly in the dust ;

They bode not till the reckenyng were discust;
What shuld I flatter? what shuld I glose or paint?
Fy, fy for shame, their hartes were to faint.

In England and Fraunce which gretly was redouted,
Of whom both Flaunders and Scotland stode in drede,
To whom great estates obeyed and lowted,
A mayny of rude villayns made hym for to blede;
Unkyndly they slew him, that holp them oft at nede:
He was their bulwark, their panes, and their wall,
Yet shamfully they slew hym; that shame mot them
    befall

I say, ye comoners, why wer ye so stark mad?
What frantyk frensy fyll in your brayne?
Where was your wit and reson ye should haue had?
What wilful foly made yow to ryse agayne
Your naturall lord? alas, I can not fayne:
Ye armyd you with will, and left your wit behynd;
Well may ye be called comones most vnkynd.

He was your chefteyne, your shelde, your chef defence,
Redy to assyst you in euery time of nede;
Your worshyp depended of his excellence:
Alas, ye mad men, to far ye did excede;
Your hap was vnhappy, to ill was your spede
What moued you againe him to war or to fyght?
What alyde you to sle your lord again all ryght?

The ground of his quarrel was for his souerain lord,
The well concerning of all the hole lande,
Demandyng suche duties as nedes most acord
To the ryght of his prince, which shold not be with-
    stoud;
For whose cause ye slew him with your owne hand:
But had his noble men done wel that day,
Ye had not bene able to haue sayd him nay.

But ther was fals packing, or els I am begylde;   May, 1489.
How be it the mater was euydent and playne,
For if they had occupied their spere and their shilde,
This noble man doutles had not bene slayne.
But men say they were lynked with a double chaine,
And held with the comones vnder a cloke,
Which kindeled the wild fyr that made al this smoke.

The commons renyed ther taxes to pay,
Of them demaunded and asked by the kynge;
With one voice importune they playnly sayd nay;
They buskt them on a bushment themselfe in baile to
        bring,
Againe the kyngs plesure to wrestle or to wring;
Bluntly as bestis with boste and with crye
They sayd they forsed not, nor carede not to dy.

The nobelnes of the north, this valiant lord and knight,
As man that was innocent of trechery or traine,
Presed forth boldly to withstand the myght,
And, lyke marciall Hector, he faught them agayne,
Vygorously vpon them with might and with maine,
Trustyng in noble men that were with him there;
But al they fled from hym for falshode or fere.

Barones, knyghtes, squiers, one and all,
Together with servauntes of his famuly,
Turned their backis, and let their master fal,
Of whos [life] they counted not a flye;
Take vp whose wold, for ther they let him ly.
Alas, his gold, his fee, his annual rent
Upon suche a sort was ille bestowd and spent!

He was enuirond aboute on euery syde
With his enemyes, that wer starke mad and wode;
Yet while he stode he gaue them woundes wyde
Allas for ruth! what thoughe his mynd wer gode,

His corage manly, yet ther he shed his blode :
Al left alone, alas he foughte in vayne !
For cruelly among them ther he was slayne.

Alas for pite ! that Percy thus was spylt,
The famous Erle of Northumberland ;
Of knyghty prowes the sword, pomel, and hylt,
The myghty lyon doutted by se and lande ;
O dolorous chaunce of Fortunes froward hande !
What man, remembryng howe shamfully he was slaine,
From bitter weping himself can restrain ?

O cruell Mars, thou dedly god of war !
O dolorous tewisday, dedicate to thy name,
When thou shoke thy sworde so noble a man to mar !
O ground vngracious, vnhappy be thy fame,
Which wert endyed with rede bloud of the same
Most noble erle ! O foule mysuryd ground,
Whereon he gat his finall dedely wounde !

O Atropos, of the fatall systers iii
Goddes most cruel vuto the lyfe of man,
All merciles, in thé is no pite l
O homicide, which sleest all that thou can,
So forcibly vpon this erle thou ran,
That with thy sword, enharpit of mortall drede,
Thou kit asonder his perfight vitall threde !

My wordes vnpullysht be, nakide and playne,
Of [l]aureat poems they want ellumynynge ;
But by them to knowlege ye may attayne
Of this lordes dethe and of his murdrynge ;
Which whils he lyued had fuyson of euery thing,
Of knights, of squyers, chyf lord of toure and towne,
Tyl fykkell Fortune began on hym to growne :

Paregall to dukes, with kynges he might compare, May, 1489.
Surmountinge in honor al erlis he did excede ;
To all countreis aboute hym reporte me I dare ;
Lyke to Eneas benigne in worde and dede,
Valiant as Hector in euery marciall nede,
Prouydent, discrete, circumspect, and wyse,
Tyll the chaunce ran agayne hym of Fortunes duble dyse.

What nedeth me for to extoll his fame
With my rude pen enkankered all with rust,
Whose noble actes show worshiply his name,
Transendying far myne homly Muse, that muste
Yet somewhat wright supprised with herty lust,
Truly reportyng his right noble estate,
Immortally whiche is immaculate ?

His noble blode neuer destayned was,
Trew to his prince for to defend his ryght,
Doblenes hatyng fals maters to compas,
Treytory and treason he banysht out of syght,
With truth to medle was al his holl delyght,
As all his countrey can testify the same :
To sle suche a lorde, alas, it was a great shame !

If the hole quere of the Musis nyne
In me all onely wer set and comprysed,
Enbrethed with the blast of influence deuyne,
As perfytly as could be thought or deuised ;
To me also allthough it were promised
Of laureat Phebus holy the eloquence,
All were to lytell for his magnificence.

O yonge lyon, but tender yet of age,
Grow and encrease, remembre thyn estate ;
God thé assyst unto thyn herytage,
And geue thé grace to be more fortunate !

Agayn rebellyones arme thé to make debate ;
And, as the lyone, which is of bestes kynge,
Unto thy subiectes be curteis and benynge.

I pray God sende thé prosperous lyfe and long,
Stable thy mynde constant to be and fast,
Ryght to mayntayn, and to resyst all wronge ;
All flateryng faytors abhor and from thé cast ;
Of foule detraction God kepe thé from the blast !
Let double delyng in thé haue no place,
And be not lyght of credence in no case.

With heuy chere, with dolorous hart and mynd,
Eche man may sorow in his inward thought
This lordes death, whose pere is hard to fynd,
Algife Englond and Fraunce were thorow saught.
Al kynges, all princes, al dukes, well they ought,
Both temporall and spiritual, for to complayne
This noble man, that crewelly was slayne:

More specially barons, and those knyghtes bold,
And al other gentilmen with him enterteyned
In fee, as menyall men of his housold,
Whom he as lord warshyply mainteyned ;
To sorowful weping they ought to be constreined,
As oft as they call to theyr remembraunce
Of ther good lord the fate and dedely chaunce.

O perlese Prince of heuen emperyall !
That with one word formed al thing of noughte ;
Heuen, hell, and erthe obey unto thy call ;
Which to thy resemblaunce wondersly hast wrought.
All mankynd, whom thou full dere hast bought,
With thy blond precious our finaunce thou did pay,
And vs redemed from the fendys pray ;

THE RISING SUPPRESSED 79

To thé pray we, as Prince incomparable,
As thou art of mercy and pyte the well,
Thou bring unto thy joye eterminable
The soull of this lorde from all daunger of hell,
In endles blys with thé to byde and dwell
In thy palace aboue the orient,
Where thou art Lord and God omnipotent.

May,
1489.

O quene of mercy, O lady full of grace,
Mayden most pure, and Goddes moder dere,
To sorowful hartes chef comfort and solace,
Of all women O flowre withouten pere!
Pray to thy Son aboue the sterris clere,
He to vouchesaf, by thy mediacion,
To pardon thy seruaint, and brynge to saluacion.

In joy triumphant the heuenly yerarchy,
With all the hole sorte of that glorious place,
His soull mot receyue into theyr company,
Thorow bounty of Hym that formed all solace;
Wel of pite, of mercy, and of grace
The Father, the Sonn, and the Holy Ghost,
In Trinitate one God of myghtes moste!

Non sapit, humanis qui certam ponere rebus
Spem cupit : est hominum raraque ficta fides.

55.

[The northern rebellion, Kingsford's "Chronicles," p. 194.]

In this yere the comons of the north made an Insur-reccion and slewe Therle of Northumbirland, of which comones and Rebelles was Capetayne one called John a Chamber.[1] Wherfore the kyng went Northward ; but before the kynges comyng therle of Surrey had distressid

May-Oct-ober.

[1] John a Chambre had served Henry well at Bosworth, and had been rewarded with various offices in Yorkshire; see Campbell's "Materials," i. 36, 431 ; ii. 61, 443.

the Rebelles and takyn the said Capyten, which w^t other of his accessaries was hanged at york. Also this yer was graunted vnto the kyng toward the deffence of Brytayn, whervpon he had exspended grete summys of goodes, the xth peny of mennys landes and goodes meovable; but it was so favorably set by the commyssioners that it amounted nothyng so moche in money as men demed it wolde haue doon. Also in this yere the lord Dawbeney leeftenaunt of Caleys, made a Journey vnto Dykysmewe [1] in fflaunders, leyng sege vnto the said Towne, the which Towne was strongly fortified w^t ffrenshemen and fflemynges; notw^tstondyng the said lord Dawbeney with thassistance of the lord Morley gat hym there great worship, and wan of his Enemyes many greate Gvnnys, which he brought w^t hym to Caleys; but there was slayn vpon the Englissche party the said lord Morley and vpon an C of Englisshemen, and vpon xxviij C. of the other party. And after he cam agayne to Caleys w^t greate Daunger, for the lord Cordes lay fast by w^t a company of xiiij or xv m^l men.

56.

[Extract from the memorial inscription on the Duke of Norfolk's monument at Thetford, Weaver's "Funerall Monuments," p. 386.]

And wythin ten wekes after hys [the Earl of Surrey's] comyng out of the Towre, ther was an Insurrection in the Northe, by whom the Erle of Northombrelond was sleyn in the feld; and also the Citee of York wonne with asawte by force: and for the subduyng of those Rebells the Kynge assembled a grete Hoste of hys sub-

---

[1] Cf. "Chron. of Calais," p. 2: "The battayle of Dickysmewe was on the xiii day of June, that day beyng satterday, and the 4 yere of Henry the Seventh, anno 1489, where the Ynglishe men had great vyctorye, for there was taken and slayne a greate nombar, and there was slayne the lorde Morley an Englishe mane."

gettis, and toke his journey towards them, from the May, 1489-
April, 1492. Castell of Hertford ; and the seid Erle of Surrey made chief Captain of his Voward, and apoynted under hym in the seid Voward the Erle of Shrewesbury, the Lord Hastyngs, Sir William Stanley, then beyng the Kyng's Chambrelayn, Sir Rice ap Thomas, Sir Thomas Bouser, Sir John Savage, Sir John Rysely and divers other.

And when this Jorney was doon the Capiteynes of these Rebelles, and many other of them were put to execution. And for the syngular truste, that the Kynge had to the seid Erle, and the activyte that he saw in hym, he left hym in the Northe, and made hym hys Lyvetenant-generall from Trent Northward, and Warden of the Est and Middle marches of Englond ageynst Scotlond, and Justice of the Forests from Trent Northwards. And there he contynued ten yeres and kepte the Country in peace, wyth Policy and many paynes-takyng wythoute whyche it wold nat have been, for that the Countrey had been so lately ponyshed, and nat wythoute desert.

And thus he dide the whole time of ten yere, savyng in the second yere of hys beyng, there was an Insurrection in the West part of the Country, with whom the seid Erle, wythe the helpe of the Kyngs true Subgetts, fought in the felde, and subdued them at Ackworth,[1] besides Pomfrett. And besydes divers of them that were slayne in the Felde, he toke the Capytaynes, and put them to execution ; and the residue he sued to the Kynges Hyghnes for ther Pardones, whiche he obteyned, and wan therby the favour of the Countrey.

[1] See also "Plumpton Correspondence," pp. 96-7, 265. This inscription is the only authority for this battle or affray at Ackworth, except the vague allusion in the "Plumpton Correspondence". The inscription is also given in Dugdale's "Baronage," ii. 269. The date of Ackworth field was apparently April, 1492.

1490.

57.

[A "Writing[1] sent from oon John Tailour, your Rebell and Traitour, beyng in Normandy in the service of your auncien Enemye of Fraunce the tenoure of whiche Writing herafter foloweth," "Rot. Parl.," vi. 454.]

Rouen, 15 September. Right Reverend and Worshipfull Sir, I hertely recomaunde me unto you, prayeng you to take to your remembraunce the wordes we spake togeders in Seynt Peters Churche of Excestre, and at the Blak Freres, when ye were at your brekefast, and y made myn erand unto you, for seyng of evidence. Sir, ye shall understand, that the Kynges grace of Fraunce, by th' advyse and assent of his Counsell, woll aide and support your maisters son to his right, and all his lovers and servants, and take theym as his frendys, bothe by land and by water, and all they may well be assured savely to come unto Fraunce, both bodyes and goodes, and suche as have no goodes they may come bedre and be releved, if they be knowen for true men to the quarell; and over that, he woll geve help of his own subgiettes, with shippes, gold and silver, to come into England, and with suche nombre as shall be thought by you, and by other youre maisters sonnes freinds, necessarie and behofull for his helpe and sucour, and they to be redy and land at such tyme and place, as ye with othre shall appoynt; and therfore I pray you shewe this matier unto suche as ye knowe well woll geve their gode counsell and assistance to the same; and if ye may, bring the answer of the mynde theryn your selfe, or ellis send it by Thomas Gale of Dertemouth; and ye may speke

---

[1] Addressed to John Hayes, late of Tiverton, Devon, and received by him at Winchester on 26 Nov., 1490. John Taylor fell into Henry's hand many years later (see below, pp. 208-9).

with him by the same token, that he and y comyned togeder of matiers touching your maisters sonne in Stokingham Park, when Sir John Halwell hunted theryn ; and be you not aferde to shewe all youre mynde unto hym, for he is trusty in this matier. Sir, ye muste come youre self, or send him, or ellis send Maister John Atte Will, whom ye well trust, and y also yf ye aunswere for him, or ellis ye may send John Aleyne of Pole, whom ye trust and y also, or John Affright, servant to my Lady Warwyk, or any other trusty body of your knowlege. I pray you make laboure unto my Lady Warwyk to write to the King of Fraunce, and to suche of his Counsell as she is best accointed with ; and that doon, she and ye, and all other of our partie, shall have all thinges necessarie as is afore rehersed. And if therto any man of gretter name, that thinketh he may owe more goode here then at home, he may suerly, come hedir and welcome, and yit it nedith not to send hedir any grete nombre, for here shall be enough redy furnished of all thinges, and the King and his Counsell sey they woll aske nothing in recompence, but to do it for the wrong he dyd, in making Henry Kyng of England, and for the gode will he oweth unto the sonne of youre maister, for they be nere of kyn. Sir, ye remembre, that the token betwene you and me is, that such as y shall send unto you, shall take you by the thombe, as y dyde you, when ye and y wente up out of the Cloister into Seynt Petres Chirche, and by that token ye shuld be assured of all thinges, and fere nothing, and so ensure ye all youre frendis and myne. Sir, ye shall here by othre frendis. Sir, the convenable tyme of helpe is come, and therfor nowe endevour youre self, and put to your hand, and spare for no cost, for there shall be helpe in thre parties oute of Royalme, but here is the place most metely for you, and where ye shall lak nothing ; the berer herof

6 *

shall shewe you more, to whome y pray you give credence. Writen att Roan in Normandye, the xv day of
Septembre, by youre old accoyntaunce, John Tayllour
th'elder.

58.

[The first coinage of sovereigns, Campbell's "Materials," ii. 522.]

29 October. The King to his trusty counsellor Giles, Lord Daube-
nay and Bartholomewe Rede, of London, goldsmith,
masters and workers of the king's moneys within the
tower of London :—Greting. We for certain considera-
ciouns vs moeving wol and charge you that of suche
bolion of gold as shalbe brought vnto you into oure
mynte within oure seid toure ye make or doo to be
made a new money of gold acordyng to the prynte and
fourme of a pece of leed to thies oure presentes lettres
annexed ; and the same money of gold to be of the
fynesse of the standard of oure moneys of gold of this
our realme of England, according to the indenture betwene vs and you in that partie made ; and we wol that
euery pece of gold of the said money be of double the
weght of the pece of gold called royalle, of which peces
xxii and an half shal make a pounde weght toure ; and
the same pece of gold shalbe called the soueraign, and
shal go and haue cours in receipte and paiement of money
for xxs. sterlinges ; and in euery pounde weght of golde
that shalbe made within our said toure, we wol that ye
make or warraunte and discharge at al tymes anenst vs
in this behalue.

59.

[Treasonable practices, "Rot. Parl.," vi. 436.]

Forasmoche as John, Abbot of the Monastery of our
Lady of Abyngton in the shire of Berk', John Mayne of
the same towne, Christofre Swanne late of the same

towne and shire Yoman, the first day of January
[1487], the second yere of the raigne of the Kyng oure
Soveraigne Lorde Kyng Henry the VIIth, at the said
towne of Abyngton, falsly and traiterously compassyng,
conspiryng and ymaginyng the destruction of the Kyng
our said Sovereygne Leige Lorde, and the subversion of
all this his Realme, falsly and trayterously assemblyng
them togeder, assented, covenaunted and agreed, that
the said John Mayne shuld departe out of England, to
the helpe and ayde of John then Erle of Lincoln then
beyng a great rebell, enemy and traitour to the Kyng
oure said Sovereygne Lorde, and for the perfourmans of
that traiterons purpose and congeiture, the said Abbot
gave to the said John Mayne a certeyne somme of
money; and ferthermore the said John Mayne about
the first day of December, the vi[th] yere[1] of the reigne
of the Kyng oure Sovereigne Lord, at London, had
communycation with oon Thomas Rothwell, otherwise
called Thomas Even, late of London, priste, and then
and ther confedred, conspired, falsly and trayterously imagined and commoned, howe they myght have taken out
of the Kyng oure said Sovereigne Lords warde, Edward
the Erle of Waruyk, then thynkyng that he had beyn
where indede he was not, intendyng, imagynyng and
conspiryng by that, to have made grete dyvysion,
rumour and insurrection within this realme, and to
have levyed warre ayenst the Kyng oure said Sovereigne
Lorde, to th'entent to have destroyed his moost royall
persone, and utterly to putt this hole realme in confusion : upon the whiche communycation, the said John
Mayne, and the said Thomas, went to the house of one
Henry Davy in London, and there they mete with the
said Herrye, and Edward Frank, and then and there
they four persones had ferther communycation howe

[1] A mistake in "Rot. Parl." for "v[th] yere," i.e. 1489.

they myght perfourme and put in execution the said
false and traiterons purpose; and there they iiii concluded to take th'advyse of the said John, Abbot of
Abyngton, to perfourme the said coursed and false dede.
Wherupon they sent to the said Abbot the said John
Mayne, the which John Mayne came to the said Abbot,
and told to hym, that a preste shuld come to hym, that
shuld shewe to hym the clerness of the said compassed
treason; wherof the said Abbot was joyous, and bad
the said John Mayne chose what he would drynke, and
said this acte must be wisely wrought, and when yt is
done, ther must be a lettre left in maner as yt were
lost, in the place where the said Erle shuld be, directed
to some good felowe, that he shuld come unto theym to
Colchester.   And after the said John Mayne brought
the said prest to the said Abbot, when the Abbot sawe
hym, he told the same John Mayne that he would not
shewe his mynd unto the said preste, for he saw by
hym, that he was but light witted, but he said he would
shewe his mynd in this mater to Edward Frank, when
he came to London.   And also the said John Mayne,
Christofre Swanne, Thomas Rothwell, otherwise called
Thomas Even, preste, the xxth day of Decembre, the
said vth Yere, at the said towne of Abyngton, in like
wyse confedred, conspired, and trayterously imagyned
and compassed the meanes how they myght have perfourmed the said false, coursed and trayterous dede, intendyng therby to have made warre and great rebellion
ayenst the Highnes of the Kyng our said Sovereigne
Lorde, intendyng and compassyng the destruction and
deposition of his most roiall persone, and the subversion of all this realme.   And for the perfourmyng of
that false and traiterous purpose, Dan' Myles Salley,
comen to the said Abbot, delivered to the forsaid
Cristofre Swanne then, and then and ther, a certain

somme of money, to execute and perfourme the false January,
and trayterous purpose aforsaid; the which Cristofre, 1490.
then and there delyvered the same somme of money
with more, to the said John Mayne; and the said John
Mayne, then and there delivered the said somme of
money, to the said Thomas Rothwell, preste, for the
performance of the said false and traiterous intent.

1491.

60.

[Execution of Sir Robert Chamberlain, Kingsford's "Chronicles,"
p. 195.]

In March was sir Robert Chambyrlen, knyght 12 March.
Rayned and adiugged at Stratford of the Bowe, and
then brought vnto the Tower.   And from thens he and
other ij were drawen from Westmynster vnto the Tower
hyll; where the ij persons were saued, and he was beheded.[1]

61.

[Opening of Henry VII's fourth parliament, "Rot. Parl.," vi.
440.   Parliament met on 17 October, sat until 4 November,
and was then prorogued until 26 January, 1492.   It was dissolved on 5 March.]

Memorandum, quod die Lune, decimo septimo die 17 October.
mensis Octobris, anno regni Regis Henrici Septimi
post conquestum septimo; videlicet, primo die Parliamenti, Reverendissimus Pater Johannes Archiepiscopus
Cantuariensis, Cancellarius Angliæ, etc. . . . pronunciavit & declaravit; assumens pro themate " Expectavi-
mus pacem & non est bonum, & tempus curacionis &

---

[1] "Dict. Nat. Biogr.," x. 7; his son Sir Edward obtained a re-
versal of the attainder on March, 1531.

ecce turbacio ". Jeremie ca' xiiiiº. In quo Gaii Salustii
viri illustris in bello Jugurtino historiam lucide per-
lustrans, Jugurtham pre omnibus fama laborantem,
sed libidine dominandi, premissis paccionibus dulcibus-
que eloquiis pacem pre se ferentem similatam & fictam,
ac consanguineos Romanosque juramento inter se
astrictos armorum strepitu violata fide jugulantem,
Senatus Romanus seclusa mora punire decrevit, & suas
interponere partes, snorum confederatorum neces vindi-
care, antequam in illud regnum Numidarum Jugurtha
confirmatus esset. Eadem nobis causa belli est contra
Francorum Regem, qui similata fronte fide mortua
nostros confederatos devicit; sed temporisare facta
summe prudencie est, & negligencia temporis plurima
sepenumero emergunt pericula. Sed tempus pacis
belli tempore laudabilius est, nisi pax fantastica, sophistica vel diabolica fuerit; ad pacem ergo laudabilem,
internam fraternam, domesticam & supernam summarie
sua dominatio reverendissima auditores invitans, omnes
politicam amplexari decrevit. Quo fit ut bellum spiri-
tuale inire possumus cum Apostolico, & corporale,
non presumptuosum, non temerarium, non voluntarium,
sed bellum corporale justum, universale & publicum.
In quo quinque memorie commendanda sunt primo,
ut arma capiens sit persona non ecclesiastica. Secundo, quod bellans non cupiditate nec crudelitate ulciscendi
ductus sit. Tertio quod sit ex causa justa. Quarto,
quod sit urgente necessitate & manifesta lesione,
hostibus non paratis ad satisfaciendum. Quinto, quod
bellum ejus fiat auctoritate qui id licentiare valeat.
Quare cum Princeps & Rex noster Anglie invictissimus
Francorum Regi pacem obtulit, nec optinere valuit,
precemur Deum ut in hoc justo bello felicem sortiri
possit effectum. Amen.

62.   1491.

[Attainder of Sir Robert Chamberlain and Richard White, "Rot. Parl.," vi. 455.]

Forasmoche as Sir Robert Chamberleyn, late of Berk- 17 October.
ing in the Shyre of Essex, knyght, and Richard White,
late of Thorpe beside Billingforde in the Shire of Norffolk, gentilman, the xxiiii day of Auguste, [1490] and
the said Sir Robert the xvii day of January, [1491] the
vith yere of the Reigne of oure Sovereign Lord the
Kyng that now is, at Berking aforsaid, traitorously
ymagined and compassed the dethe and destrucion of
oure said Sovereign Lord, and also the subversion of all
this roialme, then and there traitrously levyed guerre
ayen oure said Sovereign Lord, and adhered theym
traitrously to Charles the Frenche Kyng, auncient
enemye to our said Sovereigne Lord and this realme,
ayen their duetie and alligeaunce. Be it therfore ordeyned and enacted by auctorite of this present Parliament, that the said Robert and Richard stande and be
atteynted of High Treason. . .

1492.

63.

[William Paston to Sir John Paston, "Paston Letters," iii. 929.]

Aftyr all dew recomendacion, lyke it yow to undyr- London, 18
stond that Syr Herry Heydon schewyd me that it is February.
agreyd be Syr Edmond Bedyngfeld, that the mater be-
twyx hym and my brodyr Yelverton, schalbe comynd
at Norwyche, and there a dyreccion to be takyn in the
same mater, mete for them bothe.
Syr, the Kyng sendythe ordynaunce dayly to the see
syde, and hys tentes and alys [pavilions] be a makyng
faste, and many of them be made; and there is also

grete provysyon made be gentylmen that scholde goo
wythe Hys Grace or hors, harnese, tents, halys, gardy-
vyans [*knapsacks*], cartes, and othyr thynges that scholde
serve them for thys jurney that the Kynge entendythe
to take on hand, soo that belykelyod Hys Grace wolbe
goyng sone upon Ester.   And so I entende, aftyr that I
here heaftyr, to goo to Caleys to purvey me of harneys,
and suche thynges as I schall nede besydes hors, undyr
that forme that my costes schalbe payd fore   ⸱

Syr, I am as yet no bettyr horsyd than I was whan I
was wythe yow, nor I wote not where to have none,
for hors flesche is of suche a price here that my purce
schante able to bye one hors ; wherfor I beseche yow to
herkyn for some in youre contre.   Syr, my cosyn, John
Heydon, tolde me that the Prior of Waburnes horse was
rially amendyd, and that the Abott of Seynt Benetes
schewed hym there was a bay hors of a persons nyght
onto Seynt Benetis, and that the abot wolde gete hym
for my cosyn Heydon at a resonable price.   Syr, my
cosyn, John Heydon, woll geve me hys entrest in that
hors, if the abot have bowght hym, and so ye may lete
the abot have knowlege ; and if he have not bowght
hym, I beseche yow sende to see hym, for I wote not
how to do withowt youre helpe aswell in horsyng of me
as in other thynges.

At the makyng of thys lettyr, I cannot acerteyn yow
what person it is that owythe thys hors.   If I can know,
I wolle send yow worde in a bylle I sende to Thomas
Jullys be the berer herof.

Syr, as towardes my jurney to Caleys, the whyche I
entende[d] to have tane at my laste beyng with yow, it
was so, I was dysapoyntyd of Thomas Dey and an other
man I scholde have had be hys menys, as ye have had
knowlege of or now ; and also I had went [*weened*] to
have had folkys a mette with me at Hedyngham, whyche

ded nolt.   My lorde [Oxford], seyng me dysesyd, and February, 1492.
also none otherwyse purveyd, wyllyd me in ony wyse to
tary on tyl hys comyng to London, and sent myn excuse
to my Lorde Dawbeney undyr thys forme how that I
was sore disesyd ; notwythestondyng I was welewyllyd
to have come to fulfyll my promesse, but he cowde not
sofyr me, seyng me soo dysesyd ; and so my Lord Dawbeney was sory of my dysese and content that I taryd.

Syr, I beseche yow to holde me excusyd for kepyng of
Thomas Lynsted, yowr servaunt, and hym bothe.   It is
soo that he and I bothe have ben in hand with my unkyll
for hys mater, and yett wee have hym at noo good poynt ;
but I troste we schall have.   Syr, if I take thys jurney
to Caleys, I moste beseche yow to forbere hym lenger,
and if I goo not to Caleys, thow I be lothe to forbere
hym, yet I schall brynge hym with me schortly in to
Norfolke, ye to have hym, if ye lyste, with the Grace of
God, Who have yow in kepyng.

64.

[Conquest of Granada, and Treaty of Étaples, Kingsford's
" Chronicles," p. 197.]

This yere the vj day of Aprill was shewed by my lord 6 April.
of Caunterbury, Chaunceler of England, how the kyng
of Spayn had conquerid the Cyte and Contre of Grenade,
and aftir was there a Solempne procession generall and
a noble Sermon.   And after *Te Deum* solempnely song
in Seint powles quyre.   And in the said Sermone was
shewed, that the same yere in Rome was ffounden in
an old wall a pese of the holy Crosse.

In this yere the ix^th day of September the kyng de- 9 Septem-ber.
partid from Grenewich towards the Sees side ; and the
vj day of October he toke shippyng at Sandewiche, and
the same day landed at Caleys.   Item the ix^th day of 9 Novem-ber.
Nouember was Red in the Guyldehall before the Mayr,

Aldermen and Comon Counsaill, a letter sent from the
kyng vnto the Cite, of the conclusion of the pease
bitwene the kynges of England and of ffraunce for the
terme of either of their lyves and for a yer after of hym
that lengest lyved. And for to haue this peas establis-
shed the ffrensshe kyng graunted vnto our souerayn
lord to be payed in certayn yeres vij C and xlv M¹ Scutis,
[= *écus*] which amounteth in sterlyng money to an C
and xxvij M¹ vj Clxvj li. xiijs and iiijd. And aftir it was
showed by the mowth of my lord Chaunceler in powles
Chirch, wher aftir was songyn wᵗ greate solempnyte
Te Deum, wherat the Chaunceler was present.

65.

[" Chronicle of Calais," Camden Soc., p. 2.]

Kyng Henry the Seventh landyd at Caleys toward
Boleyne the 2. of Octobar in the 8 yere of his raigne,
and in anno 1492. And the 19. of Octobar he departyd
from Caleis toward Boleyne with his army, and lay the
first night Sandynfelde, the next night at Margyson,
and ther met with hym therle of Oxenforde, chefe
capytayne of the forwarde, then comynge from the
betinge downe of the towne of Arde, and with the erle
of Oxenforde cam the erle of Shrowesbery, the erle of
Devonshire, the erle of Suffolke, the erle of Essex, the
lorde Gray [of] Codnor, the lorde Straunge, the lorde
Powise, the lorde Hastings, the lorde Awdley, the lorde
Latimere, the baron of Dudley, and dyvers knyghts
and esquiers, and laye the same night at Margyson
before the kinge, and the next night bothe wards lay at
Wymelle, and the next night both ostes cam before
Boleyne, and there at the seige still unto viij day of
Novembar nexte folowyng. Than the Frenche kynge
sente unto oure sovereigne lorde kynge of Englande be

the lorde Cordes, chefe capitayne under the Frenche October-
kynge, beschinge the kynge of England of his pease, November, 1491.
whiche the kynge of England graunted upon a condi-
tion that the Frenche kynge shuld paye every yere lii
thowsand crownes to the kynge of England during
bothe theyr lyves; the Frenche graunted thereunto,
and the kynge of England brake up his sege and cam
agayne to Calleys, the xij of November, and the xvij
day he toke his shipe and sayled to Dovar.

66.

[Henry VII's return from France, Kingsford's "Chronicles,"
p. 197.]

In this yere, the xvij^th day of December,[1] the kyng 17 Decem-
landed at Dovir, and so came to Grenewich wher he ber.
rested hym; and the Satirday before Cristemasse he
he was met w^t the Mayr, Aldermen and certayn
comoners at blakheth clothed in violet, and so brought
through the Cite and so to Westmynster.

1493.

67.

[Henry VII to Sir Gilbert Talbot, Halliwell, "Letters," i. 172-3.]

Trusty and well-beloved, we greet you well; and not Kenil-
forgetting the great malice that the Lady Margaret of worth, 20 July.
Burgundy beareth continually against us, as she showed
lately in sending hither of a feigned boy, surmising him
to have been the son of the Duke of Clarence, and
causeth him to be accompanied with the Earl of Lincoln, the Lord Lovel, and with great multitude of Irish-

---

[1] This date is adopted by Hall, Stow, and other chroniclers. The
"Chronicle of Calais," however, has 17 November, and there is
nothing to account for Henry's delay at Calais for a whole month.

men and Almains, whose end, blessed be God, was as
ye know well. And foreseeing now the perseverance
of the same her malice, by the untrue contriving eftsoon
of another feigned lad called Perkin Warbeck, born at
Tournay, in Picardy, which at first into Ireland called
himself the bastard son of King Richard; after that the
son of the said Duke of Clarence; and now the second
son of our father, King Edward the IVth, whom God
assoil; wherethrough she intendeth, by promising unto
the Flemings and others of the archduke's obeissaunce,
to whom she laboureth daily to take her way, and by
her promise to certain aliens, captains of strange nations,
to have duchies, counties, baronies and other lands,
within this our royaume, to induce them thereby to
land here, to the destruction and disinheritance of the
noblemen and other our subjects the inhabitants of the
same, and finally to the subversion of this our royaume,
in case she may attaine to her malicious purpose, that
God defend. We therefore, and to the intent that we
may be alway purveied and in readiness to resist her
malice, write unto you at this time; and will and desire
you that, preparing on horseback, defensibly arrayed,
four score persons, whereof we desire you to make as
many spears, with their custrells, and demi-lances, well
horsed as ye can furnish, and the remainder to be
archers and bills, ye be thoroughly appointed and ready
to come upon a day's warning for to do us service of
war in this case. And ye shall have for every horseman
well and defensibly arrayed, that is to say, for a spear
and his custrel twelvepence; a demi-lance ninepence;
and an archer, or bill, on horseback, eightpence by the
day, from the time of your coming out unto the time of
your return to your home again. And thus doing, ye
shall have such thanks of us for your loving and true
acquittal in that behalf as shall be to your weal and

honour for time to come. We pray you herein ye will July, make such dilligence as that ye be ready with your said $^{1493.}$ number to come unto us upon any our sudden warning.

68.

[Perkin Warbeck to Isabella of Castile, "Spanish Calendar," i. 85 ; this letter is printed verbatim in " Archaeologia," xxvii. 199.]

His elder brother, the Prince of Wales, son of King 8 Septem- Edward, had been assassinated. He had himself been $^{ber.}$ delivered to a gentleman who had received orders to destroy him, but who, taking pity on his innocence, had preserved his life and made him swear on the sacraments not to divulge, for a certain number of years, his name, birth and lineage. That being done he had sent him away under the care of two persons, who were at once his jailors and governors. Had led a wandering life, in the midst of perils and misery for the period of nearly eight years, during which time his governors had kept him in concealment in different parts of the world, until at last one of them died, and the other returned to his own country. Was left alone while still almost a child. Passed some time in Portugal, then went to Ireland, where he was recognised and joyfully welcomed by the Earl of Ormond and the Earl of Kildare his relatives. Was equally well received by many of the chief men.

The King of France then sent for him, promising him aid against Henry Richmond, usurper of the Crown of England. Was shown the greatest honour by the King of France, but the promised aid was not given. Went, therefore, to the Duchess of Burgundy, sister to his father, who, moved by her humanity and virtue, welcomed him with open arms. The King of the Romans, his son, the Duke of Austria, the Duke of Saxony, and the Kings of Denmark and Scotland, re-

September,
1493. ceived him in the same way, and sent ambassadors to
him, proffering him friendship and brotherhood. Many
of the chief personages in England, whose indignation
had been roused by the iniquitous conduct of the
usurper, Henry Richmond, had done the same in secret.
Hopes Queen Isabella who is not only his relative, but
also the most just and pious of Princesses, will have
pity on him, and intercede on his behalf with her
husband, entreating that assistance may be given him.
Promises that if he regain his kingdom he will be grateful, and a better ally of theirs than King Richard had
been.

From the town of Andermund, 8 Sept. 1493.

(Signed)   RICHARD PLANTAGENET.

Second son of the late King Edward and Duke of
York. Richard.

69.

[Riot against the Steelyard, Kingsford's "Chronicles," p. 197.]

7 October.   Also this yere the Tewesday before Seynt Edwardes day in the mornyng, at vj of the Clok, was certayn
seruauntes of the Mercers assemblid and went downe
to the Styleyerd, and there wold haue dispoyled the
place; and, or the Mair come and the Shireffes, there
was gadred vnto theym a greate people, some to take
their parte and some to behold ; but the marchauntes
had warnyng therof and kept the gatis shet ; and assone
as the Mayr cam, anoon they fled aswell from the water
as from the gate.   And dyvers were takyn and sent to
pryson.   And after searche made it was found that ij
of John Pyctons seruauntes were begynners of this
mater, which were takyn ; and after theyr examynacion
they accused other parsons, which in likewyse were
sent to ward, and when they were examyned they ac-

cused other. And thus in conclusion were accused to _{October,} the number of iiij^{xx} and mo, that all or the more party ^{1493.} were sworn to kepe eythers counsaill; among the which number was nat one howsholder, but all seruauntes, and there more party Apprentices and childern. And aftir this dyuers were remaynyng in prison. And some were leten to bayle vpon Surety to be forthcomyng.

70.

[Ferdinand and Isabella to their ambassador in England, "Spanish Calendar," i. 90.]

Henry VII had sent an ambassador to Ferdinand ^{3 Novem-} and Isabella when they were at Barcelona, and they ^{ber.} have promised to send ambassadors to England.

The King of France, their "much beloved and very dear brother and ally" restored to them their counties of Roussillon and Cerdaña soon after the departure of the English ambassador on his way to the King of France.

In the treaty between Spain and England there is a clause by which they are at full liberty to receive from their "beloved brother," the King of France, their counties of Roussillon and Cerdaña, and to conclude with him alliances, fraternity, brotherhood, and confederation, such as have always existed between their predecessors and the predecessors of their "beloved brother the King of France." Roussillon and Cerdaña having been restored to them, they have concluded their alliances etc. with France, which they were the more entitled to do as Henry has signed nor sworn to nor delivered the treaties.

They intend strictly to fulfil their treaty with France; nevertheless, they are not disinclined to form a new alliance with England if Henry wish it,

1493.						71.

[Proceedings against rioters, Kingsford's "Chronicles," p 198.]

November.	In this yere, in November, the Mayr and his brethern
were sent for to the lordes of the Counsaill to Westmynster, and there by the mowth of the lorde Chaun-
celler in the kynges behalf was gyven a straite commaundement that they shuld dilygently Enquyer of the
Rebelles beforsaid [see No. 69], and aftir the knowlaige
had to bryng to the kynges counsaill Relacion, that the
kyng myght therof sufficiently be enfourmed. Wherupon
the Mair and his brethir, by a commyssion to theym
sent, set a Courte in Guyldhall; and ther was by ij
Enquestis certayn of the said yongmen Endited. And
so adiuged to prison, wherof some of theym lay in the
Tower, and some in othir prysons as the Countours,
many dayes aftir.

1494.

72.

[Trials for sedition, Kingsford's "Chronicles," p. 199.]

22-26	And this yer, the xxij^{th} day of ffebruary, was holdyn
February.	at Guyldhall an other [oyer] Determyne; wherat was
dyuers lordes and Juges and other of the Kyngis Counsaill, before whom was Rayned and Endited iiij persons
for treason; wherof the pryncipall hight Thomas Bagnall,
the second was John Scot, the third John Heth, and
the iiij^{th} John Kenyngton; which iiij persons were
taken owte of Saynt Martens, and for false and sedicious
billes makyng and settyng vp in dyuers places of
the Cite agayns the kynges persone and dyuers of his
Counsaill the same day iij of theym were dampned to
deth; and the iiij^{th}, named Thomas Bagnall, pleted
to be restored to sayntuary; vpon which ple he was

commytted agayn to the Tower till the next terme. February, And the xxvj day of the said moneth were the 1494. iij other persons [were] drawen from the Tower vnto Tyburn, and wᵗ theym ij men more, wherof that one was named Robert Bulley, a yoman of the Chamber wᵗ the kyng, and that other was a Ducheman, which ij were dampned at Westmynster; and so the said v persons were all beheded at Tybourne, vpon whos sowles Jhesu haue mercy.

73.

[Commercial relations with the Netherlands, Kingsford's "Chronicles," p. 200.]

In this yer in the moneth of May the kyng of Ro- May. mayns and tharche Duke his son, Duke of Bourgoyngne, for cawse that the kyng of England had Banysshed befortyme all fflaunders waris, and also had Restrayned his Englissh Marchauntes and subgettes forto adventure in to any Townes of the said Dukes, the said Kyng of Romayns and Duke hath Banysshed all Englissh Cloth and Englissh yerne vpon payne of all suche cloth and yerne ther takyn to be brent, and the brynger therof to lose aboue their Cloth certayn money to the Sum for euery cloth of iiij li. iij s. iiij d sterling.

74.

[Arrest of Sir William Stanley, Kingsford's "Chronicles," p. 203.]

Also this yere the Kyng kept his cristemasse at 25 December. Grenewich, and aftir he cam to the Tower of london, where was attached sir William Stanley, called the kynges Chamberleyn. And the same season sir Robert Clyfford, wich beforetyme had fled the land, and was in fflaunders wᵗ the kynges Enemyes, cam agayn and was taken to grace.

7 *

1495.

75.

[The trial of Stanley and others, Kingsford, p. 203 ; Flenley,
pp. 164-6.]

29 Janu-
ary.

Also this yere the xxix day of January was kept at
the Guyldhall an Oyer determyner, which lasted by
the space of iij dayes, wher wer for Juges many lordes
and knyghtes, and the second day were adiuged to be
Drawen, hanged, heded, and quartered iij spirytuell
men ; that is to say the Deane of Powles,[1] the pro-
vynciall of the blak ffreres, a noble dyvyne and ffamous
precheour, And the pryour of an house of the blak
31 January. ffreres called Langley. And vpon Satirday, being the
third day, was arayned before the Mair and the forsaid
lordes the parson of Seynt Stephens in Walbrook, called
Doctour Sutton, a ffamous dyvyne, and one Maister
Thwates, sumtyme Tresorer of Caleys, which were
countermanded vnto the Tower. And the same day was
Arayned Robert Ratclyf, esquyer, somtyme porter of
Caleys, Symond Mounteford, knyght, William Daubeney,
Esquyer, and clerk of the Jewell house Sometyme w^t
kyng Edward the iiij^th. Also a Gentilman called Cres-
syner, steward w^t the lord ffitzwater, Robert Holborn,
Shipman, a Ducheman called Hans Troys, and one
Thomas Astwode, Steward of Marton Abbey ; which
vij persons were all dampned, and after commytted to
Newgate vnder the Shireffes kepyng. Also the same
day was the parson of Seynt Stephens aforsaid adiuged
vnto lyke Jugement of the other iij spirituell men. And
M. Thwaites beforenamed, and a preest called M. Lessy,

---

[1] William Worsley. According to his own statement ("Rot. Parl.,"
vi. 489), he had been attainted by a commission of oyer and terminer
on 14 November, 1494. He was pardoned by Henry in June, 1495,
and restored in blood by Act of Parliament in the following autumn.
The other two clerics were pardoned also.

Steward vnto the Duches of Yorke, were the same day January,
atteynted of mysprision, and so commytted vnto the 1495.
Tower. And the Tuesday folowyng the Mayr and ij 3 February.
Juges sat vpon an Enquery, and vpon Wednesday sat
the Mair and the said ij Juges vpon an Enquerry. And
the after none wer drawen from Newgate vnto the
Tower hill Sir Symond Mounford, Robert Ratclyf,
William Daubeney, Thomas Crassener, and the forsaid
Thomas Astwode; where iij the first were beheded, vpon
whose sowles Jhesu haue mercy. And Cressyner and
Astwode were pardoned, which gladded moche people
for they were both yong men. And vpon thursday 5 February.
before the Mair and certeyn Juges was arayned a
Straunger, called a Briton named pety John, and ad-
inged to be drawen from Newgate vnto Tybourn, and
there to be hangid, hedid and quartered. And the
same mornyng was drawen from Newgate to Tybourn
Robert Holbourne and Hans Troy aboue namyd, which
ij persons were there hanged, and after stryken downe
quyk, and then behedid; vpon whos soules Jhesu haue
mercy. And vpon ffriday was abouenamed Pety John 6 February.
drawen from Newgate to Tybourn and ther hanged.
And the same day the lord Chambirlayn, othir wise Sir
William Standley, was arayned before the lordes In the
kynges Benche in Westmynster hall, and vpon Satirday 7 February.
he was there agayn areyned before the said lordes, and
found gilty of treason by a queste of dyuers knyghtes
and worshipfull Gentilmen. And vpon their verdyte
gyven adiuged to be drawen, hanged, and quartered,
and so conveyd ageyne vnto the Tower by M. Dygby
and his seruauntes. And vpon Wednesday next folowyng 11 Febru-
sat the Mair and ij Juges in Guyldhall, and Iniournyd ary.
the other [oyer] till monday next folowyng. And vpon 16 Febru-
the monday abowte xj of the Clok, the xvj day of ary.
ffebruary, was sir William A stanley lad bitwene ij men

February, 1495.
owte of the Tower vnto the Tower hill, and there vpon the scafold behedid, whos sowle god pardon. This was a man of grete myght in his Cuntre, and a greate [   ]sman of moveable goodes, In somoche as the Comon fame Ran that in his Castell of Holt was founden in Redy coigne, and plate, and Jewelles to the value of xl m^l marces or more; And his land and ffee extended to iij m^l li. by yere. God graunt hym pardon of his mysdede.

76.

[The Archbishop of York before the Star Chamber, Flenley, "Chronicles," p. 165.]

4 February.
Also on Wedenesday the iiij^th day off ffeveryere was apeched the archebisshop of yorke [1] and cam before the lordys in the starre Chambre and there was suerty ffor hym body for body and goodes for goodes my lorde of Cauntorbury Chanceler of Englond.

77.

[The Milanese ambassador in Flanders to the Duke of Milan, "Milanese Calendar," i. 292.]

Bois-le Duc, 11 February.
These last days in England the first man [2] who had this son of King Edward, when he was in England, has run away. Many were taken, including the Bishop of London. [3] His Majesty [4] told me that this man, [5] when he was in England, divulged that this Duke of York [6]

[1] Thomas Rotherham *alias* Scot (1423-1500) ex-lord-chancellor; this incident in the archbishop's career is not mentioned in his life in the "Dict. Nat. Biog.".
[2] Sir Robert Clifford; see No. 74.
[3] Apparently a mistake for the Dean of St. Paul's.
[4] Maximilian I.   [5] Clifford.
[6] Perkin Warbeck.

was not the son of King Edward, but is the son of the February, Dowager Duchess of Burgundy and of the Bishop of $^{1495.}$ Cambrai.

His Majesty also told me that the said duke will proceed for the present to Ireland, where he has strong connections, and that island held him for its lord before he went to France, according to what the duke himself told me.

78.

[Flenley, " Chronicles," p. 166.]

Also the xvj day off feveryere moneday was Sir 16 Febru- William Stanley Lorde Chamberleyne pardoned off the $^{ary.}$ kyng off hangyng and drawyng and the seid day betwene xj and xij at noone was he ledde from the toure of london to the toure hyll and there his hed smytten off and is beryed at Saint Donnstones in the

79.

[Landing of rebels at Deal, Kingsford's " Chronicles," p. 205.]

Also the third day of July dyvers Rebelles of the kyng 3 July. aryved at a place in Kent named Dele to the numbre of v or vj C men and of the same company Remayned vpon the water xiiij Sayles, wherin by Estymacion were mo to the numbre of viij C men ; which forsaid company that were landed, when they sawe that they cowde haue no comfort of the Cuntre, they drewe to their Shippys agayn ; at which so w^{t} drawyng the Mair of Sandewiche w^{t} certayn comons of that Cuntre, to the numbre of vij or viij scor, bekeryd w^{t} the Residue that were vpon land, and toke alyve of theym an Clxix persons, among the whiche was iiij Capiteyns takyn, named Mounford, Corbet, White, and Belt ; which said Mounford was son vuto sir Symond Mounford, which was

July, 1495. before byheded.[1] And of the said Company of Rebelles was ij slayn and dyvers drowned ; and they affermed to be their hede Capitayne the second son of kyng Edward the iiij[th], which was in one of the said Shippys. And after the said discomfirture the said Rebelles w[t] in the said shippys drewe up their sayles, and sailed westward.

12 July. And the xij day of July the Shiref of Kent, called John Peache, Esquyer, brought vnto London Brigge Clix of the forsaid prysoners ; where the Shyreffes of London receyued theym, and conveyd theym in Cartis and long Ropys vnto the Tower of London. And there lefte all the said prisoners, except xlij persons wich the said Shireffes conveied streyte vnto Newgate ; of which said persons the substaunce of theym were Duchemen and Alyauntes ; which xij[th] day was Relyk Sonday. Also vpon the monday next ensuyng, at afternone, was a Chapleyn of the Bisshop of London, callid Doctour Draper, takyn by force oute of powlis Chirch, and thens conveied vnto Lambhyth by certeyn Gentilmen, as it was Reported, of my lord Cardynalles.[2] Also vpon the

16 July. Thursday next folowyng was the aforenamed Belt, Mounford, Corbet and one Malyverey, w[t] other of the fornamed prisoners to the numbre of lj, had from the Tower vnto Grenewich, and there areyned ; and after their endytementes to theym Red, they confessid theym self worthy to dye, and vtterly put theym silf in the

24 July. kynges mercy and grace. And xxiiij day of July was many of the Duchemen and Alyauntes abouesaid areyned at Westmynst[r] in the White hall, and there adjuged to suffre deth.

[1] No. 75.   [2] John Morton, Archbishop of Canterbury.

80.   1495.

[The Corporation of Yarmouth to Sir John Paston ; plans of the
rebels, " Paston Letters," iii. 936.]

Right wurchipfull ser, we recomaund us onto your Yarmouth
good maistership, sertefyeng you that Robart Albon of ¹¹ ᴶᵘˡʸ·
Yermouth with many more of our neybors, this Saterday arn comen hom from Caunterbury. And Robart
Albon hath spokyn with the English captayns of the
Kynges rebellys ther, part of theym that arn takyn ; and
Robert Albon and his company seith that ther wer
takyn and slayn to the noumbre of vijˣˣ, wherof were
v capteyns, iiij of them he named, oon Mounford,
Whyght, Belt, and Corbett : he coude nott telle the
fyfft capteyns name. And they told hym that they
have apoynted to have a town of strength, for they
wold an had Sandwich, and the countre had nott a resisted them. And so Belt seid on to Robart Albon he
wyst weell that he was but a deed man, and for asmoche
as he wist that he was of Yermouth, he shewid hym
that they woll have Yermouth or they xall dye for it,
as Robart seyth to us.

And this is a mater of trewth, and therfore we desyre
and pray your good maistership, that we may have your
myghty help of ayde and socowr, and that it woll please
you to comon with Maister Mayer of Norwiche, to move
hym of hys sokour, but in especyall that we may have
your maistership amongs us, with suche strength of
your good councell, as your maistership shall thynk most
best for the Kynges pleasur, and for the sewyrtye of us
alle ; for we putt us in devyr to furnysh the town with
all that we can doo, for we know noon oder but that
they may be here by possybylyte this nyght or to morow
att nyght at the ferdest. No more to you, but Jesu
preserve you. Wretyn at Yermouth, in hast, this

July, 1495. Saterday, the xj day of July. Be your owyn, the Balyffes of Yermouth, with our Brethern and Comons of the same Town.

81.

[Robert Crowmer to Sir John Paston ; news of the rebels, "Paston Letters," iii. 937.]

Yarmouth,
12 July.

Wurchipfull ser, I recomaund me on to you. Maister Balyffes, with alle myn Maisteris of the town of Yermouth, thankith you hartilly, and trustyng feythfully of your ayde and comford at neede ; and if any suche cause happith with us, they woll feythfully send you word in all the hast possyble, up on the syght of the shippis.

Ser, ferdermor, ther is a ship of our town come hom from Seint John of Amyas, and he seyth that on Seint Thomas Day ther came to Seint Wallrens, in Normandie, an hoye of Dorderyght, with viij horsis, with many saddilles and brydilles ; ther in wer viij or ix Englysh men, the wiche toke the shippes boot, and went on lond at Staplis, and arn renne- a wey up in to the cuntre. And the Admiralles Depewty sesonyd the ship and hors, and all that they found ther in, to the Kyng our soverayn Lordes behooff ; and the Duche men were leyde in pryson. This is a mater of trowth, for William Carre of our town, maryner, and oder of our town, see this doon in deed. And as for the shippes with the Kynges rebellars, they be furth out of Cambyr westwards ; whyder they be, thei can not sey, but the Duche men seid to William Carre that they trustid on one man shuld help them with many men. Thes is suche tydynges as the Amyas men brout hom.

Ser, if it woll please your maistership that ye myght have leyser, I desyre and pray you to come sporte you, and to see how weell we have appareld and furnyshid

our town, I wold be right gladd, and I trust to Almyghty July, 1495.
God that it wold please your maistership right weell,
and with your betyr advyce we woll doo more to our
power, that knowith God, the wiche Lord preserve you.

82.

[De Puebla to Ferdinand and Isabella, "Spanish Cal.," i. 98.]

Friday the 3rd of July, the so called Duke of York London,
came to England with all the ships and troops he had 19 July.
been able to obtain from the Duchess Margaret, the
Archduke, and Flanders.   A portion of his troops disembarked, but the people rose up in arms against them
without the intervention of a single soldier of the King.
The peasants of the adjacent villages made great havock
on the troops, who had disembarked, and if the vessels
had not been at hand not a single man of them would
have escaped alive.   A hundred and fifty were slain,
and eighty made prisoners, among whom were eight
captains, two of them being Spaniards, Don Fulano de
Guevara (he is said to be a brother or nephew of Don
Ladron) and Diego el Coxo (the Lame), the name which
all the villagers gave him, saying that the *King* came,
and that he may go to his father and mother, who still
live in France, and are well known ; and they hold it
to be as true as Gospel, as it really is, that this affair is
like that of the Duke of Clarence, who was crowned
King of Ireland, and afterwards discovered to be the son
of a barber.   They had no great reasons for congratulating themselves, and had gone, it is believed, to Ireland
or Scotland ; for it is not probable that they would return
to Flanders, because the whole of that country is almost
ruined, in consequence of their staying there, the King
of England not having permitted any commerce with
the Flemings, in which their principal riches and their

July, 1495. life consists. Doctor De Puebla is very sorry for these foolish things, for such are they generally believed to be by those who have any knowledge of the affair. Certainly, if the King of the Romans uphold the Duke of York and xxiiij [probably James IV], it would be very difficult to conclude what your Highnesses wish. I think that all that the King of Romans does is done by the instigation of the King of France. If your Highnesses had taken care earlier of the matter, all this would have been avoided. Nevertheless, it is not too late, even now, if your Highnesses like it.

83.

[Opening of Henry VII's fifth parliament, "Rot. Parl.," vi. 458 ; most of the matters touched upon in Morton's address were the subjects of legislation during this session, see below, vol. ii.]

14 October. Memorandum, quod die Mercurii, quarto decimo die Octobris, anno regni Regis Henrici Septimi post Conquestum undecimo, Reverendissimus pater Johannes Cardinalis Archiepiscopus Cantuar' Cancellarius Angliæ etc. . . . pronunciavit & declaravit ; assumens pro themate verborum seriem subsequentem ; "Custodias & facias Legem," Josue Cap⁰ primo. Super quo introduxit quomodo leges & jura habebant constitui & sanciri, per quos & quibus de causis, & hoc de Lege Nature, Jure Gencium, Lege Mosaica, Lege Civili, Lege Evangelica, & Jure Canonico ; & horum deffiniciones atque eorum differencias perlucide declaravit, divisiones dominiorum primas, insignia regum, uncciones eorundem, magistratus principatus, & auctoritatem quibus leges ministrentur, satis aperte dilucidavit. Rempublicam in ponderibus & mensuris contempnentes, [h]abutentes intercursu mercatorum per contractus, per multuram, per usuram, viisque aliis legem contra politicam confutavit. Quibusve modis usura, perjuriam

sive juramentum illicitum committitur, & penas com- October, 1495.
mittentium ratione & auctoritate divinis & humanis
modis, & viis perdocte atque peregregie regia coram
Majestate & circumstant[ibus] edocuit.

84.

[Attainder of Sir William Stanley and others, " Rot. Parl.," vi. b03-4.]

Where William Stanley late of the towne of West- October.
minster in the Countie of Middlesex, knight, otherwise
called William Stanley late of the parishe of Seynt
Martyn in the Feld besides Charyng Crosse in the same
countie, knight, Symond Mountford late of Colshull in
the countie of Warwyke, knight, William Dawbeney
late of London, gentilman, Robert Ratcliff late of
London, squier, for certeyn treasons, ymagened and
compassed traiterously, to the destruccion of the moost
roiall persone of the King oure Sovereign Lord, and
the subversion of this his realme, before his Justices
and Commissioners in severall Oyers and Determyners
by him in that partie assigned, as well in the citie of
London, as in the shire of Middlesex, by due ordre and
processe of the lawe, were, for divers sondry treasons
by theym severally commytted and doon, convicte and
atteynted of High Treason, as in the severall recordes
therof more pleynly appereth ; by the which atteyn-
dours, the said persones atteynted, forfeited not ne
myght forfeit any manours, landes, tenementes, possessions ne hereditamentes, wherof other persones
were seased to their several uses. And where also
Gilbert Debenham late of the towne of Westminster
in the countie of Middlesex, knight, and Humfrey
Savage late of the toune of Westminster in the said
countie, knight, as fals traytours and rebelles of the
King our Sovereign Lord, the xth of Feverere, the viiith

yere [1493] of his moost noble reigne, att Westminster
aforsaid, falsly and traiterously ymagened, consedered
and compassed the deth and destruccion of our said
Sovereign Lord, and subversion of this his realme;
and to accomplishe and perfourme the same false purpose, the same Gilbert and Humfrey, knowyng oon
Piers Warbek, enemye of our said Sovereign Lord, and
other his rebelles beyng beyonde the see, adherentes
to the same Piers, to levie werre ageynst our said
Sovereign Lord, receyved att Westminster aforesaid,
message by certain persones, from the said Piers, and
other his said adherentes; and to the same entent,
sent message agayn oute of this realme, to the said
Piers, and to his said adherentes, that the said Gilbert,
within shorte tyme after wold come to the same Piers,
and to his said adherentes beyonde the see, and take
his partie ageynst our said Sovereign Lord, in leveying
warre ayenst him and come into England with the
said Piers and his said adherentes, falsly and traiterously, to his power to helpe to depose and put downe
oure said Sovereign Lord. And that the said Humfrey
Savage, for the more releife and helpe of the said Piers,
and his adherentes in that behalfe, shuld abide stille in
this realme, unto the comyng of the same Piers, and
his said adherentes; and theym then and there with all
his myght and power, wold helpe and assiste to helpe
to execute all the premysses. And so the said Gilbert
and Humfrey, the said x^th day, att Westminster aforsaid,
traiterously were adherentes, helping, councelling and
comfortyng to the said Piers, and his adherentes,
enemyes to our said Sovereign Lord, to levie werre
ayenst hym; wherupon they were and yet stande and
be indited of high treason; and for that they wold not
therupon appere to be justified after the lawes of this
land, but fledde to seyntwaries, processe was awarded

ayenst theym, till they were outlawed, and so they stand October,
and yet remayn, and be therupon outlawed and at- 1495.
teynted, by the processe of the lawe, of and upon the
said treason ; by the which also atteyndre, the said
Gilbert and Humfrey so atteynted, forfeited not ne
myght forfeite any manours, landes tenementes, possessions ne hereditamentes, wherof other persones were
seased to their severall uses. And where also John
Ratcliffe of Attilborough in the countie of Norffolk,
knight, otherwise called John Ratcliff Fitzwater of
Attilborough in the countie of Norffolk, knight, otherwise called John Ratcliff of Fitzwater late of Attyl-
borough in the countie of Norffolk, knight, William
Barley late of Albury in the countie of Hertford, squier,
and Thomas Brampton late of the same toune in the
same countie, gentilman, falsely and traiterously con-
spyred and ymagyned the deth and destruccion of the
King our Sovereign Lord, and the subversion of this
his realme of England, and the same our said Sovereign
Lord, by werres ageynst him in this his said realme
of England to be levied, reared and made ageynst him,
of his corone and regallie entended to deprive, depose
and put downe ; and to execute and perfourme the
said mischevous purpose, actes and trayterous dedes,
the said John Ratclyffe, William Barly, and Thomas
Brampton, att severall tymes were to the said Piers
confederates, assenting, assistyng, adherentes, favouryng
and helpyng, wherof they be severally indited, as in the
said severall inditementes more pleynly apperith; whiche
inditementes were badde upon true matter sufficiently
and openly shewed and declared, upon the takyng of
the same inditementes in that behalf. And where also
that the said Piers Warbek of late, from the parties of
beyond the see, with grete multitude of people of the
Kinges rebelles, enemyes, and traytours, in shippes,

with all abilementes of warre necessarie for the same,
into this his realme of England entendyng to aryve
at Deele in the countie of Kent, and then and there
grette partie of the Kinges said enemyes, rebells and
traytours, with him then accompanied, that is to say,
the iii^d day of July, the xth yere of the reigne of our
said Sovereign Lord, entred and landed att Deele aforsaid, and there and then trayterously reared and levied
batell and warre, in pleyn feld, ageynst our said
Sovereign Lord, with baners displayed, and with ar-
mours defensives, as jakkes, salettis, brigandynes,
bowes, belles, haubertes, curesses, gunnes, speres,
marespikes, crossebowes, and other enhabilmentes of
warres, compassyng the deth and destruccion of our
said Sovereign Lord, and the subversion of this his
realme, where then and there were dyvers of the
persones folowing present ; and dyverse other of the
same persones, afore that tyme, to this false and traiterous purpose of the said Piers, and other of the Kinges
said enemyes, rebelles, and traytours, with him acom-
panyed, were adherentes, assistantes, confederates,
favourers, guydantes, helpers, socourers, and com-
forters.

1496.

85.

[Zacharia Contarini to the Doge and Senate of Venice, "Venetian
Calendar," i. 227-8.]

This day the ambassadors of the Holy League accredited to the King of the Romans have been assembled
by his order, and Dom. Ludovic Bruno caused to be
read to them the reply to Lord Egremont. Besides
what was contained in the copy transmitted by Contarini,
there was a justification, purporting that, the King of the

Romans having no league or relationship soever with the King of England, the Duke of York [Perkin Warbeck], whom he firmly believes to be the son of King Edward, came to him; and that he considered it his duty not to abandon the Duke, nor to fail affording him all just and fitting favour.

A second clause purported that, should the King of England approve, the King of the Romans offered to negotiate a ten years' truce or peace between him and the said Duke of York; and thirdly, there was a paragraph to the effect that, should the King of England be admitted into the League, he was to be bound to attack the King of France next Easter, with a strong and powerful armada.

To this the Spanish ambassadors said that, were the King of the Romans to dismiss Lord Egremont with such a reply, it would be tantamount to telling him that he did not choose to admit his King into the League; in the first place, because all the paragraphs alluding to the Duke of York would only irritate the King of England; and secondly, that as the King of the Romans wrote lately consenting to the King of England's joining the League unconditionally, the King of England would not now assume the obligation of attacking.

The opinion of the Venetian ambassador being next asked, he replied that his Spanish colleagues having expressed themselves sufficiently, it merely remained for him to remind his Majesty (the King of the Romans) that during the past months the Sovereigns of Spain had given the Signory to understand that it would be very desirable the King of the Romans should drop the affairs of the Duke of York as this was not the moment for disturbing the kingdom of England, the admission of whose King into the confederation would be advantageous; as he on one side, the King of the Romans on the other, and Spain in her own quarter might simultaneously invade France, to the advantage of the confederates.

The Neapolitan and Milanese ambassadors approved what had been said; whereupon Dom. Ludovic Bruno, having heard the various opinions, withdrew, and reported them to the King of the Romans. On his return he announced that the King of the Romans was content to cancel all the paragraphs relating to the Duke of York, but insisted that the obligation on the part of the King of England to attack France should stand; not so much from any hope of its being observed, but because, unless inserted, the King of England would have obtained a promise from the King of the Romans not to favour the Duke of York, the League nevertheless deriving no advantage thence.

The Spanish ambassadors rejoined that they clearly perceived that, could the King of England be included in the League with the obligation to attack, it would be more to the purpose; but, knowing him to be a most sage King and to be well advised, they were certain he would not join with heavier obligations than had been assumed by the other confederates: that, for the observance of similar obligations, King Ferdinand and his consort would pledge themselves on behalf of the King of England, whensoever the King of the Romans pleased; and that at any rate it should be taken into account that, even were the King of England not to attack, his not being the ally of the King of France would prove of great importance, as that King would thus be prevented from availing himself of English troops, and of many other favours derivable from the King of England. The ambassadors added that, should this negociation not be concluded, England would unite with France, whose King, they understood, had already sent an ambassador to England.

The Spanish ambassadors having expressed them- January, selves thus, his Majesty sent for Dom. Ludovic, and 1496. charged him to act according to their suggestion, the matter being one which their sovereigns had much at heart and held in great account. So the document was drawn up according to the copy transmitted to the Doge and Senate by Contarini, who, on the 7th of January, announced the departure of Lord Egremont, to whom the King of the Romans had given a gold cup and one hundred florins.

86.

[The Imperial ambassador in Spain to Maximilian, " Spanish
Cal.," i. 120.]

The King and Queen of Spain do not neglect the war Burgos, with France.   They hope to influence the King of Eng- 9 January land to do their will and the will of Maximilian.   For this purpose it would be well that he should send his power to the Spanish ambassador in England nominating him as his ambassador.

Has often told the King and Queen of Spain what an advantage it would be to engage the English to undertake the conquest of Guienne.[1]   If that could be carried out, the French and the English would be so much occupied with one another, that the dominions of the Archduke would be in security, and the King and Queen of Spain and he could do what they liked, and Italy would be at their disposal.

---

[1] Henry VII was not to be misled in this way, but his son's council fell into the snare in 1511-12.

8 *

1496.   87.

[Deposition of Bernard de Vignolles relative to the alleged treason
   of Sir John Kendal, grand prior of the Order of St. John of
   Jerusalem, Gairdner's " Letters and Papers," ii. 318-323 ; cf.
   Champollion Figeac's "Lettres de Rois renies," ii. 505. On
   Kendal, see "Plumpton Correspondence," pp. 117-9.]

Rou en,   Cest la disposicion que fait Bernard de Vignolles a
14 March.
          lencontre·de le Sire Jehan Quendal, grant prieur de
          lordre de Saint Jehan de Roddes, Sire Jehan Thonge,[1]
          son nepveu, pareillement chevallier dudict ordre, mestre
          archediacre Heusse, Jehan Heusse, son nepveu, ung
          nomme Lilly, et ung aultre Jehan Watre, eulx deulx
          serviteurs dudict archediacre, et ung nomme William
          Wton[2] secretaire dudict prieur de Saint Jehan, les quelz
          congnoissent lentreprinse que fist ledict prieur de Saint
          Jehan et Sire Jehan Thonge et larchediacre Heusse, eulx
          troys estans a Romme.
            Premierement, les dessudis troys personnes estans en
          Romme firent cherche de trouver moien et faczon de
          entreprendre faire mourir le roy d'Angleterre, ses
          enffans, sa merre, et ceulx qui pensoient qui estoient
          pres de sa personne et de son conseil. Et a ceste inten-
          cion saconainterent [s'accointèrent] dun nome Radigo,
          Espaigneul ; et se alla ledit archediacre loger a sa maison,
          pensant que ledict astrelogue sceut faire et acomplir
          lamprinse que ilz avoient en intencion, de quoy ledit
          Rodigo ne scent faire. Finablement firent serche tant
          que ilz trouverent ung aultre qui se nomme mestre Jehan,
          Espaigneul, astreloge, auquel ilz declairerent leur inten-
          cion, lequel mestre Jehan ouant leur demande, fist res-
          ponce, que y sauroit bien faire seus [ceux] que il luy
          desiroint. Et a ceste intencion firent marche audit
          mestre Jehan, pour une somme dargent ; et pour plus

─────────────────────────
[1] Sir John Tong, commander of Ribstone.   [2] Wotton.

grande apreuve que congneussent que ledit mestre Jehan March 1496. sauroit bien faire ce que il luy desiroint, i fist mourir ung Turc, qui estoit serviteur du frere du Grant Turc a Romme, au pallays du pappe. Et si lediz trois person-nages eusent delivre la dite somme dargent, quilz avoient promis audit astrelogue, il leur promectoit que il eust fait sens [ceux] que luy avoient desire de faire.

Item, quant lesdiz troys personnages se partirent de Rome pour venir en Engleterre, lesserent ung nomme Stefen,[1] serviteur dudit prieur de Saint Jehan, le quel est du pais de Sardine, avecques ledit mestre Jehan, Espaigneul, pour acomplir leur movais voulloir et in-tencion; et pour ce faire, firent delivrer une quantite dargent audit Stefen, et audit astrelogue, par banque, apres leur dit departement de Romme ; lequel Bernard dit, que ledit astrelogue luy a dempuis dit que y ne luy avoient point voullu bailler asses argent pour acomplir lamprinse que ilz avoint commence, et ne voulut ledit astrelogue y besoingner plus avant, jusques a ce que il eust eu nouvelles desdiz troys personnages ; et cuide ledit Bernard que ledit argent que ilz firent delivrer audit astrelogue, que ce nestoit seullement sy non pour entretenir ledit astrelogue, atendan la somme quilz luy avoint promis, et que pour lors ilz navoint granment dargent, que ilz peussent departir car ilz avoint assez necessite pour les mener en Engleterre.

Item deux ans apres que lesdiz troys personnages furent arivez en Engleterre, delibererent par entre eulx denvoier a Romme ung homme a la priorre et requeste dudit archediacre, le quel ne cessoit audit prieur que il y voulsist envoier; et sur ce furent ledit prieur et archiediacre dun commun accord, dy envoier ledit Bernart de Vinolles, les quelz lui commanderent ex-presse[ment] que i trouvant moien de faire mourir

[1] Stephen Maranecho ; see below, No. 90.

lastrelogue qui avoit reffuse faire leur desir, pour cause
que ledit prieur et archediacre avoient entendu comme
ledit astrelogue avoit dit en Romme que lesdix prieur et
archidiacre et ledit seigneure Jehan Thong avoint eu
intencion de faire mourir le roy dEngleterre. Pareillement commanderent audit Bernard come il eust parle
a lautre astreloge nomme mestre Jehan, disant que il
acomplist sa promes qui lavoit promis devant leur partement de Romme, et que i ne se soucyat du poyement
que ilz luy avoint promis, car ilz avoint peur que il ne
leur fist comme ilz avoint eu intencion de luy faire faire
a lutre, qui est a entendre la mort du roy. Et didrent
audit Bernart, que il eust dit audit astreloge que se luy
estoit posible de faire ce que il luy desiroint de pardela
sans venir en Engleterre, de peur qui i ne fust congneu ;
sur quoy ledit ostreloge fist responce audit Bernart que
pour acomplir plustost leur emprinse, que i vendroit en
Engleterre, en labit dung frere, et pource que il luy
falloit deux dens audit astrelogue, il en feroit faire deux
de yviere, de la couleur des siennes, et dist que i vendroit par mer, pour le plus sur, disant que il alloit a Saint
Jacques ; et croit ledit Bernard, que i ne tint que pour
faulte dargent, que i navoit pour despendre par chemin,
que ledict astrelogue ne fust venu ou dit royaulme dEngleterre.

Item, an partement dudit Bernart de Rome pour sen
retourner en Engleterre, ledit astrelogue luy bailla une
petite boueste de boys, en la quelle estoit ung oingnement, le quel astrelogue envoyet audit prieur de Saint
Jehan, et luy mandoit par ledit Bernart, que il eust fait
mectre ledit oingnement, qui estoit en ladite boueste, au
longc et travers de quelque huys ou porte par ou passeroit
le roy, affin que passat par dessus ; le quel astreloge disoit,
que sil est ainsy fait, que ceulx qui avoint et portoint
plus damour au roy, que seroint ceulx qui turoint le roy,

et estoit en deffault que ledit astrelogue ne pouvoit aller
en Engleterre ; et quant ledit Bernart fut a son logis
retourne, il vint en sa chambre, et ouvrit ladite boueste,
et vit que cestoit une villaine et horde puante chose,
referma ladite boueste, et la vint gecter ou retrect, et
le landemain ledit Bernart print son chemin, pour sen
retourner en Engleterre ; et quant il fut a Orleans, il
luy souvint de ladite boueste, et de peur que ledit astrelogue, neust escryst audit prieur de St Jehan, comme
il luy avoit envoye une telle boueste par ledit Bernart,
de peur que ledit Bernart ne fust blasme, sen alla ches
ung apoticaire, achater une telle boueste comme estoit
lautre, et pour ung lyart dargent viff ; et sen retourne a
son logis, et en sa chambre et print terre seche, et de la
snye de la cheminee, avecques de lean, et la destrempa,
et ledit argent viff ensemble, pour la faire de telle coulleur que celle que ledit astrelogue luy avoit baille, pour
bailler audit prieur de St Jehan.

Item, quant ledit Bernart fut arrive devers ledit prieur
de Saint Jehan, il luy conta comme ledit astrelogue luy
avoit dit, et luy delivre ladit boueste, [que] le prieur ne
voullut toucher, pour ce que ledit Bernart luy dist que
cestoit grant danger de la toucher a celuy qui avoit
en volunte den faire mal, et que si elle demouroit xxij
heures en sa meson, qui se seroit a son grant danger ;
et pource ledit prieur commanda audit Bernart, que
il allas[t] en quelque lieu, loingns de sa meson, et la
jettat la ou elle ne fust point trouvee, et ainsy ledit
Bernart fist, comme luy avoit commande.

Item, bien tost, apres troys on quatre sepmaines, ledit
prieur vint en la chambre ou estoit ledit Bernart, fort
mallade, et dist audit Bernart, sil luy estoit posible, que
y pent chevaucher pour sen aller hors du royaume
dEngleterre, dissant que il fust alle en quelque pelerinage,
ou a la ma[ison] de son perre, pour se faire garir ;

que ledict prieur luy bailleroit argent et cheval, et ne le
fasoit ledit prieur cela, cy no[n] de peur que ledit Bernart fust prins, et que il eust revel[e] leur movois voulloir et malice ; au quel ledit Bernart fist responce, que
y feroit se [ce] que il luy commandoit, mais, neantmoins
quil estoit fort faible, et que desque i pourroit
chevaucher, que il iróit voluntiers ou il luy commandoit
dalle r; et dura ladite malladie audit Bernart dempuis
lespace de demyan ou plus, par quoy ledit prieur le luy
parlla dempuis de aller della la mer ; et apres que ledit
Bernart fut query, i demanda cougie daller devers ses
parens, et de la ou il est natiff, a intencion de faire
avertir le roy de ce que est cy desus dit, car il nousoit
luy ser . . . a savoir luy estant en Engleterre, de peur
que ceulx qui ont conpille ceste traison ne luy feissent
desplesir de son corps ; et a ceste intencion pourchassa
son cougie, disant que son frere latendoi[t] a Dieppe,
lequel luy avoit escript; et pryoit ledit Bernart ledit
seigneur de Saint Jehan, que il luy vouleist donner
cougie, et sur ce ledit seigneur de St Jehan fust content,
v[u] que il luy promettoit de retourner tout incontinant.

Item, au commencement que Pierqin Warbec estoit
en Flandre, fut par ung serviter dudit seigneur escript
par plusseu[rs] foiz audit seigneur de Saint Jehan lectres,
que ledit Bernart en partie a veus, non pas toutes,
esquelles avoit contenu en parolles couvertes comme le
marchant du Ruby [Roubaix] ne pouvoit vendre sa
marchandise audit pays de Flandres pour autant quil
en demandoit, par quoy sen alloit en la court du roy des
Romains, pour voir sil en pouroit plus trouver ; qui est
a entendre, comme dit ledit Bernart, que cestoit Pierqin
Warbec, qui ne pouvoit avoir secours en Flandres, sy
graunt numbre comme y desiroit pour venir en Engleterre ; le non dudit serviteur qui escripvoit les dessus-
dites lectres est frere Guillemin de Noion.

Item, estoit ung aultre marchaunt en la ville de Bruges, qui est quatelan, nomme Daniel Beauvivre, qui dempuis que ledit Pierqin retourna de devers le roy des Romains en Flandres, ledit marchant rescript audit sieur de St Jehan par plusseurs foiz, de quoy ledit Bernart na eu congnoissance que dune lectre, en la quelle estoit contenu comme ledit marchant avoit dempuis naguerres de temps parle audit frere Guillemin de Noion, et que ledit frere Guillemin luy avoit dit, que il avoit presque tou[t] son argent prest a la somme de ix on diz mille frans, et que il manderoit audit seigneur de St Jehan par banque, et le marchant du Ruby iroit avecques.

Item au temps que le roy estoit a Ourcestre, ledit sieur de Saint Jehan estoit en la conte de Bethford a une place de la religion de Saint Jehan, nomme Milbourne, la ou y fist faire ung ce[r]tain numbre jacquettes pour ses gens de la faczon qui sensuit, de quoy le bas estoit a deux coulleurs, vert et rouge apliz, et au desus de la sainture ny avoit que deux barres, lune devant et lautre derriere, en escharpe, de la largeur de quatre doiz, ou environ, et ce cestoit pour mectre la Rose Rouge ; et pareillement avoit fait faire ung corps tout entier pour chascune jacquecte, de pareille coulleur, et disoit ledit sieur que chascun deulx le porterait a larson de sa celle ; et dit ledit Bernart que ce nestoit pour aultre intencion que pour y mectre une Blanche Rose a chascune jacquecte.

Item, vint ung Pietres, qui est serviteur dudit Guillemin de Noion, quil envoyet audit seigneur de St Jehan oue [avec] lectres, faignant avertir le roy de la venuee que entendoit faire Pierqin en Engleterre, le quel Pietres portoit lectres, de quoy le roy neut alors la congnoissance de toutes, ne pareillement le dit Bernart ; et dist ledit Pietres audit Bernart, que il avoit unnes lectres a Thomas Brandon, lesquelles ledit Pierres luy

dist, que i nosseroit les delivr[er] audit Brendon, de peu[r]
que i nen eust quelque desplesir, et les delivra audit
sieur de Saint Jehan affin que il les baillast audit
Brendon, et ne peut le dit Bernart congnoistre autre
chose dudit Pietres.

Item, toutes les foiz que ledit sieur de Saint Jehan
avoit lectres de Flandres, ou aucunes nouvelles, il alloit
ou envoyet a levesque de Winchestre, a Jehan Heusse,
a sire Thomas Tirel, et a larchediacre Heusse, et leur
donnoit a congnoistre toutes nouvelles, et pareillement
quant les dessusdits evesque et autres avoint nouvelles,
il luy fassoint savoir, ou autrement le luy venoint dire.

Item, ledit seigneur de Saint Jehan a este par deux ou
troys foiz chascun an, une foiz apres Nouuel a la
maison de sire Thomas Tirel, eulx deulx devisant plusseurs choses, et entre les aultres commencza a dire ledit
sieur de Saint Jehan comment le roy Eduard avoit autre
foiz este en ladite maison ; au quel ledit sire Thomas
respondit, que il estoit vray, et que il y avoit fait autres
foiz[fait] bonne cherre, et que il esperoit, au plesir Dieu,
que le filz dudit Edouart y feroit ausy bonne cherre, et
que ladite meson avoit [este] faite de largent de France,
et que quelque jour il avoit espoir dengaigner de quoy en
faire une aultre ausy belle : et estoit ledit Bernart et
seigneur Jehan Thonge pressens que les dites parolles
furent dites.

Item, le secretaire dudit seigneur de St Jehan, nomme
William Outon, et ung seruiteur dudit archediarce
Heusse, nomme Lilly, et ung aultre, qui se nomme
Jehan Watre, lequel est serviteur dudit archediacre,
lesquelx troys congnoissent tout la traison que lesdits
sieurs ont enterprins de faire ; ledit Lilly et ledit Jehan
Watre congnoissent lastrelogue qui a enterprins ceste
traison, car ilz ont touz deulx demoure a Romme ; et
doit le roy faire garde que ilz ne sortent hors de son roy-

aullme. Fait a Rouan, le xiiij⁰ jour de mars, lan mil March, 1496. iiij^cc. iiij^xx. xv. De part moy Bernard de Vanholes.

[*Endorsed in the King's hand :* La confession de Bernart de Vignolles.]

88.

[Sir John Kendal to William de Novion (the Guillemin de Noion of
Vignolles' deposition), Gairdner's "Letters and Papers,"
ii. 323.]

Spectabilis ac religiose in Christo frater præcarissime. Berwick, 17 April. Io me recommando ad vui. Doi mesi ha che lo mio servitore Bernard,[1] andava ad Roan per trovare suo fradello : et expectando la trovato ha doi mei amici che hanno algune cose ad vendre, de le quale me voliano fare piacere. Et per tanto ho scripto ad Bernardo, che li conduse ad vui per essere piu prope ; ali quali ve prego faciate li bona ciera, et che non manchano merite. Et venute che sarano, vorria che Bernardo me retornasse lo piu presto che potesse, et incontinente apresso sarrano avisati de la mia intensione. Altro per la presente non me occurre, salvo ad vui me recommando. Ex Baruuyk, adi xvij April 1496.

Vestro lo prior d Ingliterra

Fra Johann Chendall

Sia data ad Fra Gilgham di Novion, cavaliero de Rhodes.

89.

[Sir John Kendal to Bernard de Vignolles, *ibid.* ii. 324.]

Io me recommando ad vui. Ali 15 del presente ho Berwick, 17 April. receputo la vostra lettera scripta ad Roan, e per la decta lettera ho inteso como havite trovato li doi mercadanti che soleano vendre petri ad Roma, et chi haveano grande

[1] de Vignolles.

piacere che ve hanno trovato, et volentieri voliano intendre se io havea volunta davere alguna de decte cose. Ho grande piacere che sonno in quelle parti ; et per tanto io vorria che andasseno ad fra Gilmyn de Novion, che sta ad tre o quatro miglia de Ayre et de Doway, in lo paise d'Artoys ; et ve prego conduicite li ala et intendiate la perfeccione de dicte petre et de la retornarite asi. Et quando havero inteso per vui la sertetza de ogne cosa, subito dapoi per vui intenderanno la mia vol[unta], et in una parte o laltra trovarimo el modo per fare dispachiare loro cose ad louro utilita. Et me recommandarite ad loro et chi pigliano la presente letera per louro. Lo portatore ha restato molto per la via ad causa che fo amalato xij giorni ad Portismouuth. Non altro con la presente. Sara una lettera per lo decto fra Gilmin, chi fazia ad dicti merca[danti] bona chiera ; et de li dispesi che haveti et farite per lo vestro restare et altri spese sarrite contentato. Et se non trovate lo dicto fra Gilmyn ala casa soa, potite lassare dicti mercadanti in casa soa et andate ad trovare dicto fra Gilmyn ad Brugis, o dove sarra ; per quanto lui non po essere molto discosto. Altro per la presente non me occurre. En Baruuyk, a di xvij Aprille 1496. Et ho dato ad presente portatore, 3 ▽.

Vostro lo prior d Ingliterra
SIR JOHAN QUENDAL

Superscribed.—Sia data ad Bernardo de Binqnole servitore del prior Dingliterra, Roan.

90.

[Sir John Kendal to Stephen Maranecho, ibid. ii. 325.]

Mangnyficho Maranecho, a voi me recommando. Per lo potador ho inteso de la vostra salute, del qual ho grandi plaser, et anchora o inteso como siti partito del realme de Napoli, per quanto haveti peliato la parte April, Fransese. No obstante ho inteso como haveti portato 1496. algune bone chosi de la, de ly quale volone haver per ly mei denari alguna chosa, segundi voi dyra lo presente portador ; et segundi che apoyntera cum voi, sereti pagato et satysfato, sensa falia alguna, como soi dira lo presente portador, alo qual dati lui fede como ala mea propria persona in questa facienda. Et segundi lo meo aparer, ala fera Danvere [Antwerp] venderiti ben li vestri chosi, segundi ve ne dira lo portador ; et trovareti ala fra Gilmyn, che vene fara bona chiera. Et in quoli parti Joy (?) al presente volo ne per quanto lo rey di Romane manda la sua filia [Margaret of Savoy] in Spanya; et quando li imbassatori furono asi cyrchavano ad conporar Joy (?). Et tamen uno di louro (?) ho mandato ly moy, per quanto ala santa (?) requeste et fano bon pagamento. No altro. Di Londra lo xxv d April. Touto vostro lo prior dInglaterra Fra Johan Chendal.

91.

[Sir John Kendal to the French Prior of St. John's, *ibid.* ii. 326.]

Reverende in Christo pater et domine, d. post de- London, bitam commendationem. In questi di passati scripsi 28 April. ad vostra signoria ad complimento. Lo presente portatore Bernardo mio servitore, lo qual va ad vedere soi parenti in quelle parte, prego la signoria vostra in questa parte havere per recommandato. Non altro. Se potzo fare cosa alguna per la signoria vostra in queste parte date me aviso che lo faro de bono et optimo core. Et Dio ve donna sannitta et tutto quello che vostro core desidera. Ex Londris die xxviij. mensis Aprilis mcccclxxxxvj Fra Johan Quendal touto vostro.

1496.

92.

[Sir John Kendal to William de Novion, *ibid.* ii. 326.]

London, 28 April.

Spectabilis ac relligiose in Christo frater precarissime, io me recommando ad vui. In questi di passati ve scripsi ad complimento. La presente e solo per questa chel presente portatore Bernardo de Bingnolis, mio servitor, va ad trovare (sic) ad Roan, ad trovare suo fradello la o intorna la Piccardia. Et se caso vene ad vui fate la bona ciera. Non altro. Se potzo fare alguna cosa per vui in questa parte, sempre sto al vostro piacere. Ex Londris, adi xxviiij Aprilis 1496. Vostro lo priore dIngliterra Fra Johan Quendal.

93.

[Ferdinand and Isabella to De Puebla, " Spanish Cal.," i. No. 133.]

Almazan, 27 April.

After this courier had been despatched, we were much occupied in our thoughts with the affairs of the King of Scotland, because they are of such great importance, and we wished to get the King of England out of his troubles. Although we have hitherto occupied ourselves with the concerns of Scotland, it has only been to deprive the King of France of assistance, and to help the King of England in the difficulties into which he has been brought by the so-called Duke of York. But now that we consider the marriage as concluded, we regard his affairs as our own. It is, therefore, our wish to get as much influence over the King of Scotland as possible, in order to conclude either peace, or a long truce between Scotland and England. We believe that it would be a great impediment to the accomplishment of our intention, if we were to make the marriage (between Arthur and Katherine) public now. We are persuaded, therefore, that it would be best to conclude

a marriage contract now with the King of England, to April,
be kept secret till we see where the affairs of Scotland $^{1496.}$
will stop, or till we send a person of great experience
to procure what is necessary, and to liberate the King of
England from the danger he is in through the Duke of
York. We hope to be able to accomplish this matter,
if we do not lose our credit with the King of Scotland.
As for the alliance, it may be concluded publicly or
secretly, as the King of England prefers. We shall be
contented with either. If the alliance were to be made
public, there would be no inconvenience in it, as it could
be justified by the league. Conclude it without delay
in one way or other.

94.

[The *Intercursus Magnus* between England and Flanders, Kingsford's "Chronicles," p. 209. Dr. Busch (pp. 367, 373) thinks
Bacon first applied the phrase *Intercursus Magnus* to this
treaty, but he does not disprove Bacon's statement that "this
is that treaty which the Flemmings call at this day *Intercursus
Magnus*". For the text of the Treaty, see below, vol. ii.
No. 149.]

Also in the moneth of Aprill was concluded an Amyte April.
and Entercourse bitwene this land and fflaunders. And
for the assurance of the same, above and besyde both
the Seales of either prynces, was graunted dyvers Townys
of this land to be bounde, among the which London
was One; and vpon the Dukes party the quater Mem-
bris w^t other; which sealyng when it shold haue been
perfourmed, the Comons of the Cite wold nat be aggreable that their Seale shuld passe. And all be it that
mylord of Derby, my lord Tresorer, the Chyef Justice
of England, Maister Bray, and the M. of the Rollys, by
the kynges commaundement come vnto Guyldehall to
exorte the said comons for the same, yet in no wise
they wold nat be aggreable that the Towne Seale shuld

passe : But besought the said lordes to graunt vnto
theym Respite of vj dayes, trustyng by that Season to
shewe in wrytyng soche Consideracions vnto the kynges
Grace and his Counsaill, that his grace shuld be ther-
with well contentid ; which was to theym graunted,
and ther vppon dyvers billes were dyuysed. Albe it
that for the hasty spede of my lord Chambyrlen, which
at that tyme was Redy to departe to Caleys to kepe
suche appoyntement as was before concluded, The
Mayrs seale was taken only as in the maner ffoloweth. . . .

95.

[Zacharia Contarini to the Doge and Senate of Venice, " Venetian
Calendar," i. 241-2.]

On Wednesday last the King of the Romans returned
to Augsburg, on the morrow gave audience to the
English ambassador, and yesterday assigned him audi-
tors, namely the Count of Cornia, Dño Vito Ulchstaner
(Wolckenstein), and Dño Conrad Sturcen, who held a
long conference with him.

To-day his Majesty convoked all the ambassadors of
the League, including the writer, and through Monsr.
de Lupiano (Lupyan?) and Dño Ludovico Bruno intimated to them, that the English ambassador had been
twice with the King and once with the commissioners
appointed him : that from what each of them could
apprehend, he was merely come to spy, and investigate
the projects of the King both about the League and the
Duke of York, notwithstanding which his Majesty had
not failed urging him to join the confederation ; and the
discovery made by them was, that King Henry does
not intend to break with the King of France, but wishes
to join the League merely on the condition that it
should not give subsidy, or favour to any party waging
war on him. The King of the Romans wished there-

fore to have the opinion of the ambassadors whether May, 1496. he should dissemble with Sir Christopher Urswick and dismiss him with fair words, or, on the contrary, let him see that he did not approve of his policy.

After a preamble setting forth the great benefit that would accrue to the Holy League by rendering Henry VII a member of it, most especially with the obligation to attack France, the ambassadors answered unanimously that he (the King of the Romans) should by no means dissemble with Sir Christopher, or dismiss him ; but in such form as of his wisdom he should deem most expedient, request the King of England to join the League, with the obligation to attack France. Should all such exertions fail to obtain this result, the ambassadors proposed that the King of England should be admitted on the mere terms imposed on the other confederates, expressing their conviction that this second arrangement would not be rejected by King Henry, as he had already declared to the ambassadors at his court that he was well disposed so to do.

Contarini and his colleagues then offered, should the King of the Romans approve, to mediate with Sir Christopher Urswick and do all that was possible to bring the matter to the desired conclusion ; whereupon Dom. Ludovic Bruno and Monsr. Lupiano took leave, saying they would acquaint the King of the Romans with the views of the ambassadors.

96.

[Zacharia Contarini to the Doge and Senate of Venice, "Venetian Calendar," i. 242-4.]

After the despatch of his last letters on the 17th, con- Augsburg, ferred again with the English ambassador, who repeated 20 May. the statement made by him to the King of the Romans,

namely, that the King of England, having been requested
by the Pope, the King of the Romans, Spain, Venice,
and Milan, to join the Holy League, was well disposed
to do so, but that, being now at enmity with the Kings
of Scotland and of Denmark, and entertaining suspicion
of the Duke of York and of other rebels in Ireland, he
does not see how he can wage offensive war against the
King of France, or even furnish the subsidies required
by the clauses for a defensive war, both on account of
his being at so great a distance from the confederates
and by reason of the enmity and suspicions aforesaid.
Remarked it was better not to promise than to make
default, and that were the clause relating to subsidies
cancelled, and the articles of the confederation revised and
equalised, that part most especially being limited, and
mention made solely of those having territory in Italy,
the King of England would join the League; and,
should his affairs subsequently assume a firm footing,
he would then do all in his power compatible with his
own honour and the safety of his subjects, adding that
much might be hoped from him.

On the 20th May Contarini and the ambassadors
from Spain and Milan went to the King of the Romans,
on a summons from him, to discuss the despatch of Sir
Christopher Urswick. The King told them that in
execution of their recent suggestions he had again con-
ferred with Urswick, but being unable to obtain any
addition to the original offer, he expressed himself thus :
" Your King refuses to wage war on the King of France
and also to afford subsidy to the confederates in a defensive war, by reason of the suspicion he entertains of
his enemies, and then proposes a compromise with us,
promising not to help any one who may attack us!
This promise amounts to nothing, for if unable to
succour us, neither could he aid our enemies ".

The King of the Romans then said that he would ask Urswick, in the presence of the ambassadors, whether the King of England would aid the Pope, the King of the Romans, and the other kings and princes of the Holy League, and be bound by the same clauses and obligations as the other confederates; stating further to him the perils and accidents which might befall England should the French King's affairs proceed according to the latter's plans, and on the other hand the great benefits that would accrue to the King of England in the event of his joining the League and waging war on France: and that on hearing Urswick's rejoinder he (the King of the Romans) would consult with the ambassadors upon the ultimatum to be given.

Thereupon Sir Christopher Urswick was sent for to the court, and on his arrival Dñs Conrad Sturzen explained to him, in a suitable and very flowery discourse, what the King of the Romans had proposed. The ambassador's reply was in accordance with the statement already made; and when urged to levy war and invade France, he stated he was not aware that any of the allies had proceeded to such an act save the Sovereigns of Spain, nor was it just that his King being the last to join the confederation, should be amongst the first to invade: and that, speaking for himself, it seemed to him fitting, should this war be waged, to stipulate the amount of troops with which each of the allies was to make the attack; how long the war was to last; in what manner the conquered provinces and places were to be distributed; and that none of the parties should be at liberty to make peace, truce, or any other agreement without the express consent of the rest. He ended by saying that, not having any commission, he would acquaint his King with what the King of the Romans had caused to be intimated to him.

9 *

When he had done speaking, the King of the Romans made him withdraw, and said to the ambassadors: " Should you approve, we will dismiss this ambassador, and send our own ambassadors immediately after him to negotiate this affair with the representatives of the other confederates, and also to negociate some form of agreement between him, the King of Scotland, the Duke of York and others his enemies, provided he bind himself to attack the King of France;" and the King of the Romans asked us our opinion, to which he said he should adhere. We answered unanimously that although he needed no counsel, nevertheless we would tell him that we deemed it more expedient to detain the ambassador here, and ask him to write to his King what had been told him, so that the King of England being thus acquainted with the intention of the other confederates, might deliberate and conclude with less loss of time : on the other hand, should Sir Christopher Urswick seem more disposed to depart than to remain, in that case he (the King of the Romans) should give him good and gracious leave, and refer these negociations to the commissioners in England, without sending other ambassadors there.

Says that the reason for persuading the King of the Romans not to send ambassadors was twofold—first, because his commission was already in the hands of the Spanish ambassadors, who would doubtless negotiate the matter with greater care and pains, so as to bring it to a good end, than the proper ambassadors of the King of the Romans, who indeed, to confess the truth, assented with some little difficulty, on account of the Duke of York ; and, secondly, because the missions of the King of the Romans were wont to be more tardy than the need required.

The King of the Romans replied, that were Sir Christopher Urswick of another nature than he is, the sug- May, 1496. gestion of the ambassadors to detain him would have been excellent, but that as he (Urswick) had been previously accredited to the King of the Romans, and having been suborned by the French, made an unfavourable report of the King of the Romans to King Henry VII, which induced the latter to make peace with France, the King of the Romans knew that to detain Urswick could not produce any good result, and he also believed Urswick would not remain willingly. The King of the Romans assented not to send ambassadors, but said that until the King of England was safe from the Duke of York, and from those who favour the latter, he would never attack the King of France, nor give subsidy to the confederation ; and he therefore thought it advisable to promise that immediately on the King of England joining the League, the confederates would send their ambassadors to arrange these differences. Thus in substance was Urswick told in our presence, and that within three days the King of the Romans would give him gracious leave.

97.

[De Puebla to Ferdinand and Isabella, "Spanish Cal.," i. p. 103.]

Henry esteems Flanders more than any other power. London, If Rojas had accomplished what he was requested to 13 June. do, anything whatever might have been obtained from Henry. But Rojas did not only not accomplish it, but did not even prevent the ambassadors of the Archduke from doing everything that was disagreeable in England, giving Henry to understand that the marriage was "nichil". They do not believe it even to this day. Has in vain implored the ambassadors of the Archduke, and sworn to them that Ferdinand and Isabella would regard the affairs of Flanders as their own, and not

June, 1496. have concluded with England, except for the sake of Flanders. There are very few honest servants in that country. They are all influenced by personal interest. Rojas, too, has not done his duty, since he has not excepted Spain, or included her in this treaty. The affairs of Spain are conducted quite differently in England. "Would to God that the Archduchess (Doña Juana) would soon go to Flanders. She will be able to do much good in England and in Flanders, especially if she is as wise as the daughter of such parents is expected to be. Only a few words more about Scotland. If your Highnesses have the so-called Duke of York in your power, and hold him in your Royal hands, you may be sure, according to what I am told, that you can absolutely do your will *in omnibus et per omnia* in England." They are very angry in England with the King of the Romans, for having sent the so-called son of Edward to England.

If they can now accomplish what is stated above, they will have " all the glory before God and the world " to themselves. But they must be very careful, for the Scotch "are astute in the highest degree ".

98.

[Zacharia Contarini to the Doge and Senate of Venice, " Venetian Calendar," i. No. 706.]

Augsburg,   Has been told by Dom. Erasmo Brascha that the
14 June.   King of the Romans was greatly surprised at hearing, by the courier from Milan, that the King of England had sent an ambassador to France, to arrange the disputes with the King of Naples ; and that Sir Christopher Urswick made no mention soever of this to him (the King of the Romans). Brascha affirmed what the King of the Romans said heretofore, namely, that by reason of the King of England's suspicion of the Duke

of York, he will endeavour to be on good terms with June, 1496.
everybody, and on no account quarrel with the King of
France.

99.

[Giovanni de Bebulcho to the Milanese secretary, "Milanese
Calendar," i. 299.]

When I asked what news there was of the Duke of Milan,
York, he [1] replied that the duke was in Scotland, making 3 July.
a marriage with a cousin of the king there. I asked
him if he had heard anything about the Scots invading
England. He said he had not, and that the king of
Scots was very poor as regards money, but he had an
abundance of men, and that the Scots were the enemies
of the English and the friends of the French. I asked
him about English affairs. He said that the king is
rather feared than loved, and this was due to his avarice.
I asked who ruled him and had control over him. He
said there was only one who can do anything, and he is
named Master Bray, who controls the king's treasure.
The king is very powerful in money, but if fortune
allowed some lord of the blood royal to rise and he had
to take the field, he would fare badly owing to his
avarice ; his people would abandon him. They would
treat him as they did King Richard, whom they abandoned, taking the other side because he put to death
his nephews, to whom the kingdom belonged.

I asked if the King of England had received regularly
every year the sum promised by the King of France.
He said that the last two payments were in arrear,
amounting to 40,000 crowns each. I asked if any
Italian had influence with Master Bray : he said that
Benedetto Bonvixi of Lucca has a good deal. I asked

---

[1] A Florentine, Aldobrandini, who had been in London at Easter
and then at Bruges.

July, 1496. about the feeling of the English towards the French ;
he said it could not be worse, and whenever the king
wished to cross he would find no lack of as many men
and as much money as he wanted. That is all I learned
from him.

100.

[Sir John Ramsay, Lord Bothwell to Henry VII, Ellis's "Original
Letters," 1st Ser. i. 23. Bothwell's services to Henry VII
were not gratuitous, cf. Bentley's "Excerpta Historica,"
p. 108 : "May 24, To the Lorde Bothwell, £10".]

September.   Pleaise zour Graice anet [1] ye mater yat master Wyot
laid to me I have ben besy about it, and my lord of
Boughcan [Buchan] takis apon hym ye fulfilling of it,
gyf it be possible ; and thinks best now in yis lang nyt
within his tent to enterprise ye mater ; for he has na
wach bot ye Kings apoinctit to be about him. I pnt' [2]
my Lord zour Letter of ye quhilk he was full glaid and
weill contentit.

I past to Santandr [3] and commonit at lenght with ye
kings broder [the archbishop], and gaff him ye cros bow.
He commends his servis humbly to zour Graice, and
sayes he intendis to do zour Grace serves, and will not,
for ought ye King can do, cum to yis ost [4] againis zour
Graice.[5] And now my lord of Mrray pass' or [over] to
him gyff ye King cummis to yis Jornay, as I dout not he
will, in contrar his barronr' willis and all his hail peplen,
and my Lord will solist yis zoung Prince [James IV's
brother] to cum to zour Graice.

Sr, I ondirstand, ye xxviii day of August, yar com a
man out of Carlell to Perkin, and eftir Perkin brought
him in to ye King I remanit to ondirstand ye mater.

---

[1] Anent, concerning.   [2] presented.
[3] St. Andrews.   [4] host.
[5] James IV invaded England in September, 1496.

I was informit secretely yat yis man sould have commyn September, 1496.
fra Randell of Dacre, broder to ye lord Dacre, and fra
the Sceltonis for mekyll [Michael?] Scelton yat is her
had ye convoyanc[e] of him.

Sr, ondoutitly thir Northumbirland men commonys
schrevitly[1] at dayis of meting, and at dayis secretly
apoinctit betwix yam and Scottsmen ; and evere day
throw yam yir[2] vacabunds escapis, cummyn to Perkin ;
and sundry w'tings cummys; and now newlinge an[3]
Hatfeld yat was wonnt dwell with my lord of Oxinfurd,
and he tellis mony tydings.

Sr, sen it is yat ye King of Scotts will in no wyse be
inclinit to ye gud of peax nor amyte, without he haf
his mynd fulfillit efter our last commonyng with my
lord of Duresme [Richard Foxe] in Berwick, I trast
verraly zour Graice sall have zour intent sa zour sud-
getts her indevor yam well, for surly yis Jornay ye king
intends to mak, is contrar ye will of ye haill pepill, and
yai ar not well apoinctit therfore, and will zour Grace
send bot douxen[4] Chyftains and men of autorite to
reulle, I dout not, with ye fok[5] yat ar her, zour Grace
sall have ye best daywerk of zour inemys yᵗ ony King
of Englond had yis jC. zers.

Sr, I have shewin ye King of Scotts yis band of ye
erle of Deschemonds, and he will scarsly beleve it.
And now I send it to zour Grace agan be this berrar.

101.

[Bothwell to Henry VII, Ellis's " Original Letters," 1st Ser. i. 25.]

Schir, I commend my servis humbly to zour Hightnes, Berwick,
and all this lang tyme I have remaint oudir respit and 8 Septem-ber.
assurans within ye realm of Scotland, and mast in ye

---

[1] shrewdly.   [2] their.   [3] one.
[4] a dozen.   [5] folk.

court about ye King, geven [1] attendans and making lauboris to do zour Graice ye best serves I can, and has full oft tymes solist ye Kings hightnes and all ye weill avisit lordes of his Realm to lef ye favor and supports ya [2] geve to yis fenyt boy, and stand in amyte and gud love and peax with zour hightnes, to ye quhilk ye King in his ansurs and wourdis sayis alwayis he wald erest [3] sa he myt have sic things concludit as my lord of Duresme com for ; an gyf yat be not, I ondirstand without dout yis instant xv. day of September the King, with all ye haill [4] peple of his realm he can mak, wilbe at Ellam kyrk within x myll of ye marchis of England, and Perkin and his company with hym ; the quhilk ar now in noum' xiiijC. of all maner of acionis ; [5] and without question has now concludit to enter within yis zour Realm ye xvij day of ye sam monetht in ye quarrell of yis said fenit boy, notwithstanding it is agens ye mynds of nerrest ye hall [6] noum' of his barronr' and peple, bat [7] for ye danger yt ylof [8] myght follow, and for ye inconvenience of ye ceaison ; notwithstanding yis sempill woulfulnes can not be removit out of ye Kings mynd for na persuasion nor mean, I trast verraly, that God will he be punyst be zour mean, for ye cruell consent of ye mourdir of his fadyr.

Sr, ye secund day of September ye King send for his lords yt war nerrest about hym, and causit yam to pas in ye chambre of counsall, and thareftir callit Perkyn to yam, and yai laid mony desiris to him bat anent ye restorance of ye vii Hesdomis, [9] ye deliuerie of ye castell and toune of Bervek, and also for ye listing of ye kings arme, and for charges maid apone him and his company to bind him to pay jC thousand marks within v. zers

---

[1] giving.	[2] they.	[3] first.
[4] whole.	[5] nations.	[6] whole.
[7] both.	[8] that thereof.	[9] Sheriffdoms.

efter his entre.   To yis askit he delay quhill ye morne ; September 1496.
and on ye morn enterit he in ye counsall and touk with
him Sir George Nevall, Lovnd ye prest,[1] and Herron,
and efter lang commonyng has bound him to deliver
Bervik, and to pay for ye costs maid on him fyfty thousand marks in tua zers, and yus is yis takin up in wryting.

Alsa I past to Santandr' with ye King and yar saw ye
rassavyng of ye lord Conquersalt and I did sa mekle yat
ba[t] I red his letter and credence, ye quhilks war ryght
thankfully wretin, bering in effect how ye king of Franc
ondirstud yat yar [2] was ingenering [3] a great apperans
of debat betwixt zour Hightnes and ye King of Scotts,
and how y[t] he of consideracion thar of had sent ye lord
Conquersalt to ondirstand ye Kings mynd and ye occasions of ye sammyn, quhidder zour Grace or the said
King of Scotts war in ye falt ; and becaus of ye tendernes
of blud and also ye tendir amyte he stands in with zou
ba[t], he prayit ye King y[t] he myt be anonper [4] betuix zu
to set zu at concord, for he ondirstud be zour writings
send be Richmound and Gyenis y[t] mekell of this onkynd-
nes movit of ye party of ye king of Scotts.   And efter
yis ye king past to counsaill and touk ye lord Conquersalt and sheu how it was all movit on ye party of England, and how he had lost sa mony schippis, sa great
herschippis of catall on ye bordors ; and efter yis ye
lord Conquersalt was bot right soft in ye solistacion of
yis peax, and to myn apperance maid bot litill diligens
herin, saying to my selff, efter I desirit him to mak diligens, it was no wounder zo[t] ye king war sterrit to on-
kyndnes.

Fordir I have sought out of yis said lord Conquersalt,
and ondirstande werraly,[5] he has laid to ye King to

---

[1] See below, No. 123.   [2] there.   [3] engendering.
[4] an umpire.   [5] verily.

have yis said Perkin send in to France ; and he sall mak
myance ¹ ye king of Scotts sall have for him jC. thousand
crounis, and zit lauboris apone ye sammyn. This I
knaw for certain, to quhat purpos I ondirstand not, bot
I wait ² well ye lord Conquersalt show me ye king of
Franc wald not ye King maryt ³ with zour Grace ; ⁴
alsoo he schow me how great inquesicion was maid to
onderstand of Perkins byrthe bat be ye admirall and
him ; and than I schew him ye Wryting I had of
Meantes, and he planly said he nevir ondirstud it bot
rather trouit ⁵ ye contrary, and I think his cummyn
hudyr ⁶ has don bot litill gud, for he and ye boye ar
everie day in counsaill.

Sr, zot yis be prevy, and zot he be my cuntreman,
I beand zour servand, I welbot schew ye treucht ; and
ford' ⁷ I sall schew zour Grace at my cummyn.

Sr, I wrait how Sr George Nevill and his complices
war bondid befor my lord of Murray and me ; and
anon efter I gat zour last wryting to yat effect I assayit
ye said Sr George and he ansuerid me yat he was
inclinit to be at ye commandement of the King of
Scotts and gyf zour Grace and he agreet he sould tharin
quyt him of Perkin ; and now yai stand in anew coun-
sort ; and yus I will not schew zour wryting, bot I
dont not he and all ye remanent will repent it ; but
surly in ye counsaill he desirit yis Dyet sould be put
of quhill ye next somer, & yt he said me was for ye
pleasor of zour Grace ; and I answerit ze karit not for
his pleasor or displeasor.

Sr, and it be not yat zour Grace pas in agrement
with ye King of Scotts, as me semes ze neid litill, and
zour Graice ondirstud all things, I dout not ye zoung

---

¹ means.   ² wot.
³ married.   ⁴ Into your Grace's family.
⁵ trowed.   ⁶ hither.   ⁷ further.

aventurusnes of ye King will bat joupert himselff, ye September, boy, and all his peple : and will zour graice do a part of 1496. my sempill avertisement, I dout not yar Journay salbe repentit in to Scotland yis hundret zer to cum : and be God him selff, yar sal be na her [1] in England sall mar willingly nor treuly help yarto, becaus I find him sa fer oute of reason, and sa litill inclinit to gudnes, bot all to traublen and cruelte, without his wilbe fulfillit in all poincts ; and wat he avis weill snybbit,[2] he wald be ye better avisit quhill he leuit.[3]

Sr, king Edward had never fully ye perfit love of his pepleu quhill he had wer off Scotland ; and he mad sa gud diligence and provision tharin, that to yis our [4] he is lovit ; and zour Grace may als well, and has als gud atyme as he had ; for I tak on me ye King of Scotts had not a C. pounds quhill now yt he has cunzet [5] his chenys, his plat, and his copbords, and yar was nevir pepill wars [6] content of ye kings guvernans yan yai ar now. Notwithstanding I have ben sa lang and desirusly inclinit to ye amyte, now seing ye falt in ye king of Scotts, I salbe als willing to do ye contrar ; and, cum it to apruff,[7] yar vill meny be contrar his opunion. Thar is mony of his faderis servants wald se a ramedy of ye ded [8] of his fadyr zit.[9]

Please your Graice to send me wourd quhat serves or oder thing I sall do, for I salbe redy to do zour commandements at my power ; and now Is cum [10] in within zour Realm to avait opon zour Grace or on quhom zour Grace will apoinct me ; and I sall not faill be Godds grace in yis besinis to do gud and exceptable serves, and yar salbe na preve thing don, noudyr about

[1] No lord ?   [2] snubbed.   [3] till he leave it.
[4] hour.   [5] coined.   [6] worse.   [7] a proof.
[8] death, though Sir Henry Ellis suggests " deed ".
[9] yet.   [10] I am come.

ye king nor in his ost, bot zour Grace sall have knau-
lage tharof ; and that that is trew and onfenit, for I
have stable sit sic myance or I departit.[1]

Sr, her is cummyn out of Flandrs Rodyk de la Lane
with twa litill schippis and iij[xx]. off Almans. I stud by
quhen ye King ressavit him in presence of Perkin ; and
thus he said in Franch. " Sr, I am cummyn her
accordyng to my promys, to do zour Hightnes servis,
and for non oder mans saik am I cum her, for and I had
not had zour letters of warand I had ben arrestit in
Flandrs, and put to great trouble for Perkins sak ; "
and he com not ner Perkin ; and than cam Perkin to
him, and he salut him, and askit how his Ant did ; and
he said " well " ; and he inquirit gyf he had ony letters
fra hir to him, and he sad he durst bring nan, bot he
had to ye King.   And surly he has brought ye king
sundry pleasant things for ye wer,[2] bat for man and
hors.

Sr, and zour Graice have agud [3] army on ye see, ze
myt do a great act, for all ye schipmen and inhabitants
[of] ye havin towns pass with ye king beland and yus
myt all thar navy be distroyit and havin touns brynt.

I past in ye Castell of Edinburght, and saw ye provision of Ordinance, ye quhilk is bot litill, that is to say
ij. great curtaldis [4] yt war send out of France, x. falconis
or litill serpentinis,[5] xxx cart gunnis of irne with
chawmeris,[6] and xvi clos carts for spers, powder,
stanis [7] and odir stuf to yir gunnis longin.

Sr, I dout nathing, bot gyf thar folkis at yar entre
within iiij or v nyghts be so wery for waching and for
lak of wetaillis [8] yat ya sall call on ye king to ratorne

---

[1] I have established such means before I departed.
[2] war.   [3] a good.   [4] short pieces of ordnance.
[5] small artillery.   [6] chambers.
[7] stones used as cannon balls.   [8] victuals.

hame, and yus ratornyng ya sall not be foughten septemSeptember
withall. That it wald pleas zour Grace efter yar entre ^{1496.}
in England y^r ye folkis of Northumbreland and ye
byschoprek[1] rate it to ye hed of Northumbreland west-
wart, and sa com northwart, noght streight apon ye Scotts
ost, bot sydlings, quhill yai war ba^t elyk[2] northt and
southt apon yam; and yan I wald yir said folks fell in
on yar bakks, and before yame to encounter yam ye
power of Zorkschir ; and yus gyf yai oudyr[3] ret'it or
fled abak, ya myt not escap, bot be foughtin with all ;
for considering yis lang ny^t and ye great baggage and
cariags, xx M men war als sufficient as jC. thousand :
and yir folks behind yam wald put yam to agrettar
affray yan twys samony[4] effor yam. Sr, I have herd
the disputacionis of my cuntremen, and yarfor I wryt
yis clause. Fordyr ye holy T'nite manten zour honor
and estat in eternall felicite. W'tin at Bervek ye viij
day of Septembre.

102.

[The Scottish invasion, Kingsford's " Chronicles," p. 210.]

And this yere in the moneth of Septembre the kyng 17 Septem
of Scottes, w^t baner displayd, w^t greate nombre of ^{ber.}
Scottes Entred iiij myle w^tyn this land, and brent
housis and cast downe ij smale Towers or pyles, makyng
greate bost and brag. But when he vnderstood of the
lord Nevelles comyng w^t iiij m^l men, and other of the
March party comyng after to haue given hym bataill,
at mydnyght aftir, he w^t his people departed in such
hast that ovir the water of Twede, which in his
comyng in to this land he was ij dayes in conveyng,
at his Rotournyng home he was, and all his people
sette ouer in viij owres.

[1] I.e. of Durham. [2] alike. [3] either. [4] so many.

1496.   103.

[Ayala's mission to England, "Milanese Calendar," i. 307.]

1 October.　The sovereigns of Spain also have a hand in them
[English affairs], and although an ambassador is resident
there, they have sent Don Pedro de Ayala, who should
have arrived several days ago; and thereby depend the
laws and the prophets,[1] that the king may act as we
desire. You will hear things to please you for the
king's service.

                              104.

[A loan from the city; Lord Fitzwalter's execution, Kingsford's
                "Chronicles," p. 212.]

18 November.　Also vpon the Sonday folowyng [the xviijth day of
Nouembre] was sent from the kyng M. sir Regnold
Bray, with other of the kynges Counsell, to the Mair
to borow of the Citie xm^l li. And vpon the Thursday
next folowyng was graunted by a Comon Counsell to
lende to the kyng iiij m^l li

Also the same weke at Caleis was beheded the lord
ffitzwater, which before season for his offence had de-
serued to dye, albe it that the kyng of his mooste specyall
grace pardoned hym of his lyf, commyttyng hym to
Guynys, there to haue remayned as prisoner where he
wold haue broken prison, ffor the which and other
offences approved ageyn hym he dyed; vpon whose
soule Jhesu haue mercy!

[1] Cf. Bacon's passage, "Amongst these troubles both civil and
external, came into England from Spain Peter Hialas, some call
him Elias (surely he was the forerunner of the good hap, that we
enjoy this day. For his ambassage set the truce between England
and Scotland; the truce drew on the peace; the peace the marriage; and the marriage the union of the kingdoms)."

1497. 1497.

105.

[Opening of Henry VII's sixth parliament, "Rot. Parl.," vi. 509.]

Memorandum quod die Lune, sexto decimo die 16 Janu-
Januarii, anno regni Regis Henrici Septimi post ary·
Conquestum duodecimo ; . . . Reverendissimus Pater
Johannes Cardinalis, Archiepiscopus Cantuar', Cancellarius Angliæ   pronunciavit & declaravit; assumens
pro exordio quandam Romanorum notissimam historiam diu per Hannibalem suosque complices fatiga-
torum peneque devictorum post cladem Canensem,
nisi bonorum virorum consilio potiti, quasi de gravi
sompno evigilantes, resumptis viribus, Scipionem cum
exercitu Cartaginem destinassent. Et prosecutus est
palam ac dilucide commemorando, primo facta & exempla
majorum & strenuorum virorum, licet gentilium &
paganorum, ut puta Curcii, Scevolæ, Reguli & aliorum,
qui rempublicam sue saluti preferentes, potius morte
crudelissima mori elegerunt, quam patriam periclitari
conspicerent ; quorum exemplo patriam ante omnia
tutandam liberandamque esse persuasit : neque avaricie
vel private utilitati inhiandum esse, quemadmodum
temporibus Marii & Sille, Pompei & Julii Cesaris factum
intelleximus, quorum finis repentinus preproperusque
interitus fuit. Neque hiis modo paganorum exemplis
aut historiis pro patria pugnandum moriendumque
esse ostendit ; verum eciam id jure divino, canonico
& civili faciendum fore, exemplo Machabeorum,
aliorumque sanctorum patrum comprobandum, alle-
gando pro suo proposito Sanctorum Augustini, Thome,
aliorumque theologorum auctoritates, necnon decreta,
decretales leges, legumque doctores copiosissime. Sec-

undo, declaravit dilucide treugam & guerrarum absti-
nentiam initas & conclusas, inter commissarios serenissi-
mi domini nostri, & Scotorum regem, Anno Domini
millesimo quadragentesimo nonagesimo quarto, mense
Aprili, usque ad septennium proximum sequendum
pleneque complendum duraturas . . . Tercio, ultimoque
ostendit qualiter, non obstante dictarum treugarum
firmissimo ut estimabatur federe percusso, inviolabilique
ex parte illustrissimi domini nostri regis observancia
ejusdem, dictus Scotorum rex temerarie, contra omnem
fidem, equitatem & justiciam, sine causa, occasione vel
monicione aliqna, paucis ante diebus, regnum hoc
invictissimi domini nostri regis, cum innumerosissimo
exercitu, vexillis extensis, hostiliter invasit, cede &
incendio multa comminuens : cui malo mature opor-
tuneque prospicere omnes ad presens Parliamentum
convocatos esse denunciavit, quibus patria non minus
quam vita chara esse deberet.

106.

[The Cornish rebellion, Kingsford's "Chronicles," p. 213. Compare Fenley's "Town Chronicles," p. 173, and the "Greyfriars'
Chronicle," p. 25. The latter chronicle says that 30,000 rebels
rose.]

In the latter Ende of May the Comons of Cornewaill
assembled theym in greate numbre, of the which was
capeteyn a blak smyth ; and so came to Exetir, wherfore
the kyng in all hast departed w^t a few people from
Shene Towardestheym. And where my lord Chamberleyn
was before appoynted that at that season he shuld haue
goon north ward for the defence of the Scottes w^t viij m^l
Sowdiours, he was sent by the kyng towardes the said
Cornysshe men ; and he departid from the kyng from
Shene the Sonday before Saynt Barnabes day. And
the kyng went from Shene the Monday next folowyng ;

and the Quene w^t my lord of York came vpon Tuesday June, 1497.
to Coldharborough, and there lay till the Monday folow- 12 June.
yng, from whens her grace w^t my said lord of york,
of the age of vj yeres or thereaboute, Removed vnto
the Toure of London. And vpon the same Monday certeyn tydynges wer brought vnto the Mair that the said
Comons wer in fernam,^{1} In whose cumpany was the
lord Awdley. And their cumpany was at that day
accompted to the numbre of xv m^l men. And the Tuesday folowyng, which was the xiijth day of Junii, was a 13 June.
generall Wacche in London. And the same after none
my lord Chamberleyn w^t other knyghtes, accompanyed
w^t viij or x m^l horsemen, came vnto hounslow heth,
whether was sent by the Mair certeyn Cartes w^t wyne
and vitaile.

And vpon Weddensday, in the tyme of the generall
procession, came certeyn tydynges vnto the Mair that
the forsaid Comons wer at Guylford, and vpon gille
downe the same day certeyn Sperys of my lord
Chamberleyns Cumpany to the numbre of vC. bekered
w^t theym, and slew some of theym and hurt and toke
ij of their Sperys, which ij Spere men wer brought vnto
my lord Chamberleyn. And the Thursday, at nyght 15 June.
after x of the Clok, the Oost of my lord Chamberleyn
came into Saynt Georges ffelde, and there lay that nyght.
And the same Thursday all the Cornysshe men removed
to Bansted Downe, and the nyght after in to Sussex
toward Rayle. And the kyng w^t his people and Ost
lay that nyght aboute Henley vpon Themys. And the
said nyght was Secret Meanes made vnto my lord
Chamberleyn by dyuers of the Cornysshe men, that it
wold please his lordship to be a meane vnto the kynges
grace that the said Comons of Cornwaill myght haue
for theym a generall pardon; And they wold of a

^{1} Farnham
10 *

148   THE REIGN OF HENRY VII

June, 1497. Suyrtie bryng in to my said lord Chamberleyn the said lord Awdeley, And their other hede capitayne the Smyth.

16 June.   Vpon the ffriday folowyng in the mornyng, aboute viij of the Clok, the Ost of my lord Chamberleyn Removed out of the ffeeld, and went toward Croydon; but they after Retourned agayn, so that by ij of the Clok they wer all in the forenamed ffelde of Saynt Georges. And that after none came also thider the kynges Oste w^t many of his lordes. And when the Mair with his Brethern and all the chief craftes of the Citie were rèdy standyng in harneys from the Brigge vuto Graschurche to Receyve the kyng, which as the Mair had vnderstandyng that his grace that nyght wold haue comen to the Tower, tydynges came to the Mayr that the kyng entendid that nyght to lye at Lambhith, so that then euery man departid home; and the kynge was after seen in the ffeelde, and abrewyng and comfortyng of his people, the which wer numbred vpon xxv m^l men. And the Cornysshe men this after none came agayn vnto the blak heth, and there pitched their ffeeld, and there lay all that nyght in greate Agony and variaunce; ffor some of theym were myended to haue comyn to the kyng, and to hau yolden theym and put theym fully in his mercy and grace, but the Smyth was of the contrary myende. And vpon the mornyng, aboute vj of the Clok

17 June.   of the Saterday, beyng the xvij^th day of Juyn, sir Humfrey Stanley w^t his Cumpany set vpon theym, and my lord of Oxinford and other vpon all other partes, so that w^tin a short season, or evir the kyng myght approche the ffeld, they were distressid; Albe it that my lord Chamberleyn hastid hym in all possible wise, in such maner that hym self was in greate daunger, at whos comyng anon they fledde. And there was taken [1]

---

[1] Bentley, "Excerpta Historica," p. 112: "23 June. To one that toke the Lorde Audeley, £1. To my Lorde Dacres servant that

the lord Awdley, and a Gentilman called fflammok, and June, 1497. their Capitayn the Smyth, all three on lyve and vnhurt, and moche of their people slayn, and many taken prisoners. And this done the kyng Rode to the place where they had pitched their ffelde. . . . And after was dyuers of the said Prisoners sold, some for xii d. and summe for more. And upon Monday folowyng the lord Awdeley, the forsaid flammok, and the Smyth, whos name was Mychaell Joseph, wer before the kyng and the lordes of his counsaill within the Tower, and there examined.

107.

[The execution of Lord Audley and other rebels, Kingsford's "Chronicles," p. 215.]

Ye haue hard before how that the Smyth, Capitayn 26.28 June. of the forsaid Comons of Cornewaill, wer taken at the blak heth w^t many moo, as the lord Awdley, flammok, and many other; which said Smyth and fflammok wer vpon the Monday, beyng the xxvj day of Juyn, Arayned in the White hall at Westmynster, and there adiuged; and vpon the morow, Tuesday folowyng, the said Smyth and fflammok wer drawen from the Tower through the Citie vnto Tiborn; and ther hanged till they wer dede, and after stryken downe, and heded and after quaterid.

And the same day was the lord Awdley had from the Tower to Westm', the Axe of the Tower borne byfore hym. And there in the White hall a-Reyned and adiuged; and that after none drawen from Westm' vnto Newgate, and there Remayned all nyght. And vpon Weddensday in the mornyng, aboute ix of the Clok, drawen from the said Gaole of Newgate vnto the

toke the Lorde Audeley, for his costs, £1 6s. 8d. . . 30 June. To one that toke the Lorde Audley, £2."

June, 1497. Tower hill w^t a cote armour vpon hym of papir, all to torne ; and there his hede stryken off : vpon whos Soule, and all christen god haue mercy ! amen ! And after his hede set vpon the Brigge. The cause of Rysyng of those Comons was after the Comon ffame for the graunt of swich money as was graunted at the last parliament, for the which the said Comons put in blame the Archbisshop of Caunterbury, my lord Cardynall, also the Archebisshop [sic] of Durham, the Bisshop of Bathe, Sir Reynold Bray and Sir Thomas Lovell, knyghtes, w^t other ; which persones their myendes was to have distroyed ; this was their owteward Colour, what their Inward intent was God knoweth, but what hath ensued of like besynesse is euydent, as by Jak Straw, Jak Cade and other.

108.

[Perkin Warbeck's proclamation, Brit. Mus. "Birch MS." 4160. This MS. was transcribed in 1616 from an original in the "Cotton MSS.," which was subsequently destroyed by fire ; another transcript, which is identical except for some variations of spelling, is in "Harleian MS.," 283 f. 123b ; and a third, which is less accurate, is in "Egerton MS.," 2219.]

July. Richard by the grace of God King of England, and of France, Lord of Ireland, Prince of Wales. To all those, that these our present letters shall see, hear or read, and to every of them greeting. And wheras We in our tender age, escaped by God's great might out of the Tower of London, and were secretly conveyed over the sea to divers other countries, there remaining certain years as unknown. The which season it happened one Henry son to Edmond Tydder—Earl of Richmond created, son to Owen Tydder of low birth in the country of Wales—to come from France and entered into this our realm, and by subtle false means to obtain the crown of the same unto us of right appertaining :

Which Henry is our extreme, and mortal enemy, as soon
as he had knowledge of our being alive, imagined, compassed and wrought, all the subtle ways and means he
could devise, to our final destruction, insomuch as he
has not only falsely surmised us to be a feigned person,
giving us nicknames, so abusing your minds; but also to
deter and put us from our entry into this our realm, hath
offered large sums of money to corrupt the princes of
every land and country, and that we have been retained
with, and made importune labour to certain of our servants about our person—some of them to murder our
person, and other to forsake and leave our righteous
quarrel, and to depart from our service, as by Sir Robert
Clyfford and other was verified and openly proved; and
to bring his cursed and malicious intent aforesaid to his
purpose, he hath subtilly and by crafty means levied
outrageous and importable sums of money upon the
whole body of our realm to the great hurt and im-
poverishing of the same.   All which subtle and corrupt
labours by him made to our great jeopardy and peril
we have by God's might graciously escaped and over-
passed as well by land as by sea, and be now with the
right high and mighty prince, our dearest cousin the
King of Scots; which without any gift or other thing
by him desired or demanded to the prejudice or hurt of
us or our crown or realm hath full lovingly and kindly
retained us, by whose aid and supportation we in proper
person be now by God's grace entered into this our
realm of England, where we shall shew ourselves
openly unto you; also confounding our foresaid enemy
and all his false sayings, and also every man of reason
and discretion may well understand that him needed
not to have made the foresaid costages and importune
labour if we had been such a feigned person as he untruly surmiseth, ascertaining you how the mind and

July, 1497. intent of the foresaid noble prince our dearest cousin, is, if that he may or see our subjects and natural liege people according to right and the duty of their allegiance, resort lovingly unto us with such power as by their puissance shall move, be able of likelyhood to distress and subdue our enemies, he is fully set and determined to return home again quietly with his people to his own land, without doing or suffering to be done any hurt or prejudice unto our realm or the inhabitants of the same. Also our great enemy to fortify his false quarrel, hath caused divers nobles of this our realm, whom he hath suspect and stood in dread of, to be cruelly murdered, as our cousin the Lord Fitzwalter,[1] Sir William Stanley, Sir Robert Chamberlayne, Sir Simon Montford, Sir Robert Radcliffe, William Daubeney, Humphrey Stafford among other besides such as have dearly bought their lives ; some of which nobles are now in the sanctuary. Also he hath long kept and yet keepeth in prison, our right intirely well-beloved cousin Edward son and heir to our uncle Duke of Clarence, and others, withholding from them their rightfull inheritance, to the intent they ne should be of might and power to aid and assist us at our need after the duty of their leigeance. He hath also married by compulsion certain of our sisters, and also the sister of our foresaid cousin the Earl of Warwick, and divers other ladies of the blood royal, unto certain his kinsmen and friends of simple and low degree and putting apart all well disposed nobles he hath none in favour and trust about his person but Bishop Fox, Smith, Bray, Lovell, Oliver King, Sir Charles Somerset, David Owen,

---

[1] Fitzwalter was executed at Calais in November, 1496 (see above, p. 144). This allusion shows that this proclamation should be associated with James IV's invasion of July, 1497, rather than with that of September, 1496.

Rysley, Sir James Turborville, Tylere, Robert Litton, July, 1497. Guildeforde, Chumley, Empson, James Hobart, John Cutte, Garthe, Hansey, Wyat, and such others, caitiffs and villains of simple birth, which by subtle inventions and pilling of the people have been the principal finders, occasioners and counsellors of the misrule and mischief now reigning in England.

Also we be credibly informed that our said Enemy not regarding the wealth and prosperity of this land, but only the safeguard and surety of his person, hath sent in to divers places out of our realm the foresaid nobles and caused to be conveyed from thence to other places the treasure of this our realm, purposing to depart after in proper person with many other Estates of the Land, being now at his rule and disposition. And if he should be so suffered to depart, as God defend, it should be to the greatest hurt jeopardy and perill of the whole realm that could be thought or imagined ; wherefore we desire and pray you and nevertheless charge you and every of you, as ye intend the surety of yourself and the commonwealth of our land your native ground, to put you in your most effectual devoirs with all diligence to the uttermost of your power to stop and let his passage out of this our realm ; ascertaining you that what person or persons shall fortune to take or distress him shall have for his or their true acquittal in that behalf after their estate and degrees, so as the most low and simplest of degree that shall happen to take or distress him shall have for his labour one thousand pounds in money and houses and lands to the yearly value of one hundred marks to him and his heirs for ever. We remembering these premises with the great and execrable offences daily committed and done by our foresaid great enemy and his adherents in breaking the libertys and franchises of our Mother Holy Church, to the high dis-

July, 1497. pleasure of Almighty God, besides the manifold treasons, abominable murders, manslaughters, robberies, extorsions, the daily pilling of the people by dismes, taskes, tallages, benevolences and other unlawful impositions and grievous exactions, with many other heinous offences, to the likely destruction and desolation of the whole realm, as God defend, shall put ourself effectually in our devoir, not as a stepdame, but as the very true mother of the child, languishing and standing in perill to redress and subdue the foresaid mischief and misrule, and to punish the occasioners and haunters thereof after their deserts in example of others. We shall also by God's grace and the help and assistance of the great Lords of our blood with the Council of other sad persons of approved policy, prudence and experience, dreading God and having tender zeal and affection to indifferent ministration of Justice, and the public Weal of the land, peruse and call to remembrance the good Laws and Customes heretofore made by our noble progenitors Kings of England and see them put in due and lawfull Execution, according to the effect and true meaning they were first made ordained for ; so that by virtue thereof, as well the disinheriting of rightfull heirs, as the injuries and wrongs in any wise committed and done unto the subjects of our realm, both spiritual and temporal shall be duly redressed, according to right, law and good conscience : and shall see that the commodities of our realm be employed to the most advantage of the same intercourse of merchandise betwixt realm and realm to be ministred and handled as shall now be to the common weal and prosperity of our subjects, and all such dismes, tasks, tallages, benevolences, unlawfull impositions and grievous exactions as be above rehersed, utterly to be fordone and laid apart and never from henceforth to be called upon but in such causes, as our noble progenitors, Kings of England, have of old time July, 1497. been accustomed to have the aid succour and help of their subjects and true liegemen.

Also we will that all such persons, as have imagined, compassed or wrought privily or apparently since the reign of our foresaid enemy, or before anything against us, except such as since the reign have imagined our death, shall have their free pardon for the same of their lives lands and goods ; so that they at this time, according to right and the duty of their allegiances, take our righteous quarrell and part, and aid, comfort and support us with their bodys and goods.

And over this we let you wit, that upon our foresaid enemy, his adherents and partakers, with all other such as will take their false quarrel and stand in their defence ag^st us with their bodys and goods, we shall come and enter upon them as their heavy lord, and take and repute them and every of them as our traitours and rebels ; and see them punished according ; and upon all other our subjects, that according to right and the duty of their liegeaunce will aid succour and comfort us to their powers with their lives or goods or victual our host for ready money ; we shall come and enter upon them lovingly as their natural liege lord, and see they have justice to them equally ministered upon their causes.   Wherefore we will and desire you and every of you that incontinent upon the hearing of this our pro- clamation ye, according to the duty of your allegeances, arready yourselves in your best defensible array, and give your personal attendance upon us where we shall then fortune to be, and in your so doing ye shall find us your right speciall and singular good lord, and so to see you recompensed and rewarded as by your service shall be unto us deserved.

[Henry VII to the Mayor and citizens of Waterford, Halliwell's
"Letters," i. 174.]

Wood-
stock,
6 August.

Trusty and well-beloved, we greet you, and have received your writing, bearing date the first day of this
instant month; whereby we conceive that Perkin
Warbeck came unto the Haven of Cork the 25th day
of July last passed, and that he intendeth to make sail
thence towards our county of Cornwall: for the which
your certificate in this part, and for the true minds that
you have always borne towards us, and now especially for
the speedy sending of your said writing which we received the 5th day of this said month, in the morning,
we give unto you our right hearty thanks, as we have
singular cause so to do; praying you of your good perseverance in the same, and also to send unto us by your
writing such news from time to time as shall be occurr-
ent in those parts; whereby you shall minister unto us
full good pleasure to your semblable thanks hereafter,
and cause us not to forget your said good minds unto
us in any your reasonable desires for time to come.

Given under our signet, at our manor of Woodstock,
the 6th day of August.

Over this we pray you to put you in effectual diligence
for the taking of the said Perkin, and him so taken to
send unto us; wherein you shall not only singularly
please us, but shall have also for the same, in money
counted, the sum of a thousand marks sterling for your
reward; whereunto you may verily trust, for so we
assure you by this our present letter, and therefore we
think it behoveful that you set forth ships to the sea
for the taking of Perkin aforesaid. For they that take
him or bring or send him surely unto us, shall have undoubtedly the said reward.

JAMES IV'S SECOND INVASION   157

110.   1497.

[News received from England, by letters dated 24 August, "Milanese Calendar," i. 320.]

First of all, by God's grace, the king and the whole London,
Court were in good condition, and on the 17th August
were at a place called Woodstock, fifty miles from London, where it is said they would reside until Michael-
mas, more or less according to circumstances.[1] That
in that place on the 14th July, there had been firmly
concluded and published the marriage of the daughter
of the King of Spain to the eldest son of the King of
England, and she was to come over next spring. That
the King of Scotland with his whole army, accompanied
by the individual who styles himself the Duke of York,
had been besieging a place in England on the seashore,
and King Henry had sent his forces, numbering 40,000
men, by sea and land to give battle. So they fought
and many fell on both sides, the King of Scotland being
put to flight, abandoning all his artillery; but as the
matter is very recent, the writer was unable to learn
the numbers of the slain. The English were pursuing
the Scots and following up the victory. The truth
would soon be heard and he would then write to his
Excellency.

Also that Monsignor de Deber and two other captains [2] who had lately rebelled against the king had been
beheaded and quartered in the city of London on the
28th of June, many others being put to death, so that

[1] Henry's movements can be traced in his privy purse expenses.
He was at Woodstock from 30 July to 18 August and from 22 August
till 27 September. Then on the news of Perkin's landing he moved
westwards by way of Cirencester, Malmesbury, Bath, and Wells
("Excerpta Historica," p. 113).

[2] Lord Audley, Flammock, and Michael Joseph.

his dominion may be considered much strengthened and permanent.

Also some months ago his Majesty sent out a Venetian, who is a very good mariner, and has good skill in discovering new islands, and he has returned safe, and has found two very large and fertile new islands. He has also discovered the seven cities, 400 leagues from England, on the western passage. This next spring his Majesty means to send him with fifteen or twenty ships.[1]

Also the kingdom of England has never for many years been so obedient to its sovereign as it is at present to his Majesty the King.

111.

[The Milanese envoy, Raimondo de Soncino, to Ludovico Sforza, duke of Milan, "Venetian Calendar," i. 751 ; "Milanese Calendar," i. 323.]

8 September. In many things I know this sovereign (Henry VII) to be admirably well informed, but above all because he is most thoroughly acquainted with the affairs of Italy, and receives especial information of every event. He is no less conversant with your own personal attributes and those of your duchy than the King of France ; and when the King of France went into Italy, the King of England sent with him a herald of his own called "Richmond," a sage man who saw everything, until his return.[2] Then the merchants, most especially the Florentines, never cease giving the King of England advices.

Besides this, his Majesty has notable men in Rome, such as Master Giovanni Zilio (de Giglis) a Lucchese, and Master Adrian (Castellesi), clerk of the Treasury,

[1] For further details of Cabot's voyage, see below, Vol. ii., Nos. 169-171.
[2] See below, Vol. iii., No. 6.

who have been benefitted and enriched by him, so that
we have told him nothing new; and the courtiers likewise have a great knowledge of our affairs, in such wise
that I fancy myself at Rome : so I am of opinion, that
should it be chosen to give any intelligence, it would be
well to impart it either more in detail than the others
do, or to be beforehand with them. To this effect the
Genoa letter bag will be of good use, but yet more such
Florentine merchants as are in your confidence, as their
correspondence passes through France without impediment and is but little searched.

The letter of congratulation dated 17 July, on the
victory gained by the King, was to the purpose, though
rather late. The victories were two—the first against
the Cornishmen, who, some ten thousand in number,
took up arms under a blacksmith, saying they would
not pay the subsidy—the other against the King of
Scotland, who raised his camp " not very gloriously,"
to express myself no less modestly than this most sage
King himself did. Another matter also, which his
Majesty did not tell me, is that the youth, the reputed
son of the late King Edward has fled incognito ; and
his wife is said to be a prisoner ; so I consider that this
youth called Perkin has vanished into smoke. The
King of England's dynasty is likewise established
through a successor, whom it may please God to preserve, for his virtue deserves it—I allude to the Prince
(Arthur) ; and your Excellency may surely congratulate
the Sovereigns of Spain on so distinguished a son-in-
law ; and the succession may the more be relied on
should the matrimonial alliance, which I am told is in
negotiation, between Spain and Scotland take place,
and a Spanish ambassador is now with the King of
Scotland. But even should that marriage not be
solemnized, this kingdom is perfectly stable, by reason,

September, 1497. first, of the King's wisdom, whereof every one stands in awe ; and, secondly, on account of the King's wealth, for I am informed that he has upwards of six millions of gold, and it is said that he puts by annually five hundred thousand ducats,[1] which is of easy accomplishment, for his revenue is great and real, not a written schedule (*non in scriptis*) nor does he spend anything. He garrisons two or three fortresses, contrary to the custom of his predecessors, who garrisoned no place. He has neither ordnance nor munitions of war, and his body guard is supposed not to amount to one hundred men, although he is now living in a forest district which is unfortified. He well knows how to temporise, as demonstrated by him before my arrival in this kingdom, when the French ambassadors wanted to go to Scotland under pretence of mediating for the peace, but he entertained them magnificently, made them presents, and sent them home without seeing Scotland ; and now he sends one of his own gentlemen in waiting to France. The Pope is entitled to much praise, for he loves the King cordially, and strengthens his power by ecclesiastical censures, so that at all times rebels are excommunicated. The efficacy of these censures is now felt by the Cornishmen, for all who eat grain garnered since the rebellion, or drink beer brewed with this years crops, die as if they had taken poison, and hence it is publicly reported that the King is under the protection of God eternal.[2]

The Caesarean ambassador and the papal nuncio have not arrived. The Spanish ambassador, in my opinion a very able man, is here. He gives me very good greeting, possibly from the extravagant compliments paid by me to his sovereigns at our first interview. The

[1] A ducat was then reckoned at 4s. 2d.

[2] See below, Vol. iii., part 2.

Neapolitan ambassador is about to depart, which I much September, regret, as he would have enlightened me vastly, and ^{1497.} has done so already to his utmost.

112.

[The Venetian ambassador, Andrea Trevisano, to the Doge, " Venetian Calendar," i. 754.]

On the 24th of August wrote from Stimburg (sic) after- 9 Septem-wards crossed over to the island, and at Dover found the ^{ber.} Prior of Canterbury and Master Corino (sic ; Curzon), gentlemen sent by the King to do him honour. Twenty miles from London was met by the Dean of Windsor and Master Russell, knight, men of great repute, with many other knights and gentlemen, and who delivered a message in the King's name making offers etc ; and riding on, was joined by other parties, so that he entered London with 200 horse on the 26th of August, and great honour was done him. The King being absent, he wrote to his Majesty, who answered that he was to come to Woodstock to have audience ; so he quitted London on the 1st of September, accompanied by the Dean of Windsor and Master Russell, and on the morning of the 3rd arrived at the royal palace of Woodstock.

The king was in the country, at a distance of two (sic) miles, hearing mass, and sent the Bishop of London and the Duke [Earl] of Suffolk, two of the chief personages of his court, to meet the ambassador, who, in a gown of crimson damask, presented himself there to his Majesty. The King received him in a small hall, hung with very handsome tapestry, leaning against a tall gilt chair, covered with cloth of gold.   His Majesty wore a violet coloured gown, lined with cloth of gold, and a collar of many jewels, and on his cap was a large diamond and a most beautiful pearl.   The ambassador having presented the ducal letter made a Latin speech, on the con-

clusion of which the King drew aside, and, having
discussed the reply, caused him to be answered by the
Chancellor Cardinal (Morton), to the effect that he was
glad to see him etc.

Beside the King and the Prince, his eldest son, by
name Arthur, 12 years old, were the Duke of Bucks
("Ducha de Suich") and other lords and prelates were
present ; and throughout the ambassador's speech the
King remained standing. In the reply the Cardinal
evinced great love towards the Signory, and on its conclusion the ambassador was taken into a hall where
dinner had been prepared, and there he dined with
four lords ; and after dinner the King gave him private
audience, which lasted two hours. The King is gracious,
grave and a very worthy person.

He finally visited the Queen, whom he found at the
end of a hall, dressed in cloth of gold ; on one side of her
was the King's mother, on the other her son the Prince.
The Queen is a handsome woman. Having presented
his credentials and said a few words in Italian, the
Queen answered him through the Bishop of London.

He then also visited the Cardinal Lord Chancellor,
presenting the letter of credence, and, after the exchange of suitable compliments, departed for London,
there to await the King, who was expected in a fort-
night, Woodstock being a sorry village, eight (sic)
miles from the palace.

113.

[Henry VII to Sir Gilbert Talbot, Halliwell's "Letters," i. 179.]

Trusty and well-beloved, we greet you well, signifying
unto you, that whereas Perkin Warbeck and his wife
were lately set full poorly to the sea by the King of
Scots, and after that, landed within our land of Ireland,

in the wild Irisherie, where he had been taken by our ^{September,} cousins, the Earls of Kildare and of Desmond, if he and ^{1497.} his said wife had not secretly stolen away. The same Perkin, being so upon the sea, is coming to land in our county of Cornwall, with two small ships and a Briton pinnace, whereupon we have sent our right trusty counsellor, the Lord Daubeney, our Chamberlain, by land, towards those parties to arredie our subjects for the subduing of him, and our right trusty counsellor, the Lord Broke, steward of our household, by water, with our army on the sea, now late returned, to take the said Perkin, if he return again to the sea. And we shall in our own person, if the case so require, go, so accompanied thitherward, with our Lord's mercy, without delay, as we shall subdue the said Perkin, and all other that will take his part, if any such be. And therefore we heartily pray you to address you unto us with six score tall men on horseback, defensibly arrayed, and no more, without any long delay ; and to meet with us, at our manor of Woodstock, the twenty fourth day of the present month ; and at your coming unto us we shall so content you for your and their conduct money, and also wages, as of reason, ye shall hold you pleased, and that ye fail not hereof, as our especial trust is in you.

114.

[Summary of a letter from Raymondo de Soncino, dated 16 September, " Milanese Calendar," i. 325.]

On the 8th September the Duke of York descended ^{London, 16} upon Cornwall with 80 savage Irishmen, and was re-^{September.} ceived by the Cornishmen, who made a rebellion there last month, which was reported, and although the Lord Chancellor offered him full pardon from his Majesty, yet they did not think it possible that he should be pardoned,

11 *

but everyone judges that this will be the final ruin of
the Cornishmen and the end of the Duke of York, because the king with all promptitude had sent troops
against them, and it was announced throughout the
army that he would go there very speedily in person,
and it was considered impossible for him to escape from
his hand, and it was thought that the affair would be
settled within a month.

It might be that the duke trusted that some of the
nobles near Cornwall would move in his favour,' but
they have all learned to their cost the impossibility of
getting out of this country, where owing to the heavy
ground and the marshes it is difficult to ride in winter,
which . . . this kingdom. In the meantime the Scots
are contriving some stroke, although we understand
that between England and [Scotland] the marshes are
so extensive that it would be all but impossible for the
Scots to move in the winter, moreover such a movement
is not expected in these countries, and the Duke of York,
like a desperate man, did not think to drag out the affair
at length.

Everything favours the king, especially an immense
treasure, and because all the nobles of the realm know
the royal wisdom and either fear him or bear him an
extraordinary affection, and not a man of any consideration joins the Duke of York, and the state of the realm
is in the hands of the nobles and not of the people.

Nothing revolutionary occurs, except what may be
compared to the generation of aerial bodies. Thus some
years ago these same Irish took the son of an English
barber and announcing that he was of the blood royal,
proclaimed him as king, subsequently taking him to
England. However, when they encountered the royal
army, the Irish all came off badly and the youth was
taken. By the royal clemency he is living in the Tower

of London, under the very slightest restraint. They September, 1497.
say that his Majesty, out of respect for the sacred
unction, wants to make a priest of him.[1]

As already reported, letters from the king have
reached the Mayor and Council of London with the
news that the Duke of York has escaped from Scotland
and gone to Ireland. There some Irish lords proposed to
apprehend him, but he found some fishermen's vessels,
and got away, and together with his wife he has arrived
in Cornwall. The king says he has sent the Earl of
Vincier,[2] who is near Cornwall, to oppose them, as well
as the Lord Chamberlain,[3] and if necessary he will go
himself in person. The Londoners do not believe what
is told them, because when the time comes, his Majesty
will make provision for everything. In the meantime
they are taking steps that no one shall create any disturbance, and it is practically certain that similar pre-
cautions have been taken not only in this city but
throughout the whole kingdom.

In London they say that the Duke of York is drawing
nigh and that he is bearing three standards, one representing a little boy coming out of the tomb, the second
with a little boy coming out of a wolf's mouth, and
the third with a red lion. They say he has about five
thousand peasants with him. It is supposed that these
little boys are intended to signify that human wisdom,
represented by these same boys, will make things bad
for his enemy. In any case the Duke of York will fall
into the king's hands, and he cannot possibly escape.

[1] Apparently an allusion to Simnel's unction at his coronation at
Dublin. Cf. Shakespeare's
> Not all the water in the rough rude sea
> Can wash the balm from an anointed king.

[2] " De Vincier " probably signifies "Devonshire ".

[3] Daubeny.

1497.   115.

[Sanuto's abstract of a missing despatch from Andrea Trevisano
to the Doge and Senate of Venice, " Venetian Cal.," i. No. 755.]

London, 17   By a letter from the same ambassador dated London
September. 17 September, and received at Venice on the 9th October, the news of those parts purported that " Perichino " (Perkin), called the son of King Edward,—who
styles himself Duke of York, had been in Scotland, and
was the cause of the whole war between the Scotch and
the English,—on hearing of the proposed treaty of
peace, quitted Scotland and came with two ships to
Cornwall.   He had again raised from six to eight
thousand insurgents, and marched sixty miles inland,
leaving his wife and children at a place on the coast
called Penryn.   The King had sent against him the
Captain Chamberlain [Giles, Lord Daubeny] (the same
who gained the victory over the Cornish men), and also
the Earl of Kent [George Grey], with some 12,000 men
in all.   He has likewise ordered many captains and
lords to put themselves in readiness; should need be,
he will march in person.   The ambassador is of opinion
that events will turn out well for the King, who has
also sent the fleet towards Cornwall to prevent the
escape of Perkin by sea.

" Mem. [by Sanuto].—How the courier said, by word
of mouth, that the ambassador had been to a place [1] on
the island where there were the entire ten decads of
Livy, and also some books on astrology, unknown to
the Italians, and that he meant at any rate to obtain
them.   The ambassador from the Duke of Milan [2] was
with ours, and had audience at the same time, but he
referred himself to what ours said.   He had, however,
a lodging of his own, but few horses."

[1] Oxford.   [2] Soncino.

116.

[The Earl of Devonshire to Henry VII, Ellis's " Original Letters,"
1st Ser. i. 36.]

After most humble recommendation had unto your Exeter, 18
September.
Grace, please it your Grace to knawe as I sent unto your
Grace by myne other wryteinge of yesterday of the
demininge of Perkin, and of diverse assaults made by
his company unto the two gates of your Citty of Excester,
and of the defence of the same. It may like your Grace
to understand further, that this morninge, of new, the
said Perkin and his company made fresh assaults upon
the said two gates ; and especially at the North gate,
which was againe well and truly defended, and put
Perkin from his purpose there ; and your said Citty
surely keped and shall bee to the behoofe of your
Grace : in soe much as when Perkin and his company
had well assaid and felt our Gunns, they were faine to
desyre us to have lycence to geder theire company
togeder, and soe to depart and leave your Citty, and to
put us to noe more trouble ; which because wee bee
not able to recounter them, and that our company were
weary and some hurt, therefore it was granted unto
them that they should depart, and not to approch the
Citty in noe wyse. And soe the said Perkin and his
company bee departed from us this day about eleven of
the Clocke in the forenoone, and bee twelve were out
of sight, and which way they would hould I cannot
yet acertayne your Grace ; But as it was said amongst
them they would go to Columpton this night, and
thanked bee God there is none of your true subjects
about this business slayne, but diverse bee hurt. And
doubt not againe, one of yours is hurt, there is twenty
of theires hurt and many slayne. And now I understand certainly that Perkin is to Columpton, and many

September, of his company departed from him, and more will as
1497.   I sell [*sic*] well, and trust verely that your Grace shall
           have good tydings of him shortly.

                              117.

      [Henry, VII to the Bishop of Bath and Wells, Halliwell's " Letters,"
                              i. 183.]

Wood-20   Right reverend father in God, right trusty and well
st°ck,
September. beloved, we greet you well, and have received your
           writing, by the which we conceive how there is word
           that Perkin is landed.   Truth it is that he is so landed,
           and that our commons of Cornwall take his part,
           amongst whom, on Monday last, the eighteenth day of
           September, there was not one gentleman.   On Sunday,
           the seventeenth of September, Perkin and his company
           came afore our city of Exeter, about one after noon, and
           there inranged themselves in the manner of a battle, by
           the space of two hours.   Within that our city were our
           cousin of Devonshire, Sir William Courtney, Sir Jo.
           Sapcotes, Sir Piers Edgecombe, Sir Jo. Croker, Sir
           Walter Courtney, Sir Humfrey Fulforth, with many
           other noblemen, both of our counties of Devonshire and
           Cornwall.   This Perkin sent for to have deliverance of
           our said city, which was denied unto him by our said
           cousin.   Whereupon Perkin and his company went to
           the east gate, and to the northern gate, and assaulted
           the same, but it was so defended, (blessed be God!) that
           Perkin lost above three or four hundred men of his com-
           pany, and so failed of his intention.   On the morrow
           after, the eighteenth day, Perkin and our rebels made a
           new assault at the said northern gate, and eastern gate,
           like as by the copy of the letter from our said cousin
           of Devonshire enclosed, ye shall move [?] to understand
           more at large.   Then Perkin and his company if they

come forward, shall find before them our chamberlain, September, our steward of household, the Lord Saint Maurice, Sir ^{1497.} John Cheney, and the noblemen of the South Wales, and of our counties of Gloster, Wiltshire, Hampshire, Somerset, and Dorset, and at their back the garrison of our said city of Exeter. And we, with our host royal, shall not be far, with the mercy of our Lord, for the final conclusion of the matter. We have proclaimed also, that whoso bringeth the said Perkin alive unto us, he shall have the sum of a thousand marks, and all their offences forgiven, first and last. We trust soon to hear good tidings of the said Perkin.

118.

[Raimondo de Soncino to the Duke of Milan "Milanese Cal.," i. 327.]

On the 19th inst., by Vadino Gambarana of Saona, I advised your Excellency of the coming of Perkin to this realm and what was the general opinion about it; and on the 25th by way of the Genoese at Bruges, I sent word that Perkin had fled. Now with the arrival of the Venetian packet I will send a detailed account of what has taken place according to the relation of Messer Fra Zoan Antonio de Carbonariis of Milan, who was actually present in the city of Exeter.

On the 6th of this month Perkin landed in Cornwall at a port called Mount St. Michael with three small ships and about three hundred persons of various nationalities, who had followed him for some time before. As he had so few with him, it is thought that the Cornishmen must have invited him. In fact eight thousand peasants were forthwith in arms with him, although ill disciplined and without any gentlemen, who form the governing class of England.

The proclaimed -Perkin as King Richard, and they

paid for the victuals with which the communes provided them, as they had done when the Cornishmen were routed at London. They marched towards his Majesty, who did not hear of this movement until the 10th, although it is not more than two hundred miles from Mount St. Michael to Woodstock. Without awaiting the royal command, the Earl of Devon, a lord of the County, opposed these people with about 1,500 men, but owing to the multitude of the enemy he withdrew to the city of Exeter. Perkin arrived at that place at the 22nd hour of the 17th of the month, and being refused admission, he began the attack on two of the gates. He burned one, but the earl drove him off with stones, so that at the second hour on the following day Perkin asked for a truce for six hours. This was granted on the understanding that no one of Exeter should be allowed to follow him. The moment the truce was made, Perkin departed and went to a village called Minet, ten miles from Exeter, where he passed the night. On the 19th he came to another good village called Taunton, twenty-four miles from Exeter, and stayed there until the 21st. During this time he issued some orders. Among other things he published certain apostolic bulls affirming that he was the son of King Edward and that he meant to coin money and give money to all. In the meantime his Majesty had sent the Lord Chamberlain against him with a good number of men, and announced that he would pardon all who laid down their arms. Accordingly the numbers with Perkin constantly lessened. He began to declare that he had a close understanding with some lords of the realm. As the bridges on the straight road were cut, he proposed to turn somewhat to the right and take another way. Subsequently at the fourth hour of the night, he silently departed from the camp with some ten persons September, and at dawn the next morning the unfortunate Cornish- 1497. men discovered their plight and took to flight, to such an extent that by the third hour of the day not one was left in Taunton.

His Majesty had already assembled an army of 30,000 men, and still kept increasing his forces; but this Fra Zuan Antonio went with all speed to Woodstock[1] and brought word of everything. Accordingly his Majesty dismissed all his army except 6000 men, with whom he himself is going into Cornwall. Including the Chamberlain's forces he will have 10,000 men, and it will be the holy oil of the Cornishmen. God grant it be not the same for others also, as they have taken Perkin's chests, and these will probably have papers inside, although we have not heard anything.

As I have already written to your Excellency, this movement was considered puerile by everybody, and the Cardinal, whom I visit frequently, had no other fear except that the man would escape, as he has done. Although I have tried hard to gather from the Cardinal who it is that supports Perkin, I have not succeeded. He only mentioned the King of Scotland and the old Duchess Margaret of Burgundy, King Edward's sister, who has at times written to the Cardinal recommending Perkin as the son of King Edward, by whom the Cardinal was raised up. The Cardinal replied: But indeed he is not reputed the son of King Edward in this kingdom.

Accordingly I repeat that this present state is most stable, even for the king's descendants, since there is no one who aspires to the Crown. With concord at home they have no occasion to fear, and nothing to do with

[1] Henry left Wells on 1 October and reached Taunton on the 4th ("Excerpta Historica," p. 114).

any foreigner, especially as his Majesty has a very great treasure, which increases daily.

What I wrote about the captivity of Perkin's wife was not correct, and I do not believe that she ever left Scotland.

119.

[Perkin Warbeck's letter to his mother, Gairdner's "Richard III," p. 384. Perkin had been brought from Beaulieu to Taunton on 5 October, and was taken thence with the king to Exeter on the 7th, "Excerpta Historica," p. 114.]

Ma mère,—Tant humblement comme faire je pnis, me recommande à vous. Et vous plaise sçavoir que par fortune, soubz couleur de une chose controuvée, que certains Engletz me ont faict faire et prendre supz moi que je estoie le filz du Roi Edouart d'Engleterre, appellè son second filz, Richart duc d'Yorck, je me trouve maintenant en tele perplexite que se vous ne me estes a ceste heure bonne mere, je suis taillie de estre en grand dangier et inconvenient, a cause du nom que je ay a leur instance prins supz moi, et- de l'entreprinse que je aye faicte. Et afin que entendez et cognoissiez clerement que sui vostre filz et non aultre, il vous plaira souvenir, quand je parti de vous avec Berlo pour aller en Anvers, vous me deistes adieu en plorant, et mon père me convoia jusque a la porte de Marvis ; et aussi de là dernière lettre que me escripvistes de vostre main a Medelbourcq que vous estiez accouchiée de une fille, et que pareillement mon frère Thiroyan et ma sœur Jehenne moururent de la peste à la procession de Tournay ; et comment mon père, vous et moi allasmes demeurer à Lannoy hors de la ville ; et vous souvienne de la belle Porcquiere. Le Roi d'Engleterre me tient maintenant en ses mains ; auquel je ay déclaré la vérité de la matière, en lui suppliant très humblement que son plaisir soit moi par-

donner le offense que lui ai faicte, entendu que je ne sui October, 1497.
poinct son subject natif, et ce que je ai faict a esté au
pourchas et desir de ses propres subjectz. Mais je ne
ai de lui encores heu aucunne bonne response, ne ay
espoir de avoir, dont je ai le coer bien dolant. Et
pourtant, ma mère, je vous prie et reqnier de avoir pitè
de moy, et pourchasser ma délivrance. Et me recom-
mandez humblement à mon parin, Pierart Flan, à
Maistre Jean Stalin, mon oncle, à mon compère Guil-
laume Rucq, et à Jehan Bourdeau. Je entends que
mon père est allé de vie à trespas (Dieu ait son ame!),
que me sont dures nouvelles. Et à Dieu soyez. Escrips
à Excestre, le xiije jour de Octobre de la main de vostre
humble filz,

PIERREQUIN WERBECQUE.

Ma mère, je vous prie que me voelliez envoier un
petit de argent pour moi aidier, afin que mes gardes me
soient plus amiables en leur donnant quelque chose.
Recommandez-moi à ma tante Stalins, et à tous mes
bons voisins.

A Mademoiselle ma mère Catherine
Werbecque, demourant à Saint Jehan
supz l'Escauld.

120.

[Henry VII to the mayor and citizens of Waterford, Halliwell's
"Letters," i. 175.]

Trusty and well-beloved, we greet you well; and Exeter,
whereas Perkin Warbeck, lately accompanied by divers 17 October.
and many of our rebels of Cornwall, advanced themselves to our city of Exeter, which was denied unto
them, and so they came to the town of Taunton. At
which town, as soon as they had knowledge that our
chamberlain, our steward of household, Sir John Chynie,

[Cheyney] and others our loving subjects with them, were
coming so far forth towards the said Perkin, as to our
monastery of Glastonbury : the same Perkin took with
him John Heron, Edward Skelton, and Nicholas Ashley,
and stole away from his said company about midnight,
and fled with all the haste they could make. We had well
provided beforehand for the sea coasts, that, if he had
attempted that way, (as he thought indeed to have done)
he should have been put from his purpose, as it is coming to pass. For, when they perceived they might not
get to the sea, and that they were had in a quiet chase
and pursuit, they were compelled to address themselves
unto our monastery of Beaulieu ; to the which, of chance
and of fortune, it happened some of our menial servants
to repair, and some we sent thither purposely. The
said Perkin, Heron, Skelton and Ashley, seeing our said
servants there, and remembering that all the country
was warned to make watch and give attendance, that
they should not avoid nor escape by sea, made instances
unto our said servants to sue unto us for them, the said
Perkin desiring to be sure of his life, and he would come
unto us, and show what he is ; and, over that, do unto us such service as should content us. And so, by
agreement between our said servants and them, they
encouraged them to depart from Beaulieu, and to put
themselves in our grace and pity. The abbot and convent hearing thereof demanded of them why and for
what cause they would depart. Where unto they gave
answer in the presence of the said abbot and convent,
and of many other, that, without any manner of con-
straint, they would come unto us of their free wills, in
trust of our grace and pardon aforesaid. And so, the
said Perkin came unto us to the town of Taunton, from
whence he fled ; and immediately after his first coming,
humbly submitting himself unto us, hath of his free

will openly showed, in the presence of all the council here with us, and of other nobles, his name to be *Piers Osbeck*, whereas he hath been named Perkin Warbeck, and to be none Englishman born, but born of Tournay, and son to John Osbeck, and sometimes while he lived comptroller of the said Tournay ; with many other circumstances too long to write, declaring by whose means he took upon him this presumption and folly.

And so, now this great abusion, which hath long continned, is now openly known by his own confession. We write this news unto you, for we be undoubtedly sure, that calling to mind the great abusion that divers folks have been in, by reason of the said Perkin, and the great business and charges that we and our realm have been put into in that behalf, you would be glad to hear the certainty of the same, which we affirm unto you for assured truth.

Sithence the writing of these premises, we be ascertained that Perkin's wife is in good surety for us, and trust that she shall shortly come unto us to this our city of Exeter, as she is in dole.[1] Over this, we understand by writing from the Right Reverend Father in God, the Bishop of Duresme, that a truce is taken betwixt us and Scotland; and that it is concluded that the King of Scots shall send unto us a great and solemn ambassady for a league and peace to be had during our lives. And sithence our coming to this our city of Exeter for the punition of this great rebellion, and for so to order the parts of Cornwall, as the people may live in their due obeisance to us and in good restfulness unto themselves for time to come : the commons of this

---

[1] " To Robert Suthewell for horses, sadells, and other necessarys bought for the conveying of my Lady Kateryn Huntleye, [Perkin's wife] £7 13s. 4d., 15 October " ("Excerpta Historica," p. 115). On 1 December Henry gave her £2 (*ibid.*).

shire of Devon come daily before us in great multitudes in their shirts, the foremost of them having halters about their necks, and full humbly with lamentable cries for our grace and remission, submit themselves unto us; whereupon, doing, first, the chief stirrers and misdoers to be tried out of them, for to abide their corrections according, we grant to the residue our said grace and pardon. And our commissioners, the Earl of Devon, our chamberlain, and our steward of household, have done and do daily likewise in our county of Cornwall.

121.

[Raimondo de Soncino to the Duke of Milan, "Milanese Calendar,"
i. 329.]

21 October. By the enclosed extract your Excellency will have full information about the end of Perkin. However I will also relate what was told me by the royal herald Richmond, who is a man of wit and discretion. When Perkin fled from Taunton, in the company of John Aeron,[1] sometime a merchant of London and two other English gentlemen, he came to an abbey called Diodle,[2] where there is a noble franchise with a circuit of thirty miles and touching the coast. The abbot of this place happened to know the said John and the two gentlemen, and sent word to his Majesty about them, feeling sure that the youth must be with them, as indeed he was. Some of the Royal Council went thither, and came to the following arrangement with John and his fellows, to wit, that John should go to his Majesty and either bring back a pardon for himself and his companions, or should be put back into sanctuary, while in the meantime the two companions should stay behind

[1] Heron.
[2] Beaulieu, sometimes anglicized as "Bewdley",

and guard the youth, so that he should not escape, _{October,} despite the fact that about the franchise, especially on ^{1497.} the sea side, there were so many royal guards that not one of them could get away.

John, who swore to the king that he had never known Perkin except as Richard II [sic], son of King Edward, returned with the offer of a pardon to the young man if he would go to the king's presence. The youth agreed to go, and renounced the franchise into the abbot's hands. He put aside the habit in which he had disguised himself in this place, and clothing himself in gold, he set out with some of the king's men, among whom was this Richmond. He tells me that the young man is not handsome, indeed his left eye rather lacks lustre, but he is intelligent and well spoken.

The young man was brought into the royal presence, where many nobles of the realm were assembled, some of whom had been companions of Richard, Duke of York. He kneeled down and asked for mercy. The king bade him rise and then spoke as follows : We have heard that you call yourself Richard, Son of King Edward. In this place are some who were companions of that lord, look and see if you recognize them. The young man answered that he knew none of them, he was not Richard, he had never come to England except that once, and he had been induced by the English and Irish to commit this fraud, and to learn English. For quite two years he had longed to escape from these troubles, but Fortune had not allowed him.

Richmond was not present at this interview, at which there were none besides princes, but I believe it all, because he is a wise man, and because he showed me a sheet, written in French, signed in a different hand, thus "Per Pero Osbek," which he says is in Perkin's hand, in which he names his father and mother, his

grandparents on both sides, his native city of Tournay,
his parish, his schoolmasters, the places where he was
brought up and to which he has been up to the present
time. Many similar sheets have been made, to be sent,
so I take it, to various places.[1]

I asked Richmond whether those who led this young
man thought he was the Duke of York, or if they knew
he was not. He told me that Perkin had informed the
king that of the three English who were with him at
the franchise, two thought he was the duke, but John
Aeron knew he was an impostor. As it appears that
John lied to the king, he has been arrested by a person
who has recently come from the king.

The King of Scotland, Perkin's father-in-law, and the
King of the Romans, have been taken in. Madame
Margaret of Burgundy knew all, according to what this
one says. The Most Christian King a long time ago
had been put right as to the truth of the matter, and
he wrote a letter to the king here saying it was quite
clear that Perkin was a burgess of Tournay. Nevertheless Perkin deposes that the last French ambassador
in Scotland advised him, Perkin, to go to France, with
the promise of an ample safe conduct and of a yearly
pension of 12,000 francs.[2] But either the English or
the others who have supported Perkin have allowed him
to come to want, as they found no more than ten crowns
at the franchise.

I asked Richmond if Perkin would escape with his
life. He told me that he would, but it was necessary
to guard him well, in order that the men of Cornwall
may not murder him, as they are incensed since they
have learned from the king that they have been worship-
ping a low born foreigner as their sovereign.

The king here is most clement and pardons every-

[1] See below, No. 124.   [2] See pp. 139-40.

body, even the common people of Cornwall, although if October, he wished to do strict justice he would have to put to 1497. death more than 20,000 men. I think it most likely that the heads will be headless.

Tomorrow or the day after, this Richmond is to cross the sea to go to the court of the Most Christian King, where he will stay until he is recalled, and within a few days three of the king's men will be in France, the chamberlain and the doctor, who are there, so they say, about the reprisals, and this herald, who is worth two doctors.

There is nothing remarkable about his Majesty having various persons in one place, because he is cautious and reflects deeply over all his proceedings, although from this time forward he is perfectly secure against Fortune, and has no one else to fear, while his treasure will remain like leaven

122.

[Sanuto's abstract of a missing despatch from Trevisano, "Venetian Cal.," i. No. 759.]

Receipt of letters from .the ambassador Andrea 6 Novem- Trevisan, dated London, 6 November, stating that the ber. rest of the insurgents fled into sanctuary after the retreat of "Perkin who styled himself Duke of York, and son of King Edward," and that Perkin was now come to humble himself before King Henry, saying it was not true that he was the son of King Edward, but that he had been instigated by certain people in Cornwall. The King treated him kindly, and had marched from London towards Cornwall to crush the rebels. There had lately arrived in England an ambassador from the King of France, by name Monsieur de Duras, a man of high rank, with ten horses. He went to the King, while Andrea Trevisan remained in London, but hearing of this ambassador, wrote to the King saying he would join his Majesty, who desired him not to stir. The Spaniard Don Pedro de Ayala was gone as ambassador to the King of Scotland, to negotiate an agreement between him and the King of England, and a marriage between a daughter of the King of Spain and a son of the King of Scotland.[1] If this be effected, the discord in the island will be quelled, the son of the King of Scotland becoming brother-in-law of the eldest son of this King Henry,

123.

[Perkin Warbeck's defeat and capture, Kingsford's " Chronicles,"
p. 217.]

Also this present moneth of Septembre landed in Cornewaill Perkyn Werbek w^t iij smale Shippes only, and w^t hym to the numbre of an hundred or vj score persones, which entred ferther vnto a Towne called Bodman, where he was accompanied w^t iij or iiij m^l men of Rascayll and most parte naked men. And there proclaymed hym silf kyng Richard the iiijth, And Second Son vnto kyng Edward the iiijth late kyng of Englond.

And vpon Saynt Mathewes day [21 Sept.] came certeyn tydynges vnto the Mayre that vpon the Sonday before, beyng the xvijth day of Septembre, the said Perkyn and his complices assawted the Citie of Exetir at ij Gates, that is to sey the Northgate and the East Gate, where by the power of therle of Devenshire and the Citezeins he was put of, and to the numbre of CC men of the said Perkyns slayn.

And vpon the Monday folowyng he and his people made a new assawte vpon the said Citie, where agayn they wer put of to their more Damage. Albeit that

[1] On 18 December Henry paid him £66 15s. for his services ("Excerpta Historica," p. 115).

they fired the Gates; at which said Second assawte the
Erel of Devenshire was hurt in the arme w^t an arowe.
And when the said Perkyn and his Companye Sawe
they myght not opteyne their purpoos agayn the Citie
of Exetir they w^tdrew theym toward Taunton; where
vpon the Weddensday folowyng [20 Sept.] he mustrid,
havyng to the numbre, as it was said, of viij M^l men;
how be it they wer pore and naked. And the nyght folowyng aboute mydnyght the. said Perkyn w^t lx horsmen
accompanyed fled secretly fro the pore Comons levyng
theym amased and disconsolat. And after my Lord
Chamberleyn, havyng knowlege of this his departure,
sent toward the Sees side CC Sperys to Stoppe hym
from the See, and to Serche the Cuntrey yf they myght
take hym.

And vpon the ffriday John Heyron, Mercer, which
before tyme had fledde the Citie of London for dette,
and one Skelton w^t one Asteldy [or Ashley], a Scryvainer,
which iij persones wer the moost worthy of his Counseill,
came vnto Bewdely, a Sayntwary beside Southhampton;
and there Registred theym self. And in this while one
James a Rover, which had gadered in his cumpanye to
the numbre of vj or vij C Rebelles, Sechyng the forsaid
Perkyn to haue assisted hym, mette w^t the Provost of
Peryn, and brought hym vnto Taunton aforsaid; and
there in the Market place slewe hym pytuously, in such
wise that he was dismembred and kutte in many and
sundry peces. The cause as it was said was for that
he was one of the Occasioners of the Rebellyng of the
Cornysshemen; for he was one of the commyssioners
in that Cuntre and gadered, as they say, more money
than came vnto the kynges vse. But what so euer the
cause was, foule and piteously was he murderid; vpon
whose Soule and all Christen Jhesu haue mercy! Amen!

And the Tuesday folowyng [26 Sept.] came vnto Westmynster a chapeleyn of the said Perkyn, and one of his Chief Counseill w^t other also to Seynt Martyns; and thus his disciples fled from theyir fayned Maister; the forsaid preest was named Sir William Lounde,[1] sumtyme chapeleyn and Stieward of houshold w^t Sir Rauf Hastynges, knyght, from whome full falsly and trayterously the said preest w^t certeyn money and Juelles to a good Substaunce stale away from the said Sir Rauf, and so departed ouer the see vnto the said Perkyn; and there abode still w^t hym by the Space of iij or iiij yeres to the grete trowble and daunger of the forsaid Sir Rauf Hastynges.

And vpon the Sonday next folowyng [1 Oct.] came certeyn tydynges from the kyng vnto the Maire, of the takyng of the said Perkyn w^t in the Sayntwary of Bewley aforsaid; wherfore the Mair, w^t his Brethern assemblid, went forthw^t aboute x of the Clok in the mornyng vnto poules, and there caused Te Deum to be solempnly songen, which was the first day of Octobre:

And after this came certeyn wrytyng vnto the Maire that the said persone was brought vnto the kynges presence vnto Taunton, where the kyng pardoned hym of his lif and John Heron also; and so from thens he awayted vpon the kynges grace Rydyng his progresse westward. And vpon Tuesday, beyng Saynt Lukes Even, the Quene, comyng from Walsyngham, came through the Citie Receyved by the Mair and his Brethern vpon horsbak at Bisshopes Gate. And from thens so conveyed vnto the warderobe by the blak ffreres, where she loged that nyght and the Day folowyng; and from thens to Shene, where to her Grace was brought, the Saterday [7 Oct.] before Saynt Symon and Jude, the wif of Perkyn aforsaid; which said wif was a Scottish woman and doughter vnto the Erle of Huntley of Scotland.

[1] See above, p. 139.

124.

[Perkin Warbeck's confession, Kingsford's "Chronicles," p. 219.]

This yere the Saterday, beyng the xviij[th] day of Nouembre, the kyng came vnto his manoir of Shene after his long beyng at Excetir.[1] And vpon the Weddensday folowyng he came by land to Lambhith, and there toke his Barge and came vnto Westm', where the Mair, w[t] his Brethern, receyved hym in the paleis, w[t] dyuers of the Citesyns to the numbre of iiij[xx], of euery ffeliship a certeyn assigned in their last lyuereys. At which Seasone the forsaid Persone Perkyn came also before the kyng, vpon whom the same season and other dayes folowyng was moch wonderyng, and many a Curse throwen at his hede.

18 November-4 December.

Here after ensueth the Confession of the said Perkyn and Pedygre.

" ffirst it is to be knowen that I was born in the Towne of Turney, and my ffaders name is called John Osbek ; which said John Osbek was controller of the Towne of Turney. And my moders name is Kateryn de ffaro. And one of my Grauntsires vpon my ffaders side was called Deryk Osbek, which died ; after whos deth my grauntmother was maried vnto the w[t]in named Petir flam, which was Receyvour of the forsaide Towne of Turney and Deane of the Botemen that be vpon the watir or Ryver of Leystave. And my Grauntsire vpon my moders side was called Petir ffaro, the which had in his kepyng the keys of the Gate of Seynt Johns, w[t]in the abouenamed Towne of Turney, Also I had an Vncle named Maister John Stalyn dwellyng in the parisshe of Saynt Pyas w[t]in the same Towne, which had maried my ffaders Sister, whose name was Johane

---

[1] According to the itinerary in " Excerpta Historica," p. 115, Henry did not reach Sheen until 21 November.

or Jane, w^t whom I dwelled a certeyn season ; and
afterward I was led by my moder to Andwarp for to
lerne flemmysshe in an house of a Cosyn of myne,
officer of the said Towne, called John Stienbek, w^t
whome I was the Space of half a yere. And after that
I retourned agayn vnto Turney by reason of the warres
that wer in fflaunders. And w^tin a yere folowyng I
was sent w^t a Merchaunt of the said Towne of Turney
named Berlo, and his Maister's name Alex., to the
Marte of Andwarp, where as I fill syke, which sykenesse
contynued vpon me v monethes ; and the said Berlo
set me to boorde in a Skynners hous, that dwelled beside
the hous of the Englessh nacion. And by hym I was
brought from thens to the Barowe Marte, and loged at
the Signe of tholde man, where I abode the space of ij
monethes. And after this the said Berlo set me w^t
a merchaunt in Middelborough to seruice for to lerne
the language, whose name was John Strewe, w^t whome
I dwelled from Cristmas vnto Easter ; and than I
went into Portyngale in the Cumpany of Sir Edward
Bramptons wif in a Ship which was called the Quenes
Ship. And whan I was comen thider I was put in
seruice to a knyght that dwelled in Lusshebourne,
which was called Petir Vacz de Cogna, w^t whome I
dwelled an hole yere, which said knyght had but one
Iye ; and than because I desired to se other Cuntrees
I toke licence of hym. And than I put my silf in
seruice w^t a Breton, called Pregent Meno, the which
brought me w^t hym into Ireland. And whan we wer
there aryved in the Towne of Corke, they of the Towne,
because I was arayed w^t some clothes of silk of my
said Maisters, came vnto me and threped vpon me that
I shuld be the Duke of Clarence sone, that was before
tyme at Develyn. And for as moch as I denyed it
there was brought vnto me the holy Euaungelist and

PERKIN IN IRELAND 185

the Crosse by the Mayre of the Towne, which was called John Lewelyn; and there in the presence of hym and other I toke myn Othe as trouth was that I was not the forsaid Dukes Son, nother of none of his blood. And after this came vnto me an Englissh man, whose name was Steffe Poytron, w^t one John Water, and said to me in sweryng grete Othis, that they knew wele I was kyng Richardes Bastarde Son; to whome I answerd w^t hie Othis that I were not. And than they advised me not to be afferd but that I shuld take it vpon me Boldly, and iff I wold so do they wold ayde and assiste me w^t all theyr powr agayn the kyng of Englond; And not only they, but they were well assured that therles of Desmond and Kildare shuld do the same, ffor they forsid not what party so that they myght be revenged vpon the kyng of Englond; and so agaynst my will made me to lerne Inglisshe, and taughte me what I shuld doo and say. And after this they called me Duke of York, the Second Son of kyng Edward the ffourth, because kyng Richardes Bastarde Son was in the handes of the kyng of Englond. And vpon this the said John Water, Steffe Poytron, John Tiler, Huberd Bourgh, w^t many other, as the forsaid Erles, entred into this fals Quarell. And w^tin short tyme after this the ffrensshe kyng sent vnto me an Embasset into Irelond, whose names was loyte Lucas and Maister Steffes ffrion,[1] to aduertise me to come into ffraunce; and thens I went into ffraunce, and from thens into fflaunders, and from fflaunders into Ireland, And from Ireland into Scotland, and so into England."

The Tuesday before Seynt Andrewis day, beyng the xxviij day of Nouembre, the sayd Perkyn was conueyd vpon horse bak thorowh Chepe and Corne hyll vnto the

[1] Formerly French Secretary to Henry VII. See Campbell, ii., 60.

November-
December,
1497.

Towr of London ; and after hym was also on horse bak,
clad in armittes abyt, a man, ffast bound hondes and
ffete, which some tyme was, as it was reportyd, Sargeaunt
fferrour vnto owir Souerayn Lord the kyng Henry
the vijth, also lad vnto the said Towir and ther lefte
as prisoner; which said fferrour departyd oute of the
kynges seruice long tyme before and went vuto the
said Perkyn, and became his seruant and was w^t hym
yeris and days, and after the said Perkyns takyng,
wandrid abowte in the habit and ffourme of an Ermyte,
and so was takyn and browght vnto the kyng. And
after thys prisoner thus lafte in the Tower the said
Perkyn was conueyd ayen thorwth Candylwyke strete,
and so ageyn thorwth Chepe toward Westmynst'. with
many a curse and wonderyng Inowth. The Monday
next ffolowyng, beyng the iiijth day of Decembre, the
forsaid fferrour and one callid Edwardes, which some
tyme had ben in seruice w^t the Quens grace in the
Roume of a yoman, wer drawen from the towir to
Tiborne and ther hangyd, and the said fferrour hedyd
and quarteryd, and after bothe buryed in the ffrere
Austyns : vpon whos sowlys god haue mercy! Amen!

125.

[Sanuto's abstract of despatches from Trevisano, "Venetian Cal.,"
i. No. 760.]

28 Novem-
ber.

Receipt of letters from the ambassador Andrea
Trevisan, dated 28 November, stating that on the 22nd
the King returned from the camp to London, having
been against the Cornish men. He did not enter the
city with any triumph, whereas on the former occasion
when he returned it was his wont to come with pomp,
neither did he choose any of the resident ambassadors
to go out to meet him, saying that he had not gained a

worthy victory, having been against such a base crew November, 1497.
as those Cornish men.

Subsequently the [Venetian] ambassador went to the King, who gave him a gracious greeting and chose to give audience to an ambassador from the King of Scotland, who was come to negotiate an agreement, in the presence of all the ambassadors, including the one from the King of France. The King was well arrayed with a very costly jewelled collar. Has also seen that Perkin, who was in a chamber of the King's palace and habitation. He is a well favoured young man, 23 years old, and his wife a very handsome woman ; the King treats them well, but did not allow them to sleep together. Asks leave to return home, perceiving that his stay in England is of no importance

126.

[Queen Elizabeth to Isabella of Castile, Wood's " Letters of Royal and Illustrious Ladies," p. 114.]

To the most serene and potent princess the Lady Westminster, 3 December.
Elizabeth, by God's grace queen of Castile, Leon, Aragon, Sicily, Granada, etc. our cousin and dearest relation, Elizabeth, by the same grace queen of England and France, and lady of Ireland, wishes health and the most prosperous increase of her desires.

Although we before entertained singular love and regard to your highness above all other queens in the world, as well for the consanguinity and necessary intercourse which mutually take place between us, as also for the eminent dignity and virtue by which your said majesty so shines and excels that your most celebrated name is noised abroad and diffused everywhere ; yet much more has this our love increased and accumulated by the accession of the most noble affinity which has recently been celebrated between the most illustrious

December, 1497.

Lord Arthur, prince of Wales, our eldest son, and the most illustrious princess the Lady Catherine, the infanta, your daughter. Hence it is that, amongst our other cares and cogitations, first and foremost we wish and desire from our heart that we may often and speedily hear of the health and safety of your serenity, and of the health and safety of the aforesaid most illustrious Lady Catherine, whom we think of and esteem as our own daughter, than which nothing can be more grateful and acceptable to us. Therefore we request your serenity to certify us of your estate, and of that of the aforesaid most illustrious Lady Catherine our common daughter. And if there be any thing in our power which would be grateful or pleasant to your majesty, use us and ours as freely as you would your own ; for, with most willing mind, we offer all that we have to you, and wish to have all in common with you. We should have written you the news of our state, and of that of this kingdom, but the most serene lord the king, our husband, will have written at length of these things to your majesties. For the rest may your majesty fare most happily according to your wishes.

127.

[Raimondo de Soncino to the Duke of Milan, "Milanese Calendar," i. 335.]

London, 6 December.

To tell the truth, his Majesty is right in behaving well to the French, as every year he obtains 5,000 [50,000] crowns from them, some say for observing the peace made between King Edward and King Louis ; others, whom I believe, say that it is because his Majesty, having supplied the Duchess of Britanny with much money, receiving in pledge some fortresses which the King of France afterwards captured, the king here, among other articles arranged with the French when he went to

Picardy, provided that the money lent to the duchess, December
now Queen of France, should be restored by the pay- 1497.
ment of 50,000 crowns yearly. The French not only pay
this sum to his Majesty, but with his knowledge and
consent they give provision to the leading men of the
realm, to wit, the Lord Chamberlain, Master Braiset
[Bray], Master Lovel, and as these leading satraps are
very rich the provision has to be very large. I hear also
that they give to others, but this is not so well established as in the case of these three.

. . . .

Perkin has been made a spectacle for everybody and
every day he is led through London, in order that everyone may perceive his past error. In my opinion he
bears his fortune bravely.

1498.

128.

[Perkin Warbeck's escape and recapture, Kingsford's " Chronicles,"
p. 223.]

Ye haue hard before of the takyng of the Perkyn, 9-17 June.
and his confession and pedigrew; and how graciously
it plesyd the kynges grace to Deale w^t hym, and after
kept hym in his court at liberte ; which grete benefetes
vpon the said Perkyns party forgotyne, he vpon Trinite
Sonday evyn, vpon Saterday, beyng the ix^th day of Junii,
aboute Mydnygth, stale A way owte of the Court, the
kynge beyng then at Westmynst.' for whom was made
grete serch.[1]

The said Perkyn after he was departed, as before is

---

[1] "9 June. To Steven Bull and Barnsefeld sekyng for Perkyn,
for there costs, £1 6s. 8d." (" Excerpta Historica," p. 118). " 10
June. To Bradsha riding for Perkyn, 13s. 4d. To four yomen
watching one night with four botes, 6s. 8d." (ibid.).

June, 1498. said, went vnto shene ; and ther made swych petyous mocyons vnto the ffader of the plaise, that after he had set hym in Suyr kepyng went vnto Westmynst' and ther gate pardon of the kyng for hys lyffe, and so was browgth Agayne to the kyng. And the ffriday next folowyng was made w⁴in the palays at Westmynst' a scaffold of pipis and of hoggysshedes ; and there vpon a peyr of stakes he was set A good part of the fore none ; And ther was wondred agene vpon, as he had ben ofte tymys before.

And vpon the monday folowyng was a scaffold made in Chepyssyde, foreagayn the kynges hede, where vpon the said Perkyn stood from x of the mornyng tyll iij of the clok at after none, where he was excedyngly wondred vpon. And the same after none abowte thre of the Clok he was browgth from the said place thorwth Cornhylle vnto the Towir of London, w⁴ Officers of the Cite and also of the said Towir folowyng.

129.

[De Puebla to Ferdinand and Isabella, "Spanish Cal.," i. 198.]

London,
12 June.

I wrote a long while ago to your Highnesses, supplicating you to give your opinion and advice as to how the King of England ought to deal with Perkin. Your Highnesses have not to this day, no doubt for some just reason and impediments, sent a word in reply, or written anything. I say this because the said Perkin fled a few days ago, without any reason. Your silence causes much pain to me, because I am sure the King of England would do what your Highnesses might advise. God be thanked ! Perkin is already captured. The same hour that he was arrested the King of England sent one of his gentlemen of the bedchamber to bring me the news. I have not yet had time to ascertain what will become

of Perkin, because I am writing these lines at the same June, 1498.
hour that the King of England sent me the news. I
think he will either be executed, or kept with great
vigilance in prison.

130.

[Agostino de Spinula, Milanese agent in England to the Duke of
Milan, " Milanese Calendar," i. 348.]

There is little fresh to advise except that on the 12th London,
inst.[1] at midnight Perichino Oxbeke, when sleeping ^{20 June.}
between two warders in the wardrobe of the king's
palace at Westminster, escaped through a window, but
was found on the following day in the Carthusian
monastery of Sheen, seven miles from that place. He
was brought here, and after receiving much contumely,
he remains in the Tower of London, under better
guard.

131.

[Skelton's attack on Perkin Warbeck, " Works," ed. Dyce, i. 15.]

Skelton Laureate
agaynst.

A comely coystrowne that curyowsly chawntyd, and
    curryshly cowntred, and madly in hys musykkys
    mokkyshly made agaynste the ix Musys of polytyke
    poems and poettys matryculat.
Of all nacyons vnder the heuyn,
These frantyke foolys I hate most of all ;
For though they stumble in the synnys seuyn,
In peuyshnes yet they snapper and fall,
Which men the viii dedly syn call.
This punysh proud, thys prendergest,
When he is well, yet can he not rest.

                    [1] The 9th seems the more correct date.

June, 1498. A swete suger lofe and sowre bayardys bun
Be sumdele lyke in forme and shap,
The one for a duke, the other for dun,
A maunchet for morell theron to snap.
Hys hart is to hy to haue any hap;
But for in his gamut carp that he can.
Lo, Jak wold be a jentylman!

Wyth, Hey, troly, loly, lo, whip here, Jak
Alumbek sodyldym syllorym ben!
Curyowsly he can both counter and knak
Of Martyn Swart and all hys mery men.
Lord, how Perkyn is proud of his pohen!
But ask wher he fyndeth among hys monacordys
An holy water clarke a ruler of lordys.[1]

He can not fynd it in rule nor in space:
He solfyth to haute, hys trybyll is to hy;
He braggyth of his byrth, that borne was full bace;
Hys musyk withoute mesure, to sharp is hys my;
He trymmyth in hys tenor to counter pyrdewy;
His dyscant is besy, it is withoute a mene;
To fat is hys fantsy, hys wyt is to lene.

He lumbryth on a lewde lewte, Roty bully joyse,
Rumbyll downe, tumbyll downe, hey go, now, now!
He fumblyth in hys fyngeryng an vgly good noyse,
It semyth the sobbyng of an old sow:
He wold be made moch of, and he wyst how;
Wele sped in spyndels and turning of tauellys,
A bungler, a brawler, a pyker of quarellys.

Comely he clappyth a payre of clauycordys;
He whystelyth so swetely, he makyth me to swete;
His descant is dasshed full of dyscordes;

<hr/>

[1] Possibly a reference to William Lound, chaplain and steward
of the household to Sir Ralph Hastings, see pp. 139, 182.

A red angry man, but easy to intrete :
An vssher of the hall fayn wold I get,
To poynte this proude page a place and a rome,
For Jak wold be a jentylman that late was a grome

Jak wold jet, and yet Jyll sayd nay ;
He counteth in his countenaunce to checke with the best :
A malaperte medler that pryeth for his pray,
In a dysh dare he rush at the rypest ;
Dremyng in dumpys to wrangyll and to wrest ·
He fyndeth a proporcyon in his prycke songe,
To drynk at a draught a larg and a long.

Nay, jape not with him, he is no small fole,
It is a solemnpne syre and a solayne ;
For lordes and ladyes lerne at his scole ;
He techyth them so wysely to solf and to fayne,
That neyther they synge wel prycke songe nor playne :
Thys docter Deuyas commensyd in a cart,
A master, a mynstrell, a fydler, a farte.

What though ye can cownter *Custodi nos?*
As well it becomyth yow, a parysh towne clarke,
To syng *Sospitati dedit aegros :*
Yet bere ye not to bold, to braule ne to bark
At me, that medeled nothyng with youre wark :
Correct fyrst thy self ; walk and be nought !
Deme what thou lyst, thou knowyst not my thought.

A prouerbe of old, say well or be styll :
Ye are to vnhappy occasyons to fynde
Vppon me to clater, or els to say yll.
Now haue I shewyd you part of your proud mynde ;
Take thys in worth the best is behynde.
Wryten at Croydon by Crowland in the Clay,
On Candlemas euyn, the Kalendas of May.[1]

[1] A purposely absurd date ; Candlemas was the 2nd of February.

1498.   132.

[Londoño and the sub-prior of Santa Cruz to Ferdinand and Isabella, "Spanish Cal.," i. pp. 161-3.]

London,
18 July.

The Doctor (De Puebla) is in such a state of irritation with Don Pedro de Ayala that it has been the cause of many disagreable scenes which are notorious in England. There is no remedy for it. De Puebla cannot bear any other ambassador. He has been unable to conceal his fear and distrust towards them, though he had been told that his services are fully appreciated in Spain. Have observed that he is a great partizan of the King of England. He magnifies everything that relates to Henry as much as possible. He thinks that the affairs of the King of England are to be considered as more important than those of any other prince. King Henry says that he is very well satisfied with De Puebla, who is a good servant of the King and Queen of Spain, and that no other ambassador could conduct the negociations so well as he does, adding, that he makes these observations only in order to recommend De Puebla to his masters. Suspects, however, that De Puebla had begged the King to speak of him in that way, as De Puebla had gone alone to the palace the day before, and had not liked to accompany them the next day. Moreover, some persons have told them that De Puebla had besought the King to commend him. King Henry is certainly satisfied with De Puebla, not because he thinks him a good man, or a good servant of the King and Queen of Spain, but because he carries on negociations rather in the interest of England than of Spain.

De Puebla is a quarrelsome intriguer. He is disliked by the Spanish merchants in England. They say that he could easily have induced Henry to abolish the extra duties imposed upon them when the last treaty was July, 1498. concluded. The King was then in such difficulties that he would not have refused even the half of his revenues if De Puebla had asked it. But De Puebla is more an agent of the exchequer of the King of England than ambassador of Spain. He is under such subjection to Henry that he dares not say a word, but what he thinks will please the King. The Spanish merchants had told them all this without being asked. Intend to send the complaints of the merchants in writing.

Doctor Peter Panec [?], a privy counsellor of Henry, who had transacted business with De Puebla, asked them whether he had been sent to superintend the affairs of the King and Queen of Spain, or those of the King of England and his own? He added that De Puebla had conducted the business of Spain very badly. Many things have been left entirely to his decision, and he has not decided them in favour of Spain. This has especially been the case with respect to the marriage. Henry was then in the midst of his difficulties with Scotland and Perkin. The Cornish rebels were in arms against him, and had even advanced to within a few leagues of London. If any other man had been the ambassador of Spain, Ferdinand and Isabella could, in that conjuncture, have dictated conditions to England. In fact, Doctor Panec says Henry is indebted for his crown to Spain, because, as soon as the marriage was known to be concluded, all became quiet. But De Puebla, during all that time, went from one privy counsellor to another, begging that the marriage might be concluded, as though there were no other means to do it. He had said everywhere that King Henry had made great difficulties about concluding the marriage. If another ambassador had been in the place of De Puebla, Henry would have begged exactly the same things of him which De Puebla

13 *

has been begging of Henry. The King would have given much money besides. There is only one opinion about these things in England. The same informant said further that the peace with Scotland had been delayed by De Puebla, who had falsified the letters of Don Pedro de Ayala, which the King had asked him to translate from Spanish into French. King Henry was very angry with De Puebla on this account, and De Puebla had the insolence to say that everywhere he regretted he had concluded the marriage because Henry had not been so liberal towards him as his services deserved.

Henry is rich, has established good order in England, and keeps the people in such subjection as has never been the case before. He is on good terms with the King of France, to whom he has sent an embassy. He is a friend of peace.

To the Italian ambassadors he answered that he liked to live on good terms with France, and that Italy is too far distant for an alliance. The ambassadors from Milan are expected.

The persons who have the greatest influence in England are the mother of the King, the Chancellor, Master Bray, the Bishop of Durham, Master Ludel [Lovell], who is treasurer, the Bishop of London, and the Lord Chamberlain.

A short time ago ambassadors arrived from the King of the Romans. De Puebla says that they have asked Henry to take part in the war against France.

Remained a few days longer in England, because the ambassadors from France were hourly expected. The ambassadors are, the Bishop of Cambray, and two literary men. They say that they are come to conclude peace, and to bring about an understanding respecting English commerce in Flanders. The truce with France, they say, is converted into a perpetual peace.

[Ayala's description of James IV of Scotland, " Spanish Calendar,"
i. 169.]

Obedient to their orders, sends them a description of 25 July.
the King and the Kingdom of Scotland.

The King is 25 years and some months old. He
is of noble stature, neither tall nor short, and as handsome in complexion and shape as a man can be. His
address is very agreeable. He speaks the following
foreign languages; Latin, very well; French, German,
Flemish, Italian and Spanish; Spanish as well as the
Marquis, but he pronounces it more distinctly. He
likes very much to receive Spanish letters. His own
Scotch language is as different from English as Aragonese from Castilian. The King speaks, besides, the
language of the savages who live in some parts of Scotland and on the islands. It is as different from Scotch
as Biscayian is from Castilian. His knowledge of
languages is wonderful. He is well read in the Bible
and in some other devout books. He is a good historian.
He has read many Latin and French histories, and
profited by them, as he has a very good memory. He
never cuts his hair or his beard. It becomes him very
well.

He fears God, and observes all the precepts of the
Church. He does not eat meat on Wednesdays and
Fridays. He would not ride on Sundays for any consideration, not even to mass. He says all his prayers.
Before transacting any business he hears two masses.
After mass he has a cantata sung, during which he
sometimes despatches very urgent business. He gives
alms liberally, but is a severe judge, especially in the
case of murderers. He has a great predilection for
priests, and receives advice from them, especially from

the Friars Observant, with whom he confesses. Rarely, even in joking, a word escapes him that is not the truth. He prides himself much upon it, and says it does not seem to him well for Kings to swear their treaties as they do now. The oath of a King should be his royal word, as was the case in bygone ages. He is neither prodigal nor avaricious, but liberal when occasion requires. He is courageous, even more so than a King should be. I am a good witness of it. I have seen him often undertake most dangerous things in the last wars. I sometimes clung to his skirts, and succeeded in keeping him back. On such occasions he does not take the least care of himself. He is not a good captain, because he begins to fight before he has given his orders. He said to me that his subjects serve him with their persons and goods, in just and unjust quarrels, exactly as he likes, and that, therefore, he does not think it right to begin any warlike undertaking without being himself the first in danger. His deeds are as good as his words. For this reason, and because he is a very humane prince, he is much loved. He is active and works hard. When he is not at war he hunts in the mountains. I tell your Highnesses the truth when I say that God has worked a miracle in him, for I have never seen a man so temperate in eating and drinking out of Spain. Indeed such a thing seems to be superhuman in these countries. He lends a willing ear to his counsellors, and decides nothing without asking them; but in great matters he acts according to his own judgment, and, in my opinion, he generally makes a right decision. I recognise him perfectly in the conclusion of the last peace, which was made against the wishes of the majority in his kingdom.

When he was a minor he was instigated by those who held the government to do some dishonourable

things. They favoured his love intrigues with their July, 1498.
relatives, in order to keep him in their subjection. As
soon as he came of age and understood his duties,
he gave up these intrigues. When I arrived, he was
keeping a lady with great state in a castle. He visited
her from time to time. Afterwards he sent her to the
house of her father, who is a knight, and married her.
He did the same with another lady, by whom he had
had a son. It may be about a year since he gave up,
so at least it is believed, his lovemaking, as well from
fear of God as from fear of scandal in this world, which
is thought very much of here. I can say with truth
that he esteems himself as much as though he were
Lord of the world. He loves war so much that I fear,
judging by the provocation he receives, the peace will not
last long. War is profitable to him and to the country.

134.

[De Puebla to Ferdinand and Isabella, "Spanish Calendar," i. pp.
185-6.]

With respect to the observations of your Highnesses 25 August.
on Perkin, there is nothing to be said, except that he is
kept with the greatest care in a tower, where he sees
neither sun nor moon. The Bishop of Cambray, ambassador of the Archduke, wished to see Perkin, because
he had formerly transacted business with him. The
King, therefore, sent a few days ago for Perkin, and
asked him in my presence why he had deceived the
Archduke and the whole country. Perkin answered as
he had done before, and solemnly swore to God that the
Duchess, Madame Margaret, knew as well as himself
that he was not the son of King Edward. The King
then said to the Bishop of Cambray and to me, that
Perkin had deceived the Pope, the King of France, the
Archduke, the King of the Romans, the King of Scot-

land, and almost all Princes of Christendom, except
your Highnesses. I saw how much altered Perkin
was. He is so much changed that I, and all other
persons here, believe his life will be very short. He
must pay for what he has done. I do not remember
whether I have already written to your Highnesses
respecting what the Biscayans did who brought him
from Ireland to Cornwall. The ship in which Perkin
was, falling in with the fleet of the King, was boarded.
The commander of the said fleet called the captain and
the crew of the ship into his presence and told them,
that, as they were aware, the Kings of Spain and
England were living on terms of intimate friendship,
that the Prince of Wales has now married the Princess
Katharine, and that the marriage has been really contracted, I acting as proxy for the Princess. He then
exhorted them, as faithful subjects of your Highness, to
deliver up Perkin if he were hidden in their ship. The
English did not know him. The commander of the
fleet promised them 2,000 nobles in the name of the
King, besides many other favours, and showed the
letters patent under the royal signature, signed with
the royal seal, which they had on board the fleet. The
obstinate Biscayans, however, swore, in spite of all this,
that they had never known or heard of such a man.
Perkin was all this time in the bows of the ship, hidden
in a pipe. He told me all this himself; and the man
who came to ask letters for your Highnesses, recommending the said Biscayans to mercy, gave the same relation.

135.

[De Puebla to Ferdinand and Isabella, "Spanish Calendar," i.
p. 188.]

25 August.   But as the King of France is so near and so powerful a neighbour, and yet pays tribute to the King of

England, and pensions to the English, Henry esteems August,
his friendship more than the whole of the Indies, especi- 1498.
ally when he sees that the whole Christian world com-
bined can scarcely resist the King of France.

136.

[Raimondo de Soncino to Ludovico Sforza, Duke of Milan, " Venetian Calendar," i. No. 776.]

The King of England sent for him on the 11th instant, London, 17
and replied according to the accompanying note.   That November.
he might understand thoroughly what he was to write,
the King, with his natural condescension, repeated the
words the second time.   Thereupon he (Raimondo)
said he would draw up a minute of the message, and
present it for correction to his Majesty.   This pleased
the King, to whom he took the draft in Latin on the
15th instant, when the King said, that although it contained the sense of the reply, he wished it written more
fully and that he would order a draft to be prepared in
such form as seemed fitting to him.

Accordingly last evening, the 16th, Messer Pietro
Carmeliano,[1] who had drawn up the minute in his own
hand, the King correcting it, delivered the document
to him, requesting him, in the King's name, not to
alter the words.   Promised obedience and then copied
it verbatim.   Encloses it, and would gladly have sent
the original, but Pietro Carmeliano said the King
chose that should be returned to him.   Deems it requisite to make the following remarks concerning this
reply.

On the King's becoming acquainted with his arrival
in London his audience was delayed for about forty
days.   Is of opinion that this was solely to avoid giving

[1] Henry VII's Latin secretary, a humanist, and a friend of
Erasmus.

umbrage to the King of France, from whom he understands that his Majesty extorts more money than from
the late King, most especially on account of the arrears
of ransom for the late Duke of Orleans.[1] Although he
had had four private audiences, the King never repeated any of the expressions uttered by him last year,
as for instance, that " he was to write to the Duke that
should the French King choose to invade Italy there
would be remedies," and when he charged him to tell
the Duke that he " held his alliance in account, as it
might aid him vastly by way of Genoa," together with
similar expressions.

Is aware, partly from the King's conversation and
partly through inquiries made by him in other quarters,
that the changes in Italy have altered the King's
opinions vastly : he is not so much disturbed by the
discord between the Venetians [and the Florentines]
about the affairs of Pisa, concerning which he daily
receives advices, as by this tacit yet manifest confederation between the Pope and the King of France, which
he expects the Venetians will join, to the Duke's detri-
ment ; nor can he believe, even should they lose Pisa
(which he considers a difficult matter), that they will
fail to attack Milan.

Raimondo is also of opinion that the King of England
esteems the present King of France [2] more highly than
he did his predecessor, either because he extorts more
money from him, or because he rates his personal
qualities more highly, or else by reason of their ancient
mutual friendship, when they jointly defended the
Duchess of Brittany against the French. Moreover,
the peace stipulated between the Sovereigns of Spain
and France makes him act with more reserve ; and

[1] See also p. 217 n.
[2] Louis XII who succeeded Charles VIII on 7 April, 1498.

above all the large pensions paid in the English court with the King's knowledge have much influence.

The King of England, who, in addition to his other good qualities, is very communicative, complained and expressed surprise that the League formed with so many ties should have been thus dissolved.

Is of opinion, and the English themselves say so, that the King has need of no one, and being at peace with all, and perceiving so much disunion, believes he will not compromise his reputation. Considers it certain that the King will never stir against France until he sees it in confusion ; neither will he ever cause her any suspicion unless for his own security and advantage.

There will be no change in England whilst the present King lives. It is understood that the King of Scotland, whom the English hold in very great account, is on excellent terms with the King of England, and that some negociation is on foot for marrying him to the eldest daughter of England (Princess Margaret), who is not more than eight years old, the project with Mons. de Rohan, of Brittany, being at an end. The King of England, however, is more inclined towards the eldest son of Denmark, who is fourteen years old. Is of opinion that the King is right, not only on account of the respective ages of the parties, but because England has more to fear from Denmark than from Scotland.

The English and Flemings are angry with each other, by reason of fresh duties laid by the Flemings on English cloths, and the English public threaten war against Flanders, under which name of war, possibly by way of fifteenth (*quindena*), a certain sum of money may find its way to the King's purse ; but the sovereigns are certain to come to terms, and the losers will have to bear their loss.

1499.

137.

[Raimondo de Soncino to the Duke of Milan, "Milanese Calendar,"
i. 364.]

26 Janu-
ary.

In his Highness's [Henry VII's] opinion he has need
of no one, while everyone needs him, and although he
clearly sees what may happen to the world, yet he considers it so unlikely as to be practically impossible. In
the midst of all this, his Majesty can stand like one at
the top of a tower looking on at what is passing in the
plain. He also seems to believe that even if the King
of France became master of Italy, which he would not
like, he would be so distracted in ruling it that no harm
would ensue either to his Majesty or to his heirs.
Although I may answer this and similar propositions
with all diligence, he always seemed to hold to his
opinion.

138.

[A fresh conspiracy, Kingsford's "Chronicles," p. 225; the pretender's name was Ralf Wulford, see Fabyan's "Chronicle,"
pp. 685-6, and "Dict. Nat. Biogr.," lxiii. 172.]

22 Febru-
ary.

This yere vpon Shrove Tuesday was hangid at Seynt
Thomas Wateryng a yonge ffelowe of the age of xix
yeres, which was son of a Cordwainer dwellyng at the
Bulle in Bisshoppesgate strete; for somoche as he en-
tendid to haue made a new Rumour and Insurrexcion
wᵗin this lande, callyng and namyng hym self Erle of
Warwyk; where he hynge in his Shirte from the said
Tuesday till the Satirday agayne nyght next folowyng.

139.   1499.

[Pedro de Ayala to Ferdinand and Isabella, "Spanish Calendar," i.
pp. 206-7.]

Has on former occasions written that the people of London,
England believe in prophecies. In Wales there are ^{26 March.}
many who tell fortunes. In the same way that people
in Galicia tell fortunes from certain signs on the back
of a man, they believe here in other signs and cere-
monies which they perform. A few days ago the King
asked a priest, who had foretold the death of King Edward and the end of King Richard, to tell him in what
manner his latter end would come.[1] The priest, according to common report, told the King that his life would
be in great danger during the whole year, and informed
him, in addition to many other unpleasant things,
that there are two parties of very different political
creeds in his kingdom. The King ordered the priest to
speak to nobody about this prophecy. But he could not
keep the secret; he told it to a friend of his, and that
friend to another friend. Thus the King found out the
indiscretion of the priest. The friend of the friend is in
prison, but the other two persons have fled. "Henry
has aged so much during the last two weeks that he
seems to be twenty years older." The King is growing
very devout.[2] He has heard a sermon every day during
Lent, and has continued his devotions during the rest
of the day. His riches augment every day. "I think
he has no equal in this respect." If gold coin once
enters his strong boxes, it never comes out again. He

---

[1] Cf. Henry's privy purse expenses (Bentley's "Excerpta," p.
121). "1499, 6 March. To Master William Paronus, an astrony-
myre, £1." There are similar references (ibid. pp. 110, 123).

[2] "1499, 8 February. To Olyver Tonor for relikes, in rewarde,
£2 13s. 4d" (Bentley, p. 121).

always pays in depreciated coin. His ordinary expenses for his house, table, kitchen, pension, council, chapel, servants, liveries, hunting, etc., for his own person, the Queen, the Prince of Wales, and all his children together, is about one hundred thousand scudos [1] a year. Parliament has lately made him a grant of 300,000 crowns, on condition that he leave the money of the country unaltered. According to the laws of England, any person can have his own gold or silver coined in the Mint; he has, nevertheless, altered these laws. He is said to gain, over and above the usual profits, seven reals in the mark of silver.[2] All his servants are like him, they possess quite " a wonderful dexterity in getting other people's money ". A short time ago, a certain Bernay from Avila, a merchant, incurred a penalty. Asked Henry to treat the said Bernay leniently, because he was a Spanish subject, who had failed from ignorance. The King answered, without a moment's hesitation, and very graciously, that he would not be hard on Bernay, in order that they might not be hard on English merchants in Spain. "He is so clever in all things, and in this matter shows it so much, that it is a miracle."

140.

[Marriage of Prince Arthur and Catherine of Aragon, "Spanish Calendar," i. 241.]

19 May.

On the 19th of May 1499, being Whit-Sunday, after the first mass, and at about 9 o'clock in the morning, Arthur, Prince of Wales ; Doctor de Puebla in his quality of proxy of Katharine, Princess of Wales; William, Bishop of Lincoln ; John, Bishop of Coventry and Lichfield, with many other persons, entered the

---

[1] About 20,880 pounds sterling.

[2] Henry also spent various sums on experiments to turn the baser metals into gold (Bentley, pp. 121-2).

chapel of the manor of Bewdley, in the diocese of Here- May, 1499.
ford, in order to perform, and respectively to witness,
the nuptial ceremony *per verba de præsenti*, between
the said Prince and Princess of Wales.

The Bishop of Coventry and Lichfield said in a clear
voice to the Prince of Wales that it was well known
how much King Henry wished that the marriage between him and the Princess of Wales should be contracted *per verba de præsenti*, that is to say, that it was
to be henceforth indissoluble. Doctor De Puebla, duly
authorized by the Princess of Wales, had come to this
holy place, in order to perform, in the name and in the
stead of the said Princess, the rites prescribed by the
Church. Moreover, the Pope had dispensed with all
obstacles to this matrimonial union. It was therefore
his duty, there to declare his opinion and his will.

After this peroration, the Prince of Wales said in a
loud and clear voice to Doctor De Puebla that he was
very much rejoiced to contract with Katharine, Princess
of Wales, daughter of King Ferdinand and Queen Isabella
of Spain, an indissoluble marriage, not only in obedience
to the Pope and to King Henry, but also from his deep
and sincere love for the said Princess, his wife.

De Puebla answered the Prince of Wales that he was
the more gratified by this declaration, since the marriage
was the fruit of his incessant labours. In the name of
the Princess Katharine he declared that he was willing
to conclude an indissoluble marriage.

The Bishop of Coventry and Lichfield then asked
De Puebla whether he had sufficient power to act as
proxy of the Princess Katharine. The power was delivered by De Puebla to the Bishop, and read in a loud
voice by Doctor Richard Nic. [The power of the Princess of Wales to Doctor de Puebla, dated " in the town
of Mayorete, 12th March, 1499," follows.]

May, 1499. After the power had been read, the Prince of Wales took, with his right hand, the right hand of Doctor De Puebla ; and Richard Peel [Pole], Lord Chamberlain of the Prince, and Knight of the Garter, held the hands of both in his hands. In this position the Prince declared that he accepted De Puebla in the name and as the proxy of the Princess Katharine, and the Princess Katharine as his lawful and undoubted wife.

The same ceremony was repeated, and De Puebla declared in the name of the Princess Katharine that she accepted the Prince of Wales as her lawful and undoubted husband.

141.

[Raimondo de Soncino to Ludovico Sforza, Duke of Milan, "Venetian Calendar," i. 799.]

London, 13 July.

There is nothing to write, save that, after the departure of Dr. Ruthal for France, Master (Sir Thomas) Lovel, the King's chief financier crossed to Calais, and returned with a good sum of crowns, paid by the French King on account of his obligations to the King of England. Has been unable to ascertain the precise sum ; some say 50,000 ducats, others 100,000. Antonio Spinola said he had heard 200,000. Does not believe the amount to be so large, for having had a long conversation with the King, who holds his own glory in becoming account, and having assiduously endeavoured to learn the sum, he thinks it impossible that, if it had been 200,000, the King would have failed to tell him so. The French respect the King greatly, and having lately seized in France a partizan of King Edward's, by name John Taylor, who devised Perkin's expedition to Ireland when the latter first declared himself the son of King Edward, they have surrendered the prisoner to the English ambassadors. Dr. Ruthal has already returned, but his colleague, a layman, remains behind to bring July, 1499. the prisoner with him. Believes that this thing will be held in great account by his Majesty ; much more than 100,000 crowns, as the English may say "Whither shall I go then from thy spirit, or whither shall I flee from thy presence?"[1]

142.

[The Earl of Oxford to Sir John Paston and another, "Paston Letters," iii. 942.]

Right trusty and welbeloved councellours, I com- Godshill, aunde me to you. And where the Kiuges Grace is lately acerteinyed that th' Erl of Suffolk is departid owt of this his Realme, Hys Grace hath commaundid me to wryte unto you that ye incontynent uppon the sight of this my writing endeovour you to enquyre aswell of such persones as be departid over with the seid Erle as of theim that accompanyed hym in his repayre to the see, and retornyd ageyn, or in any wyse were prevy to the same, and theruppon, in as goodly hast as ye kan, to put them and every of them in suertie savely to be kept, and therof t' acerteyn me, to th'entent ye maye knowe his ffurther pleasure in the same. And if ye shall at any tyme herafter perceyve any suspect person nyghe unto the see costes which shall seme unto you to be of the same affynyte, than His Grace will that ye put them in lyke suertie. And Almighti God have you in His keping.

143.

[John Pullan to Sir Robert Plumpton, "Plumpton Correspondence," p. 141.]

. . . Sir, so yt was that Parkin Warbek and other iij London, 21 Nov-

[1] Another translation of this despatch is given in the " Milanese ember. Calendar," i. 380. For Taylor, see above, pp. 82-4. He was, with the mayor of Cork and the mayor's son, sentenced on 16 November to be hanged, drawn, and quartered (Kingsford, p. 227).

were arreyned, on satterday [1] next before the making herof, in the Whithall at Westmynster, for ther offences,
afore Sir John Sygly, knight marshall, and Sir John
Trobilfeild ; and ther they all were attended,[2] and judgment given that they shold be drawn on hirdills from
the Tower, throwout London, to the Tyburne, and ther to
be hanged, and cutt down quicke, and ther bowells to be
taken out and burned : ther heads to be stricke of, and
quartered, ther heads and quarters to be disposed at the
Kyngs pleasure. And on munday next after,[3] at the
Gildhalle in London wher [4] the Judges and many other
knyghts commysioners to inquer and determayn all
offences and trespasses ; and theder from the Tower
was brought viij presoners, which were indited, and
parte of theme confessed themselfe gyltie, and other
parte were arreyned : and as yet they be not juged. I
thinke the shall have Judgement this next fryday. Sir,
this present day was new baresses made in Westmynster hall, and thether was brought Therle of War-
wek, and arrened afore Therle of Oxford, being the
Kyngs grace comyssioner, and afore other Lords,
(bycause he is a pere of the Realme) whos names
followeth ; the Duke of Bokingham, Therle of Northumberland, Therle of Kent, Therle of Surrey, Therle of
Essex, the lord Burgenny, lord Ormond, lord Deyngham,
lord Broke, lord of Saynt Johns,[5] lord Latymer, lord De
la Warre, lord Mountioy, lord Daubeney, lord Hastings,
lord Barns, lord Zowch, lord Sentmound, lord Willughby,
lord Grey of Wylton, and lord Dacre. And ther Therle
of Warweke confessed thenditments that were layd to his
charge, and like Judgment was given of him, as is afore
rehersed. When thes persones shalbe put in execution
I intend to shew to your mastership right shortly ; and

---

[1] 16 November.   [2] Attainted.   [3] 18 November.
[4] were.   [5] The prior of St. John's.

give credence unto this berrer.   From Lyncolns Inne November, 1499.
at London, this xxi day of November.

144.

[Trial and execution of Perkin Warbeck, the Earl of Warwick,
and their accomplices, Kingsford's " Chronicles," pp. 227-8.]

And vpon the Monday [1] after [the xvj day of Nouem-18 Novem-
bre] sate at the Guild hall of London vpon an Oyer ber-4 December.
determyn the Mayre, w^t my lord Chief Juge, w^t dyuers
other Juges and knyghtes ; and there before theym was
endyted viij prisoners of the Tour, among the which
was Thomas Mashborwth, sometyme bowyer vnto kyng
Edward, ij Citezeins of the Citie, that one named
ffynche, that other Prowde, and 6 other, which were
seruauntes to M. Dygby, Marshall of the Tour, entendyng aftir the Comon ffame to haue slayn their said M.,
and to haue set at libertie therle of Werwyk and
Perkyn.

And vpon the Tuysday next ensuyng was arayned in
the greate hall at Westm' the said Erle of Warwyk,
beyng of the age of xxiiij yeres or thereaboute ; vpon
whome sate for Juge the Erle of Oxinford, vnder a
Cloth of Astate : where w^{t}out eny,processe of the Lawe
the said Erle of Warwyk, for tresons by hym Confessed
and doon, submytted hym to the kynges grace and
mercy ; And so was there adiuged to be hangid, drawen
and quartered.

And vpon the satirday folowyng next, beyng seynt
Clementes day,[2] was drawen from the Tour vnto Tybourne Perkyn or Peter Warbek, and one John a Water,
sometyme Mair of Corf[k], as before is said, at which place
of Execucion was ordeyned a small Scafold, whervpon
the said Perkyn stondyng shewed to the people there in

[1] 18 November.   [2] 23 November.
                14 *

greate multitude beyng present, that he was a straunger
born accordyng vnto his former confession ; [1] and took
it vpon his dethe that he was neuer the persone that he
was named for, that is to say the second son of kyng
Edward the iiij[th]. And that he was forsed to take vpon
hym by the meanes of the said John a Water and other,
wherof he asked god and the kyng of forgiveness ; after
which confession he took his dethe meekly, and was
there vpon the Galowes hanged ; and with hym the said
John a Water; And whan they were dede, stryken
downe, and their hedes striken of ; and after their bodies
brought to the ffrere Augustynes, and there buryed, and
their heedes set after vpon London Brigge.

And vpon the Thursday folowyng, which was the
xxix day of Nouembre,[2] was therle of Werwyk before-
said brought out of the Tour bitwene two men, and so
ledde vnto the Scaffold and there beheded ; and after
the body w[t] the hede leide Into a Coffyn and born ageyn
vnto the Tour; which execucion was done bitwene ij
and iij of the Clok at after none : vpon whose Soule
and all christen Jhesu haue mercy !

And at the next tyde folowyng the body was conveied
by water vnto Byrsam, a place of Religion beside
Wyndesore, and there by his Auncesturs entered and
buried.[3]

And vpon the ffriday next folowyng, beyng seynt
Andrewes even,[4] Sat ageyn at the Guyld hall the Mair
w[t] the Chief Justice and other Juges and knyghtes ;
before whom was arayned the fore named viij prisoners
for lyf and deth, beyng charged one Quest with v

---

[1] See above, pp. 173, 183-5.

[2] Thursday was the 28th of November.

[3] " December.   Payd for the buriell of therle of Warwic by iiii
bills, £12 18s. 2d." (Bentley, p. 123).

[4] 29 November.

prisoners, and that other enquest w^t iij ; of the which November-
said viij persones, iiij of theyn named Strangwissh, December 1499.
Blowet, Astwood, and long Roger were adiuged to be
hanged, drawyn and quartered ; which Jugement was
given vpon seynt Andrewes day,[1] the Mayre and the
forsaid Juges there agayn sitting.

And vpon Monday folowyng, sittyng at the said place
the said Justices, was brought before theym the fore
named ffynch, Girdeler, and there Juged in like manner.

And vpon Weddensday next ensuyng was drawen
from the Tour vnto Tiborn the forenamed Blewet and
Astwode, both vpon one herdell ; and there hanged, and
after heded, and their bodies brought vnto the ffreres
Augustynes, and there buryed ; which forenamed Astwod
was, in the yere [1494] that Richard Chawry was mayre
drawen w^t other transgressours from Westm'. vnto the
Towre hill there to haue been beheded ; whome the
kyng at that season, of his most bountevous grace,
pardoned ;[2] wherfore as now his offence was the more
heynous and Grevous.

1500.

145.

[De Puebla to Ferdinand and Isabella, "Spanish Calendar," i. 249.]

England has never before been so tranquil and obedi- London, 11 January.
ent as at present. There have always been pretenders
to the crown of England ; but now that Perkin and the
son of the Duke of Clarence have been executed, there
does not remain "a drop of doubtful Royal blood," the
only Royal blood being the true blood of the King, the
Queen, and, above all, of the Prince of Wales. Must
forbear from importuning them any more on this sub-

[1] Saturday, 30 November.   [2] See p. 100.

January,
1500.

ject, as he has written so often concerning the execution of Perkin, and the son of the Duke of Clarence.[1]

146.

[Henry VII to Sir John Paston, "Paston Letters," iii. 943.]

Richmond,
20 March.

Trusty and welbeloved, we grete yow well, letting yow wete that our derest cousins, the Kinge and Queene of Spaine, have signified unto us by their sundry letters that the right excellent Princesse, the Lady Katherine, ther daughter, shal be transported from the parties of Spaine aforesaid to this our Realme, about the moneth of Maye next comeinge, for the solempnization of matrimony betweene our deerest sonne the Prince and the said Princesse. Wherfore we, consideringe that it is right fittinge and necessarye, as well for the honor of us as for the lawde and praise of our said Realme, to have the said Princesse honourably received at her arriveall, have appointed yow to be one amonge others to yeve attendance for the receivinge of the said Princesse; willinge and desiringe yow to prepare yourselfe for that intent, and so to continue in redynesse upon an honres warninge, till that by our other letters we shall advertise yow of the day and time of her arrivall, and where ye shall yeve your said attendance; and not to fayle therin, as ye tender our pleasure, the honor of yourselfe, and of this our foresaid Realme.

147.

["Chronicle of Calais," pp. 3-4; cf. "Greyfriars' Chronicles," p. 26, and Kingsford, p. 229.]

8 May-16
June.

Kynge Henry the Seventh and quene Elizabeth his

[1] For Catherine of Aragon's later belief that "her marriage had been made in blood," and was consequently ill-starred because her father had required these executions as a preliminary, see my "Political History of England," vi. 116 n. and "Henry VIII," p. 179.

wyffe, comynge out of England, landed at Caleis on the May-June, 1500.
8. day of May, being friday at night, in anno 1500, and
in the 15. of his raigne. With hym came the duke of
Buckynham, the erle of Surrey, the erle of Essex, the
lorde Dawbeney, being then lorde lyvetenaunt of the
towne and marches of Caleis, and lord chamberlayn of
the kyng's house, the bysshope of London, the lorde of
Burgaveny, the lorde Dakers of the Northe, the lorde
William of Suffolke, and the lord Souche. . . .

The 9th of June kynge Henry the Seventh and qwene
Elisabethe his wyfe, with many lords, ladyes, knights,
esquiers, gentlemen and yemen, met with the duke of
Burgoyne at owr lady of St. Petar's without Calays.
Saint Petar's churche was richely hanged with arras,
and ther they all dyned, for the churche was partyd
with hangings into dyvers offices, and when they had
dyned and comunyd ther was a rich banqwete, and
after the duke of Burgoyne dauncyd with the ladyes of
England, and then toke leave of the kynge and qwene,
and rode that nyght to Gravenynge, for he would not
come within the towne of Caleys.

The 16. day of June the kynge, the qwene, and all
the lordes and ladyes, landyd at Dover from Calleys.[1]

148.

[Death of Henry VII's youngest son Edmund, Duke of Somerset
(b. 20 February, 1499), Kingsford's " Chronicles," p. 231.]

Also this yere, the ffriday next folowyng Whitson 19 June.
Sonday, died at a place of the Bisshop of Elys, called
hatfeld, vpon a xx myle from London, my lord Edmond,
yongest Sone vnto the kyng, and the third Sone, vpon
whole Soule and all Christen Jhesu haue mercy ! Amen !

[1] "Paymentes made in the Kinges journey frome Grenewiche
to Calais, and from Calais to Grenewiche agen, by the space of 9
weeks, £1589 12s. 10d." (Bentley, p. 124).

June, 1500. And the Monday, beyng the xxij day of Juyu, was
the Corps of the said lord Edmond brought and conveyed honourably through fflete strete w^t many noble
personages, the Duke of Bokyngham beyng the Chief
mournour, the Mair and all the Craftes In their lyuereys
standyng in ffletestrete after their orders ; and the said
Corse so conveyed in a Chare, and all the mournours
Ridyng toward Westmynster, where he was the said
day buried by the Shryne of Saynt Edward.[1]

149.

[Death of Cardinal Morton, Kingsford's "Chronicles," p. 232 ;
cf. "Greyfriars' Chronicle," p. 26, "and the same yere dydo
the archbysshoppe of Yorke,[2] the bysshoppe of Norwyche,[3] and
the bysshoppe of Elye." [4]]

12 October. Also this yere in the begynnyng of the moneth of
Octobre departed out of this world Doctour Moreton,
Archebisshop of Caunterbury, Cardynall, Chaunceler
and prymat of this Realme, a man worthi of memory
for his many greate Actes and specially for his greate
wisdom, which contynued to the tyme of his Disease,
passyng the yeres of iiij^{xx} and odde ; in our tyme was
no man lyke to be compared w^t hym in all thynges;
Albeit that he lyved not w^{t}oute the greate Disdayn and
greate haterede of the Comons of this land ; his body
is entered at Caunterbury, caryed from Knoll, where
he died: vpon whos Soule and all Christen Jhesu haue
mercy ! Amen !

[1] " May.   Paid for the buryall of my Lorde Edmund   £242
11s. 8d. " (Bentley, p. 124).

[2] Thomas Rotherham *alias* Scott.

[3] Thomas Jane, d. September, 1500.

[4] John Alcock, d. 1 October, 1500.

1501.   1501.

150.

[Margaret Beaufort to her son, Henry VII, Ellis, "Original
Letters," 1st Ser. i. 46. Ellis has given no year to this letter,
but it may be inferred from the next letter.]

My oune suet and most deere Kynge and all my Coly-
weston,
worldly joy, yn as humble maner as y can thynke y 14 Janu-
recommand me to your Grace, and most hertely beseche ary.
our lord to blesse you ; and my good herte wher that
you sa [say] that the Frenshe Kyng hathe at thys
tyme gevyn me courteyse answer and wretyn . . . lettyre
of favour to hys corte of Parlyment for the treve ex-
pedicyon of my mater [1] whyche soo longe hathe hangyd,
the whyche y well know he dothe especially for your
sake, for the whyche my . . . ly beseeche your Grace
yt . . . to gyve hym your favourabyll . . . thanks and to
desyr him to contenew hys . .   And, yeve yt soo
myght leke [like] your Grace, to do the same to the
Cardynall, whyche as I understond ys your feythfull
trew and lovyng servant. Y wysse my very joy, as y
efte have shewed, and y fortune to gete thys or eny
parte therof, ther shall nedyr be that or eny good y
have but yt shalbe yours, and at your comaundement
as seurly and with as good a wyll as eny ye have yn
your cofyrs, as wuld God ye cowd know y^t as veryly as
y thinke yt. But my der herte, y wull no more en-
combyr your Grace with ferder wrytyng yn thys matter,
for y ame seure your chapeleyn and servante Doctour
Whytston ihathe shewed your Hyghnes the cyrcom-
stance of the same. And yeve yt soo may plese your

[1] Apparently her claim for repayment of money lent by her
mother the Duchess of Somerset, to the Duke of Orleans, Louis
XII's father, while he was a prisoner in England (Halsted's "Life
of Margaret Beaufort," p. 205 ; see "Milanese Calendar," i. 353).

Grace, y humbly beseche the same to yeve ferdyr
credense also to thys berer. And Our Lord gyve you
as longe good lyfe, helthe, and joy, as your moste nobyll
herte can dessyre, with as herty blessyngs as our Lord
hathe gevyn me power to gyve you. At Colynweston
the xiiij[th] day of January, by your feythfull trewe bed-
woman and humble modyr.—MARGARET R.[1]

151.

[Margaret Beaufort to Henry VII, Wood's " Letters of Royal and
Illustrious Ladies," i. 118. Miss Halsted, who has also
printed this letter, assigns it to 26 July, which was St. Anne's
day; but Dr. Gairdner says the allusion at the end to Henry
VII's birthday must refer to St. Agnes' day, 28 January.]

My dearest and only desired joy in this world.

Calais, 28
January.
With my most hearty loving blessings and humble
commendations I pray our Lord to reward and thank
your grace, for that it hath pleased your highness so
kindly and lovingly to be content to write your letters
of thanks to the French king, for my great matter, that
so long hath been in suit, as Master Welby hath shewed
me your bounteous goodness is pleased. I wish, my
dear heart, an my fortune be to recover it, I trust you
shall well perceive I shall deal towards you as a kind,
loving mother; and, if I should never have it, yet your
kind dealing is to me a thousand times more than all
that good I can recover, an all the French kings might
be mine withal. My dear heart, an it may please your
highness to license Master Whitstone, for this time, to
present your honourable letters, and begin the process of
my cause—for that he so well knoweth the matter, and
also brought me the writings from the said French king
with his other letters to his parliament at Paris—it

_____
[1] Margaret had no technical right to this royal signature.

should be greatly to my help, as I think : but all will I January, 1501.
remit to your pleasure. And if I be too bold in this, or
any my desires, I humbly beseech your grace of pardon,
and that your highness take no displeasure.

My good king, I have now sent a servant of mine into
Kendall, to receive such annuities as be yet hanging
upon the account of Sir William Wall, my lords chaplain, whom I have clearly discharged; and if it will
please your majesty's own heart, at your leisure, to send
me a letter, and command me that I suffer none of my
tenants be retained with no man, but that they be kept
for my lord of York, your fair sweet son,[1] for whom they
be most meet, it shall be a good excuse for me to my
lord and husband; and then I may well, and without
displeasure, cause them all to be sworn, the which shall
not after be long undone. And where your grace
shewed your pleasure for . . ., the bastard of King
Edward's, sir, there is neither that, nor any other thing,
I may do by your commandment, but I shall be glad
to fulfil to my little power with God's grace. And, my
sweet king, Fielding, this bearer, hath prayed me to
beseech you to be his good lord in a matter he sueth
for to the Bishop of Ely, now (as we hear) elect,[2] for a
little office nigh to London. Verily, my king he is a
good and wise, well ruled gentleman, and full truly hath
served you well, accompanied as well at your first as all
other occasions, and that causeth us to be the more bold
and gladder also to speak for him;[3] howbeit, my lord
marquis[4] hath been very low to him in times past, because he would not be retained with him; and truly,

---

[1] Afterwards Henry VIII.

[2] Richard Redmayne was elected Bishop of Ely early in 1501.

[3] This passage is hardly consistent with the account of Redmayne given in the "Dict. Nat. Biogr.," xlvii. 483.

[4] Thomas Grey, first Marquis of Dorset.

my good king, he helpeth me right well in such matters
as I have business with in these parts. And, my dear
heart, I now beseech you of pardon of my long and
tedious writing, and pray Almighty God to give you as
long, good, and prosperous life as ever had prince, and
as hearty blessings as I can ask of God.

At Calais town, this day of St. Anne's, that I did
bring into this world my good and gracious prince, king,
and only beloved son.

By your humble servant, headwoman, and mother.—
MARGARET R.

152.

[Building of Richmond Palace, Kingsford's "Chronicles," p. 233;
cf. "Greyfriars' Chronicle," pp. 26-7.]

In this yere the kyng, after he had ffynysshed a greate
parte of the buyldyng of his Manoir of Shene, which as
before is said was consumed by ffire,[1] ffor consideracion
that in the tyme of the said brennyng greate substaunce
of Richesse, as well in Juelles and other thynges of
Richesse, was perisshed and lost; And also that the
Reedifiyng of the said Manoir had cost, and after shuld
cost or it wer pursued, grete and notable sumes of money,
where before that season it was ones called or named
Shene, ffrom this tyme forward it was commaunded by
the kyng that it shuld be called or named Rich mount.

153.

[Flight of the Earl of Suffolk, Kingsford's "Chronicles," p. 233.
Suffolk had already fled once, in August, 1499, but had returned (see above, p. 209, and "Dict. Nat. Biogr.," xlvi. 22).]

August. In this yere in the moneth of August departed
Secretely out of the lond the Erle of Suff., and so sailed
vnto fraunce, where he accompanyed hym with Sir

[1] 21 December, 1497.

Robert Cursun, knyght, before season in like maner August, departed; ffor the which the kyng charged all officers, as serchers and other, to make due serche euery man in his Cuntre to se that noon other in like maner departed his land w^toute his licence.

154.

[Arrival and marriage of Catherine of Aragon. Henry VII to Ferdinand and Isabella, "Spanish Calendar," i. 311.]

Has already told them that the Princess Katharine Richmond, arrived on the 2nd of October at the port of Plymouth. 28 November. Is very glad that the Princess and her companions are well. Had felt great anxiety about her during her voyage from Spain to England. Has sent some of his officers to bring her by short and easy journeys to London. Has likewise told them that he and the Prince of Wales went to meet the Princess on her way. Have much admired her beauty, as well as her agreeable and dignified manners. On the 12th of November [1] the Princess made her entry into the capital, accompanied by such a multitude of prelates, high dignitaries, nobles and knights, and with the acclamation of such masses of people as never before had been seen in England.

On the 14th of November the Princess was conducted, with great splendour, to the Cathedral of St. Paul, where both the primates of England, a great number of Bishops, and the first secular and ecclesiastical Lords of the kingdom were present. The Archbishop of Canterbury said high mass before the principal altar of the church, and the Prince and Princess of Wales were solemnly wedded. Although the friendship between the houses of England and Spain has been most sincere and

[1] "November 12.   Ista die venit Domina Ispan. London" (Bentley, p. 126).

intimate before this time, it will henceforth be much more intimate and indissoluble.

Great and cordial rejoicings have taken place. The whole people have taken part in them. Begs them to banish all sadness from their minds. Though they cannot now see the gentle face of their beloved daughter, they may be sure that she has found a second father who will ever watch over her happiness, and never permit her to want anything that he can procure for her. Has already written to them about all this, but such things cannot be too often repeated.

The Archbishop of Santiago, the Count de Cabra, the Bishop of Majorca, and all the other ambassadors who have accompanied the Princess, have secured for themselves his love and esteem.

The union between the two royal families, and the two kingdoms, is now so complete that it is impossible to make any distinction between the interests of England and Spain. Promises punctually to fulfill all his obligations, and even more if they wish it.

1502.

155.

[Excommunication of Suffolk, "Greyfriars' Chronicle," p. 27.]

22 February. And the second Sonday of lent after was sir Edmonde de la Poole pronuncyd accursed opynly with boke, belle, and candell, at Powlles crose at the sermonde before none.

156.

[Arrest of Sir William Courtenay, Sir James Tyrrell, and others, Kingsford's " Chronicles," p. 255.]

February. And sone after [the ende of ffebruary] was the lord

William of Devenshire,[1] Sir James Tyrell[2] and his February, Eldest Son, and one Wellesbourne, a servaunt of the said James Tirell, taken and comytted to sauff kepyng for ffauouryng of the party of the erle of Suff.

157.

[Death of Prince Arthur, Kingsford's "Chronicles," p. 255.]

Also in the moneth of Aprill next folowyng, that is to 2 April. say the second day of Aprell, or nere aboute, died the noble prynce Arthure, the Eldest Sonne of our soueraign lord, at Ludlow; ffor whose soule the ffriday next folowyng at London was kept a Generall procession; and vpon the same Daye at after none   In euery parisshe Chirche of London a Solempne Dirige by note, and on the morow a masse of Requyem; And all the honest inhabitauntes of euery parisshe warned to be there present, to pray for the said Soule. And at Powles was doon a Solempne Dirige; where the Mair and his brethern were present in blak, and offred on the morne at Masse.   And the body was entred [interred] at Worcetir;[3] vpon whose soule and all Christen Jhesu haue mercy!   Amen!

158

[Trial and execution of Sir James Tyrrell and his accomplices, Kingsford's "Chronicles," p. 256.]

Vpon Monday, beyng the second day of May, was 2.9 May. kept at the Guyld hall of London an Oyr determyne,

[1] Sir William was eldest son of Edward Courtenay, Earl of Devonshire; it was not unusual in those days to describe the sons of an earl in the fashion of the chronicler. His arrest is dated 1503 in the "Dict. Nat. Biogr.," xii. 336.

[2] Sir James Tyrell was afterwards accused of complicity in the murder of the princes in the Tower.

[3] "June 18. Payd to the Under Treasurer, the rest of his boke made for the buriall of my Lorde Prince, £566 16s." (Bentley, p. 128).

where sat the Mayre, the Duke of Bokyngham, Therle of Oxenford, w^t many other lordes, Juges, and knyghtes, as commyssioners, before whome was presented as prisoners to be enquyred of, Sir James Tyrell, and sir John Wyndam, knyghtes, a Gentilman of the said Sir James, named Wellesbourn, and one other beyng a shipman.

Vpon the day folowyng, beyng the day of the halow-yng of the Invencion of the Crosse sat agayn there the said Mair, Lordes and other; where before theym ageyn were brought the said iiij persones, and there for certeyn tresons by theym commytted were adiuged to be drawen, hanged and quartered.

Vpon ffriday folowyng, beyng the vi^th day of May and the morowe after the Ascension of our Lord, Sir James Tyrell and the forsaid Sir John Wyndam, knyghtes, were brought out of the Toure, to the scaffold vpon the Toure hill, vpon their ffete; where they were both beheded.

And the same day was the forsaid Shipman laied vpon an herdyll, and so drawen from the Toure to Tybourne, and there hanged, hedid and quartered. And the forenamed Wellysbourn Remayned still in prison at the kynges commaundment and pleasure.

Vpon the Saterday folowyng was arayned before my lord of Derby and other lordes in the Whitehall at Westm' the sone of the forsaid Sir Jamys, one named Mathew Jonys, a yoman of the Croun, and a pursevaunt, and theder was brought the forsaid Wellesbourne for to geve Evidence agayne theym.

And the same day sat at Guyld hall the Mair and certeyn other commyssioners, before whom was arayned Sir John Wyndam's sone, and a barbour, dwellyng aboute the stile yerd in London, called James Holand.

And vpon the Monday folowyng sat agayn at the

yeldhall the said commyssioners, where for certeyn May, 1502.
tresons by theym commytted were Juged to be drwen,
hanged, and quartered, the forsaid ij persons.

And sone after the forsaid Mathew Jonys, and the
pursevaunt, which was called pursevaunt Cursum, were
sent to Guynes, and there were put to deth. And the
Residue Remayned in prison at the kynges grace.

159.

[Capture of a famous highwayman, Kingsford's "Chronicles,"
p. 257.]

Abowte Midsomer folowyng was taken a land Rover, 24? June.
or theff, the which named hym silff Greneleff; the
which, as it was Reported, had many Thevis at his
Retynew, and Robbed moch people aboute London; of
the which was Reported dedes and doynges after Robyn
hode. '

160.

[Isabella of Castile to Ferdinand, Duke de Estrada, Spanish ambassador in England, "Spanish Calendar," i. No. 327.]

Know that the King of France is on his way to Milan Toledo,
with an armed force, and has sent a force against us 12 July.
with the intention, it is said, of endeavouring to take
from us our possessions there. He has also sent to the
frontier of Perpignan many armed men, foot and horse,
and has commanded that ban and reban be proclaimed.

All the time this was going on we were at ease here,
for we did not believe that he would break the agreement which he had made and sworn.

But now you must see of how great importance it is
that there should be no delay in making the agreement
for the contract of marriage with the Prince of Wales
who now is. It is the more necessary, as it is said that
the King of France is endeavouring to hinder it, and is
intending to obtain the said alliance for his daughter,

or for the sister of Monsieur d'Angoulême. Therefore, without saying anything about this, since it is already known for a certainty that the said Princess of Wales, our daughter, remains as she was here (for so Doña Elvira has written to us), endeavour to have the said contract agreed to immediately without consulting us; for any delay that might take place would be dangerous. See also that the articles be made and signed and sworn at once, and if nothing more advantageous can be procured, let it be settled as was proposed. In that case let it be declared that the King of England has already received from us 100,000 scudos in gold, in part payment of the dowry, and let that be made an obligatory article of the contract, with a view to restitution, in accordance with the former directions given you. Let it be likewise stipulated that we shall pay the rest of the dowry when the marriage is consummated, so please God ; that is, if you should not be able to obtain more time. But take heed, on no account to agree for us to pay what still remains of the dowry until the marriage shall have been consummated. See, moreover, that the King of England give immediately to the Princess of Wales, our daughter, whatever may be necessary for her maintenance and that of her people. Provide also that, in the arrangement of her household, everything should be done to the satisfaction of the King of England. Take care that Doña Elvira remain with her, and any other persons whom she may wish to retain, according to the number which was agreed upon for her service.

Be very vigilant about this, and endeavour to have the contract made without delay and without consulting us. Do not, however, let them see you have any suspicion of hindrance, or show so much eagerness that it may cause them to cool. But set about it prudently, and in the manner which may seem best to you, so that there may be no delay in making the contract, and July, 1502. let us know immediately what you have done in it.[1]

Notwithstanding that a league of amity has been concluded between us and the King of England, binding us to aid each other in the defence of our possessions, yet the treaty says, *in what we possess at present,* that is to say, what we possessed when the treaty was made. According to that treaty, therefore, he is not obliged to aid us in the defence of Apulia and Calabria, because we have obtained those countries since. Consequently, we desire that at the time when the treaty of marriage is made, you should say to the King of England that it is reasonable, since the treaty of kinship is being settled afresh, he should renew the treaty of amity in such a manner that, without altering anything in it except the date, all that we have mentioned may be remedied.

The clauses of the treaty are very clear in this respect. If you think well of it, you may make use of the old treaty.

Before you say anything to the King of England respecting the King of France, we desire that the affair of the treaty of marriage should be settled, so that the one matter may not hinder the other. On this account, it would be well that it should be done quickly. In case that you hear anything of the King of France, appear as if you did not believe it, until after the treaty of marriage is concluded. Afterwards you must show to the King of England the relation which we send you herewith of the matters between us and the King of France. Let the King of England know that he is sending against our frontiers of Perpignan a large armed force of infantry and cavalry, and that he has proclaimed throughout all our frontiers ban and reban, and that he is intending to attack us in our possessions.

[1] See below, Vol. iii., Nos. 13-14.

15 *

July, 1502. The King of England, our brother, knows that in accordance with the treaty of amity which has been agreed on between us, we are bound to aid one another in the defence of our possessions. Learn, therefore, what it is which he desires we should do in the matter, and let us know.

If by chance the rupture between the King of France and ourselves should be already known in England, and there should be a disposition in the King of England to recover Guienne and Normandy by uniting himself with us, and we with him, in that case the King of the Romans will also be on our side. So, if you see that your negociation will be benefitted by it, and that the state of affairs between us and the King of France renders it necessary, endeavour to get the King of England to take part in it, saying that he will never have such an opportunity of recovering his own possessions. We believe that it would be well to make use of Doctor De Puebla for this negociation. Therefore, if you think he will be of use, impart the business to him, and let him aid you in the way that may seem best. Try to induce the King of England to take part in this matter, and use the skill that we look for from you, and the necessary diligence. If anything be said to you about it, listen and negociate with prudence, and consult with us. But do not speak of it without being first certified of our rupture with the King of France.

161.

[Ferdinand of Aragon to the Duke of Estrada, "Spanish Calendar,"
i. pp. 287-8.]

1 Septem- Now this enterprise of the King of France cannot be
ber. hindered except by putting him under the necessity of defending his kingdom of France. This, to be of any use, cannot, as you know, be done by means of one King

only. But if we and the King of England were to join together to make a descent upon France, each one with all his forces, we might then attack Guienne and Normandy ; or we might descend upon Languedoc and the parts about Fuentarabia while the King of England attacked the duchies, in the hope, with God's assistance, that, our army might then effect a junction there with the army of the King of England. For, if we and the King of England could meet in France, he might recover, by God's help, the said duchies of Guienne and Normandy, or a large portion of them. By these means the King of France would be obliged to quit Italy, in order to come to the defence of his own kingdom.

As soon as he had left Italy, having within his kingdom two such Princes as his adversaries, it is very certain that all the people of Italy would join together to take from the King of France and his people that which he holds in Italy, so that he would lose it all. Moreover, it is probable that in order to deliver his kingdom he would, in such a case, consent to all that we and the King of England might require. On the other hand, no great forces being sent against the King of France, the people of Italy would dare to do nothing except what he might command. Therefore what above all things we now desire is, that the King of England should be induced to take part in the matter in the way we have pointed out.

Having regard to what we have said, you will on this account give this business precedence of all others, for you must see how much it imports our royal state and service. And you will tell the King of England, immediately, from us, how the King of France, without any just cause or reason, and without wishing to find any means of maintaining peace and concord, has broken all that he had capitulated and sworn to with us, we having kept our faith very entirely with him. You will also say that, after having seized upon our country of Sicily by means of his fleet and army, we being quite at ease the while, confident as we were of peace and un- prepared for war, he made war upon us there, saying that he desired to have our duchies of Apulia and Calabria and our kingdom of Sicily, and has already proceeded from words to deeds. Moreover, show him how little security he, or any one, can have that the King of France will keep that which he has confirmed and sworn, after breaking with us in the way he has done. For even if there had been no treaty of amity agreed to and sworn between us and the King of Eng- land, by which he would have been bound to take part in this matter, there would still be sufficient reason for him to join with us in remedying the evil. How much the more need then is there for him, being, as he is, obliged thereto on account of the treaty of amity settled between us, to aid us in the defence of our kingdom of Sicily and of those our other realms.

We therefore pray him that he will be willing to do this, because, as we said before, the matter requires strong and speedy measures to be speedily taken. For, we are quite determined to aid him, with all our power. God willing, to recover his duchies of Guienne and Normandy, if he will aid us to recover our possessions. You will also tell the King of England that suitable security must be given on the one side and the other, that, God willing, we should not dissolve our confedera- tion against the King of France, or make peace or truce with him without the King of England, or the King of England without us. Above all, give this business precedence of all others, and use your best endeavours in it, making the strongest representations to the King

of England respecting it, and endeavouring in all pos- September,
sible ways to get him to take part in it.

1503.

162.

[Death of the Queen, Kingsford's "Chronicles," p. 258.]

And vpon Candelmas day, in the nyght folowyng the 2-11 February.
day, the kyng and the Quene then beyng loged in the ^{ary.}
Towre of London, the Quene that nyght was delyuered
of a doughter; where she entendid to have been delyuered at Richmount, and vpon the Saterday folowyng
was the said doughter Cristened w^tin the parisshe
chirch of the Towre, and named Kateryn. And vpon
that day vij nyght or vpon Saterday, beyng the xjth day
of ffebruarij, in the mornyng, dyed the noble and vertuous
Quene Elizabeth in the said Tour;[1] vpon whose Soule
and all Christen Jhesu haue mercy! Amen!

163.

[Death of the Queen, "Venetian Calendar," i. No. 833.]

Receipt of letters from the ambassador, Alvise Antwerp,
Mocenigo, dated Antwerp 19 February. News had 19 February.
been received that the Queen of England, after giving
birth to a female child, had died, though the English
ambassadors said they did not know this for certain.
Writes that this Queen was the daughter of the late
King Edward; a very handsome woman and of great
ability.

[1] "March 16. Delivered to Sir Robert Hatton in prest at two
tymes for the buryall of the Quenes grace, £433 6s. 8d. " (Bentley, p.
130). " 31 May. Delivered to thunder-treasurer in full payment
of £2832 7s. 3d. for thentirment of the Quenes grace, £2389
0s. 7d. " (*ibid.*).

February,
1503.

By a letter from the same of the 23rd, the death of the Queen was confirmed; she was 35 years old, a very handsome woman, and in conduct very able; has left a son and three daughters. It is supposed that although King Henry has made the agreement with the King of the Romans, England will make a stir, and affairs there be in commotion.

164.

[Excommunication of Edmund de la Pole and Sir Robert Curzon, Kingsford's "Chronicles," p. 259 ; cf. No. 155.]

5 March.

Vpon Sonday, beyng the first Sonday of Lent, and the vth day of March, was at Poules Crosse executed a Solempn Curs w^t book, bell, and Candell; by Reason or auctorytie wherof there was solempnely accursid Edmond De la Poole, Sir Robert Cursun, and other, w^t all such as theym ayded or favered In Will or in dede.

165.

[Murder of the prior of Sheen, Kingsford's "Chronicles," p. 259.]

March.

In the Ende of the moneth of March the priour of the Charterhous of Shene was murdered w^t in the place by meanes of a monk of the same hons, named Goodwyn ; and an other Monk also by hym and his complices was there also murdred.

166.

[Margaret, Queen of Scotland, to her father, Henry VII, Ellis, "Original Letters," 1st Ser. i. 41. Margaret Tudor was married to James IV by proxy on 25 January, 1503 ; she left Richmond on 27 June, and made her state entry into Edinburgh on 7 August.]

Edin-
burgh (?)
Aug. 1't.

My most dere lorde and fader in the most humble wyse that I can thynke I recummand me unto your

Grace besechyng you off your dayly blessyng, and that August 1503.
it will please you to yeve hartely thankes to all your
servauntts the whych by your commaundement have
geven ryght good attendaunce on me at this tyme, and
specially to all thes ladies and jantilwomen which hath
accompeneyed me hydder, and to geff credence to thys
good lady the berar her off, for I have showde hyr mor
off my myud than I will wryght at thys tyme. Sir, I
beseche your Grace to be good and gracious lorde to
Thomas, whych was footman to the Quene my moder,
whos sowle God have soyle;[1] for he hath byn on[2] off
my fotemen hydder with as great diligence and labur to
hys great charge of his awne good and true mynde. I
am not able to recumpence hym, except the favor of
your Grace. Sir, as for newys I have none to send,
but that my lorde of Surrey ys yn great favor with the
Kyng her that he cannott forber the companey off hym
no tyme off the day. He and the bichopp off Murrey
orderth every thyng as nyght[3] as they can to the Kyngs
pleasur. I pray God it may be for my por[4] hartts ease
in tyme to come. They calnot[5] my Chamberlayne to
them, whych I am sur wull speke better for my part
than any off them that ben off that consell. And iff he
speke any thyng for my cause my lord of Surrey hath
such wordds unto hym that he dar speke no furder.
God send me comford to hys pleasur and that I and
myne that ben lefftt her with me be well entretid such
wayse as they have taken. For[6] Godes sak Syr, oulde[7]
mea escusyd that I wryt not my sylf to your Grace, for
I hav no laysyr thys tym, bot wyt a wishse I would I
wer wyt[8] your Grace now, and many tyms mor, wan I
wold andsyr. As for thys that I have wrytyn to your

---

[1] assoyle.   [2] one.   [3] nigh.   [4] poor.
[5] call not.   [6] These last lines only are in the Queen's hand.
[7] hold.   [8] with.

August,
1503.

Grace, yt ys wery tru, bot I pray God I may fynd yt
wel for my welefer[1] efter. No more to your Grace at
this tym, bot our Lord hau you en ys kepyng. Wrytyn
wyt the hand of your humble douter, Margaret.

1504.

167.

[Henry VII's last parliament, "Rotuli Parliamentorum," vi. 520.]

25 January.

Memorandum quod die Jovis, xxv die Januarii anno
regni Regis Henrici Septimi post conquestum decimo
nono. . . Dominus W. Archiepiscopus Cantuariensis
. . . causam summonitionis Parliamenti . . . declaravit.
. . . Nam, ut ait Augustinus, sublata justicia, quid
aliud sunt regna, quam magna latrocinia; unde
scriptum est in Ecclesiastico, "Propter injusticias
transfertur regnum de gente in gentem". Et quoniam
inter multa que regnis ac civitatibus sunt necessaria,
leges precipuum obtinent locum, sola justicia optim-
arum legum conditrix est, eademque conditarum con-
servatrix; cum alioquin leges aut condantur inique,
quarum auctores execrantur, unde Propheta dicens
" Ve qui condunt leges iniquas; " aut pervertuntur bene
condite. De quo Cicero, Existunt, inquit, sepe injurie,
calumnia quadam & nimis callida juris interpretacione,
ex qua illud " summum jus summa injuria " factum est
jam tritum sermone proverbium. Ex hiis itaque liquet
in rebus humanis utilius nichil esse posse justicia.
Postremo, quid preterea voluptatis habeat ipsa justicia,
certissimis argumentis ostendit. Nam quantumcumque
sit utilis, quantumvis honesta, nisi delectet, amari non
potest. Non enim amatur, nisi quod delectat; ut ait
Augustinus, quamquam parum ei videtur delectare
justiciam nisi eciam inter omnia que delectant, plus te

[1] welfare.

delectet ipsa justicia; delectant enim quedam naturali- January,
1504.
ter propter infirmitatem nostram, ut cibus & potus
delectant esurientes & sicientes; delectat nos hec lux
que de celo funditur sole exorto, vel que syderibus &
luna fulget, vel que in terra accenditur, luminibus
consolantibus tenebras oculorum; delectat corona, vox
& suavissima cantilena; delectat odor bonus; delectant
eciam tactum nostrum quecumque pertinent ad carnis
aliquam voluptatem; & que delectant nos in sensibus
corporis, aliqua licita sunt, aliqna illicita : justicia sic
delectare debet ut vincat eciam licitas delectaciones,
nedum illicitas; quamquam ne id quidem satis sit, ut
Angustino placet, pro amore justicie, contempsisse
quicquid te delectabat, nisi eciam contempseris quicquid te terrebat; contempne carceres, contempne
vincula, contempne exilium, contempne tormenta,
contempne mortem. Hiis ac aliis nonnullis tam divin-
arum quam humanarum legum antiquissimis ration-
ibus & argumentis, omnium circumstancium animos ad
justiciam summe collendam mirifice inflamavit.

168.

[The Doge and Senate of Venice to Nicolo Giustiniam, Venetian
consul in London, "Venetian Calendar," i. No. 837.]

He is aware that during the lifetime of Pope Alex- Venice,
27 Janu-
ary.
ander VI, the Duke of Valentinois (Cæsar Borgia)
ceased not by all possible ways and means to plot against
the Signory, trying to seize their towns and fortresses.
The Republic having been thus provoked by him, on
the death of Pope Alexander (18th August, 1503), and
also as a measure of self-defence, took Faenza by force
from Valentinois, he having occupied and usurped it
from the Church, together with many other cities, towns,
and fortresses.

The Republic also obtained the city of Rimini from

its lord, Pandolfo Malatesta, who recovered it from
Valentinois ; but who, not having the means either to
reduce the castle, or to maintain himself in that state,
ceded the said city to the Republic, in exchange for
three times as much, as will appear by the enclosed
note ; the Signory keeping for itself that which had been
tyranically held by Valentinois, and restoring to the
Church the supremacy and acknowledgement of tribute.
Declare that the appropriation of this territory can not
be attributed to covetousness, the Republic having already ample possessions, whereas the cost of the newly
acquired places far exceeds their revenue ; and that what
has been done was solely for the honour and advantage
of holy Church, and to secure the Republic against competitors already in the field, and who sought to seize
these towns, having sent troops to Faenza, putting
forward one Franckscheto de Manfredi, a bastard, for
whom, however, the State of its munificence provided
suitably.

Assert that this is what the Republic has done in the
affairs of the Romagna ; for which impartial and unim-
passioned minds would award praise and commendation,
and not blame, which is constantly cast on the State,
at the instigation of rivals and malignants, by the Pope,
at the Courts of the Christian powers, amongst whom
is understood to be the King of England.

Are assured that his Holiness has written to the said
King a brief, accusing the Republic heavily for the
aforesaid acts, and referring to Cesena, Imola, and
Forli, which places have been hitherto respected out of
consideration for his Holiness, although they might
easily have been seized ; the State occupying Rimini and
Faenza, and the territories thereof, by reason of state
policy, and for the advantage of the apostolic see and of
his Holiness, but restoring to him his tributes, and

paramount rights—the Republic constituting itself his January, 1504.
tributary. The Pope and apostolic see can thus have
the assistance of the Signory in place of Valentinois—
an irreverent and most cruel tyrant, of whose fellow no
record exists in any history, ancient or modern ; notwithstanding which, the Pope at the suggestion of bad
men, lays blame on the Republic, which has always
been of such service to Christendom and holy Church
as seen by innumerable proofs and instances. Without
referring to circumstances of ancient date, they would
mention what had been done recently by the State for
the election of a pontiff on the demise of Pope Alexander,
when the Signory opposed Valentinois, who had a
strong force in the apostolic palace for the purpose of
coercing the sacred College of Cardinals to elect a pope
after his fashion, and prevented these his plots and
iniquitous designs from taking effect. The consul is
charged to obtain audience of King Henry, and in detail
to acquaint him with all the aforesaid justifications in
such terms as his ability and prudence may suggest.
He is to explain the course of events to every one, as
shall seem necessary, so as to make a favourable impression. The King himself, the State is convinced, will
expect the Pope to be well disposed towards the Signory.

The consul to omit no assiduity. They rely much on
his prudence and ability. To write back word of the
execution of these commands.

169.

[The Duke of Estrada to Isabella of Castile, "Spanish Calendar,"
i. 398.]

The King had taken the Princess of Wales to Rich- London, 10 August.
mond, and from Richmond to Windsor. There they
stayed twelve or thirteen days, going almost every day
into the park and the forest to hunt deer and other

game. From Windsor they returned to Richmond, where they passed a week.

The Princess had been unwell for three days, suffering from ague and derangement of the stomach. She soon got better. From Richmond the King proceeded to Westminster, leaving the Prince of Wales behind, but taking the Princess of Wales, the Princess Mary and all the English ladies with him. A few days later they all went together to Greenwich. After staying six or seven days in Greenwich the Princess fell ill again, and much more seriously than before.

Before she had recovered, King Henry was obliged to leave on a visit to Kent. The Princess of Wales then returned to the house in which she had formerly lived. She had, however, not improved. She is rather worse, for she now suffers every day from cold and heat. The illness seems sometimes serious, for the Princess has no appetite and her complexion has changed entirely. Nevertheless the physicians have much confidence and say that the patient will soon recover.

.   .   .   .

The King left Greenwich the same day on which the Princess of Wales went away. He sends messages to her very often, and offers to visit her. He offers to convoke all the physicians of the kingdom, and is very courteous. The Prince of Wales is with the King. Formerly the King did not like to take the Prince of Wales with him, in order not to interrupt his studies. It is quite wonderful how much the King likes the Prince of Wales. He has good reason to do so, for the Prince deserves all love. But it is not only from love that the King takes the Prince with him; he wishes to improve him. Certainly there could be no better school in the world than the society of such a father as Henry VII. He is so wise and so attentive to every-

thing; nothing escapes his attention.   There is no August, 1504.
doubt the Prince has an excellent governor and steward
in his father.   If he lives ten years longer he will leave
the Prince furnished with good habits, and with immense riches, and in as happy circumstances as man
can be.

Wishes very much to leave England as soon as
possible.   Was told last year that there was no
money to defray the expenses of his journey.   Had,
therefore, already remained one year longer in England
than was necessary.

Expected the brief of the Pope containing the dispensation [1] would have come a long while ago.   As it
had not come, doubts arose whether the dispensation
would be given at all ; and a brief, of which a copy is
added, even seemed to confirm these doubts.   Went to
King Henry in order to take leave of him.   The King
was much surprised, and asked him to remain till the
dispensation arrived.   Promised to stay in England till
the end of August.   Said that if the dispensation did
not arrive during that time it would then be clear that
the Pope did not like to give it.

At last, after the King had left Greenwich, the dispensation arrived.   Henry sent it directly to him, in
order that he might show it to the Princess.   If the
Dean,[2] who is ambassador of the King of England in
Rome, should have to bring the papal bulls, they will
not arrive before the middle of October.   The King,
wishing to make the marriage very solemn, will communicate the bulls to the principal personages of the
kingdom who usually assemble in Westminster on the
Day of All Saints.   Thus November will come on be-

[1] For the marriage between Prince Henry and Catherine of
Aragon ; see also Vol. iii., Nos. 14 ff.
[2] Robert Sherborne, Dean of St. Paul's.

fore it will be possible for him to leave England, and
a voyage in that season is by no means an agreeable
thing, especially for so bad a sailor as he is. Begs her
to send him money, and a positive order to return to
Spain, which, if necessary, he can show to the King of
England.

170.

[Ferdinand of Aragon to Henry VII, " Spanish Calendar," i. 409.]

Informs him that that self same day it had pleased
God to take to Himself Queen Isabella. Her death is
the greatest affliction that could have befallen him.
Does not doubt but that the King will feel her loss as
a brother. Expresses his assurance that she is in glory,
and his desire to be resigned to God's will. Acquaints
the King that she has ordained by her will that her
husband should be administrator and governor of the
kingdoms of Castile, Leon, and Granada etc., as he
already is, on behalf of their daughter Queen Juana.
On all these matters the King of England will be informed by De Puebla.

171.

[Treasonable words about Henry VII reported by John Flamank,
" Letters and Papers," i. 231-240. Dr. Gairdner dates this
document 1503 ; but the reference on p. 245 to a prophecy
that Henry would not reign more than twenty-two years seems
to indicate a later date. The " Lady Luse " on p. 246 was Sir
Anthony Browne's wife, Lady Lucy Neville, niece of the
" Kingmaker," and daughter of John, Marquis Montagu.]

About the last day of Septembre last past, beyng in
a secrett counter within your deputie [1] is place at Calis,
he, Sir Hughe Conway, your treserer ther, and Sir
Sampson Norton, master porter of that your sayd toune,

[1] Sir Richard Nanfan.

cald to them my brodre William Nanfan and me.   Then 1504 or
said my master your depute to us " Sirs, we must comyn 1505.
here now of many great matres touchyng the kyngis
grace and the surtie of this hys toune of Calis.   Therfore by cause ye be next unto me, I must some tyme
put you in tryst more then other.   Ye shall hyre here
thees matrys that we intend to comyn of ; but first ye
shall be boythe sworen upon a boke that ye shall never
utter nothyng that is now here spoken, without it be to
the kyngis grace yf nede shall require, or els to non
lyvyng creature."   Then after many matris spoken by
my master your depute and resonned to the same by
your treserer and porter, wiche matres and wherof they
were I ame and shalbe [ready] to shew to your hygnes
at suche tyme or tymes that best shall plese your grace
that I so do.

Then seid Sir Hughe Conway, " Master depute, yf ye
knew as moche as I do, ye wolde saye that ye hade
as grett cause to take kepe to your sylfe as ony lyvyng
creature ; and therto ye be asmuche bownden to thank
God for that ye have askaped hetherto as ye have, for
I know thoos persons that have be sett to murdre you,
and by whoos cause and menys they so dyde."   Mi
master askyd hym what they were he wold then shew
hym, but seid that he wold shew hym more of that
mater at a nodre tyme when we shall have more layser.
So for what he said now ame I and master porter as fyr
into the daunce as ye be, for I promyse you of my faythe
that all thoos that be and were proffered hydre into ther
romes by my Lord Chamberlayn [1] shall never love non
of us, and specially thoos that were his houssold servauntis tofore.   The cause whij they soo do I cannot
tell, but for that we folow the kyngis plesure and wil do.
Therfore good yt is that we see to our owne surtie, as

[1] Giles, Lord Daubeney.

1504 or
1505.

well as fore the surtie of this the kyngis toune, that yt may be sure to hym and his, wat world so ever shall hapen to fall here after, to have in remembrans that the gretter and more partie of thoos that be in the kyngis retenu here be of my lordis prefferment. Also loke hoo stronge he is in the kyngis courte of his houshold servauntis, for the more partie of his garde be of thoos that were my Lord Chamberlayn servauntis tofore, and hard hyt is to know mennys myndis yf God should send a soden change, as he hayth here tofore.

Then said my master, your depute, that "I darst reseive the sacrament that my lord is as true to the kyngis grace as ony man lyvyng;" and in lyke wyse seid master porter.

Item, my master your depute said " My lord Chamberlayn was very shlake in oone jorny, wherwith I knowell that the kingis grace was discontent; for and he had done his parte welle, the Cornyshe men hade never made the kynge feld at Blake hethe, but had all ben distroyed longe before ther comyng thedre, that I knowell the kyngis grace hade lever hade be done then xxᵐ₁ li for his honour.

Item, after many wordes spoken, Sir Hughe Conwey seid, " Mastres, I hanot spoken theys wordis for no untrothe that I do thynk be now in my lord Chamberlayn, for I dar say now as ye do that he lovyth the kynge aswell as any man can do lyvyng; but yt haith be sene in tymys past that chaynge of worldis hayth caused chaynge of mynd."

Item the same Sir Hughe said, that " we be here now togedres the kyngis true servauntis to lyve and dy, and also to spend all that we have in the world to do his grace servis. Therfore watt so ever we speke or comyn for his surtie, and for the surtie of this his toune, can be no tresone; so good yt is that we loke and

speke of thyngis to come as well as thoos present. I 1504 or
do speke this for a cause that is good that we loke sadly 1505.
to, for the kyngis grace is but a weke man and syklow,
not lykly to be no longe lyvis man. Yt ys not longe
sithens his hygnes was syke and lay then in his maner
of Wangsted.[1] Hyt hapned the same tyme me to be
emonges many grett personages, the whiche fele in
communicacion of the kyngis grace and of the world
that should be after hym yf hys grace hapned to depart."
Then he said that some of them spake of my lorde of
Buckyngham, saying that he was a noble man and
woldbe a ryall ruler. Other ther were that spake, he
said, in lykwise of your traytor Edmond De la Pole,
but none of them, he said, that spake of my lord prynce.
Then said master porter to hym, "Have ye never
broken to the kyngis grace of this mater?" Then said
Sir Hughe Conway to hym agayn, "I pray you souffer
me to tell forthe my talle, for I am not yet athe ynd.
Ye have in mynde wat that I have shewed you touchyng
this matris. Of my faith, in lyke wise sithens my
comyng I have shewed the same to Sir Nycholas Vaux,[2]
lieutenant of Gysnes, and to Sir Antony Bronne, lieutenant of the castell here, and they answeryd me both
this, that they had to good holdes to resorte unto, the
wiche thay seid sholdbe sure to make their paxce, ho
so ever the worlde tourne." Then my master youre
depute, and master porter boyth said to hym that he
could no lase doo but shew thes matres unto your
hyghnes. He said that, "Hyt ware good that the
kyngis grace knew thees sayyngis, but asyet I have not
shewed hym no part theroff, nother never I wildo."
Then said master porter to hym angrely, and sware by

---

[1] Henry VII bought Wanstead in 1499 (Bentley, "Excerpta,"
p. 122).

[2] Vaux was appointed lieutenant of Guisnes in 1502.

Godis precious soule he be the more to blame to kepe
suche matris from his hygnes; and in lyke wyse said
my master your depute, and all we beyng there.

Item, after many wordis spoken touchyng the same,
Sir Hughe Conway said, " Yf ye knew kynge Harry oure
master as I doo, ye woldbe ware how that ye brake to
hym in ony suche matres, for he wold take yt to be said
but of envy, yll wille and malis. Then should ani on have
blame and no thanke for his trouth and good mynd; and
that have I welle proved here to fore in lyke causes, for
that tyme that the lord Lovell lay in Colchester a trysty
frend of myn came to me and shewed me in councell the
day and tyme of hys departyng, and of alle hys purpos.
I was sworen to hym that I should never utter thys to
man lyvyng to his hurte; butt yet forthwith after-
wardis by cause of myn alegens, I came to Sir Raynold
Bray and shewed hym all as is abowe, and forthwith he
said that Master Bray shewed the same unto the kyngis
[grace]. Wher uppon I was brought before hys hygnes
and I affermed all to be true as my said frend hade
shewed; and the kynge said that hyt could not be so, and
resoned with me always to the contrary of my said
sayynges. At last he asked what he was that told me
thus tale of hys departyng. I prayed hys hygnes to
pardon me, for I said that I was sworen to hym that I
should never utter hym, to be drawen with wyld horsses;
wherewith the kynge was angry and displesed with me
for my good wille. I shall no more tempt hym wile I
lyve in suche causes." Then said Master porter "I
thynk that ye drast never speke thees wordes to the
kyngis grace as ye have rehersed them now here," and
he sware many grett othes that he dyde.

Item, my master youre deputie said that "I knowell
that the kyngis hyghnes is harde of credens in suche
matres; and that knowe ye," he said, "master porter,

aswell as I, for howe longe was yt er hys grace and hys 1504 or
councell wold belyve ony thyng of untrothe to be in Sir 1505.
Jame Tyrell ; and some said I dyd seke to do hym hurte
for malis.

"Item, a nodre tyme I dyd wryt unto his hygnes
that oone hade shewed me that Sir Robert Clyfford
should say here in this toune to a lady that Perken
Warbeke was kynge Edwardes sone. Never wordes
went coldre to my hart then they dyd. Hys hygnes
sent me sharpe wrytyng agayn that he wold have the
prouffe of this matier. I hade no wittnes then but my
sylfe ; but as hyt hapned afterwardes I caused hym by
good crafte to confesse the same he had said to me before hym that was marshell here at that tyme, and els I
hade lykly to be putt to a grett plonge for my trothe. At
the last al thought that hit was not to shewe this to
youre grace without better proffe; yet master porter
said yt was grett pitty that the kinge dyd not tryst hys
true knyghtes better, and to geve them credens in suche
thynges as they should shew for hys surtie, for grett
hurt may come by that mene."

Item, after this the treserer said, " Master depute and
master porter, what daunger be we in now, remembryng
all thynges welle, for we have no suche holdes to resort
unto as thees other men have, considryng also oure
many enymies that we have in this toune and els where
that wilbe glade to distroy and murdre us all yf other
should come to the kyngis grace then wele. And for
trothe I knowell that he cannot longe contynu for hyt
is wryten of hym that he shall no longer raygne than
dyd kynge Edward, wiche," he said, "was but xxij^te
yere and lytle more." Then said my master youre
depute, "I bysherwe hys hart that so dyde wryte, and
also I pray God send all them that thynk the same to
be true a shorte shamfull dethe ". The treserer said

agayn " We may not be angry in this matris when we shall comyn for the surtie of oure sylfes aswell as of this the kyngis toune, for I thynk not veryly thus to be all true that I have said, but I knowell that every manys mortall and must dij, and that that I have said I shall shew you my boke that shall declare you the same playnly to be as I have said and spoken ". Master porter said, " Then I pray you, master tresere, brene that boke, and a vayngens take the first wryter ".

Item, then said my master your depute to master Convaye, " I pray you leve thys profyciyng of the kynge, for ye speke of thynges that I never kepe never hire nor see, and that my prayer is that I never leve day nother oure longer then the kyngis grace and hys chyldre shall have and inyoye the realme of Inglond." And likevise spake master porter and we all beyng there.

Item, then said master Conway, " All this that I have spoken is to thentent to have all thynges to be made sure for the kynge and hys childre, and specially this hys toune of Calis ; and that cane never be done without good and wyse communycacion had of the same byfore ; for I tell you for surtie that that shall never be aslonge as the lady Luse shalbe in the castell, that we cane sure the kynge of thys hys toune, for the castell is the kay of this toune ; he that is therin beyng of a contray mynd may lett men inow in oone nyght to distrij us alle wyle we shalbe in oure beddes sleepyng. I know, masters," he said, " wat longeth to suche matres better then ye do ; therfore I pray you seuffer me for to speke. Lett nott us thynk the contrarij but and the kyngis were ons departyd, she beyng in the castell here and Edmond De la Pole hire cosen at hys lyberte, but that she wolde helpe hym in hys causes with all hire poure and to lett hym come into this toune by the

postren of the castell to the distruccion of us alle. Re- 1504 or 1505.
membre welle how ny that Kent is hydre, wat a lyans
thay be of thers." He spake of Sir Edward Poynynges,
Sir Rychard Gylforth, Sir Thomas Bonchir. Wat he
said of ther demener, master porter, yf youre grace
exammen hym cane shew youre hygnes better then I
can do. Also he said, "Remembre all the company of
this the kynges retenu here, wat ille mynde they bere
unto us that wilbe all redy then to folow hyre mynd as
they doo now, and to doo us the most myschyffe they
cando," and named Rychard Wodhouse and John
Clynton speris. Item, Raynold of the Chambre, a con-
stable of the retenu, with other. "Thees men," he
said, "never lovyd the kyngis grace, nor never woldo,
with many mo of the same mynd within this toune.
Now I have shewed all the wyrst. This be a sherwde
company sett in yll mynde. Dout ye not but this will
falle in dede but good provysion be made for the remedy
in tyme."

Item, then said my master your depute, " Yf suche
thyng shall happen, as I pray God that I never leve to
se, the kyngis grace to departe byfore me, but and yt
please God that he shall so do, to be for the surte and
use of my lorde prynce and for all my mastris childre
to have this toune alle tymes at ther owne wille and rule ;
and rather then yt shouldbe otherwyse I had lever
souffer dethe. And we do wysly, I dont not but by
good counsell we shalbe able by good polici to distrii
alle the captayns and ryngledres that be of yll and contrarij mynde ; that done the other wilbe good to rule.
So I tryst that we shall alwayes kepe the toune and
marches to the kyngis use and hys." More of this
touchyng this last artycle was spoken, wiche is not now
perfetly in my remembrans ; but well I remembre that
everyman named oone to ryde the world of, yf suche

daunger should come to pase, as I tryst never to se by Godis grace, whoo ever preserve youre hygnes.

Item by the fayth that I bere unto my Savyour Cryst Jhesu and to youre hygnes, this before rehersed was the sayyng of every of them as nyghe as I kan call now to my remembrans.

Thees folwyng be the wordys that Sir Hughe Conway dyd speke in the hyryng of Sir Rychard Nanfan, knyght, your depute of Calis, Sir Sampson Norton, your porter there, Welyam Nanfan and John Flamank.

First, he said that the kynge is but a weke man and syklow, and not lykly longe to contynue ; therfore good yt is that we see for our owne surties aswell asfor the surtie of this hys toune of Calis.

Item, he said that my lorde chamberlayn was a strongeʰandʰmighti man of men in the kyngis courte aswell as within this the kyngis toune of Calis and els were, and said, " Put yt that he be true as ony man lyvyng to the kyngis grace now, yet chaynge of worldes haith caused change of men myndes, and that haith be sene many tymes.

Item, he said that the firthermust that he could ever se or rede of the kyngis grace was that he should raygne but as longe as kynge Edward dyde, whiche he said was but xxij^ti yere or lytle more.

Item, he said that when my master youre depute, and master porter wolde have hym, he wolde brynge hys boke of profici to Welyam Nanfan, and he should rede y^t, wiche should playnly declare the same.

Item ; he seid that the kyngis grace lay seke aboute a iiij yers past in hys maner of Wangsted ; " At wiche tyme," he said, " fortuned me to be in the company of many dyvers and grett personnages, the wiche as at that tyme hapned to commune of the kynge oure master, and wat world shouldbe yf his grace deperted, and hoo should have the rule in Inglond then.   Some, he said spoke of my lorde of Buckyngham, that said that he woldbe a ryall ruler, and so gave hym grett prees; and other of them in lykwyse spake of the traytour Edmond De la Pole, but non of them, he said, spake of my lorde prynce."

Item, he said that he hade shewed all this mater to Sir Nycholas Vaux, lieutenant of Gysnes, and to Sir Antony Browne, lieutenant of the castell in Calis, and said that ther answere to hym was saying that they had too good sure holdes to resort unto, the wiche should make ther peaxce hoo ever the worlde tourne.

Item, he said that the lady Luce was a proude hij mynded woman, and lovyth not the kyngis grace, and that Edmond De la Pole was hyr kynnysman, to whom, he said, she wildo all the plesure and helpe she cando in the world, and that yf anythyng should come to youre grace other then wele he douted not but she wolde lett hym by the postren of the castell to the distruccion of us all.

The cause and ground whij and to what intent he spake all thes wordes by me herè wryten, my master your depute, and Sir Sampson Norton, whoo herd all the same, and soo dyde Weliam Nanfan in lykwyse, that cane shew and declare alle unto youre hygnes moche better then I cando.   Butt by the faythe that I owe and bere unto my Savyoure Cryst Jhesu, and to youre most noble grace, I herde hym speke all thees wordes in ther presens, with more then my poure mynd cane serve me to declare untò your hygnes.

Item, I have herd master porter and Welyam Nanfan saij dyvers tymes, that they have herd Sir Hugh Conway say that ther shuldbe never more popys in Rome after hym that is now, nother kynges in Inglond after youre grace.

Item, upon a tyme I brought a letter to Sir Hughe Conway, that Sir Nycholas Vaux had sent to my master. After that he had rede the same letter to theend, he toke me by the arme and said to me, " Brodre Flamank, thij master and master porter be not aswyse as I wold that they were; for now may ye see that other men cane have knowlyche dayly of every thyng or grett mater that is done in Inglond and we cane have no knowlych of nothyng but by them. This is not good, nother no sure waye for us. I have often tymes spoken to them to have a sure and a wyse man to lij a boute the court styll at oure coste and charges; he may all tymes send us how the world goyth. I pray you tell them that I wille bere halfe yf this to be done, for God knoweth how sodenly a change may fall;" with many more wordes touchyng grett peryll that my fall yf this be not don.

1505.

172.

[Silvester de Giglis, Bishop of Worcester, to Henry VII, "Letters and Papers," i. 243-5.]

Sacra Regia Majestas, post humillimam commendationem etc. Jam arbitror intellexisse potuit majestas vestra per breve apostolicum, et per instructiones ad Johannem Paulum fratrem meum una cum ultimis litteris missis, placuisse summo pontifici ut ad majestatem vestram venirem, et bullas originales dispensationis matrimonialis afferrem, legitimasque causas dilationis earundem, et animi dolorem ac molestiam quam Sanctitas sua contraxit ex transmissione ab Hispaniis in Angliam copiæ dictarum bullarum, quam ad ultimam consolationem serenissimæ ac Catholicissimæ dominæ Helisabeth Hispaniarum reginæ morientis oratori istic suo concessisset sub fide et sacramento silentii ac taciturnitatis, coram majestati vestræ exponerem, cum nonnullis aliis privatis negotiis, quæ mihi in mandatis datura erant; et insuper sacrum ensem, quo potissimum majestatem vestram ex omnibus principibus Christianis hoc anno insignire voluit eidem præsentarem. Sane si quid unquam votis optare, vel non immerito forsitan expectare potni ex hoc pontificatu Sanctissimi Domini nostri, cui me Altissimus affinitatis vinculo astringere dignatus est, satisfactum est amplissime desiderio et expectationi meæ, assequutus sum cumulate, et supra votum quod continue expectavi ex eo tempore ex quo aliquid esse incepi sola gratia et benignitate majestatis vestræ. Tandem concessum est creaturæ vestræ ad auctorem factoremque suum redire, et eum coram intueri revisere et venerari, cui non solum fortunas et facultates debeo, sed quod vivo, quod spiro, quod omnino aliquid sum eidem acceptum refero. Quam profectionem meam ad majestatem vestram, quoniam præcæteris omnibus mihi gratissimam habeo, brevi accelerabo, et intra paucos dies ex Urbe me expediam. Non dubito quin adventum meum clementia vestra pro sua erga me benignitate et humanitate lætanter suscipere dignetur, et humilem creaturam suam eo vultu aspicere quo me ab humo tollere dignata est, et tot immortalibus beneficiis, honoribus ac dignitatibus honestare. Quibus cum nullæ gratiæ meæ pares esse possint, silebo potins quam infinita ejus erga me merita inepte recensendo minora faciam; sed me ipsum personamque meam eidem coram reverenter tradam; suum est quicquid ago, quicquid cogito, quicquid cupio. Rogo non verba, quæ debitum meum exprimere non possunt, sed corpus, spiritum et animum qui totus ex illa pendet, benigne accipiat, et ita de me sentiat, meipsum mihi ipsi tum demum placere

posse, si cum ad illam venero inveniam aliquid a me
factum quod majestati vestræ placere intelligam. Quam
opto ut Altissimus diutissime conservet felicem, et cui
interim me quam humillime commendo.

Novitatum nihil in præsenti est quod auribus majestatis vestræ dignum putem, præterquam quod superioribus diebus Sanctissimus Dominus noster in ægrotatiun-
culam levem incidit, quam acceptis quibusdam pilulis,
statim rejecit, atque in pristinam salutem continuo
Sanctitas sua restituta est. In rebus autem quæ
Sanctæ Romanæ Ecclesiæ statum concernunt Sanctitas
sua die noctuque vigilantia quadam mira repetitura creditur quicquid occupatum superioribus annis fuerat, et
nunc cum Venetis egit ut magna terrarum pars quas sibi
ab ecclesia verterant, eidem Sanctæ Romanæ Ecclesiæ
restituatur. Reliquum est ut me iterum clementissimæ
majestati vestræ quam humillime commendem.

Post scripta venit in mentem meam dignum esse
ut majestatem vestram certiorem facerem de legatis
sive oratoribus regis Poloniæ, qui superioribus diebus
de consuetudine in Urbem suscepti, primam eorum
audientem a Beatissimo Patre nostro in publico
auditorio die x Martii superioris habuerunt, atque ipsi
Sanctissimo Domino nostro obtulerunt varia munera,
et quæ summam duorum millium ducatorum caperent.

173.

[Henry VII's instructions to Anthony Savage, sent on a mission to
Ayala, who was then in Flanders, "Spanish Calendar," i. 429.
They throw some light on Henry's dealings with the Archduke
Philip. Bergenroth assigns them to the "spring or summer" of
1505 ; it seems probable that they are earlier than Henry's loan
in April to Philip ; see pp. 257-8, note.]

There are the articles which Anthony Savage shall
communicate to the Reverend Father, Pedro de Ayala,

Apostolic Prothonary, and about which he shall hear his opinion.

The said Anthony shall first deliver the letters of the King to the said Prothonotary, and then tell him what follows. A long time has already elapsed during which his Royal Majesty has heard nothing from the Prothonotary respecting . . . of that country. As the Prothonotary had written to the King's Majesty a letter, forwarded by Garter King-at-Arms, and asked him to send the said Anthony to him, in case he had anything to communicate which could not be safely entrusted to writing, his Royal Highness, wishing to inform him of something, and to hear his opinion, sends him the said Anthony.

After this preamble, the said Anthony shall tell the said Prothonotary that the most Serene King of the Romans had sent Herman Rimbre, with credentials and instructions, to his Majesty, by virtue of which the said Herman had showed and explained to his Majesty the following matters:—

1. The King of the Romans wishes to refer the differences about the fairs of Calais to the decision and arbitrament of the King of England.

2. He offers the King of England his daughter in marriage.[1]

3. The same Herman informed the King's Majesty of the quarrel of the King of the Romans with the King of Hungary, and begged his Majesty to send an embassy about this affair to the King of Hungary and his subjects.

4. The said Herman further told the King of England that the King of the Romans intends to go to Rome, in order to be crowned there. From Rome the King of the Romans intends to go to Hungary, to take posses-

---

[1] Margaret of Savoy.

sion of his rights.   He begs for this purpose, one thousand archers from the King of England, who are to be paid for by the King of the Romans.

5. The said Herman said to the King of England that the King of the Romans had had very great expenses in Germany and in Gueldres, and would be obliged to spend much more money on his expedition to Rome and Hungary.   The King of the Romans asked, therefore, the King of England to lend him money, without, however, stating the amount.

Anthony Savage shall communicate, confer, and treat with the Prothonotary, separately, on each article contained in the credentials of Herman Rimbre, ask his advice, and send his answer in writing to the King of England.

He shall also inquire whether the Prothonotary knows anything about these articles.

He shall further beg the Prothonotary to make very diligent search, and to communicate the truth, in this matter, through the said Anthony to the King's Majesty, especially with respect to the marriage, that is to say, whether the King of the Romans means it earnestly and sincerely, or is playing the hypocrite, and whether he has other intentions.   If the latter be the case, what may his intentions be?

He shall also inquire to how much the dowries amount, which the daughter of the King of the Romans has in Spain and in Savoy?

Do the dowries consist in real estates and other property, or in pensions; and what is the amount of the property, and how large are the pensions?

What security has the Princess for her dowries, and how would she be provided for in case her property should be taken from her, or the payment of her pensions suspended?

Is she reputed to be rich, and in what do her riches consist?

Would her father and brother, or either of them, give her, in addition to what she now possesses, a dowry for her marriage with the King's Majesty, and what and how much would that be?

He shall inquire whether any other Prince is asking her in marriage, and who the Prince is, and whether she has a liking for him, and wishes to be married to another Prince, and who that Prince is?

He shall inquire what sentiments, intentions, dispositions of mind, and affections the King of the Romans entertains towards the King of England, and whether the King of England can confide in him as in a good, true and constant brother?

He shall also ask the Prothonotary what is the mind, and what are the intentions of the King of Castile [1] towards the King of England.

He shall question the Prothonotary whether the King of Castile intends to go to Spain this summer or next winter, and whether by land or by sea, with an army or without an army?

He shall endeavour to find out whether the King of the Romans, after the conclusion of the war in Gueldres, will make over a portion of his army to the King of Castile? How great that portion would be, and who would be the captains? Would it be foot or horse, and what purpose would it serve?

He shall ask what intentions the Queen of Castile has; whether she is of the same mind with the King of Castile, and whether she will accompany him to Spain?

Are the Kings of Aragon and of Castile friends or foes; and if they are foes, what is the reason of their enmity?

[1] Philip,

What is likely to become of Edmund de la Pole?

Does the King of the Romans favour him by deed or by words?

Does the King of the Romans favour the said Edmund?

Has the King of Castile concluded a convention with the Duke of Gueldres respecting the said Edmund, and what are the articles of that convention?　　✔

He shall inquire what the Duke of Gueldres intends to do with the said Edmund; whether he has a liking for him, or only esteems him a little? How is the said Edmund now watched; is he kept like a prisoner in strict confinement, or does he enjoy freedom, although not complete freedom?

The said Anthony shall very often repeat to himself all these articles, and afterwards frequently confer about them with the Prothonotary. As often as he learns anything worth writing or communicating, he shall send speedy messengers to the King of England, or return in person to England in order to speak to the King.

The said Anthony shall tell the Prothonotary that the King of England, intending to give a suitable answer to the King of the Romans on all subjects contained in the instructions of Herman Rimbre, will very soon send some privy counsellors to the King of the Romans. These privy councillors, or ambassadors, shall first confer with the Prothonotary about the answer to be given in the name of the King of England to the King of the Romans.

He shall inquire for what reasons the King of Aragon sends ambassadors to the King of France, and whether there is hope that these two Kings will conclude a peace?

The King of England communicates all these secret matters to the Prothonotary as though he were one of his most intimate councillors, and expects that the March, Prothonotary will communicate these secrets of the ^{1505.} King of England to no person living. His Majesty has the greatest confidence in the Prothonotary and is persuaded that he will make all these inquiries by safe and secret ways and means

174.

[Vincenzo Quirini to the Signory, "Venetian Calendar," i. No. 850.]

Had been informed by the Spanish ambassador that Antwerp, the Princess of England sent a messenger lately to the ^{26 July.} King of Castile,[1] urging his Majesty, after obtaining Guelderland, to come to Calais, to which place she would proceed, and would also bring the King of England, to effect an agreement and compromise, and adjust all disputes between them and their subjects. The commendator (De Haro) considers this the device of Don John Manuel, who with such a plausible pretext seeks to bring about an interview between these two kings, in order through his craft and cunning to compass an agreement, or something not beneficial to all parties.

Don John induced the Princess to take this step by means of her governess, his cousin, giving her to understand that it will prove highly advantageous.

The commendator De Haro trusts, however, that nothing will come of this, as he has acquainted the Princess with all the villainy of these people, and feel sure that she will immediately intercept and thwart this negotiation, by reason of her being the obedient daughter of the King of Spain.[2]

[1] I.e. Philip, Archduke of Austria, who claimed the government of Castile in the right of his wife Juaña, eldest daughter of Ferdinand of Aragon and Isabella of Castile.

[2] Three months before this, on 25 April, 1505, Henry had already lent £108,000 to Philip "for his next voyage into Spayne, upon

1505.   175.

[Quirini to the Signory, "Venetian Calendar," i. No. 851.]

Antwerp,   Announces the receipt of letters from the camp, pur-
1 August.
porting that peace had been concluded between the
King of Castile and the Duke of Guelders, who, on the
29th ultimo, was to be at Arnheim to swear to it.
The Duke (*sic*) of Suffolk, called " White Rose," concerning whom he wrote to the State that he was besieged in a castle in Guelderland, is now in the power of
the King of Castile,—intelligence which greatly delights
this country, and his Majesty hopes by means of this
individual to keep the bit in the mouth of the King of
England.

176.

[Cardinal Hadrian de Corneto to Henry VII, "Letters and Papers,"
i. 247.]

Rome,   Nova nulla hic sunt, nisi de matrimonio Hispaniæ,[1]
23 October.
et multi multa loquuntur de vestra majestate, sed quid
sit verum adhuc nos latet.   Veneti continuant occupare
illas duas Ecclesiæ civitates, tamen sunt valde territi de
pace ista quæ dicitur inter hos duos reges,[2] et etiam
acceperunt magnam jacturam in aromatibus quæ pas-
sim veniant de illis insulis per Portugallenses repertis.
Florentini quiescunt sine civitate Pisarum.   P[a]pa,
intellecta compositione hujus pacis quæ dicitur facta
inter istos duos reges, dixit mihi et multis aliis cardinalibus dum essemus'in civitate Corneti, in qua ego natus
sum, " Isti duo reges diviserunt sibi vestimenta mea, sed

sertain writings made betwen the Kinges grace and hym " (Bentley,
p. 132) ; and another sum of £30,000 was lent on 27 September
(*ibid.* p. 133).
   [1] Ferdinand's second marriage with Germaine de Foix.
   [2] Ferdinand and Louis XII.

illis significari fecimus aliqua super his. Videbimus October,
quæ sequentur ". Postea dixit mihi soli post cœnam quod 1505.
offerebant Ecclesiæ suum annuum censum, et quod
habebat literas a Gallia quod vestra majestas dabat
illustrissimo principi suo nato illam puellam Danguleme
in uxorem. Dixi non posse me hoc credere cum jam
essent contracta sponsalia per verba de præsenti cum
filia Hispaniæ, media dispensatione suæ Sanctitatis, et
quod hoc . . . regi Hispaniæ. Respondit quod scribitur
sibi quod in hoc consentit ipse rex Hispaniæ. Nunc
vestra majestas habet quæ nova audivi a sua metuendis-
sima Sanctitate.

177.

[Catherine of Aragon to her father Ferdinand, Wood's "Letters
of Royal and Illustrious Ladies," i. 131.]

Hitherto I have not wished to let your highness know 2 Decem.
the affairs here, that I might not give you annoyance, ber.
and also thinking that they would improve; but it
appears that the contrary is the case, and that each day
my troubles increase; and all this on account of the
doctor de Puebla, to whom it has not sufficed that from
the beginning he transacted a thousand falsities against
the service of your highness, but now he has given me
new trouble; and because I believe your highness will
think that I complain without reason, I desire to tell
you all that has passed.

⌐Your highness shall know, as I have often written to
you, that since I came into England I have not had a
single maravedi,[1] except a certain sum which was given
me for food, and this such a sum that it did not suffice
without my having many debts in London⌐and that
which troubles me more is to see my servants and

---

[1] See below, Vol. iii.

17 *

maidens so at a loss, and that they have not wherewith
to get clothes ; and this I believe is all done by hand of
the doctor, who, notwithstanding your highness has
written, sending him word that he should have money
from the King of England, my lord, that their costs
should be given them, yet, in order not to trouble him,
will rather intrench upon and neglect the service of
your highness. Now, my lord, a few days ago donna
Elvira de Manuel [1] asked my leave to go to Flanders to
get cured of a complaint which has come into her eyes,
so that she lost the sight of one of them ; and there is
a physician in Flanders, who cured the infanta donna
Isabel of the same disease with which she is affected.
She laboured to bring him here so as not to leave me,
but could never succeed with him ; and I, since if she
were blind she could not serve me, durst not hinder her
journey. I begged the king of England, my lord, that
until our donna Elvira should return his highness would
command that I should have, as a companion, an old
English lady, or that he would take me to his court ;
and I imparted all this to the doctor, thinking to make
of the rogue a true man ; but it did not suffice me—
because he not only drew me to court, in which I have
some pleasure, because I had supplicated the King for
an asylum, but he negociated that the king should dismiss all my household, and take away my chamber
(equipage), and send to place it in a house of his own,
so that I should not be in any way mistress of it.

And all this does not weigh upon me, except that it
concerns the service of your highness, doing the contrary
of that which ought to be done. I entreat your highness that you will consider that I am your daughter,
and that you consent not that on account of the doctor
I should have such trouble, but that you will command

[1] See No. 174.

some ambassador to come here, who may be a true servant of your highness, and for no interest will cease to do that which pertains to your service. And if in this your highness trusts me not, do you command some person to come here, who may inform you of the truth, and then you will have one who will better serve you. As for me, I may say to your highness that, in seeing this man do so many things not like a good servant of your highness, I have had so much pain and annoyance that I have lost my health in a great measure; so that for two months I have had severe tertian fevers and this will be the cause that I shall soon die. I supplicate your highness to pardon me that I presume to entreat you to do me so great favour as to command that this doctor may not remain; because he certainly does not fulfil the service of your highness, which he postpones to the service of the worst interest which can be. Our Lord guard the life and most royal estate of your highness, and ever increase it as I desire. From Richmond, the second of December.

My lord, I had forgotten to remind your highness how you know that it was agreed that you were to give, as a certain part of my dowry, the plate and jewels that I brought; and yet I am certain that the king of England, my lord, will not receive anything of plate nor of jewels which I have used; because he told me himself that he was indignant that they should say in his kingdom that he took away from me my ornaments. And as little may your highness expect that he will take them in account and will return them to me; because I am certain that he will not do so, nor is any such thing customary here. In like wise the jewels which I brought came from thence (Spain) valued at a great sum. The king would not take them in the half of the value, because here all these things are esteemed much cheaper, and the king has so many jewels that he rather desires money than them. I write thus to your highness because I know that there will be great embarrassment if he will not receive them, except at less price. It appears to me that it would be better that your highness should take them for yourself, and should give to the king of England, my lord, his money. Your highness will see what would serve you best, and with this I shall be most content.

1506.

178.

[Arrival of the Archduke Philip, "Greyfriars' Chronicle," p. 28. A detailed contemporary narrative of Philip's stay in England until 12 February is printed in Gairdner's "Memorials," pp. 282-303.]

Thys yere the xv day of January at twelve of cloke at none rose soche a tempest of wynde tyll it was twelve at mydnyth, that it blew downe tres and tyles of howsys, and that same nyght it blewe downe the weddercoke of Powlles Stepulle the lengthe of the ende of Powlles church into the syne of the black egylle; at that tyme was lowe howses of bokebynderes wher nowe is the scole of Powles. And that same nyght was the duke of Burgone that was callyd Phyllype with hys lady and many shepes of hys, the wyche intendyd to a gone into Spayne to a bene crownyd kynge, but by tempest were drevyne to Porchemoth havyne, and soo the kynge send many of the nobyll lordes and states of the realme both sperituall and temporall to reseve hym and all hys pepull, and soo browte them to London; and there the kynge nobylly reseved them and made them grete chere and soo departyd them home agayne. And that same yere at that tyme was soch a sore snowe and a frost

that men myght goo with carttes over the Temse and January-
horse, and it lastyd tyll after candlemas. And then it $^{April,}_{1506.}$
was agreed betwene the kynge and the duke of Burgone
that Edmond de la Pole shulde be send home agayne,
and so he was.

179.

[William Makefyrr to Roger Darcy and Giles Alyngton, "Paston
Letters," iii. 953.]

Ryght worschypfull masters, I recomend me un to Windsor,
you, certyfying you that the Kynges Grace and the $^{17, Janu-}_{ary.}$
Kyng of Castyle mett this day at thre of the cloke, apon
Cleworth Greyn, ij mylle owt of Wyndesower, and ther
the Kyng reseyvyd hym in the goodlyest maner that
ever I sawe, and ech of them enbracyd oder in armys.

To schew you the Kynges aparell of Yngland, thus
it was :—hys hors of bay, trappyd with nedyll warke ;
a gown of purpuyr velvyt, a cheyn with a jeorge of
dyamondes, and a hood of purpuyr velvyt, whych he
put not of at the mettyng of the seyd Kyng of Castylle ;
hys hatt and hys bonett he avalyd, and the Kyng of
Castylle in cas lyke. And the Kyng of Castyll rod apon
[a] sorellyd hoby, which the Kyng gave un to hym ; hys
apparell was all blak, a gown of blak velvytt, a blak
hood, a blak hatt, and hys hors harnes of blake velvytt.

To schew you of the Kynges company, my Lord
Harry of Stafforth rod in a gown of cloth of tuyssew,
tukkyd, furryd with sabulles, a hatt of goldsmyth worke,
and full of stons, dyamondes, and rubys, rydyng apon a
sorellyd courser bardyd with a bayrd of goldsmythes
wark, with rosys and draguns red.

And my Lord Markas [of Dorset] rydyng apon a bald
sorelyd hors, with a deyp trapper full of long tassels of
gold of Venys, and apon the crowper of hys hors a whytt

fedyr, with a cott apon hys back, the body goldsmyths
wark, the slevys of cremysyne velvyt, with letters of gold.
My Lord of Kent, apon a sorelyd hors, bald, the
harnes of Venys gold, with a deyp frynges of half zerd
of lengh.   My Lord of Kent cott was on barr of cloth
of gold, an oder of cremysyn velvyt, pyrlyd with a demy
manche cut of by the elbowe.   Thyes be the lords that
bare the bruyt.

Sir Hew Waghan apon a bay hors trappyd with
cremysyn velvyt full of gylt bels, a gown of blak velvyt,
and a cheyn of gold, bawdryk wys, worth v. hondreth
pownd.

Theys be the sperys : Master Sant John apon a blak
hors, with harnes of cloth of gold with tasselles of
plunkytt and whytt, a cott of plunkytt and whytt, the
body of goldsmyths werk, the s[l]evys full of spanguls.

John Carr and William Parr cotts lyke, the horsys
gray, of Parr trappyd with cremysyn velvyt with tasselles of gold, and bels gylt.   Carr hors bay with an
Almayn harnes of sylver, an ynch brod of betyn sylver,
both the cottes of goldsmythes wark the bodys, the
slevys on stryp of syllver, the oder gylt.

Edward Nevell apon a gray hors trappyd with blak
velveyt full of small belles, hys cott the on half of greyn
velvyt, the oder of whytt cloth of gold ; thyse to the
rutters of the spers, with oder dyvers well appontyd.

On the Kyng of Castylles party, the Lord Chamberlayn cheyff, I can not tell hys name as yett ; hys apparell was sad, and so was all the resydeu of hys company
with clokes of sad tawnye blake, gardyd, sum with
velvyt and sum with sarsnyt, not passyng a dosyn in
nowmber.   It is sayd ther is many by hynd, wych
cums with the Queyn of Castyll, wych schall cum apon
Teyusday.

When the Kyng rod forth to Wyndesouer Castyle,

the Kyng rode apon the ryght hand the Kynges of January, Castylle, how be it the Kynges Grace offeryd hym to take·hym apon the ryght hand, the whych he refussyd. And at the lyghtyng the Kyng of Castylle was of hys hors a good space or our Kyng was a lyght ; and then the Kynges Grace offeryd to take hym by the arm, the whych he wold not, bot toke the Kyng by the arme, and so went to the Kynges of Castylle chamber, whych is the rychestly hangyd that ever I sawe ; vij chambers togeder hangyd with cloth of arras wroght with gold as thyk as cowd be ; and as for iij beds of astate, no kyng Crystyned can schew sych iij.

Thys is as fer as I can schew you of this day, and when I can know mor, ye schall have knowlege.

180.

[Vincenzo Quirini to the Signory, "Venetian Calendar," i. No. 869.]

King Philip and Queen Juana embarked at Armuy- Falmouth den on the 7th instant with their whole retinue, but, in ₂₃ January order to await the full moon, the fleet did not go out of port until the morning of the 10th. The wind was then fair, and continued so the whole of that day and the next until off Hampton, when towards midnight, after a dead calm, every ship having all sail set, so violent a storm sprang up from the N.N.E., as greatly to alarm the oldest and most experienced hands, for the night was dark and the channel unsafe, and great was the labour and peril of lowering the sails. That night one third of the fleet parted company ; and the wind lasted the whole of the 12th, taking them to the edge of the Bay of Biscay, so far as the pilots could ascertain from their soundings. A calm then ensued, and continued until the evening of the 13th, when the wind rose from the W.S.W., full upon the coast of England. Orders

were then given to tack throughout the night, in the
hopes of a change for the better, but the sea and wind
rose so highly, that about midnight, when possibly not
more than 50 miles from the shore, and when such was
the darkness that not an object could be distinguished
one span a head, a terrible hurricane commenced, of
which the oldest mariners in the fleet say they have
not experienced the like within the last half century.
All now sought for safety as they best might : some
ships stood out to sea, others made for land ; amongst
the latter was his (Quirini's) ship. At daybreak eighteen
sail found themselves in a denze haze so close upon the
land that all gave themselves up for lost. Attributed
their safe arrival in Falmouth to the miraculous mercy
of the Almighty, to whom they had addressed vows and
prayers, despairing of any other succour.

King Philip and Queen Juana took the other tack
and remained out at sea in the gale the whole of the
14th and 15th, when, with only two ships, they were
driven into Portland, a road and not a port, ten leagues
from Hampton.

Of the rest of the fleet, four ships got into Plymouth
and three into Dartmouth, off which harbour three
others foundered, though the greater part of the crews
were saved. Nothing has been heard as yet of any of
the other vessels. On making Portland, King Philip
immediately sent expresses to Plymouth, Dartmouth,
and Falmouth announcing his safety, and desiring the
vessels to await further orders.

Has heard nothing of the King, he (Quirini) being in
Cornwall at the extremity of the island, 250 miles from
Hampton, in a wild spot where no human being ever
comes, save the few boors who inhabit it. Considers
it impossible that King Philip should have left Portland, the weather having never been fair for one single

hour, but always blowing a gale either from the W.S.W., January.
or W.N.W., or else from the S.E.; everybody declaring 1506.
that in the memory of man a worse month of January
had never been seen. Mentions the arrival at Falmouth
of some sailors out of a Brittany ship, which had also
foundered in the storm: on the road they fell in with
a man who had saved himself from some wreck, and
from his garb, and so far as they could comprehend his
language, believed him to be a Venetian galley oarsman.
Was therefore apprehensive for the Flanders galleys,
and had sent all along the coast to enquire, but no one
could be found who knew anything about them; and
has received assurance from many quarters that they
have not been seen in the Channel.

181.

[Edmund de la Pole's commission to treat with Henry VII,
"Letters and Papers," i. 278-85.]

Be hit knowen to alle princes, nobles and true Namur,
Cristen men, by this present writing, that we, Edmund 24 Janu-
duke of Suffolk, of England, on the xxvj day of De- ary.
cember last passed had certain comynycacions and
wordes towching the troubles that ar in the reame of
England, by reason that it standeth by twixt the king
of England and me as hyt doeth.

Wherupon my servant, Thomas Kyllyngworth,[1] my
stewerd, axked me wheder my mynd and entent was
as I spake it. I answerde "Ye on my faith;" and soo
I, the said duc, shewed to hym more largely my said
entent and mynd concernyng the same playnely as
it is.

The said Thomas therupon hath retorned to me the
xxij day of this instant moneth of January, shewinge

[1] See Vol. iii.

and acerteyning me that he hath openned and disclosed my said entent and myud to the kinges servant, John Chamberlayn, and that the same John is goon to the kyng to thentent to yeve the king undrestanding and knowleage of the same. Wherwith I am contented and pleased. Wherupon I have nowe eftsones of newe comyned in this matier, and shewed my full entent and playne mynd to the said Thomas Kyllyngworth, and also to my servant John Gryffyth. And for the trust I have in the trowthes to me of the said Thomas and John, I have openned at large to theym my hert in this behalve. And by vertue and auctoritie herof I have yeven to the said Thomas and John, and by thise presentez yeve to them jointely full power and anctoritie to have comynycacion with such person or persones, honnest, God dreding, as shalbe by the said king of England sufficiently auctorized ordenned and assigned. And whatsomever they shal on my behalve promise by their worde or writing touching the premisses, I, the said Edmund duc of Suffolk, promise and bynde me by this my present writing upon myn honnor and faith to God of a true Cristen prince that I shal and wolle faithfully and truely kepe and observe the same in eche point and article, like as I have further auctorized theym in that behalve. In witnesse wherof I, the sayd duke, have sette my signe manuell and seall to thise presents, and also undre written the same with myn own hand, the xxiiij day of January, the yere of our Lord God a thousand fyve hundreth and sex.

I seste [1] my hand to thest yn tent that ale manner of mene sale chake [check] that I vele parforme thest be fore vrytvn, and also vat that the [they] prommes on my be havalf EDMUND SUFFOLK.

---

[1] This last paragraph is added in Suffolk's own writing.

182.   1506.

[De la Pole's instructions to treat with Henry VII, "Letters and Papers," i. 280-285.]

Instructions yeven by the right excellent prince my Namur, lord Edmund duc of Suffolk, the son and heire of my 28 January. lord John sometyme duc of Suffolk, to his trusty and welbeloved servantes Thomas Kyllyngworth his steward and to John Griffith, howe and undre what maner the said ducis full mynd, entent, and plaisir ar, that the said Thomas and John shal demeane and handell theym selfes on the said ducis behalve with the kinges highnesse for the pacifieng and fynal determinacion of suche gruges, variances, and causes as ar depending at this tyme, and long saison have doon, bytwixt the kinges said highnesse and the said duc their maistre.

EDMUND SUFFOLK.

Furst, and principally the said ducis myud is that the said Thomas and John on his behalve shal humbly beseche the kinges highnes to bee his good and gracious souverain lord, and that it maye please his grace to withdrawe from the said duc his high displaisir, and to putte clerely oute of his hert suche grugge and malice as his grace hath had ayeinst the said duc. And that it also maye like the kynges highnesse to accepte and admitte the said lord Edmund to his estate as my lords his grantfader and fader were accepted and taken in tyme passed : and the said duc is and shalbe redy to receive the kinges pardon and wolbecomme his true sobget and liegeman, and semblably after the king our souverain lordes decesse contynue to my lord prince the kinges son and to his heires, withoute erring or declynyng from the same whyles he lyveth.

EDMUND SUFFOLK.

Secondarily, the said Thomas and John shal on the said ducis behalf humbly beseche and require the kinges grace that it may please his highnesse, as honour and noblesse and right require, to restore to the said duc and to his heires alle the honours, castelles, maners, lordships and heriditamentes apperteynyng to the said duchie of Suffolk, holly and entierly as the same were lefte to the possession of the said nowe dukes fader, with suche offices as my lordes his grantfader and fader have had of the yefte of the kynges or princes aforetyme or by inheritance. And over this, that they shal beseche the kinges grace that it maye please his highnes, as right and conscience requiren, to restore to the said duc alle suche sommes of money as his grace or any persones by his auctoritie and commaundment have received, aswele touching thannuyties of creacions yeven by kinges for thestat of the said duchie, as of the revenues of thin-heritances aforsaid, from the tyme of the deth of the said duc John to this day ; and also to bee restored to such goodes and stuf of howsehold as the same duc had at his departing fro England.

EDMUND SUFFOLK.

Thirdly, as to the town of Leighton Buzard, which king Edward enforced the said ducis fader to relesse to the colleage of Windesor, the said duc besecheth humbly the kinges highnesse to bee good lord to him therein, and that he maye be restored therunto, and that al things therin doon by my lordes fader maye bee disannulled by the lawe and by the parliament, the said duc restoring to the said colleage suche money as can bee duely proved that my lord his fader received for the same of king Edward, or of the said colleage. Semblably for the towne and castell of Orford with thapportenances, whiche the lord Willoughby hath ; the maner of Filberdes which Sir Richard Gyldeford hath; the maner of Hanwel, whiche the Coferer hath; and al othre lands alienned by the said duc, or by his fader to Sir Water Herbert, or any other. And also as to the maners of Bulcamp, Hynham, Sidesterne, and Newton, whiche were relessed to Sir Tirry Robsertson at the labour of Sir William Carewe, that the said duc maye bee also restored to eche of the same, restoring again the money of theim received.

EDMUND SUFFOLK.

Fourthly, if it shulde soo happenne that the king of Castelle, or the gouvernors of his landes in his absence, after the tyme that the kinges grace and the said duc bee accorded, wil not bee aggreable ner suffre that the said duc shal departe oute of their hands, but kepe him by force, the said duc then beseecheth the king to helpe him to his libertie under the maner as his grace shal seme best. And wher no creatur is sure of his lif it mighte peradventure in the mean tyme happe the said duc to dye, as God forbydde; neverthalas whatsoever maye fortune in this behalf the said duc wol bee and contynue the kinges true subject to thend of his lif. Beseching therfor humbly the kinges highnes that incontinent upon the said aggrement hit maye please his grace to suffre my lady the said ducs wif tordre and make officers in his lands as he shuld doo him sylf and to receive the revenues of the same during the tyme he shalbe kept as prisoner by the king of Castelle or any othre.

EDMUND SUFFOLK.

Fyftely, if it soo shal fortune, as Almighty God forbydde, that the said duc decesse withoute issue male of his body lieufully begotten and commyng in the mean tyme and saison of his keping prisoner as afore is saied or afterward. That then ymmediately after the said dukes decesse hit maye please the kinges highnesse to permitte and suffre my lady the said ducis wiff to have, holde, and enjoye, paicibly and frely her jointour in the said lands for the terme of her lyff, according to the lawe of the land and her right. And that also at the humble request, desir, and supplication of the said duc, hit maye like the kinges said highnesse to bee agreable and to accorde, and that at this present comynycacion and tract hit maye bee accorded and finally concluded, that my lady Elizabeth, the doughter of the said duc, shalbe reputed, accepted and takenne as the doughter and heire of the said duc, and that the same lady Elizabeth and the heires of her body lieufully begotten and commyng for evermor maye holde, possede, and enjoye the hole enheritaunces of the said duchie of Suffolk, as above is saied.

EDMUND SUFFOLK.

Sextly, that it maye plese the kinges grace, aswele for the part of his grace and my lord prince as for the part and suretie of the said duc and his heires, upon such pointz and causes as shalbe accorded and concluded herupon by twix the king and the said duc, or by twix the king and the said Thomas and John, in the said ducis name, wheder the said pointz and causes bee herin expressed or not, of whatsoever weight and substance they bee, that the same maye bee engrossed under the writing or seales of the king and my lord prince, and also enacted and conformed by auctoritie of parliament under suche maner a shalbe to the king thoughte moost expedient. And also such writinges and bondes as shalbe divised by the king, and made for the part of the said duc by the said Thomas and John in his name and under his seal. For whiche entent the said

duc hath to theym delivered his seal and certain blanks
signed with his hand, or ells that shalbe made by the
said Thomas and John, for the part of the said duc in
theire owne names, as it shal please the king, the said
duc promiseth and obligeth hym self truely to observe
and performe the same in eche behalf at the kinges
plaisir in his own person, yf God sende hyme his lif and
libertie, or larger as it shalbe devised by the king's
grace.

EDMUND SUFFOLK.

Sevently, that it maye please the kinges highnesse at
the humble request of the said duc that, incontinent
upon this aggrement, his grace wil putte to libertie my
lord William of Suffolk, and al suche gentylmen and
othre persones, whatsoever personaiges they bee, whiche
ar in prison for the said ducis sake or cause, or at the
kinges commandement under suretie ; and that he and
they maye bee restored frely to their goods and lands, or
their sureties to bee dischargeth, as the caas requireth.
And that al suche gentilmen or othre persones, whatsoever they bee, that been dede, and have lost their landes
for the cause of the said duc that theire heires maye bee
restored to their enheritances.   And over this, that it
maye like the kinges said highnesse to have respect
unto Sir George Nevyll, and that the same Sir George
maye have and enjoye such landes as he hath right unto
in his own title, or in my lady his wifes touching her
jointour and dower in therl Ryvers lands

EDMUND SUFFOLK.

Eightely, the said duc faithfully byndeth him by thise
presentez, and promiseth on his faith of a true Cristen
prince, or elles uttrely to bee reputed the contrary, that
never whiles he lyveth he shal breke nor doo contrary
to the said promesses and aggrements, ner defaulte in
VOL. I.   18

hym shalbe founden; yeving by thise presentz full
power and auctoritie to the said Thomas and John to
conclude thorougly with the kinges grace, or with his
deputies, in this behalf having the kinges power, likewise as the said duc shulde doo if he were present hym
sylf, the suretie for the said ducis person except, and
for his submission and the maner of his commyng to
the kinges presence, which the said duc reserveth, to
commone therin hym silf, as he shal see cause to require, with suche nobles and men of honnour of the
kinges counsail as shalbe in this partie deputed, and as
therin he hath somewhat opened his mynd to his said
servantes. And to thentent that thissame maye bee
groundely and playnely knowen to all kinges princes
and nobles, aswele in England, as elleswher that it is
the full mynd, dede, and commandement of me the said
duc, I have caused the said Thomas Kyllyngworth to
write thise articles, to everyone of which I have sette
my hand for record, At the castel of Namure, the
xxviij^{ty} day of January, the yere of our Lord God a
thousand V^c and sex.

EDMUND SUFFOLK.

183.

[Vincenzo Quirini to the Signory of Venice, "Venetian Calendar,"
i. No. 865.]

Falmouth,
30 Janu-
ary.
Whilst waiting for a messenger to convey the accompanying letter to the Consul in London, a gentleman
arrived at Falmouth, sent by King Philip to notify his
well being and his determination to come towards Falmouth by land.

Never had man a narrower escape from drowning
than the King. His ship was at sea all Wednesday
and until Thursday evening, unable to make any port;

the guns and everything else on deck were thrown over-
board. When attempting to lower the mainsail, a gust
of wind laid it on the sea, carrying the ship gunwale
under; nor did she right for half an hour. Had it not
been for the aid given by one single mariner, who thrice
plunged into the waves and, by cutting away the shrouds,
righted the vessel, their plight would have been irre-
mediable; for both the master, the pilots and the crew
were utterly bewildered, and had given themselves up
for lost. In the meanwhile the vessel caught fire
thrice, so that the chance of death in the flames or in
the deep was equal. For a long while the King bore
up manfully, always in his doublet about the ship, en-
couraging everybody; but at length a sea struck him,
and he was hurled below with such violence that everybody thought he was killed. Thenceforth he remained
with the Queen, who evinced intrepidity throughout;
and the King and some of his gentlemen to whom he
is affectionately attached, having embraced each other
mutually, awaited immediate death, without any hope
of escape. The King declared that he did not regret his
own death, since such was the will of God; but deeply
lamented first of all, that he should cause the death of
so many brave men whom he had brought with him, as
he firmly believed that since his own ship, which was
the biggest, and manned by so many pilots and skilful
mariners, perished, there could be no salvation for the
rest of the fleet. Secondly, he grieved to leave his
children orphans at so tender an age; and thirdly, he
deplored the ruin and confusion that might ensue in
his territories.

The King of England, on hearing of the arrival of the
King of Castile, immediately sent his master of the
horse to him, requesting him to go to London, or, if
the distance should be inconvenient, to wait at Win-

18 *

January,
1506.

chester. An interview had been appointed at Winchester for last Monday, the 26th, and it was expected that the marriage with Madame Margaret and the confederation would then be concluded.

184.

[Quirini to the Signory of Venice, "Venetian Calendar," i. No. 867.]

Falmouth,
25 February.

Since his last of the 23rd and 30th ultimo, has been daily expecting the arrival of the King of Castile. A messenger has now arrived, saying the King of Castile is still with the King of England, who has shown such kindness, made such entertainments, and lavished so many honors on his guest, that it would have been impossible to do more. The Kings of England and Castile have concluded and proclaimed a new and very close alliance,[1] which was ratified and sworn to at the altar, after a solemn mass on the consecrated wafer, of which both their Majesties partook. The King of Castile has accepted the "Garter" from the King of England, and given the "Fleece" in exchange to the Prince of Wales. The King of Castile has sent Monsr. de la Chau, his trusty privy councillor, to Flanders, for the purpose, as generally credited, of removing hither the Earl of Suffolk, called "White Rose," in order to deliver him to the King of England. The opinion may be false, though it is not formed without reason. Queen Juana is to leave Romford (14 miles from London) for Falmouth; and on the same day the King of Castile, out of compliment to the King of England, is going to visit Richmond, to remain eight days, and then proceed to Falmouth to join his fleet, which has assembled there.

Was extremely anxious to join the King of Castile, for the better performance of his duty to the State; but

[1] See below, Vol. iii.

in the first place, Falmouth is 250 miles distant, and February, 1506. the road is represented as the worst possible. Again, he is without horses, having sent his own to Spain by land, as already mentioned, and in a very wild place which no human being ever visits, in the midst of a most barbarous race, so different in language and custom from the Londoners and the rest of England that they are as unintelligible to these last as to the Venetians. From these people, pay what he might, he could obtain no horses but pack horses, nor any other accommodation.

185.

[Sanuto's abstract of missing despatches from England, "Venetian Calendar," i. No. 868.]

Receipt of letters from England how the Archduke Venice, 13 March. or King of Castile had arranged matters with the King, and promised to give him his adversary "White Rose" for whom he had sent; also that the Archduke's sister, the widow of the Duke of Savoy, was to marry the King of England.

186.

[Quirini to the Signory of Venice, "Venetian Calendar," i. No. 869.]

Until the 16th instant the lords and gentlemen at Falmouth, 17 March. Falmouth, who constituted almost the entire retinue of the King of Castile, had not received any letters or certain news from his Majesty; for two days after taking leave of the King of England, the King of Castile fell sick and was obliged to stop at Reading, where he remained some days indisposed, but did not write word of this to the Queen, who had been for some time at Exeter, or to Falmouth, lest the Queen should take alarm and his troops make some stir.

Has had the greatest difficulty in forwarding his letters from Cornwall.

Yestereven the King of Castile's master of the horse arrived at Falmouth with money for the pay both of the German infantry and of the ships which had arrived in that port. By order of the King the master of the horse visited him, and assured him that his Majesty was quite recovered, and would be in Falmouth in a week, with the intention of setting sail with the first fair wind.

Has been told by a cordial friend, a person of great prudence, who accompanied the master of the horse, that Monsieur de la Chau, who had according to report been sent to Flanders, went to Spain with such speed that he reached the court in 14 days, letters having been already received announcing his arrival there. Some persons fancied that the object of this journey was to ascertain whether, on the receipt of the news of the storm, and of the king of Castile's landing in England, any change had taken place; others were of opinion that Monsieur de la Chau was charged to negociate a triple league between the Kings of Spain, England, and Castile.

Was also told by the same friend, that three gentlemen had been sent to Flanders to bring to England the Duke of Suffolk, called " White Rose ; " but the council of Mechlin refused to give him up, and wrote that they would be very willing to surrender him on hearing that their King had quitted England, as they did not choose the King of England, after obtaining " White Rose," to have power to demand some other greater concession. The King of Castile, on the other hand, having pledged himself to the surrender before he embarks, keeps his word, and has written back to Mechlin, and sent another of his gentlemen, a dear favourite, to bring the aforesaid Duke of Suffolk at any rate, as he is determined not to quit this country until "White Rose" be in the hands of the King of England. It is suspected that this circumstance may delay the departure for some days. March, 1506.

187.

[Adrian de Croy to Maximilian, King of the Romans, "Spanish Calendar," i. 456.]

King Philip of Castile had been urged so strongly by the King of England that he had decided to deliver up Suffolk into his hands. He had not done so, however, until the King of England had given him a solemn promise in writing, sealed with his seal, that Suffolk should receive a full pardon for all his past offences, and not be exposed to persecution during the whole remainder of his life. Mechlin, 23 March.

The Kings of England and Castile separated on terms of the greatest friendship.

188.

[Surrender of De la Pole to Henry VII, "Chronicle of Calais," pp. 5-6.]

Edmond a Poole late erle of Suffolke was browght owt of the Duke of Burgoyn's lande to Calleys the xvi of Marche, and was convayd over to Dovar on the xxiiii of Marche by Sir Henry Wiette knight and Ser John Wilshere knight and comptrowler of the towne and marches of Calleys, and lx sowldiars of Calleys all in harneys; where he was receyved by Ser Thomas Lovell and othar, and conveyed to the towre of London. 16-24 March.

189.

[Quirini to the Signory of Venice, "Venetian Calendar," i. No. 870.]

Announces the arrival at Falmouth yesterday of the King and Queen of Castile, who have been long expected. Falmouth, 27 March.

They were in good health, and very glad to find themselves with so many of their servants, whom they at
one time feared never to see again. Although not very
strong, rode forth a distance of five or six miles from
Falmouth to meet the King, and received such greeting
as to prove that companionship in distress greatly increases affection. On seeing his pallid face, the first
words the King said were " Ambassador, it is very
evident you love me, for not merely by sea, but
likewise in sickness have you followed me "; and
added many other expressions, evincing to everybody
his great satisfaction at being attended by a Venetian
ambassador, in order that the Lord Treasurer and the
master of the horse of the King of England, with a
number of other lords who had accompanied him to
Falmouth, should have ocular demonstration of the
fact.

The King of Castile and all his attendants bestow the
highest praise on the King of England, who could not
have done more even had he been the King of Castile's
father; and whilst the Kings were together, and also
afterwards all through the country, the King of Castile
received as much honour as if he had been the Prince
of England. The whole way along the road, thus far,
the King of Castile and all his retinue had their expenses
defrayed, but are henceforth to be at their own cost, as
has been the case with himself (Quirini) and all the
others during their stay at Falmouth.

Touching the negociations between the two Kings,
has not as yet been able to learn more than the confirmation of what he wrote heretofore, namely, the
alliance and close friendship ratified between them, and
the surrender of the Duke of Suffolk as promised by the
King of Castile, with a promise and public oath, however, from the King of England to forgive him every

injury, to restore to him his confiscated property, and to March, 1506.
treat him as his loyal kinsman.

Understands, moreover, that whilst the two Kings were together at Richmond, two French ambassadors accredited to the King of England arrived there, and went to visit the King of Castile, condoling with him in the name of King Lewis on the storm, and congratulating him on his escape and on having reached a spot where a warm welcome awaited him ; adding, that the like would have befallen him had he put into Britanny or any other port of France; and that they were commissioned by their sovereign to thank the King of England for the good reception given by him to his Majesty. The King of Castile answered them in a similar strain, but believes that they were sent for the sole purpose of ascertaining the conclusion of the negotiations to be effected in Spain.

The Spanish ambassador resident with the Emperor (Don Pedro de Ayala), who from ill health had remained at Bruges, has also arrived. He tells him (Quirini) that the King of Spain, having heard of the misfortunes of his son-in-law and daughter, commanded him to come to them, for the purpose, he (Quirini) supposes, of assisting at the treaty, though he came too late, for when he arrived the King of Castile had already taken leave of the King of England.

.   .   .   .

Has been assured by the King of Castile that he would sail with the first wind, and expects him to do so, both from his wish to be in Spain, and also because there is a great scarcity at Falmouth, where he incurs intolerable expense.

1506.   190.

[Quirini to the Signory of Venice, "Venetian Calendar," i.
No. 872.]

Falmouth,   Since the arrival at Falmouth of the King of Castile,
30 March.
has exerted himself vastly to learn some of the particulars concerning his conference with the King of England,
and is assured by several persons that the result is a
confirmation between the Kings of the peace and confederation, with the identical terms and clauses which
the Emperor swore three years ago in his own name
and that of his son when at Antwerp, purporting that
each of the parties was bound not to harbour the enemies
of the other; and further pledged themselves, in the
event of getting possession of such enemies, immediately
to surrender them, especial mention being made of the
Duke of Suffolk, called "White Rose," who by this
time is supposed to have been surrendered to the King
of England, but on condition that he is to be pardoned
and restored to his possessions. The marriage of
Madame Margaret is said not to be concluded, but
simply discussed; as also that of an infant daughter of
the King of England to a son of the King of Castile.
It is also reported that Monsieur de la Chau has been
sent to Spain to negotiate an agreement between
King Ferdinand and his son-in-law, to the intent that
they be the rulers and governors of Castile, as stipulated
between them, and that Queen Juana may not interfere,
nor be allowed to administer affairs of state, for the
reason that her conduct since she left Flanders has been
that of a woman whose intellects are not sufficiently
sound for such a charge; and it is strongly suspected
that husband and wife will disagree, and that the King
of Castile will speedily return to his own country; it
being evident that on reaching Spain, the Queen will

choose to govern and be mistress. This is the dread of March, 1506. the King of Castile's councillors, who know how hateful they are to the Queen, and therefore seek to make the arrangement with her father, that she may be put under restraint. Others again say that the mission of Monsieur de la Chau has for object to prevent the marriage of King Ferdinand to Madame de Foix ; this assertion being based on a belief that the King of Castile proposed doing so, had he arrived in time.

This day, whilst at mass together, the King of Castile told him he had received letters of a recent date from Spain, purporting that his father-in-law and all the rest were anxiously expecting him ; and that Monsieur de la Chau, whom he sent hence, had been at the court some time, together with the other ambassador, Monsieur de Verre.

191.

[Quirini to the Signory of Venice, "Venetian Calendar," i. No. 873.]

By his last of the 30th ultimo, acquainted the State Falmouth, 4 April. with two of the reasons assigned for the mission to Spain of Monsieur de la Chau. Has since ascertained through a trustworthy channel that he was sent by King Philip to arrange with King Ferdinand for the decorous maintenance of Queen Juana as consort, without giving her further authority, and that her father and husband should alone govern the kingdom of Castile, so that being dissimilar to her mother in intellect, she be likewise dissimilar to her in authority. This was done because in the recent arrangement between Spain and Castile, it had been stipulated that Queen Juana might intervene as a third party for the administration of the state, with power to sign and command. King Ferdinand and King Philip now, however, say that they have

discovered her incapacity for such a charge, and all the
ministers of King Philip desire and urge this arrangement, suspecting that if the Queen, who hates them
extremely, exercise authority in Spain, she may not
only seek to disgrace them with the King, and deprive
them of their influence over him, but also annul the
pensions assigned them since the adjustment in , the
kingdom of Castile; some of the ministers receiving
1,000 ducats annually, some 800, and others 500.

The ministers also seek to avoid an insurrection.
They fear lest Spaniards, who are turbulent naturally
—especially the grandees who love change and have
feuds amongst each other—might rise and make some
stir on the plea of choosing to be governed by the Queen,
who is their legitimate sovereign.   Their object now is,
that before the arrival of King Philip, his father-in-law
should circulate a report that Queen Juana is unfit to
govern, as is generally believed here ; and they hope
King Ferdinand will accede to their wishes, both as it
may prove to his interest, and also because, on the
death of Queen Isabella, amongst the other reasons
assigned by him for not ceding the government of
Castile, he alleged that his daughter was incapable and
unfit to rule ; an opinion which he seems to retain,
according to the last letters of King Philip's ambassadors, who are doing their utmost to arrange this business
as it affects them personally : Monsieur de Verre having
an annual pension in Castile of 3,000 ducats, together
with a promise of the first vacant bishopric for one of
his brothers, and Monsieur de la Chau a pension of
1,000 ducats ; and all live in hopes that King Philip may
provide their children, grandchildren, and remotest
connexions with commanderies of St. James, of Cala-
trava, or of Alcantara ; for although King Ferdinand
be the master of these three orders, and has all the

revenues, yet the vacant commanderies are in the al-
ternate gift of either sovereign, and when King Philip's
turn comes, King Ferdinand is bound to accept his
presentations.

Was informed this morning by the Spanish ambassador, who is his friend and places great trust in him,
that yesterday King Philip sent him to visit the Queen,
whom he had not allowed to see the ambassador or
anybody else for many days. When about to enter her
chamber, Don John Manuel, who accompanied him,
gave him notice that if he wished to oblige the King,
he would not stay long, and do good service. Having
entered the chamber, he received cordial greeting from
the Queen ; she would not allow her hand to be kissed,
insisted upon his being seated, and very tenderly made
many inquiries of him how her father fared, six months
having elapsed since she had received any news of him ;
and whether it was true that he wished her as much
harm as she was told he did. The Queen asked if,
after hearing of the storm, he had announced that she
and her husband were gone back to Flanders, and no
longer intended to proceed ; and last of all, whether her
going into Spain displeased him so much.

The ambassador replied that none of these things were
true ; nay, that the King her father loved her and her
husband as his very dear children, and had no greater
wish in the world than to see them. Thereupon the
ambassador took leave as quickly as he could. He told
him (Quirini), moreover, that he knew for certain that
King Philip's councillors had given the Queen to understand that her father bears her ill will, and would fain
not see her in Spain, in order that her going thither with
this impression, she might, at their first meeting, treat
him unbecomingly ; whilst King Ferdinand, being informed in like manner, that his daughter loved him not,

and was such as they described her, would the more readily consent to deprive her of the government.

192.

[Catherine of Aragon to her father Ferdinand, Wood's "Letters of Royal and Illustrious Ladies," i. 138.]

. . . .

Richmond,
22 April.

[I cannot] speak more particularly, because I know not what will become of this letter, or if it will arrive at the hands of your highness ; but when don Pedro d'Ayala shall come, who is now with the king and queen in the harbour, your highness shall know all by ciphers. I have written many times to your highness, supplicating you to order a remedy for my extreme necessity, to which (letters) I have never had an answer. Now I supplicate your highness, for the love of our Lord, that you consider how I am your daughter, and that after Him (God) I have no other good nor remedy, except in your highness ; and how I am in debt in London, and this not for extravagant things, nor yet by relieving my own (people), who greatly need it, but only for food ; and how the king of England, my lord, will not cause them (the debts) to be satisfied, although I myself spoke to him, and all those of his council, and that with tears : but he said that he is not obliged to give me anything, and that even the food he gives me is of his good will ; because your highness has not kept promise with him in the money of my marriage portion. I told him that I believed that in time to come your highness would discharge it. He told me that that was yet to see, and that he did not know it. So that, my lord, I am in the greatest trouble and anguish in the world. On the one part, seeing all my people that they are ready to ask alms ; on the other, the debts which I have in London ; on the other, about my own person, I have nothing for chemises; wherefore, by your highness' life, I have now April, sold some bracelets to get a dress of black velvet, for I 1506. was all but naked : for since I departed thence (from Spain) I have nothing except two new dresses, for till now those I brought from thence have lasted me; although now I have nothing but the dresses of brocade. On this account I supplicate your highness to command to remedy this, and that as quickly as may be; for certainly I shall not be able to live in this manner.

I likewise supplicate your highness to do me so great a favour as to send me a friar of the order of San Francesco de Osservancya, who is a man of letters, for a confessor; because, as I have written at other times to your highness, I do not understand the English language, nor know how to speak it ; and I have no confessor. And this should be, if your highness will so command it, very quickly ; because you truly know the inconvenience of being without a confessor, especially now to me, who, for six months have been near death : but now, thanks to our Lord, I am somewhat better, although not entirely well.

This I supplicate your highness once again that it may be as soon as possible. Calderon, who brings this letter, has served me very well. He is now going to be married. I have not wherewith to recompense him. I supplicate your highness to do me so great a favour as to command him to be paid there (in Spain) and have him commended ; for I have such care for him that any favour that your highness may do him I should receive as most signal.

Our Lord guard the life and most royal estate of your highness, and increase it as I desire.

1506.

193.

[Jehan le Sauvage to Maximilian, King of the Romans, "Spanish Calendar," i. 476.]

Pont de
Vaulx,
30 July.

The Archduchess Margaret decidedly refuses to marry Henry VII, although he, at first by himself, and afterwards conjointly with the Imperial ambassador, had daily pressed her during a whole month to consent. But the alliance with England is not endangered thereby. For Henry desires the marriage between his second daughter and the Prince of Castile more than his own marriage with the Archduchess.

1507.

194.

[Ferdinand of Aragon to Henry VII, " Spanish Calendar," i. 501.]

Naples,
15 March.

. Before going to Naples, sent a letter to him from Castile by his ambassador Doctor Nicholas West. That letter contained all particulars concerning the arrangements made with the late King Philip.

Has written two letters to De Puebla, one from Castile, and the other from Barcelona, and has told him all the reasons why it has been impossible to send the marriage portion of the Princess of Wales to England. Those reasons were twofold. In the first place, the death of Queen Isabella, and the disturbances which have taken place in consequence of it, have absorbed all his attention and his means. Scarcely had peace been restored, when King Philip and Queen Juana came to Spain, and the disorders were renewed.

Has left the greatest part of the marriage portion of the Princess of Wales in the hands of the trustees of the late Queen Isabella ready to be sent to England.

The small sum wanting to make up the whole amount March, 1507. of the portion was more than covered by jewels in the keeping of the said trustees, and it had been settled with King Philip that he should take them and give money in their stead. Had recommended King Philip to raise no obstacles to the trustees, and he had promised it. Before, however, the money could be sent to England, King Philip died. This death had caused him much grief, and to the Queen Juana unspeakable affliction. The consequence has been that the trustees could not send the money, because the Queen was unable to sign the order, and himself was absent in Italy. The trustees have, therefore, decided to wait for his return to Spain. That has been the will of God. Hope soon to conclude his business in Naples, and to return to Spain. Directly after his return to Spain the money shall be sent.

Begs he may be excused, and his daughter treated as he would treat a daughter of his brother, the King of England.

195.

[Ferdinand of Aragon to his daughter Catherine, " Spanish Calendar," i. 502.]

Has received her letter sent with Cavallos. God Naples, 15 (?) March. alone knows the sadness of his heart whenever he thinks of her miserable and trying life. Loves her more than ever a father loved his daughter. May God forgive King Philip; for, to tell the truth, he caused all her misery. The money of her marriage portion was ready to be sent to England, but he prevented it. He always was hostile to him, and to all his daughters. Queen Juana is unable to give orders, and the money cannot therefore be sent during his absence. Intends to return to Castile

in the spring. Queen Juana and a great many other
persons have written to him, saying that his presence is
absolutely necessary in Spain for the conservation of
peace. Directly after his arrival in Castile the money
shall be sent to England.

In Naples there is not a fit person to be found to
serve her as confessor, but a Spanish confessor will be
sent to her from Castile.

Promises to send another ambassador to England.
Don Pedro de Ayala, if he could be persuaded to go,
would perhaps be the best person for that place.

If the King of England, as she believes, be not willing
to accept the ornaments plate etc. for the price at which
they were valued in Spain, he may take them at the
price they are worth in England. She must, however,
take care that nothing of the jewels, ornaments, etc. be
lost before she is married, for they form part of her
marriage portion, and it would be difficult to replace
them. The ambassador whom he intends to send will
easily persuade King Henry to arrange the affair to her
satisfaction. Meanwhile, she must try to win the good
will of the King, and always speak of her marriage as a
thing beyond all doubt.

Has read her letter, by which she has communicated
to him the wish of the King of England to marry her
sister, Queen Juana. She must tell the King that it is
not yet known whether Queen Juana be inclined to marry
again ; but if the said Queen should marry again, it
shall be with no other person than with the King of
England, especially as he has proposed such acceptable
conditions. Expects that the King of England will
send him an ambassador with whom he can treat about
this marriage of Queen Juana, as soon as it is known in
England that he has returned to Castile. But the
affair must be kept most secret ; for if Queen Juana

should hear anything about it, she would most probably March,
do something quite to the contrary. No one knows her ¹⁵⁰⁷·
better than himself. For this reason nothing must be
done before his return to Spain.

Sends a letter for the King of England in cipher.
The person who is to decipher it must be a trustworthy
person.

Has written something concerning the marriage of
the King of England to De Puebla. She may make
use of him till another ambassador arrives.

196.

[Catherine of Aragon to her father, Wood's " Letters of Royal and
Illustrious Ladies," i. 143.]

Since your highness will provide everything so quickly, Greenwich,
I have only for the present to let you know that I gave ¹⁷ ᴶᵘˡʸ·
the letter of credence of your highness to the King of
England, my lord, and explained to him clearly that
which came in cipher.

His highness rejoiced as much as there was reason,
and sets a high value on seeing the desire that your
highness shews on this occasion to testify your good
will by acts, and expressed himself under much obligation to you for it; and that all your highness says
appeared to him so good and so much to his purpose,
that he could add nothing more than to commit himself
entirely to your highness, since he counts upon you so
certainly on his side. And that when your highness
has arrived and has seen the disposition that there is in
regard to this business, if it be that which we all desire,
the king of England, my lord, will send to your highness
his ambassadors, with full and entire power for your
highness, making himself known to you as though you
were one and the same person with himself, since he

believes you nothing less in affection, and thus will trust in your highness as much as in himself : since he holds for certain that you will regard him as your highness offered him, and that no embarrassment may cause this affair to be obstructed.

I wish to advise your highness, that by way of France and also from Spain I have learned how the king of France labours, that if the lady queen of Castile, my sister, should be married, it should be to the Conte de Foix, and this does not appear convenient to me, either for the estate of your highness or for that of the lady queen of Castile, because it would be sending discord to the very knife into that kingdom ; and your highness could never be secure, since these inconveniences which I here speak of, as resulting from such a marriage in effect, might follow.   Let not your highness think that I say this by way of advising you, since I do not say of myself anything in the world that can warn your highness which you will not have well before prepared for ; but I say it because I, in this, feel myself personally interested.   And in the negociation which I have spoken of, I supplicate your highness to give diligence that it may be held as was agreed upon ; since, as regards the king of England, my lord, they make great haste with marriages, as for that of the duchess of Savoy and others ; and his highness, as well on account of the advantage that there is in this as because he would prefer to contract kindred with your highness rather than with all the princes of Christendom, holds himself entirely in suspense, without determining anything, hoping in this other determination and answer which he expects from your highness.   And, since I see with how much affection your highness desires this may come to effect, there will be no need to supplicate you, (or) that I labour at it, except to kiss your hands for the favour that, for my part, in this affair I receive, July, 1507. who may find such new obligation to love your highness more, and give myself to serve you in every respect ; since I esteem the affairs of the king of England, my lord, more mine than my own. And since his highness writes more to your highness about this in his letter, I conclude.

Our Lord guard the most famous and royal estate of your highness, and increase it as I desire.

197.

[Catherine of Aragon to her father, Wood's " Letters," i. 148. The preceding letter was written either at Henry's dictation, or for his perusal. This expresses Catherine's own sentiments. On p. 295, l. 6, "terminate" should be "conclude".]

I received your highness' letters, which, by a servant Greenwich, of the king of England, my lord, you wrote to me ; and, 18 July. setting aside the pleasure which it gave me to know the news of the health of your highness, which I desired, since I can have no greater good after my salvation, so much did the ciphers of your highness avail here, that I have by them passed three or four days in such good spirits as are unearthly ; and they were much needed at the time that they came : for not two days before the king had said to me that the journey of your highness was postponed according to report ; and I indeed felt it was said to do me fresh displeasure, so that on all accounts the letters of your highness were necessary to me. At the conjuncture that they arrived, I gave the credence of your highness to the king of England, my lord, and he had shewed to him clearly that which came in cipher. He rejoiced so much to see them that, as I tell your highness, he told me of his great satisfaction thereupon ; and he commanded me that I should write on his part to your highness the pleasure that he had of the good will that your highness by this shewed, and that he was greatly obliged by it, and that all that your highness said appears to him so good and so much to his profit, that he could say nothing more than to commit himself entirely to your highness, since he thinks you so certainly on his side ; and that when your highness arrives and has seen the disposition that there is to execute that which he wishes in case it were that which he desires, your highness making it known to him, he will send you ambassadors with all power for your highness, as though you were the same person with himself, since he believes you no less in affection ; and thus he will trust your highness as he would himself, since he esteems it certain you will regard him as no less (person) as your highness offered yourself to him.

And since he writes himself to your highness I have no need to enlarge more on his behalf ; that which on mine he commanded me-to write was to advise your highness how, by way of France and also of Spain, they have written that the king of France was exerting himself so that if the queen should marry it should be with the Conte de Foix. He told me that I should tell your (highness) as well on my own part, that this would be great inconvenience for the estate of your highness, and of the queen, and of her sons, and that Frenchmen entering into that kingdom your highness could not be in security ; and many other things about this which I do not say, because they are more to his purpose than to that of your highness. And that your highness may provide in that which is most necessary, and that you may see what is most conducive to your service, it suffices to let you know this, without more apprehension or advices ; because as refers to your highness, I consider such things improper [? impertinent].

That which I venture to supplicate your highness is, July, 1507. that, whatever be the dispositions that your highness shall see entertained on this affair, you will not so act as that it may arrive at effect; for I thus figure it to myself, that it must be that your highness entertains this business in order to terminate my marriage; because with this bait I believe that, as to that which concerns me, things will be done better than in the past, when some one comes who knows how to arrange and disinvolve them as I have written to your highness.

And now I will not cease to return to it here, to supplicate your highness that he who shall have to come here may have the authority and rank that I have said, because he has more to do than your highness thinks, or I could tell you. For those of this kingdom are as dilatory as any in the world in negotiating; in it (this kingdom) are needed more particulars than in any other, especially since the necessity is doubled by all being in the state that it is, as he who shall come will see. And much as I say to your highness, I cannot give you to understand the state in which things are here, because, though I knew how to say it to you, I think your highness would not credit me in much of it; and thus the person who should come here, informing your highness of the truth concerning what is going on, I believe your highness would be frightened at that which I have passed through: so that as to that which pertains to me and to the service of your highness, I should, beyond a trifle, prefer to see such a person as I speak of come without the dowry, than the dowry without a suitable person. And your highness may believe I speak from experience, the which I have well learned by what has passed and continually passes concerning me, for want of such a person as I speak of; because that, if there were one here who would have devoted himself to the service of your highness, my tribulations would not have arrived at such an extreme'; since, also, they would not have placed me as a pledge to make peace—they would not have consented that I should lead such a life. But, as I have written to your highness, that which I feel as most importunate is to see myself in such a situation, and that there is no one who will contradict it. If the ambassador whom your highness has here were a man, he would not have consented—even though I were not to be married to the prince,—were it only considering whose daughter I am, that I should be in this kingdom, with such a company in my house that I am indignant to think of it; for in comparison of this, all the other things that I have passed through I think little of. And thus I am doubly desirous on this account for my remedy, that I may not see myself as never knight's daughter was seen in the kingdom of your highness.

It is certain that I desire that at the least your highness should let the king of England, my lord, know how this is felt,—above all, since you are in a case not to satisfy him, I being in such a manner in his kingdom, as I told him a few days ago. And I spoke so well that I should rejoice to give account of it to your highness, only that an affair of such length is not to be put in writing. I hope since your highness knows all, you will provide in the manner that I have entreated you, and therefore I will not detain myself in telling your highness many continual troubles that I have passed through ; because, since I expect so speedy a remedy, I do not desire to give more trouble than that which, by my past letters, I have given to your highness, since this suffices to enable you to judge that all the rest is of the same fashion.

The shortness of the return of your highness consoles

me, since with it I hope all will be remedied, since your July, 1507.
highness showed that you care for me, as indeed I need
it.

The king rejoiced much in seeing the speedy attention
that your highness intended to give about the coming of
the dowry. May it please God that it may come at the
time that is hoped for—because I fear, and not without
cause, to think that it should not be so; and for this
reason, that it concerns my interest rather than that of
your highness. I hold it for certain that it is not [? most]
necessary that I have made haste to write, although in
fear from its not being in cipher, and from not sending it by one of my own people. But I believe as to
that, that they go by as good a messenger as though he
that takes them were of my house, because I send them
by a faithful person to Martin Sanchez de Camudio, in
order that he himself may take them to your highness.

May it please our Lord that they may arrive at the
time that your highness has arrived, because, according
to what is reported, they tell me that your highness is
so already.

The king himself acknowledged the diligence which
I have given in answering your highness in that which
concerns him, and I, as well to content him, am glad
to let him (know) that which your highness commands
me; that in reference to the king, while in the meantime your highness is providing, I may act as hitherto
your highness has rightly commanded me, according to
that which falls in most with the service of your highness. And that nothing may be hindered by me, I do
as I have always done, since I cannot improve upon it;
and thus I shall act until your highness sends to give
remedy in my life, which is greatly needed. And thus
I conclude, supplicating your highness so to act that I
may be here favoured by your highness; and that you

July, 1507. may shew that you hold me in esteem, although I may
not merit it; because if your highness should desire it,
it is in your power that things may not be as they have
been hitherto.

That which I say in this letter may suffice in reference
to your highness, and that minute that I sent with the
king's packet was what I showed to the king as the
meaning of that which I wrote in his affair. And because, in truth, he might have had it shewn to him, I
sent it to your highness. He commanded me that I
should add, that if the marriage which I have spoken
of with the Conte de Foix should take place, that in
length of time Spain would come to be joined to the
crown of France; and as for himself, that he considers
himself as a true son of your highness. When your
highness writes to him, I entreat you to shew him that
in this affair I have the same good will which I shew to
him.

May our Lord guard the life and most royal estate of
your highness, and increase it as I desire.

198.

[De Puebla to Ferdinand of Aragon, "Spanish Calendar," i. p. 439.]

.   .   .   .

London,   The King of England has no confidential advisers.
5 October. The [Lord Great] Chamberlain [Lord Herbert], who
is of his blood, is, however, more in his confidence than
any other person. He is much devoted to King Ferdinand
and the Princess of Wales. Begs that a gracious letter
may be written to the Lord High Steward [Shrewsbury],
and that he may be encouraged to continue.

.   .   .   .

There is no finer youth in the world than the Prince
of Wales. He is already taller than his father, and his

limbs are of a gigantic size. He is as prudent as is to October, 1507.
be expected from a son of Henry VII.

The Princess of Wales is well, and her health constantly improves. She suffers from no other evil than the anxiety she feels because she has heard that her marriage is not yet rendered indissoluble.

199.

[Skelton's education of Prince Henry, "Works," ed. Dyce, i. 150.]

The honor of Englond I lernyd to spelle,
In dygnyte roialle that doth excelle :
Note and marke wyl thys parcele ;
I yaue hym drynke of the sugryd welle
Of Eliconys waters crystallyne,
Aqueintyng hym with the Musys nyne.
Yt commyth thé wele me to remorde,
That creaunser was to thy sofre[yne] lorde ·
It plesyth that noble prince roialle
Me as hys master for to calle
In hys lernyng primordialle.

200.

[Imprisonment of Yorkist nobles, "Chronicle of Calais," p. 6.]

Ser Richard Carow knight, lievetenaunt of the castle 18 October. of Caleys, browght owt of England, by the kyng's comaundement, the lord marques Dorset and the lord William of Devonshire the erle of Devonshire's son and heyre, whiche were bothe of kynne to the late qwene Elizabethe and of hir blode. They had bene in the towre of London a greate season. They were kepte prisoners in the castle of Caleys as longe as kynge Henry the Seventhe lyved, and shulde have bene put to deathe, yf he had lyved longar. They wer browght in to the

castle of Caleys the xviii of Octobar the xxiii of Henry
the Seventhe.[1]

201.

[Catherine of Aragon to Queen Juaña of Castile, "Spanish
Calendar," i. 553.]

Richmond,
25 October.
Most noble and most mighty Princess, Queen and
Lady, after having kissed the royal hands of your Highness and humbly commended myself to you I have to
express the very great pleasure it gave me to see you in
this kingdom, and the distress which filled my heart, a
few hours afterwards, on account of your sudden and
hasty departure.[2]

My Lord the King was also much disappointed in
consequence of it, and if he had acted as he secretly
wished, he would, by every possible means, have prevented your journey. But, as he is a very passionate
King, it was thought advisable by his Council that they
should tell him he ought not to interfere between husband and wife. On which account and for the sake of
other mysterious causes with which I was very well acquainted, he concealed the feelings occasioned by the
departure of your Highness, although it is very certain
that it weighed much upon his heart.

[1] The editor of the " Chronicle of Calais " adds " [1508] " ; and is
followed by the " Dict. Nat. Biogr.," xxiii. 202 ; but the 18th of October in the twenty-third year of Henry VII was in 1507, and Bernard
André gives this as the date (Gairdner's "Memorials," p. 100).

[2] It is almost incredible that Catherine should have written in
October, 1507, in these terms of her sister's departure in April,
1506, without the least allusion to the death in the meantime of
her sister's husband. But the contents of the letter show that its
date is October, 1507, and not October, 1506. It is, however, safer
to interpret the letter as expressing Henry VII's diplomacy
rather than Catherine's feelings.

The great affection he has felt, and still feels, towards October, your Royal Highness from that time until now, is well $^{1507.}$ known. I could not in truth express, even though I were to use much paper, the pleasure which my lord the King and I felt on hearing that the King, our lord and father, had returned to Castile, and was abiding there with your Highness, and that he was obeyed throughout all the kingdom, peace and concord prevailing everywhere.

It is true that I have experienced, and am still experiencing, some sorrow and depression of mind on account of having heard, a few days ago, that the French have taken a large and beautiful city called Tilmote, belonging to my nephew,[1] and that all his subjects and the whole land are in great fear of the French. Wherefore, as a remedy for everything, and not less for the destruction and chastisement of the Duke of Gueldres his rebel, I have ventured to write these lines to your Highness, entreating you to hearken to my wishes respecting this matter. I have, moreover, written to my lord the King, our father, about this business, which is of great advantage and importance to your Highness, to the increase of your state, the tranquillity and welfare of your subjects, and those of the said Prince, my nephew, and which also affects my lord, the King of England. He is a Prince who is feared and esteemed at the present day by all Christendom, as being very wise, and possessed of immense treasures, and having at his command powerful bodies of excellent troops. Above all he is endowed with the greatest virtues, according to all that your Highness will have heard respecting him.

If what my lord the King, our father, shall say to

[1] The future Emperor Charles V, who had succeeded Philip as Duke of Burgundy.

October,
1507.

you should please, as I think it will, your Highness, I do not doubt but that your Highness will become the most noble and the most powerful Queen in the world.[1] Moreover, nothing will more conduce to your pleasure and satisfaction, and the security of the kingdom of your Highness. In addition to all this, it will double the affection subsisting between my lord the King, our father, and my lord, the King of England. It will also lead to the whole of Africa being conquered within a very short time, and in the hands of the Christian subjects of your Highness, and of my lord the King our father.

I entreat your Highness to pardon me for having written to you, and for having meddled in so great and high a matter. God knows what my wishes are, as I have already said ; and I have not found it possible to resist the desire I felt to write to you. For it appears to me that if this be not done, it will be committing a great sin against God, against the King, our lord and father and against your Highness, whose life and royal estate may our Lord guard and increase.

202.

[Treaty of marriage between Charles and Mary Tudor concluded at Calais, " Chronicle of Calais," p. 6.]

27 October-
21 Decem-
ber.

The xxvij of October there came out of England the bysshope of Wynchestar lorde prevye seale, the erle of Surrey lorde treasurar, and the lord of Saint John's,[2] with doctor Weston, all ambassadors ; they landed at Temperlto [sic] in Pecardye, and the ij of November, there came to Caleys out of Flaunders from the duke of Burgoyne the erle of Fynes, the lorde of Barowe, and the presydent of Flaunders, with dyvers othar of the

[1] This refers of course to Henry VII's proposal to marry Juaffa himself.   [2] Sir T. Docwra succeeded Kendal in 1501.

contrye, and with them met ser Richard Carew, live- October-
tenaunt of the castle of Calleys, and syr John Wilshere December, 1507.
comptrowlar of Caleis, and Waltar Culpepar undar-
marshall of Caleys, and all the speres and archars on
horsbacke and dyvars sowldiers all in harnes, for thes
strangars feared the Frenche men ; but beinge browght
in savetie to Caleys, there the lords on bothe partyes
concluded the mariage betwixt the duke of Burgoyne and
the lady Mary dowghtar to kynge Henry the Seventhe,
where on seynt Thomas day the Apostle [1] was great
triumphe made in Calles.

203.

[Henry VII to the Mayor and Aldermen of London, Halliwell's
"Letters," i. 194-6.]

Trusty and well-beloved, we greet you well. And for- December.
asmuch as we doubt not but it is and shall be to you
and all other our true subjects right joyful and comfortable to hear and understand, from time to time,
specially of such causes and matters as redound to the
great honour and exaltation, universal weal, surety and
restfulness of us, this our realm, and our subjects of
the same ; we signify unto you that, by our great
labour, study and policy, this great and honourable
alliance and marriage betwixt the Prince of Castile and
our right dear daughter the Lady Mary, is now (our
Lord be thanked) betwixt our ambassadors and the
orators, as well of our brother and cousin, the King of
the Romans, as of the said young prince at our town

[1] 21 December. The treaty was not confirmed by Margaret of
Savoy, the regent of the Netherlands until 1 October, 1508 (see
below, Vol. iii.), after Wolsey's mission which apparently had
this object (see Gairdner's "Letters and Papers of Richard III
and Henry VII," i. 425-52 ; his despatches are too badly mutilated
to be suitable for reproduction here).

of Calais, accorded, agreed, concluded, and finally determined with a great, ample, and large amity and consideration to the surety, strength, defence, and comfort,
as well of us and the said prince, as of either our
realmes, countries, dominions, and subjects. And, considering the noble lineage and blood whereof the said
young prince is descended, which is of the greatest
kings and princes in Christendom ; remembering also
the regions, lands, and countries, wherein, by rightful
inheritance, he shall succeed, with the manifold commodities and goodness that may follow and ensue to us
and this our realm, as well by the said alliance and
amity, as also by the free and sure intercourse of mer-
chandize, that our and his subjects may and shall have
in the regions and countries specially being so nigh
joined together as they be ; we think verily that, though
the same shall be right chargeable, yet for the honour,
surety, weal and profit of this our said realm, none so
noble marriage can any where be found ; so that, by
the mean thereof and the other alliance which we have
with our good son the king of the Scots, this our realm
is now environed, and, in manner, closed in every side
with such mighty princes, our good sons, friends, confederates, and allies, that, by the help of our Lord, the
same is and shall be perpetually established in rest and
peace, and wealthy condition, to our great honour and
pleasure, the rejoicing and comfort of all our loving
friends, confederates, and allies, the fear and discomfort
of our enemies, that would intend or presume to attempt anything to the contrary.

The premises therefore considered, we do advertise
you of the same, to the intent that, like as we doubt
not but ye and every of you will take pleasure and comfort in hearing thereof ; so, with convenient diligence,
upon sight of these our letters, ye will cause demonstra-

tions and tokens of rejoicing and comfort to be made in December, sundry places within our city there, as well by making fires in such places as you shall think convenient as otherwise in the best and most comfortable manner that ye can, so that thereby ye may be evidently known what gladness and rejoicing is generally taken and made.

1508.

204.

[Doubts about Henry's marriage with Catherine ; the Provost of Cassel to Margaret of Savoy, " Letters and Papers," i. 345-9.]

. . . Affin madame, que je ne voz celle rien, je croy London, que a la fin ancoirez [1] voz ourez parler du mariage de 14 June. monseigneur le prince de Galles, et de madame Lyonoire, [Eleanor] quelque chose que je voz en ay escript parcidevant ; toutesfois de cy a ung mois je voz en escriray plus certainement que je ne sauroye faire maintenant. Tant y a que pour maintenant je say de vray et le commandeur de Haro la dit publiquement, que le roy de France comme vray allie et ami du roy Darragon a puis nagheres escript au roy Dangleterre, le pryant bien acertes pour laccomplissement du mariage de madame Katherine Despangne, avec monseigneur le prince de Galles, etc. Et ma on dit que le roy Dangleterre na point este fort content que le roy de France sen mesle si avant. Et que plus est, lon dit que mondit sieur le prince ny est gheres enclin. Toutesfois, madame, en peu de temps lon en saura plus.

Ledit de Haro a bruyt destre fort François et je le croy, car yl se declaire aulcqune fois trop quant aulcqunes nouvelles viengnent. Mais il lui fait a pardonner ; car son maistre [Ferdinand] est tel. Mais se [si] Dieu donne sa grace touchant Gheldres, madame, voz cog-

---

[1] Encores vous ouirez, you will yet hear.

June, 1508. noisterez grandz choses et toutz les amys de fortune demanderont votre ayde et assistence. Dieu voz en doint la grace, comme jespoire fermement quil fra ; mais yl est mestier que chascun se mette maintenant en œuvre plus que jamais a rebouter les Francois, si viengnent. Ne pensez point, madame, que au cas que les affaires se portent bien en Gheldres, il ny aura roy de France ne Dangleterre quil ne voz estime plus que nulle aultre princesse, et le roy Darragon avecques. Mais principalement le roy Dangleterre ; car jamais si dingue et profitable pour lui alliance ne pourra avoir en ce monde, comme quelque jour, quant yl voz plaira que je soy retourne, voz diray bien au long. Parquoy en bonne raison il pouroit avoir noz affaires pour recommandees ; mesmement considere lestat on [en] quel cheulx [ceux] de Gheldres sont maintenant, au sort yl noz fault ayder noz mesmes, dumoingz durant ses [ces] trois ou quatre mois.

Madame, comme je voz ay escript pluseures fois que le delay de la venue de messieurs les ambassadeurs nest cy [si] non pour entretempz veoir ou la Fortune favorisera, et selle [si elle] est bonne pour lempereur et votre maison, voz aurez des grandz offres de plaisirs et services.

Il y a ung astrologue par de ca quil ma dit que les le xxiie ou xxiiie de ce mois la fortune de lempereur sera si grande et si bonne plus que jamais. Dieu le face ainsi. Je ny adjouste nulle foy ; mais neantmoingz sy fault yl que chascun sy emploie a son extreme possible a la conservation de la juste querele, mesurement de celle de Gheldres, ainsi que jay remonstre par deca si a plain que nul nen pouroit dire au contraire. .

Madame si le roy Dangleterre se peult apercevoir que voz escris telles choses, yl me tiendra pour ung espye, et par avanture me vouldroit nuyre. Dieu saif de quelle foy et lealte je y procede. Parquoy, Madame, voz prye de deschirer ses [ces] lettres quant voz aurez le tout June,1508. [b]ien entendu.

205.

[The Provost of Cassel to Margaret of Savoy, "Letters and Papers," i. 365-6 ; the words printed in italics are in cipher. Compare Van den Bergh's "Correspondance de Marguerite d'Autriche," pp. 123-33.]

Ma tres redoubtee dame, je me recommande tres London, humblement a votre beningne grace. Ma dame, pour ce $^{29\,July.}$ que pas les deux derrenieres bougettes monsieur lambassadeur de Burgho ne moy avons receu aulcqunes lettres de voz, noz en sumes estez fort maris et perplex, et mesmement que entendons assez *le retardement des ambassadeurs*.

Madame, voz savez ce que ycellui seigneur de Burgho et moy voz en avons escript, et en effect je *crains que le roy Dengleterre se joindra avec le roy de France* entierement a notre *destruction*. Comme je voz ay escript par tant de fois, *le roy Dengleterre a toutjours espie la Fortune et ne vouldroit que eussions le pays de Gheldres*. A ceste fin yl fait les *difficultez* touchant *argent et le prest*.

Ma dame, au cas que *le roy Dengleterre soit* entierement *avec le roy de France* comme il fait *a craindre*, sans doubte *se [si] les ambassadeurs ne viegnent*, tout se pouroit *perdre*. Voz en saurer bien user.

206.

[Sir Edward Wingfield to Margaret of Savoy, "Spanish Calendar," i. No. 600; the editor of the "Spanish Calendar" has ascribed this despatch to "Edmund" Wingfield, but its author was clearly Sir Edward, see "Letters and Papers," ii. 366.]

Henry VII has it much at heart that the affairs of November. the Emperor, and the Prince his son, should be settled
20 *

to the greatest advantage in the approaching Congress
of Cambray, and that their enemies should be entirely
discomfited.

As long as the alliance between the King of France
and the King of Aragon continues, it is to be feared
that the principal enemy [1] of the Emperor and Prince
Charles will triumph. For if he be assisted by France,
the King of Aragon will most probably be able, not
only to keep the usurped government of Castile in his
own hands, and the other dominions belonging to that
kingdom, as long as he lives, but also to deprive the
Prince of his right of succession. To prevent this, it
seems to Henry that the best plan would be to exclude
the King of Aragon from the treaties that are to be
made at Cambray, and to sever the alliance existing
between him and the King of France. The King of
Aragon has usurped the government of Castile only by
means of the help of the King of France. If he were
to be isolated, he would be unable to preserve it, and
the Emperor would have it in his power, aided by those
who are inimical to the King of Aragon, to take the
government of that kingdom into his own hands.

Since it might be difficult to dissolve the alliance between the King of Aragon and the King of France,
has bethought himself of some expedients which might
be useful. The King of France, at divers times, has
proposed to Henry that the Prince of Wales should
marry the sister of the Duke of Angoulème, and that a
treaty of alliance and friendship should be concluded
between the Prince of Wales and the Duke of Angoulème. The King of England has constantly rejected
these offers, though the King of France has been ready
to make great sacrifices. He would not even now accept them, were it not that they would be advantageous

---

[1] I.e. Ferdinand of Aragon.

to the Emperor and the Prince. But as the King of France could not be induced to dissolve the alliance with the King of Aragon on any other terms, the King of England would condescend to accept either the marriage or the alliance.

It is known that the King of France greatly desires this marriage and alliance, and it is therefore probable that, if he could obtain them, he would make peace with the Emperor, and give up his alliance with the King of Aragon. As she and the Cardinal of Gurk are to be present at the conferences of Cambray, he begs them to broach these matters to the Cardinal of Amboise. But it must be understood that it is to be kept secret, that these proposals come from the King of England. If it should be found that the King of France is inclined to enter into the negociations, the Emperor must write to King Henry, and beg him to consent to either the alliance or the marriage.

If the King of France should abandon his alliance with the King of Aragon, a new alliance could be concluded between the Pope, the Emperor, the King of England and the King of France, from which the King of Aragon would have to be excluded. Deprived of all assistance and succour, the King of Aragon would soon be expelled from Castile by the Castilians themselves, who tolerate him only through fear of France.

The Emperor could thus easily obtain the government of Castile, and would not only be able to gain much thereby, but would also have it in his power to administer better justice and to secure the succession to his [grand] son, Prince Charles.

Another important advantage to the Emperor would be that he would gain great reputation, and considerably augment his power. He could employ the army and navy of Castile against the Venetians, take venge-

ance on them, and reconquer all of which he has been
deprived. The Emperor would, moreover, be enabled
to proceed to Rome to his coronation. The King of
England loves the Emperor and Prince Charles above
all other Princes, and would therefore gladly take all
the trouble of the negociations concerning the peace
between the Emperor and the King of France, and the
alliance of the Pope with the Princes upon himself.

207.

[The Provost of Cassel and other Flemish ambassadors to Margaret
of Savoy, " Letters and Papers," i. 368-74.]

Madame, tant et le plus humblement que povons
nous nous recommandons a vostre bonne grace.

Madame, nous avons desavant hier v[eille] de Saint
Nicolay aux champs entre Dartford et ceste ville receu
voz lettres de Cambray du second de ce mois; dont
assez humblement ne vous saurions mercyer, car vous
nous avez par icelles et par les bonnes et joyeuses
nouvelles y contenues tant confortez et resjoys que ne
le vous saurions escripre. Prians Dieu nostre Createur
vous par . . . ster jusques a lexecucion des matieres
conceues, ainsi quil a fait jusques ores, et espero[ns]
infailliblement quil fera enoultre jusques a la fin. Nous
vous supplions aussi en toute humilite que en ensuyvant
ce que de vostre grace vous a pleu nous escripre par
vosdites lettres nous vouloir signifier de la conclusion
desdites matieres quant elle se fera pour icelle nostre
joye confirmer et radoubler.

Quant a noz nouvelles, madame, depuis que derniere-
ment vous avons escript nostre arrivee a Douvres,
sommes le lendemain de la Saint Andrieu partiz dudit
lieu de Douvres, accompaigniez du gra[n]t prieur de
Canturbery, de messieurs Eduart de Pouninghe [1] et

---

[1] Sir Edward Poynings.

Gilbert de Talbot depute de Calays, chevalier de lordre, December,
et allez ledit jour au giste audit Canturberey en labbaye 1508.
illec. A notre entree devant ladite abbaye furent aude-
vant de nous [t]ous les officiers principaulx et gens de
la ley de ladite ville en grant nombre, qui nous bien-
viengnerent et feirent tant bon recueil avec offre et
presentacion de tout plaisir et service de si bonne sorte
que riens plus. Et le soir nous vindrent faire presens
de vin, cyre, espices, et pluiseurs autres choses, selon la
coustume du pays, en grant quantite et bien honorable-
ment.

Le Samedi partismes, et venismes au giste a Setim-
borch,¹ ung village a dix milles plusavant dont aussi
nous partismes le lendemain, qui fut Dimence, apres la
messe, et venismes au giste a Rochestres. Dudit Rochestres feismes une autre journee, qui fut le Lundy,
jusques a Dartfort, a douze miles pres de ceste cite. Et
partout estions recueillez et tant bien venuz que mer-
veilles. Jusques apres dudit lieu de Dartfort nous con-
voyerent et conduirent tousjours le grant prieur de
Canturbery et Messire Eduart de Pouninghe, qui furent
a nous recevoir au descendre des navires audit Douvres,
avec aussi le depute de Calays, et illec print cougie de
nous ledit sieur prieur et retourna en son eglise.

Lesdits depute et de Pouninghe nous ont tousjours
accompaignie jusques icy. Et devant h[ie]r Mardy en
deslogeant dudit Dartfort a demye lyeue pres dillec,
trouvasmes au devant de nous aux champs messieurs
lesvesque de Worcestre, le conte de Serosbery, grant
maistre Dengleterre, le commandeur de Saint Jehan,
messire Eduart Brandon, chevalier de lordre, et le
doctor West, avec grant multitude de gens de bien en
nombre de cent et cinquante chevaulx ou plus ; lesquelz
avec aussi lesdits depute de Calays et le sieur Pouninghe

¹ Sittingbourne.

nous conduirent jusques en notre logiz. A lentre de la ville trouvasmes nouvelle compaignie de gentilz hommes de lostel du roy et autres, bien accoustrez et montez. Le soir nous vint on semblablement faire des presens de par la ville, non moindres, ains plus grans que jusques ores lon avoit fait, tousjours en accroissant.

Hier, le jour Saint Nicolay, entre une et deux heures apres midy vindrent devers nous en notredit logis messieurs larchevesque de Canturberey et le conte Doxenfort, ung des grans, et, comme lon nous dit, le principal personnaige de ce royaulme. Apres la congratulacion faicte de notre bien joyeuse et desiree venue, qui seroit trop longue a escripre, nous dirent que le roy estoit prest de nous recevoir et donner audience quant nous vouldrions, et en leur disant que nous estions prestz quand il plairoit a sa majeste, nous consignerent heure ce jourdhuy devers luy en sa court de Grunevuyse, hors de ceste ville, a unze heures devant midi. Et pour y aller nous envoya sa barge avec aussi les seigneurs et personnaiges dessus nommez.

Madame, nous y sommes allez a lheure assignee. Illec venuz avons trouve ledit sieur roy accompaignie de monseigneur le prince de Gales, son filz, de lambassadeur du roy Darragon, de douze on treize evesques, et de pluiseurs et la pluspart des princes · et grans maistres de son royaulme. De vous escripre lonneur et le recueil quil nous feist et demonstra, ce seroit chose trop longue, et ne saurions. Il seroit impossible de meilleur.

Apres la presentacion et visitacion de noz lettres de credence, et lexposicion de notre charge, et responce de par luy sur ce faicte par la bouche de monseigneur de Canturbery, son chancellier, nous dit et repeta a diverses fois et de tant bonne affection quil estoit possible, que nous luy estions les tres bien venuz. Il nous dit aussi que vray estoit quil avoit eu quelque regret et anvy December, a notre retardement et longue demeure ; mais notredite 1508. venue, congnoissant par icelle la bonne et entiere affection le lempereur et de vous, madame, pour laccomplissement des choses faictes et traictees a Calays, luy fait oblier le tout.

Apres, pour la presse qui estoit en la salle ou il nous avoit receu, nous mena en sa chambre, et illec se devisa longuement et priveement de sa grace avec moy, de Berghes, et me dit tout plain de bonnes choses. En effect, pour demonstrer quil a aussi grant desir a laccomplissement des choses traictees, et a nostre despesche comme nous meismes, nous dit que demain envoyera devers nous ses deputez pour veoir et visiter les lettres, tant dun coste que dautre, et apres adviser et conclure du jour de la solempnisacion des fianchailles et des choses qui en deppendent, tellement que esperons bien brief avoir bonne expedicion du tout.

208.

[" Greyfriars' Chronicle," p. 29.]

Thys yere was many aldermen put in to the tower, and sir William Capell put toward in the shreffes howse.

209.

[Kingsford's " Chronicles," p. 262.]

This yere was Sir William Capell ayein put in vexacion, by sute of the kyng, for thinges doon by hym in the tyme of his mairaltie.

In the begynnyng of this Maires tyme Sir William Capell, after his prisonment in the Contour, and Shryvishouse, was by the kynges Counceill commaundid

December, 1508.

to the Tower, where he remayned till the kyng died. And shortly after was deliuered w⁺ many other.[1]

And in lykewise was Sir Laurence Aylemer delt w⁺, and commytted to the ward or hous of Richard Smyth, Shyryve. And there remayned as prysoner by the space abouesaid.

1509.

210.

[Membrilla to Ferdinand of Aragon, "Spanish Calendar," Suppl. to vols. i. and ii. p. 13.]

London, 4 March.

Much have I laboured to depart spotless from England, and to save your Majesty from vexation, hoping from day to day that the marriage of the Princess of Wales would take place, and that the disorders in the house of the Princess would be remedied without annoyance to your Highness. I confess that it has been an error, because if I had written it in time it might have been possible to remedy it, and not have gone too far forward; but it is better late, as they say [than never]. Your Highness should know that there is much need of a person who can rule this household, and that it should be such a person whom her Highness holds in honour, and those of this household in respect, for now the household is governed by a young friar, whom the Princess has for confessor, and who being, in my view and in that of every one, unworthy of having such a charge, causes the Princess to commit many errors.

[1] Cf. *ibid.* p. 261 : "And this yere [1506-7] was Thomas Kneysworth, late maier, and his ij shryves condempned to the kyng in great sommes of money, over peynfull prisonment by them in the Marshalsy susteyned". See also Vol. ii. Nos. 23-30. These fines and imprisonments were due to prosecution by Empson and Dudley.

As your Highness knows how full of goodness she is, March, and so conscientious, this her confessor makes a sin of 1509. all acts, of whatever kind they may be, if they displease him, and thus causes her to commit many faults. This servant of the Princess goes despatched behind my back to your Highness, to give time to those who wish to make complaints of me. I will not say now all the things which have need of correction, submitting to the opinion of those your Highness may order to interrogate him [the servant] as to the condition in which the house of the Princess is, and as to the things which for two months past have happened, and from his report you will know more of it than I should be able to write. If, after having been informed of their complaints of me, your Highness should desire to know the truth, although it may be against me, I will tell it to your Highness without lying on any point. Because, however, the beginning, and middle, and the end of these disorders is this said friar, I say that he is young, and light, and haughty, and scandalous in an extreme manner ; and the King of England has said to the Princess very strong words about him. Because I have said something to the Princess which did not appear to me right of this friar, and the friar knew it, he has been so far able as to put me so much out of favour with the Princess that if I had committed some treason she could not have treated me worse ; and I have some letters preserved to show to your Highness, which the Princess has written to me. Certainly, unless I were so faithfully devoted to the service of your Highness, neither the dread of losing that which I have, nor of putting my life in peril, would detain me longer in England. I would already be gone, had not the service of your Highness such power over me that I have not the free judgment which God gave me to do any other thing, except to die and serve you. I entreat your Highness, that, having heard the information which he who brings this letter, and who is a servant of the house and knows everything, will give, your Highness amend the life and the household of the Princess, sending her an old and honest confessor and of the order of San Francisco, because such an one might stay in England with less scandal than this one, and more according to the pleasure of the King of England. In order that your Highness may know of what kind this friar is, I will tell you what he said to me, and they were these words exactly, without making them worse or better. He said to me : I know they have told many things of me to you. I said to him : Certainly, father, they have said nothing of you to me. He said : I know it, for he who told you told me. I said to him : Well, any one can rise as a false witness but I swear to you by the Corpus Cristi that they have told me nothing which I remember. He said : Be it so, but in this house there are evil tongues, and they have slandered me, and not with the lowest in the house, but with the highest, and this is no disgrace to me, and if it were not for contradicting them I should already be gone. Certainly I tell the truth to your Highness, that I was excited and almost beyond power of restraint from laying hands on him. Moreover, the King of England, and all the English abhor so much to see such a friar so continually in the palace and amongst the women, that nothing could be more detested by them ; and it is not a good token that the King of England does not remedy a thing which displeases him so much.

211.   1509.

[Catherine of Aragon to Ferdinand, "Spanish Calendar," Suppl.
to vols. i. and ii. p. 16.]

From a letter which your Highness has written to Richmond
the ambassador I have seen that you have determined ^{9 March.}
to send hither a ·prelate to conduct these negociations.
I kiss the hands of your Highness for it, for as things
here become daily worse, and my life more and more
insupportable, I can no longer bear this in any manner.
Those [servants] whom up to this time I have had are
no longer of any use to me, because my ill fortune
wills it that those whom your Highness sends hither,
however sufficient they might be, have always so much
crippled your service, that the sending of a new ambassador is my only support and comfort.   Your Highness
knows already how much the King of England, who
does not like to see or to hear this one, would be pleased
at it.   Not that he is not loyal, but I think he does not
know how to treat matters.   For as Doctor de Puebla
conducted the affairs with too great gentleness in every
thing that regarded the interests of this King, so this
other behaves with too great rigour towards him and his
servants, especially as I, being dependent on them, cannot make use of anything that is not done with modera-
tion.   Therefore, I beseech your Highness not to forget
what I have written to you so many times, but immediately to send redress, and to determine as to the way in
which your Highness desires me to live.   It is impossible
for me any longer to endure what I have gone through
and still am suffering from the unkindness of the King,
and the manner in which he treats me, especially since
he has disposed of his daughter in marriage to the
Prince of Castile, and therefore imagines he has no
longer any need of your Highness, as this has been

done without your consent. He tries to make me feel
this by his want of love, although in secret and without
confessing it he knows that as long as he does not possess the goodwill of your Highness, he is wanting in the
greatest and best part. All this causes me much pain,
as being against the interest of your Highness, and if I
had not any other cause, this alone would not permit
me to let it pass without making you acquainted with
it. God knows how much I am grieved that I have to
write to you always of so many troubles and difficulties.
But remembering that I am your daughter, I cannot
prevail upon myself to conceal them from you, and not
to beg you to remedy them as your station and service
require. To tell the truth, my necessities have risen
so high that I do not know how to maintain myself.
For I have already sold my household goods, as it was
impossible to avoid it, and I do not know whence I can
have anything else. Some days ago, speaking with the
King about my wants, he said to me, that he was not
bound to give my servants food, or even to my own self,
but that the love he bore me would not allow him to do
otherwise. From this your Highness will see to what
a state I am reduced, when I am warned that even my
food is given to me almost as alms. What I feel most,
is to see all my servants in such a ruined state as they
are. Although not all have served me as they ought,
it gives me pain and weighs on my conscience that I
cannot pay them, and send those away who cause me
great annoyance, especially Juan de Cuero, whose
audaciousness it is very difficult for me to bear. He is
the cause that others do not do what they ought to do,
and I must be silent, owing to my necessities, of which
I have informed your Highness. What afflicts me most
is that I cannot in any way remedy the hardships of my
confessor, whom I consider to be the best that ever

woman of my position had, with respect to his life, as well as to his holy doctrine and proficiency in letters, as I have oftentimes written to your Highness. It grieves me that I cannot maintain him in the way his office and my rank demand, because of my poverty, during which he has always served me with such labour and fatigue as no one else would have undergone. He is very faithful in his office as well as in giving good advice and a good example, and it seems to me it would be ingratitude if I neglected to inform your Highness how badly the ambassador has behaved towards him. The service of your Highness suffers thereby, and I have been much annoyed. The reason of it is that the ambassador has strongly attached himself to the merchant Francisco de Grimaldo, whom he has brought over with him, and to a servant of mine, Francisca de Cáceres, who, by his favour, were about to marry, contrary to my wishes. And situated as I am, I had to conceal my feelings for the sake of the honour and honesty of my house. I found myself in so great a difficulty, that I could not help giving a bond for a certain sum of money, and I believe that if your Highness knew the reason which moved me to do so, you would not reproach me, but rather recognise me as your daughter. On account of the annoyance this woman has caused me I sent her away, but the ambassador of your Highness received her into his house and at his table, which did not seem well to me considering his official position as representative of the person of your Highness. He has caused me many annoyances every day with this merchant, giving me to understand that he wanted to go away, and to carry off my marriage portion, unless I began to pay something of what I had promised him. But if my bond is attentively considered, it appears that I owe him nothing. Because the confessor gave me advice in all this, the ambassador has quarrelled with him, and when he saw how little reason he had to do so, he tried to excuse himself by saying that the confessor meddled in the affairs of the embassy. I swear by the life of your Highness, which is the greatest oath I can make, that that is not the case. I sent him to ask for the [marriage] treaty, of which I wanted to see one article. As the King does not like that I should see it, I was forced to send and to ask it from him. On account of this he grew angry, and permitted himself to be led so far as to say things which are not fit to be written to your Highness, and of which I shall only observe that he has had no regard for the service of your Highness and the honour of my house, and said what is not true. I therefore entreat your Highness to write to him, and to give him to understand that you are not well served, and I do not consent that my confessor be treated in such a manner. Your Highness would render me a signal service if you would write to him another letter, telling him that you are satisfied with the manner in which he serves me, and commanding him to continue and not to forsake me. For, in consequence of what the ambassador has said to him, he asks me leave every day, and I think, on no condition will he remain here if your Highness does not force him to do so. As I am in great want of such a person as he is, I implore your Highness to prevent him [from going away]; and to write also to the King that your Highness has commanded this father to stay with me, and to beg him that for the love of your Highness he should order that he be very well treated and humoured ; and to tell the prelates that your Highness is pleased with his staying here. For the greatest comfort in my troubles is the consolation and the support he gives me. Your Highness may believe that I feel myself reduced to such a state, that I send almost in despair this my March, servant to your Highness to implore you not to forget 1509. that I am your daughter, and how much I have suffered for your service, and how much [my sufferings] continually increase. Do not let me perish in this way, but write directly by this messenger what you decide, otherwise, in the condition in which I am now, I am afraid I might do something which neither the King of England nor your Highness, who has much more weight, would be able to prevent, unless, and that is necessary, you send for me so that I may conclude my few remaining days in serving God. That would be the greatest good I could have in this world. God guard your Highness' life and the royal estate, and augment it as I desire.

From Richmond, 9th of March.

I beseech your Highness soon to send back this messenger, and to give him money for his return. In order to provide him for what was necessary for his journey there, I was obliged to sell from my wardrobe. I do the same always when I am unwell during fasting time, for in the house of the King they would not give meat to anyone, even if he were dying, and they look upon them who eat it as heretics.

212.

[Membrilla to Ferdinand, "Spanish Calendar," Suppl. to Vols. i. and ii. p. 23.]

Since I wrote to your Highness by Martin Sanchez London, de Zamudio, ambassadors from the King of the Romans 20 March. and Madame Margaret have come here. They arrived on the sixth day of March, and were eight days without seeing the King, because he was ill of the sickness of last year, and does not allow himself to be seen. The Prince received the ambassadors. Concerning this em-

bassy, I have understood that they have moved a marriage for the Prince of Wales with the daughter of the
Duke Albert of Bavaria, a daughter of the sister of the
King of the Romans, assuring him (the King) that if he
concludes this marriage he shall still wed with Madame
Margaret, and they will give all the securities that he
may desire that the match between the Prince of Castile
and his daughter shall be confirmed. I have not learned
this from such a source that I can hold it for certain,
but as all the affairs of this court directly that they are
negotiated become public, it may be that he who told it
me may have heard it in a good quarter. Also I am
informed that the nobles of the kingdom press the King
much that he may marry his son, above all since they
have seen him ill, and they do not speak for one more
than for the other, but tell him he should decide on that
which he wishes, or is more profitable for him, and that
he should marry the Prince, because he is already very
manly, and the kingdom is in danger with only one heir.
They tell me he has taken a period of two months to
decide, and they are all much astonished at your Highness's great delay in answering, and at the slowness of
him whom your Highness is to send. For John Stile
has written to the King that a prelate would come
quickly here, and even certified that it would be Don
Pedro de Ayala, Bishop of Canaria.[1] In order that your
Highness may be informed of everything, I decided to
send this messenger. For it appears to me that one
way or the other it would be well that your Highness
should determine that which you wish in this affair.
They do not cease to preach to the people, wherever
they can, that because your Highness does not fulfil
your obligations towards the King of England, this
marriage is not concluded ; and although on our side

[1] See below, Vol. iii.

we might have better preachers, they would not make them believe anything except that which they have already imagined.

I have not seen the King of England since he be- trothed his daughter, because he appears to be very angry with me, and he does not say that the cause is because I did not choose to be present at the espousals of his daughter, but because I had made sinister reports to your Highness, in consequence of which your High- ness has not conceded that which he asks, according as I wrote to your Majesty, and the Lord Privy Seal had sent to tell me ; and on that account he did not wish to see me unless I had business on which to talk. And neither have I seen the Princess from that time, for to those who advise her Highness it does not appear good that her Highness should see me, as the King of Eng- land is not very friendly to me, and her Highness has such faith in them, that she believes what they tell her is good. And not only does her Highness feign to be angry with me, but shows herself to be so in reality. And this they have advised because they fear that, if I go to see the Princess, I shall not be able to refrain from telling her something which does not appear to me good in those who advise her thus, and with this fear not only have they prevailed with the Princess that she is angry with me, and that she shows it, but they have managed on all sides, where they have been able to do so, in such a manner as to remove me so that I may not communicate with her Highness. Many things happen in her house which have need of amendment, but her Highness is so submissive to a friar whom she has as confessor, that he makes her do a great many things which it would be better not to do. Lately he made her do a thing which much grieved the King. It was this, that whilst staying in a lonely house which

21 *

is in a park, the King of England wished to go to Richmond, and sent to say to the Princess that next day
her Highness and Madame Mary his daughter should
be at Richmond, where he would go before or after
them. The Princess obeyed the order, but next day
when she was about to start, and Madame Mary was
waiting for her with the company deputed to go with
them, the friar came and said to the Princess, " You
shall not go today." It is true that the princess had
vomited that night. The princess said, " I am well ;
I do not wish to stay here alone." He said, " I tell
you that upon pain of mortal sin you do not go today."
The Princess contended that she was well, and that
she did not wish to stay there alone. The friar, however, persevered so much that the Princess, not to displease him, determined to remain. When Madame
Mary had been waiting for more than two hours she
sent to tell Madame Mary to go, but that she did not
feel well. The English who witnessed this, and had
seen the Princess at mass and at table, rode off with
Madame Mary and went away, whilst the Princess remained alone with her women and only the *Maestre
Sala* and her chamberlain, who had been absent and
came by chance. The distance was at the utmost less
than one league. There is no need to speak of the provisions the Princess had that night, for as the contin-
gency was not expected it was not provided for, nor did
they give themselves much trouble to provide for it.
Next day the King of England did not again give an
order to send for the Princess, as though she had been
staying in such company as suited her, and they tell
me that the King was very much vexed at her remaining there. The following day the Princess went [to
Richmond] accompanied by no other living creature
than three women on horseback, the *Maestre Sala*, the

chamberlain, and the friar, a numerous [company] l These and other things of a thousand times worse kind the friar makes her do. It is more than 20 days since the King last saw the Princess, nor has he, since her staying away, sent to know how she is, although she had been ill. ˙ May God forgive me, but now that I know so well the affairs of the Princess's household, I acquit the King of England of a great and very great portion of the blame which I hitherto gave to him, and I do not wonder at what he has done, but at that which he does not do, especially as he is of such a temperament as to wish that in house and kingdom that be done without contradiction which he desires and orders. That the King allows these things of the friar, which appear so bad to him and which are so much brought before his eyes, to go on is not considered as a good sign by those who know him. As I have written by a servant of the Princess, whose name is Juan Azcotia [or Ascuetia], and who was despatched behind my back, I shall not dilate here on this subject, because your Highness can hear from him the truth of all these things if you desire to know them. He is a loyal servant of your Highness, and, as a man, being unable to endure many things which appeared bad him, he has said something of this to the friar, for which no good has come to him. Your Highness must know that there is very great need to remedy these things of this friar, and to remove him from here as a pestiferous person, for that he certainly is.

The Chamberlain, Juan de Cuero, being a good servant, cannot do otherwise than speak the truth, which they do not desire to hear. The Princess behaves towards him as though he had committed the greatest treason in the world, and all because he hinders them from selling every day a piece of plate to satisfy the follies of the friar. I entreat your Highness to grant

him the favour of an order that he whom your Highness should send may settle with him the accounts of
the office which he has held, because he is very old and
would not wish that death should overtake him before
having accounted for all that for which he is respon-
sible.   Your Highness ought to do it, and to place a
restraint on the selling, for in fifteen days they have
sold gold for two hundred ducats, with which the
Princess has done nothing that can be seen, nor is it
known in what she spends it, except in books and the
expenses of the friar.   Fearing that this King should
resent that your Highness commanded that the Princess
should be claimed, unless he should consent to her
marriage, as he has resented and known it in conse-
quences of the little secrecy that there is in the chamber
of the Princess, I told Francisco de Grimaldo that by
degrees he should send out of the country as much money
as he could ; and so he has done, for happily there are
out of England more than thirty thousand crowns.
The remainder shall be sent away by degrees, and preserved at a place whence, if it should be necessary to
make the payment to the King of England, it could be
remitted without any inconvenience.   This I have done
to satisfy my conscience, for, according to what I have
perceived and do perceive, it seems to me that thus it
ought to be done.   If your Highness should command
anything else, inform me by the flying courier that
I may not be in error.   I desire not to err in this, I am
sure.

213.

[Membrilla to Secretary Almazan, "Spanish Calendar," Suppl. to
Vols. i. and ii., p. 29.]

London,
20 March.
In many ways I am afflicted at the delay which there
has been in this affair, for every day we lose ground,

and as I write to his Highness, out of every bush springs a hare, and considering, the time that has passed since you wrote to me from Alcala del Reyno, I know not what to think of such delay, above all as the King of England had already news of the coming of him, who has to come, before I received the letters of his Highness. As they see that he delays [his coming] they make many conjectures, and prepare themselves for whatever may happen. They will not err in the answers, as they know that which we desire. For, as some days ago I wrote to his Highness, the little secresy which there is in the chamber of the Princess has done us injury, because there is nothing which I have written recommended to secresy which the King of England does not know as I know it, and even with some additions of the reporters. For this anxiety which I have, and in order to inform his Highness of that about which I am writing, I determine to send this messenger, and I entreat of your Honour that, if this business is to be prolonged, his Highness will withdraw me hence, because I shall not be able to serve either God or his Highness, as I am at variance with every one.

I wrote to your Lordship about a friar who is here as confessor to the Princess, who would to God he were in his monastery, and not here, because he neither brings nor has brought any good, and if he is here much longer he will bring greater injury on her Highness. I write something, and not so openly as I should desire, because there goes to his Highness a servant of the Princess who is called Juan de Ascuetia [or Azcotia], who was despatched behind my back ; and because his Highness may be informed by him of what I say to him, concerning this friar, in parables. For this reason I do not write more at length on the affair since he, as a man who has seen and knows it all, and as servant of the

house, will be able well to tell, and he is a very loyal
servant of the King and of the Princess, although such
are not here held in so much esteem as good servants
are worth.

I wish' only to say here that this ought to be remedied
by withdrawing this friar from the Princess, for he is
with her Highness against the will of all the English,
and especially against the will of the King and his
Highness. You ought to consider that which ought to
be considered in this case, and may God destroy me if
I see in the friar anything for which she should have so
much affection, for he has neither learning, nor appearance, nor manners, nor competency, nor credit, and yet
if he wishes to preach a new law they have to believe it.

A bill for five hundred ducats, which I have taken in
exchange, I sent to your Lordship, the which I took
from one Pedro Centurion, a Genoese. I supplicate
your lordship that if it is not paid you will give orders
to pay it, because directly it is known that it is not
accepted they will draw upon me, and your Lordship
knows what might follow from that. I also entreat
you to send orders to provide for me ; for I swear by
my faith that this country is so expensive that what I
possess there and here does not suffice, and I swear by
our Lord that three hundred and ninety ducats, which
they sent me from Naples, with all that I received from
there and here, is spent, and if you do not supply me,
and do not pay that which I have taken, I shall not
find anyone who will give me a ducat, or who will
stand security for me, nor shall I be able to go from
here nor to remain, unless I sell that which it is not
reasonable to sell.

This Gallician is to have for the journey going and
coming, twenty five ducats ; I have given him here ten,
thus you ought to give him there fifteen ducats. May

our Lord add to the life and estate of your Lordship as March, 1509. you desire.

214.

[Catherine of Aragon to Ferdinand, "Spanish Calendar," Suppl. to vols. i. and ii. p. 33.]

The ambassador sends to tell me that it is very neces- Richmond 20 March. sary for him to despatch this messenger in all haste to your Highness, because many things have been discovered to him, and as I fear that some of them may not be true, I do not like to let him go without a letter from me, beseeching your Highness that if he writes anything about my household and especially about my confessor, your Highness will not credit it. For, by my salvation, and by the life of your Highness, he does not tell the truth if he states anything except that [the confessor] serves me well and loyally. A few days ago I wrote to your Highness, by a servant of mine, although not so much in detail as I could wish; for all that the ambassador, with his disorderly tongue, has said against my person and the honour of my house, from affection, for a certain Francisca de Cáceres, à former servant of mine, can not be put upon paper, and I would rather die than see what I have suffered and suffer every day from this ambassador and all my servants. I shall not believe that your Highness looks upon me as your daughter if you do not punish it, and order the ambassador to confine himself to the affairs of his embassy, and to abstain from meddling in the affairs of my household. May your Highness give me satisfaction before I die, for I fear my life will be short, owing to my troubles.

1509.

215.

[Henry VII's death, Kingsford's "Chronicles," p. 262.]

21 April.   This yere vppon the Saterday¹ next before Seiut
Georges Day died the king our soueraign lord at his
lodging called Richemount. Vpon whose soule and all
Cristen, Jhesu haVe mercy! Amen!

216.

["Greyfriars' Chronicle," p. 29]

Thys yere the xxii day of Aprill dyde kynge Henry
the VIIth at Richmonde, and browth to London over
the brygge and soo to Powlles the furst nyght, and the
nexte day to Westmynster nobylly and there buryd.

217.

[Sanuto's abstract of news letters relating to the death of Henry
VII, "Venetian Calendar," i. No. 942.]

Venice,   Receipt of letters from Rome, dated the 3rd and
8 May.   4th, stating that sure news had been received there of
the death of the King of England on the 20th of April,
and his son had succeeded to the kingdom peaceably ;
and this the Pope said in the Consistory. The truth
of this was also known on the 6th at Lucca, as read in
letters dated the 26th, received from London by the
bankers Bonvisi, who have a bank there ; and that
down to that day, the Flanders galleys, commanded by
Agostin da Mula, were there. The new King is——
years old, a worthy King and most hostile to France ;
it is thought he will indubitably invade France, and

¹ 21 April in 1509 was a Saturday ; the statement in the following passage from the "Greyfriars' Chronicle" to the effect that
Henry VII died on the 22nd perhaps arose from the practice of
dating Henry VIII's reign from the 22nd.

has perhaps had our galleys detained for the convey-
ance of troops. He is the son-in-law of the King of
Spain. His name——; and it seems that he was crowned
there on the 26th. The King his father was called
Henry, —— years of age ; was a very great miser, but
a man of vast ability, and had accumulated so much
gold that he is supposed to have more than well nigh
all the other Kings of Christendom. This King, his
son, is liberal and handsome, the friend of Venice and
the enemy of France ; and the ambassador Andrea
Badoer and [Nicolò] de Ponte, who is intimate with the
King, being on the spot, and his councillors being
hostile to the French, the King will assuredly take the
offensive : so that this intelligence is considered most
satisfactory.

218.

[Skelton's epitaph on Henry VII, Works, ed. Dyce, i. 178.]

Orator regius Skeltonis Laureatus in singulare merit-
issimumque præconum nobillissimi principis Henrici
Septimi, nuper strenuissimi regis Angliæ hoc epi-
taphium edidit, ad sinceram contemplationem reverendi
in Christo patris ac domini, Domini Johannis Islippæ
Abbatis Westmonasteriensis optime meriti, anno domini
MDXII pridie divi Andreæ Apostoli etc.

Tristia Melpomenes cogor modo plectra sonare,
Hos elegos foveat Cynthius ille meos.
Si quas fata movent lacrymas, lacrymare videtur
Jam bene maturum, si bene mente sapis.
Flos Britonum, regum speculum, Salomonis imago,
Septimus Henricus mole sub hac tegitur.
Punica, dum regnat, redolens rosa digna vocari,
Jam jam marcescit, ceu levis umbra fugit.
Multa novercantis fortunæ, multa faventis
Passus, et infractus tempus utrumque tulit.

Nobilis Anchises, armis metuendus Atrides,
Hic erat; hunc Scottus rex timuit Jacobus.
Spiramenta animæ vegetans dum vescitur aura,
Francorum populus conticuit pavidus.
Immensas sibi divitias cumulasse quid horres?.
Ni cumulasset opes, forte, Britanne, luas.
Urgentes casus tacita si mente volutes,
Vix tibi sufficeret aurea ripa Tagi.
Ni sua te probitas consulta mente laborans
Rexisset satius, vix tibi tuta salus.
Sed quid plura cano? meditans quid plura voluto?
Quisque vigil sibi sit: mors sine lege rapit.
Ad Dominum, qui cuncta regit, pro principe tanto
Funde preces quisquis carmina nostra legis.

ABERDEEN: THE UNIVERSITY PRESS.

Lightning Source UK Ltd.
Milton Keynes UK
UKOW05f0850151116

287623UK00002B/587/P